MW01065141

Valuing Enterprise and Shareholder Cash Flows

The Integrated Theory of Business Valuation

Z. CHRISTOPHER MERCER, ASA, CFA

Published by Peabody Publishing, LP

Valuing Enterprise and Shareholder Cash Flows:
The Integrated Theory of Business Valuation

Copyright © 2004 Z. Christopher Mercer

This publication is designed to provide accurate and authoritative information in regard to the subject matter covered. It is sold with the understanding that neither the author nor the publisher is engaged in rendering legal, accounting, or other professional service. If legal advice or other expert assistance is required, the services of a competent professional person should be sought.

From a Declaration of Principles jointly adopted by a Committee of the American Bar Association and a Committee of Publishers.

Library of Congress Control Number: 2004095964

ISBN: 0-9700698-5-5

Peabody Publishing LP
5860 Ridgeway Center Parkway, Suite 400
Memphis, Tennessee 38120
Tel: 800.769.0967
Fax: 901.685.2199

To Ashley Le Blanc Mercer, SRH,
my wife, supporter and friend,
with thanks for all you do to make life wonderful

and to all my children
Amanda Nell Mercer Thompson
Zeno C. Mercer, III
Katherine Elizabeth Forrest Mercer
Katherine Le Blanc Green
Margaret Lyon Green

for their continuing inspiration and motivation

About the Author

Z. Christopher Mercer is founder and chief executive officer of Mercer Capital, one of the leading independent business appraisal firms in the country. Mercer Capital, founded in 1982, provides business valuation and investment banking services to a national and international clientele.

Mr. Mercer began his valuation career in the late 1970s. He has prepared, overseen, or contributed to hundreds, if not thousands, of valuations for purposes related to M&A, litigation, and tax, among others. He is a prolific author on valuation-related topics and one of the most sought after speakers on business valuation issues for national professional associations and other business and professional groups.

Mr. Mercer is the author of *Quantifying Marketability Discounts* (Peabody Publishing, LP, 1997 & 2001) which deals with the central issue of marketability discounts applicable to private businesses. He is also the author of *Valuing Financial Institutions* (Business One Irwin, 1992) which was the first book of its kind to offer bank-specific valuation topics of interest both to valuation professionals and to bankers. In addition, Mr. Mercer is a contributing author to the book *Valuation for Impairment Testing* (Peabody Publishing, LP, 2001), the first comprehensive analysis of compliance issues regarding SFAS 141 and SFAS 142 from a valuation perspective for CFOs and auditors.

He is an Accredited Senior Member (ASA) of the American Society of Appraisers and holds the Chartered Financial Analyst (CFA) professional designation from the Association for Investment Management and Research. Mr. Mercer holds a bachelor's degree in economics from Stetson University and a master's degree in economics from Vanderbilt University.

Mr. Mercer is a member of the Editorial Advisory Board of *Valuation Strategies*, a national magazine published by RIA Group dealing with current appraisal issues. In addition, he has contributed numerous articles to the *Business Valuation Review*, a quarterly journal published by the American Society of Appraisers, as well as to numerous other business and professional publications.

Contact Information:
Mercer Capital
5860 Ridgeway Center Parkway, Suite 400
Memphis, Tennessee 38120
Tel 901.685.2120 • Fax 901.685.2199
e-mail: mercerc@mercercapital.com
www.mercercapital.com

Acknowledgements

So many people have kindly contributed their time and talents to *Valuing Enterprise and Shareholder Cash Flows: The Integrated Theory of Business Valuation*, and I am sincerely grateful.

The People of Mercer Capital. Mercer Capital has been the intellectual incubator for numerous ideas over the years. Because of the intellectual curiosities and capacities of my fellow professionals, the Quantitative Marketability Discount Model (QMDM), the intellectual precursor to the Integrated Theory, was forged. The QMDM was and is important because with its development we began to realize that all of valuation is interrelated. Therefore, heartfelt thanks to all the wonderful people of Mercer Capital who have provided a virtual laboratory and effective sounding board for the development of the ideas in this book and for helping me to pursue this project.

Kenneth W. Patton, ASA. Ken has been my confidant, friend and business partner for more than 20 years. Ken's skills and abilities have not only contributed to the success of Mercer Capital, but also to the development of *Valuing Financial Institutions*, *Quantifying Marketability Discounts,* and *The Integrated Theory.* His technical review of this book was excellent and very much appreciated. For those things in this book that he advised me to omit or change – and I listened – I thank him. For those same things where I chose to ignore him and it turned out he was right – I offer penance in advance. For his tireless support of our mutual efforts over these many years, I cannot thank him enough.

Barbara Walters Price, CME. Barbara is the longest-tenured employee at Mercer Capital other than me, beginning in 1983 as a part-time, all-purpose helper. She has grown with the company and today is a senior vice president of Mercer Capital and our marketing director. She has been my friend, confidant, and consultant for many years. As with my previous books, she has taken on the publication of this one as a personal challenge and objective. Barbara is my #1 sounding board for turning technical points into understandable prose. But more than that, she creates deadlines and then makes us all meet them. *Valuing Financial Institutions, Quantifying Marketability Discounts*, and now *The Integrated Theory*, have been enhanced remarkably by her efforts. Thanks again.

Travis W. Harms, CFA, CPA/ABV. It is not often that one has the opportunity to work with someone who is at once so young and who has such remarkable insights into financial theory as applied in the business environment. Travis has been instrumental in a number of our conceptual breakthroughs as *The Integrated Theory* has taken shape. Travis helped with conceptual discussions and with developing the underlying algebra and math. He co-authored Chapter 1 with me and I thank him for his able and willing assistance throughout the project.

Matthew R. Crow, ASA, CFA and *Timothy R. Lee, ASA.* Matt and Tim are senior vice presidents of Mercer Capital and are responsible for, among other things, keeping the shop moving. They have been part of the development of both *Quantifying Marketability Discounts* as well as *The Integrated Theory.* In addition, they have both taught hundreds of other appraisers how to use the QMDM based on our collective experience in applying it since 1994. They have supported this new book with critical comments and insights and I thank them for their encouragement and leadership at Mercer Capital.

There are a few others at Mercer Capital that deserve special mention. *Julie A. Reno* works with Barbara Walters Price in the Marketing Department. She has labored tirelessly on this project and was instrumental in putting the final pieces together so we could get the book to the printer. She, along with *Marty A. Drier,* also worked diligently on the footnotes. I thank them for their efforts and note that if there are any references that are missed or incomplete, I accept full responsibility.

V. Todd Lowe serves as Executive Assistant to both Ken Patton and me. Todd is a retired "Flag Writer" from the U.S. Navy, or executive assistant for Admirals of the Fleet. He brings a wealth of talent and experience to Mercer Capital. I thank him for his willingness to jump in and take care of things.

Tammy Ford Falkner serves as Mercer Capital's Strategic Sales Coordinator and does a marvelous job. Thanks are due her for her willingness to step in and help with anything that needed doing during this project.

In addition, I owe debts of gratitude to professional colleagues who have especially influenced, assisted, and/or challenged me over the past 20-plus years. These colleagues include:

- *Dr. Shannon P. Pratt, CFA, FASA, MCBA,* who has been a mentor and friend since my early days in the business appraisal field. We often agree, sometimes disagree, but always respect each other.

- *Eric W. Nath, ASA* whose 1990 article (cited in this book) raised the original challenge that forced the thinking process leading to *The Integrated Theory*.

- *Michael J. Bolotsky, ASA, CBA* whose provocative article in 1991 (cited in this book) forced even deeper thinking regarding the levels of value and the interrelationships between enterprise and shareholder valuations.

- *Dr. Wayne C. Jankowske, CPA, ASA* whose academic approach to the levels of value raised further questions for consideration.

- *Roger J. Grabowski, ASA* whose insights (along with those of *David W. King, CFA*) into the cost of capital have forced a continuing re-evaluation of how to quantify equity discount rates for closely held companies.

In addition, several professional colleagues provided technical reviews of one or more chapters of this book and I gratefully acknowledge their assistance. Also, I in no way implicate them for any errors in the book, or for disagreements regarding emphasis, omissions, assumptions, theory, or methodology. My special thanks to the following:

- *Dr. David Tabak.* I single out Dr. Tabak for a special measure of gratitude for his exhaustive and timely review of the manuscript and for his insightful comments. His help was invaluable and very much appreciated. Thank you.

- *Dr. Shannon P. Pratt, CFA, FASA, MCBA*

- *Rod P. Burkert, CPA/ABV, CVA*

- *Rand M. Curtiss, FIBA, MCBA, ASA, ASA*

- *John A. "Jack" Bogdanski, Esq.*

- *Alex W. Howard, CFA, ASA*

- *Bruce B. Bingham, ASA*

- *Dr. Tom Copeland*

If I have inadvertently forgotten someone, I sincerely apologize. This book was several years in the making and I am humbled by the amount of help and encouragement I have received from so many. Thank you to all who helped to make this book happen.

Z. Christopher Mercer, ASA, CFA
August 2004

TABLE OF CONTENTS

Chapter 5: Fundamental Adjustments to Market Capitalization Rates

Chapter 6: The Adjusted Capital Asset Pricing Model

Chapter 7: The Quantitative Marketability Discount Model

Chapter 8: Fair Market Value vs. the Real World

Chapter 9: Economic Value Added, Economic Profit and Market Value Added

Chapter 10: The Levels of Value in Perspective

Introduction

Simply put, this book helps the reader understand the *why* of business valuation. Most business valuation texts deal with the *how* by focusing on an interesting amalgamation of seemingly unrelated financial concepts. These concepts appear as pieces of a puzzle. The reader implicitly knows that the pieces somehow relate to each other and should fit together; however, the puzzle seems impossible to put together, since there is no picture on the front of the box to guide you. This book is the picture on the front of the box because once the *why* of business valuation is understood, the *how* becomes much more straightforward and, instead of dealing with disjointed pieces, the completed puzzle emerges.

Valuing Enterprise and Shareholder Cash Flows: The Integrated Theory of Business Valuation assembles these various valuation concepts into a theoretically and practically consistent whole. The reader views financial concepts not as unrelated, but as part of a complete and clear picture of business valuation.

THE INTEGRATED THEORY OF BUSINESS VALUATION DEFINED

The Integrated Theory of Business Valuation is a theoretical discussion of financial and valuation concepts designed to explain the behavior of real-world market participants in the context of financial theory and institutional reality. The broad range of observed behaviors of real-world market participants is examined in the context of the cash flows of business enterprises – and the derivative cash flows attributable to specific interests in those enterprises.

The Integrated Theory accomplishes a number of important objectives by:

- Presenting certain organizing principles of business valuation in the context of what we term the "GRAPES of Value" (Growth, Risk and Reward, Alternative Investments, Present Value, Expectations, and Sanity).

- Examining the relationships between the Gordon Dividend Discount (or Growth) Model, or the Gordon Model, and the discounted cash flow model of valuation.

- Defining the various "levels of value," ranging from strategic enterprise concepts to the level of illiquid, minority interests in those enterprises.

- Defining relevant valuation premiums and discounts (e.g., control premiums, minority interest discounts, and marketability discounts) in the context of financial and valuation theory.

- Placing business acquisition pricing decisions into practical and theoretical perspective.

- Accounting for all the cash flows from the enterprise level to the derivative cash flows of the shareholder level.

The Integrated Theory is grounded in the real world of market participants. The Integrated Theory is fully developed in Chapter 3 and elaborated upon in numerous other chapters. The Integrated Theory illustrates the normal behavior of the market participants buying and selling business enterprises and interests in them, whether in the public or private markets. Many aspects of less normal behavior can also be explained in the context of the Integrated Theory.

While grounded in the real world of market participants, it is logical to ask what the Integrated Theory says about fair market value since this is the standard under which a majority of appraisals are rendered. The hypothetical participants in the world of fair market value look at the real-world transactional data, including rational and irrational data points, in their determinations of price. But the definition of fair market value refines the behavior of hypothetical market participants (relative to real-world participants) in several specific ways by eliminating elements of compulsion found in the real world; eliminating knowledge disparities that may exist when real-world market participants engage in transactions; and equating the capacities of hypothetical buyers and sellers.

In addition, one of the most important insights of the Integrated Theory is in the focus on the relationship between enterprise valuation concepts and the valuation of shareholder interests in enterprises. The value of enterprises is based on the expectation of future cash flows from the enterprise. The value of interests in enterprises, particularly minority interests, is based on the portion of expected enterprise cash flows attributable to those interests.

In other words, the valuation of minority interests of enterprises is a derivative process. It begins with the valuation of the enterprise, then follows (projects) the derivative cash flows to minority interests for the duration of the expected holding periods of the investments, and then discounts the derivative, shareholder cash flows to the present at a discount rate appropriate for the risk of the interests (in relationship to the risk of the enterprises).

THE INTEGRATED THEORY PROVIDES ANSWERS

A series of questions that have been the subject of debate in the business appraisal profession are presented at the beginning of each chapter. We have structured the content of each chapter to provide answers to these questions. Keep in mind that it will not be uncommon to see certain questions repeated in other chapters because naturally some of the information provided overlaps chapters. These questions will be answered using the Integrated Theory, which provides the framework within which we can address these seemingly unrelated topics.

WHO SHOULD READ THIS BOOK?

A variety of business, finance, business valuation, legal, and accounting professionals should read *Valuing Enterprise and Shareholder Cash Flows: The Integrated Theory of Business Valuation.*

Corporate Finance and M&A Professionals

Valuing Enterprise and Shareholder Cash Flows is designed to be helpful for corporate finance and M&A professionals in a variety of ways. We are targeting corporate finance and M&A professionals first in this introduction because most valuation books do not address their conceptual and practical needs to understand valuation.

- Chapter 1 on the discounted cash flow (DCF) model provides helpful perspective for users of the DCF method. The discussion of the interrelationships between the Gordon Model and the DCF method provides important perspective for finance practitioners.

- This book provides thoughtful assistance in key areas of concern to all those in the corporate finance arena, including corporate finance staffs, CFOs, legal counsel, accountants, and boards of directors when examining acquisitions, investment projects, and joint ventures.

  - The analysis of the difference between the long-term growth rate used in DCF models to estimate terminal values and the earnings growth rates that are the focus of securities analysts will help avoid overvaluation of acquisitions. The discussion of the impact of expected growth on valuation should provide thoughtful guidance in this area.

  - The overall presentation of the Integrated Theory and the insights it provides regarding the appropriate discount rates for valuing acquisition subjects can also help in analyzing acquisitions.

  - The discussion of "GRAPES of Value," or organizing principles of business valuation (Chapter 2), as well as the discussion of fair market value and the real world (Chapter 8) provide food for thought.

  - Many joint ventures, partnerships, and subsidiaries of major corporations have buy-sell agreements or other repurchase or cross-purchase agreements where the valuation mechanism is set to be fair market value. An understanding of the meaning of fair market value is critical for all existing and future partnership and joint ventures.

  - Importantly, the book provides a means of articulating valuation concepts for use within the corporate structure and in negotiations with outside parties.

Business Appraisers

The Integrated Theory pulls the many seemingly unrelated financial concepts employed by business appraisers into a unified system. These multiple concepts necessitate the need for a deeper understanding of their interrelationships. A few examples of the valuation concepts that will be "integrated" include:

- Discounted cash flow model of valuation

- The Gordon Model

- Levels of value concepts

  - Marketable minority level of value

  - Marketability discounts

- Nonmarketable minority level of value
- Financial control level of value
- Financial control premiums
- Minority interest discounts
- Strategic control level of value
- Strategic control premiums

• Normalizing adjustments to the income statement (to exclude unusual, extraordinary, or otherwise non-recurring events from consideration)

• Controlling interest adjustments available to financial buyers or strategic buyers of particular subject interests

• Discount rates – required rates of return
  - Applicable to net income or net cash flow at the level of the enterprise?
  - Differences at the enterprise and shareholder levels
  - Risks attributable to the buyers rather than the sellers

• The "build-up" method for developing discount rates

• The Capital Asset Pricing Model and the Adjusted Capital Asset Pricing Model for developing discount rates

• Capitalization rates and expected growth

• Control premium studies

• The so-called "prerogatives of control"

• Restricted stock and pre-IPO studies

• Fair market value

• Investment value

• Transactional data bases

• Guideline public company information and fundamental adjustments

• S corporations vs. C corporations

• And so on….

The Integrated Theory provides the foundation for understanding business valuation concepts on a more profound level. These insights will be helpful for beginning and experienced appraisers alike. And the Integrated Theory raises (and answers) a number of questions about "standard" valuation practices employed by many appraisers, for example, the application of control premiums, minority interest discounts and marketability discounts.

Accountants Regarding Fair Value

With the implementation of numerous accounting pronouncements regarding the necessity to account for numerous assets and liabilities at their fair values, it is becoming exceedingly important for CPAs charged with auditing financial statements to understand valuation concepts. Several recent accounting pronouncements and regulations have focused on financial statement transparency and current value accounting.

While the Integrated Theory does not attempt to define fair value in the context of recent accounting statements or regulations, it does provide a vehicle to assist CPAs and appraisers as they both attempt to translate interpretations of the concept from the FASB, the SEC, or elsewhere into actionable valuation concepts. In other words, any discussion of enterprise cash flows can be placed in the context of the Integrated Theory and, therefore, within a framework where valuation can be discussed in meaningful terms.

Users of Business Appraisal Reports

The Integrated Theory will also be helpful for users of appraisal reports. The basic concepts of the Integrated Theory are not difficult, and the limited use of symbolic math is fairly easy to follow (we hope!). Informed users of business appraisals (and related products and services) are best able to benefit from their use. We have advised clients for many years: "If you don't understand it, then don't stand for it." Reading the Integrated Theory, particularly on a specific-topic basis when questions arise, can help readers develop a better understanding of business appraisal reports.

The Integrated Theory of Business Valuation takes the seemingly disjointed pieces of the business valuation puzzle and assembles them together for the first time in a complete picture.

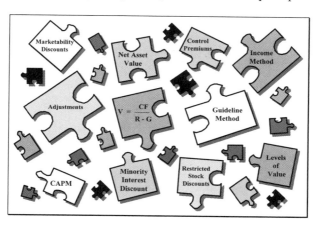

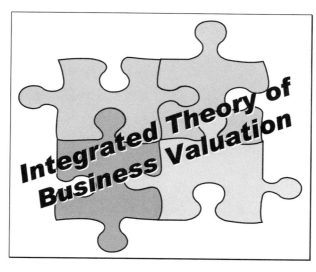

Chapter 1

Discounted Cash Flow and the Gordon Model:
The Very Basics of Value[1]

INTRODUCTION

We begin by focusing on "The Very Basics of Value," which is the subtitle of this chapter. This subtitle is intentional because our purpose here is to explore the underpinnings of both the discounted cash flow model and the Gordon Model to enhance our understanding of these basic tools of valuation and finance. As will be shown, the discounted cash flow model and the Gordon Model can be used to develop the Integrated Theory of Business Valuation.

COMMON QUESTIONS

In order to move the reader from theory to practice, we begin each chapter with a series of often vexing questions. We have structured the content of each chapter to provide answers to these questions. Keep in mind that it will not be uncommon to see certain questions repeated in other chapters because naturally some of the information provided overlaps.

1. What are the implicit assumptions of the Gordon Model?

2. Where does the generalized valuation model, Value = Earnings x Multiple, come from?

3. What are the conditions that define g, the long-term growth rate of core earnings for use in the Gordon Model?

---

[1] Co-authored by Travis W. Harms, CFA, CPA/ABV, vice president of Mercer Capital.

4. What is the relationship between the net income and the net cash flow of business enterprises?

5. When applying the DCF method, is the appropriate measure of benefits for discounting supposed to be net income or net cash flow?

6. What is the difference between the expected growth rate in *earnings* of a business and its expected growth rate in *value*?

7. What is the source of value of a *business enterprise*?

8. Are the DCF method and single-period income capitalizations intrinsically different?

9. What are the economic reasons that the long-term *g* used in single-period income capitalization methods is almost always a single-digit percentage?

10. When capitalizing net income versus net cash flow, should adjustment factors to *r*, the discount rate, be applied?

Keep these questions in mind as we begin with a discussion of the discounted cash flow model.

THE DISCOUNTED CASH FLOW MODEL

The value of a business enterprise can be described as:

- The value today (i.e., in *cash-equivalent terms* today)

- of all expected future cash flows (or benefits) of the business

- forecasted or estimated over an indefinite time period (i.e., *into perpetuity*)

- that have been *discounted to the present* (expressed in terms of *present value* dollars) at an appropriate *discount rate* (which takes into consideration the riskiness of the projected cash flows of the business relative to similar investments).

While business appraisers and finance professionals may disagree on many things, a large-scale poll of both would indicate virtual unanimity on this conceptual definition of the value of a business enterprise. In order to value a business today then, we need the following:

- A forecast of all expected future cash flows or benefits to be derived from ownership of the business; and,

- An appropriate discount rate with which to discount the cash flows to the present.

This conceptual definition of business value can be defined symbolically in Equation 1-1:

$$\text{Value} = V_0 = \left(\frac{CF_1}{(1+r)^1} + \frac{CF_2}{(1+r)^2} + \frac{CF_3}{(1+r)^3} + \frac{CF_4}{(1+r)^4} + \ldots + \frac{CF_n}{(1+r)^n} \right)$$

Equation 1-1

Where: V_0 is the value of the equity of a business today.

CF_1 **to** CF_n represent the expected cash flows (or benefits) to be derived for periods 1 to n.[2]

r is the discount rate that converts future dollars of CF into present dollars of value.

Equation 1-1 is the basic discounted cash flow (DCF) model. To employ the model in this form, however, the analyst must make a forecast of *all* the relevant cash flows into the indefinite future. For clarity, the cash flows or earnings discussed in this chapter are the net earnings and net cash flows of enterprises. V_0 is the value of the equity of the enterprise, or the present value of the expected cash flows to the owners of the equity of the enterprise.[3] Expanding the analysis to embrace the total capital (equity plus debt) of an enterprise will have to be addressed at a later time.

---

[2] The discounted cash flow model is based on periods of time of equivalent length. Because forecasts are often made on an annual basis in practice, we use the terms "periods" and "years" almost interchangeably for purposes of this theoretical discussion.

[3] For purposes of this book, we are discussing enterprises where there is little risk of bankruptcy.

THE GORDON MODEL

In his 1962 finance text, Myron J. Gordon showed that under the appropriate assumptions, there is an equivalency between Equation 1-1 and the simplified equation represented by Equation 1-2[4]:

$$V_o = \frac{CF_1}{r - g}$$

Equation 1-2

The Gordon Model initially dealt with dividends, hence it has been called the Gordon Dividend Growth Model, or the Gordon Growth Model. This equation has become so generalized that it reflects what can be called the general valuation model. CF_1 represents the estimate of earnings for the next period, so we can generalize and refer to the cash flow measure as *Earnings*. The expression $(r - g)$ is known as a capitalization rate or factor.[5]   And the expression $(1/(r - g))$ is nothing other than a multiple (of the earnings measure being used).   So the Gordon Model compresses into the general valuation model:

$$\textbf{Value} \quad = \quad \textbf{Earnings} \quad \textbf{x} \quad \textbf{Multiple}$$

Equation 1-3

These factors are so basic and so taken for granted that appraisers sometimes forget their source. "Earnings" in the generalized valuation model must be clearly defined and the "multiple" must be appropriate for the defined measure of earnings.   These comments could be based on common sense, and they are. However, as will be shown, they are also theoretically sound. Returning to the Gordon Model, the "dividend" aspect will be explored in more detail later in this chapter; however, in Equation 1-2, the "dividend" is 100% of the cash flows of the enterprise (which, as will be shown, may be less than 100% of the (net) Earnings of the business).

For there to be an equivalency between Equations 1-1 and 1-2, the following assumptions must hold:

---

[4]   Myron J. Gordon, *The Investment, Financing, and Valuation of the Corporation* (Homewood, IL: Richard D. Irwin, 1962).

[5]   See "Definitions," *ASA Business Valuation Standards* (Washington, D.C.: The Appraisal Foundation, 2002), p. 21.

- CF_1 is the measure of *expected cash flow* for the next period (sometimes derived as $(CF_0 \times (1 + g))$ or otherwise derived specifically).

- Cash flows must be growing at the constant rate of *g*.

- All cash flows must be: 1) distributed to owners; or, 2) reinvested in the enterprise at the discount rate, *r*.

- The discount rate, *r*, must be the appropriate discount rate for the selected measure of cash flow, CF.[6]

By comparing Equations 1-1 and 1-2, we see two equivalent ways to estimate the value of an enterprise. Equation 1-4 restates Equation 1-1 to share constant growth and equates it to Equation 1-2.

- Looking at the left portion of Equation 1-4, we forecast cash flows into the indefinite future (into perpetuity) and discount them back to the present.

- Alternatively, if the outlook for an enterprise calls for a constant rate of growth of cash flows, i.e., at *g*, then we can simplify the process and capitalize next year's cash flow using *(r − g)* as the capitalization factor.

$$V_0 = \left[\frac{CF_0(1+g)}{(1+r)^1} + \frac{CF_0(1+g)^2}{(1+r)^2} + ... + \frac{CF_0(1+g)^n}{(1+r)^n} \right] = \frac{CF_1}{r - g}$$

Equation 1-4

Recall the assumptions that must hold for Equation 1-4 to be an identity. This chapter is subtitled "The Very Basics of Value" for a reason. Our purpose is to go beyond mere recognition of identities such as Equation 1-4. Appraisers need to claim ownership and understanding of the implications of basic valuation principles, rather than simply acknowledge truisms.

Equation 1-1 and the left portion of Equation 1-4 require a discrete forecast to time period n, or effectively into perpetuity. This may not always be practical. Few forecasts in practice extend beyond five or 10 years, and then a terminal value is developed to represent all remaining expected cash flows.

---

[6] In the real world, businesses make reinvestments and accept the returns of these investments, some of which will exceed *r* and some of which may be less than *r*. This model assumes that all reinvestments will achieve a return of *r*.

Equation 1-2 and the right portion of Equation 1-4 require that an estimate of next year's cash flow be capitalized into perpetuity at a constant growth rate of g. This also may not be practical, given an analyst's knowledge about near-term expectations for cash flow growth, which might well be significantly different from a longer-term assumption for growth after an expected period of higher/lower/variable growth.

Equation 1-4 can be rearranged to illustrate two forecasting periods, a discrete period and then a portion representing all remaining expected cash flows. In Equation 1-5, we divide the forecast period into two portions. In so doing, we derive in symbolic form the "two-stage" DCF model most often used by appraisers and business decision-makers.

- *A finite period ending in Year f, or Interim Cash Flows.* The future is always hard to predict because it has not happened yet. However, near-term future events can usually be forecasted with more clarity than the more distant future. The left side of Equation 1-5 can therefore be used to determine the Present Value of Interim Cash Flows (PVICF).

- *All remaining cash flows after Year f, or the Terminal Value.* The Terminal Value is the present value of all remaining expected cash flows after the finite forecast period ending in Year f. When discounted to the present from the end of the year, the Present Value of the Terminal Value (PVTV) is obtained.

$$V_0 = \left[\frac{CF_1}{(1+r)^1} + \frac{CF_2}{(1+r)^2} + \frac{CF_3}{(1+r)^3} + \ldots + \frac{CF_f}{(1+r)^f} \right] + \left[\frac{CF_{f+1}/(r-g)}{(1+r)^f} \right]$$

Present Value of Interim Cash Flows (PVICF) Using this portion of the basic DCF model, the analyst is not constrained by the requirement of constantly growing cash flows during the finite forecast period ending with Year f. This part of the equation is the present value of interim cash flows through the finite forecast period ending with Year f, or PVICF.

Present Value of the Terminal Value (PVTV) Using the Gordon Model, all cash flows are capitalized after Year f, assuming cash flows are growing from that point at the constant rate of g. This portion of the equation therefore represents the present value of $CF_{f+1} = CF_f \times (1 + g)$

Equation 1-5

8/

Equation 1-5 provides a practical way to employ the DC
practical (as nearly always) to forecast expected cash f
future, or into perpetuity. Appraisers using this formulation typ-
specific forecast of earnings or cash flows for a discrete period, usually ranging
from about three to 10 years or so. They then estimate the present value of the
terminal value using the Gordon Model as shown in Equation 1-5.[7]

This methodology can be used to illustrate the equivalency between the
DCF method and the Gordon Model under appropriate assumptions. In this case,
the "proof" of equivalency will be practical and not algebraic.[8]

Practical Proof: DCF = Gordon Model

Consider a business enterprise that is expected to generate $1.0 million in net
earnings (CF_1) next year. Earnings of this business are expected to grow at 10%
per year into the indefinite future.[9] Further, assume that the appropriate discount
rate is 20%. Given these assumptions, we can value the enterprise using the
Gordon Model (Equation 1-2). And we can also value the enterprise using the
DCF methodology from Equation 1-5.

---

[7] Alternatively, in practice, many appraisers and market participants use a market-based
method that applies current market multiples to the forecasted cash flow for Year f or
Year f-plus-1. This alternative practice, if employed with reasonable multiples from the
public marketplace, should not be considered unusual or incorrect. For a further
discussion on this point, see Practical Observations at the conclusion of this chapter.

[8] In Equation 1-5, let f=0. The sum of the interim cash flows (PVICF) is, therefore, zero.

$$PVTV = \frac{CF_1 / (r-g)}{1} = \frac{CF_1}{r-g} = \text{Equation 1-2}$$

Thanks to Dr. David Tabak for this "algebraic" proof.

[9] In the Practical Observations section at the end of this chapter, I suggest that a long-
term g of 10% may be on the high side for many discounted cash flow applications. For
purposes of this example which will be used for the remainder of the chapter, I ask the
reader's indulgence. A 10% growth rate is convenient for calculations and gives a nice,
round conclusion, and therefore facilitates this discussion.

The Gordon Model valuation is in Figure 1-1:

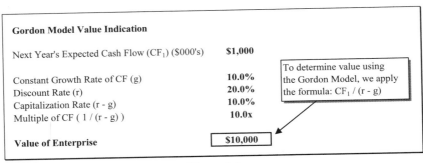

Figure 1-1

The indicated value for the enterprise using the Gordon Model is $10 million, as derived in Figure 1-1. The capitalization rate, $(r - g)$, is 10% (20% - 10%), and the multiple of cash flow is 10.0x (1/10%). The implicit assumptions of this example should also be understood: *Cash flows are growing at the constant rate of g, and all cash flows are either distributed or reinvested in the enterprise at the discount rate, r.* Another assumption is that the cash flows are reinvested (or received) at the end of each year of the forecast. This will be clear in the DCF method below.

We can now develop a parallel valuation using the DCF methodology. In doing so, we employ Equation 1-5 in Figure 1-2. First, the present value of cash flows for the finite period (PVICF) is calculated. At the end of the finite forecast period, the value of all remaining cash flows (from year 6 into perpetuity) is derived using the Gordon Model. This Terminal Value is then discounted to the present at the discount rate, r, providing the Present Value of the Terminal Value (PVTV). Recall that in this example, it is assumed that cash flows are growing at the constant rate of g, or 10%, during the finite forecast period as well as in the perpetuity calculation.

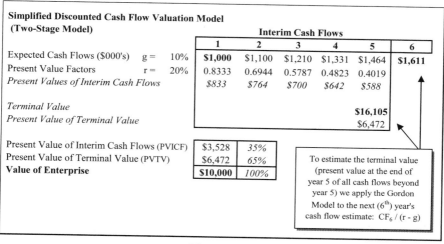

Figure 1-2

The DCF valuation conclusion is $10 million, or precisely the same as the conclusion of the Gordon Model in Figure 1-1. In the DCF model, the implicit assumptions of the Gordon Model are made explicit. Value is the sum of the present value of the five interim cash flows ($3.5 million), plus the present value of the terminal value ($6.5 million), each discounted to the present at 20%. Note the following about this example:

- The model assumes receipt of each of the interim cash flows by the owners of the enterprise.

- The Present Value of Interim Cash Flows (PVICF) represents $3.5 million, or 35%, of the concluded value of $10 million.

- The Present Value of the Terminal Value (PVTV) represents $6.5 million, or 65% of the total value. This straightforward analysis should alert readers to the importance of the terminal value estimation in DCF valuations. For example, with 10% compound growth in cash flow for five years, the terminal value accounts for almost two-thirds of the total value. If cash flow growth were faster or there were losses during the finite forecast period, the influence of the terminal value on the conclusion would be amplified.

- The starting point for the model is at the end of Year 0 (or at the start of Year 1). The cash flows are received at the end of each year of the forecast. This is clear in the DCF model above. The present value factors for Years 1 and 2 are calculated as follows:

$$(1 / (1 + 20\%)^1 = 0.8333) \quad (1 / (1 + 20\%)^2 = 0.6944)$$

These calculations clearly indicate discounting in Figure 1-2 for the whole periods, i.e., one full year, two full years, and so on. The importance of this assumption, rather than, for example, an assumption that cash flows are received (or reinvested) continuously, or as a proxy, at mid-year, is beyond "the very basics of value."[10] The purpose at this point is simply to focus on the assumptions of the model.

Owners of the example enterprise expect to receive a total return equal to the discount rate of 20%. How does this happen? There are two components of the expected return, the current return from expected distributions, and the expected growth in the value of the enterprise. The first is the expected return from interim cash flows, which can be described as the *yield on current value*. For the first period in Figure 1-2, cash flow is $1.0 million, which reflects a 10% yield on the current value of $10.0 million. We can also calculate the expected value at the end of each period and see that the return for each subsequent year is also 10%.[11]

The expected growth rate in value is also 10%, as can be confirmed by the growth of value from $10.0 million today to $16.1 million at the end of Year 5 (($10.0 x $(1 + 10\%)^5$)= $16.1). So the total expected return for the owners of the enterprise in Figure 1-2 is 20%, or the discount rate. This is comprised of the current yield on value of 10%, plus the expected growth in value of 10%. *The total return of 20% is achieved with full distribution of all interim cash flows.*

---

[10] Sensitivity to changes in assumptions is a fact of life in valuation. For example, changing the assumption to reflect receipt of cash flows at mid-year into perpetuity would raise value in this example from $10 million to $10.95 million, or increase it by 9.5%. The sensitivity of the Gordon Model and the DCF model to changes in assumptions is beyond the scope of "very basics." The basics are complicated enough, as we will soon see.

[11] For example, projected value at the end of Year 2 is equal to $12.1 million (Year 3 cash flow of $1,210 capitalized by $r - g$ of 10%). Expected cash flow for Year 3 divided by value at the end of Year 2 is 10% ($1.210 million / $12.1 million). Under the assumptions of Figure 1-2, this expected current return, or current yield, will be 10% for every year.

Intuitive Impact of Reinvesting Cash Flows

Each period, the owners of a business make one of four decisions:

- Distribute all cash flows or earnings to the owners of the business; or,

- Retain all cash flows or earnings in the business and reinvest them; or,

- Distribute a portion of cash flows and retain (reinvest) the remainder.

- Repurchases of stock could be considered a fourth decision, but repurchases, like distributions, return earnings to shareholders.

Intuitively, the value of a business whose cash flows are reinvested should grow in value more rapidly than a similar business whose cash flows were all distributed to its owners. This makes sense, because more dollars are retained in the former business upon which to achieve a return. Said another way, the business that retains all its earnings can experience more rapid growth in expected future earnings (upon which expected future value is based) than a similar business that distributes all its earnings.[12]

Revisiting the Gordon Model

Revisiting the Gordon Model and examining the basic DCF example to consider reinvestment in the enterprise will show that the intuitive analysis does indeed comport with financial theory as well as common sense. We can then consider the implications for valuation.

In Equation 1-2, the Gordon Model provided an estimate of the value of a business based upon its capitalized expected cash flows. It should be clear from Figure 1-2 and the discussion of its results that the *g* in Equation 1-2 reflects *the expected growth rate in the cash flows (or earnings)* of the enterprise. Equation 1-2 can be rewritten in generalized form as Equation 1-6 to show this relationship specifically:

---

[12]   However, retention of earnings does not necessarily imply optimal returns to shareholders. This will become clear when we focus on the importance of the expected reinvestment rate for non-distributing or partially distributing enterprises.

$$V_0 = \frac{\text{Earnings}}{r - g_e}$$

Equation 1-6 (The Earnings (CF) Growth Method)

g_e is the expected constant growth rate in earnings (consistent with the distribution of all earnings to shareholders). We stated earlier that the Gordon Model was a dividend growth model, rather than an earnings growth model. As originally formulated, the Gordon Model was designed to estimate the price of a security today based on a capitalization of its expected dividends, growing at a constant rate into perpetuity.

$$P_0 = \frac{D_1}{r - g_d}$$

Equation 1-7 (The Dividend Growth Model)

Where: P_o is the expected price of the security

D_1 is the expected dividend for the security

g_d is the expected growth rate of the dividend, D_1

D_1 represents the portion of the cash flows of the enterprise that is to be distributed. To relate Equations 1-6 and 1-7, we can express D_1 as follows:

D_1 = Earnings x DPO

DPO = Dividend Payout Ratio (dividends as a percentage of earnings)

Equation 1-7 can be rewritten as Equation 1-8:

$$P_0 = \frac{\text{Earnings} * \text{DPO}}{r - g_d}$$

Equation 1-8

If all earnings are distributed (DPO=100%), Equation 1-7 is equal to Equation 1-8 (and Equation 1-2), and the expected growth rate of the dividend (D_1) is equal to the expected growth rate of earnings (*Earnings*). Further, if we hold constant the discount rate (r), the price of the security (P_0), and its expected earnings (*Earnings*), the expected growth rate in the dividend (g_d) must vary with the dividend payout ratio.[13]

Finally, the expected growth in dividends (g_d) provides the trajectory for the expected growth in the value of the enterprise, which we denote as g_v. Using our previous assumptions and assuming earnings are $1.00 per share (D_1), we can calculate the stock price today (P_0) and next period (P_1).

Time 0	Time 1
$P_0 = \dfrac{D_1}{r - g_d}$	$P_1 = \dfrac{D_1(1+g_d)}{r - g_d}$
$P_0 = \dfrac{\$1.00}{r\,(20\%) - g\,(10\%)} = \$10.00$	$P_1 = \dfrac{\$1.00\,(1+10\%)}{r\,(20\%) - g\,(10\%)} = \$11.00$

Figure 1-3

Now we can determine the expected growth rate in value, g_v:

$$g_v = \frac{P_1}{P_0} - 1$$

$$g_v = \frac{\$11.00}{\$10.00} - 1 = 10\% = g_d$$

Equation 1-9

This insight is not particularly new; however, its implications for business valuation are not yet generally recognized. We will explore these implications in the remainder of this chapter.

If we substitute g_v for g_d in Equation 1-8, and solve for g_v, we get Equation 1-10 and Equation 1-11 following the interim substitutions:

$$P_0 (r - g_v) = Earnings * DPO$$

$$(r - g_v) = \frac{Earnings * DPO}{P_0} = \frac{D_1}{P_0}$$

$$g_v = \left(r - \frac{D_1}{P_0} \right)$$

$$g_v = \left(r - \frac{Earnings * DPO}{P_0} \right)$$

$$g_v = Discount\ Rate - Dividend\ Yield$$

Equation 1-10

$$r = g_v + \frac{D_1}{P_0}$$

$$= Growth\ in\ Value + Dividend\ Yield$$

Equation 1-11

In other words, the expected growth in value is equal to the discount rate less the expected dividend yield (Equation 1-10). If the dividend payout percentage is 100%, the expected growth in value is equal to the discount rate less the earnings yield. If the dividend payout percentage is 0% (and all earnings are retained), the expected growth in value is equal to the discount rate. Alternatively, the discount rate is equal to the expected growth in value plus the expected dividend yield (Equation 1-11). So we have confirmed the logic of Figure 1-2 and the intuitive logic that reinvestment should accelerate the expected growth in value over the base level of earnings growth without reinvestment. Reinvestment at r will achieve the required return of r for the enterprise.

The Core Business vs. Reinvestment Decisions

The Gordon Model provides an indication of the value of the equity of an enterprise if its (net) earnings are fully distributed (i.e., DPO = 100%). But what if the owners decide to reinvest all earnings in the business?[14]

In order to understand the difference between these two scenarios, it is helpful to think, conceptually (and somewhat artificially in terms of the way we look at businesses), about the future of a business enterprise as having two components:

- *The core business.* The core business is the existing enterprise. It is generating cash flows and earnings. The core level of earnings is normally expected to grow at a rate consistent with the company's market position and management capabilities (in the context of the local/regional/national/world economy). When business appraisers discuss the expected growth rate of earnings, they should be referring to the growth of this core level of earnings, or g_e.

  What is the expected growth in core earnings? This is a very important concept that needs explanation. We define g_e as the level of (constant) long-term growth available to a business assuming that all the net earnings of the business are distributed (i.e., DPO = 100%). This assumption has several important implications, including:

  - Capital expenditures are equal to depreciation

  - Positive net present value capital investments may be available

  - Inflationary price increases are achieved (to the extent reasonably available over time)

  - Productivity enhancements are also captured (to the extent reasonably available over time)

---

[14] The Gordon Model breaks down under the assumption that DPO = 0%. However, DPO = 0% is an unlikely long-term assumption. It would suggest that a company would retain all of its cash flows into perpetuity with no distributions to shareholders. Such an assumption would likely attract few investors.

Let us be clear about the core business. No investment of cash flows occurs above the level of capital expenditures equaling depreciation. There is only investment of depreciation charges to replace existing plant and equipment, but no reinvestment of cash flows into new plant or equipment for growth. Under these assumptions, value can be estimated using Equation 1-8 as follows:

$$V_0 = \frac{E_1 \times DPO}{r - g_d} = \frac{E_1 \times 100\%}{r - g_d} = \frac{Earnings}{r - g_d}$$

Equation 1-12

The long-term, core level of expected earnings growth for private companies will seldom exceed 10%. In fact, the *long-term* level of expected earnings growth for larger public companies seldom exceeds 10%, in spite of the fact that earnings for the next one, three, or five years might be expected to grow at rates of 15%, 25%, or more.[15]

- *The cumulative impact of reinvestment decisions.* Healthy business enterprises are earnings (cash flow) machines. They are designed to engage in economic activities and to generate earnings and cash flow. When earnings are retained in a business, such earnings should be viewed as being *reinvested* in the business. Over time, the bulk of all value in a business relates to reinvestment decisions, rather than to the growth in core earnings. The concept of the core business assumes no reinvestment of earnings into the business, but rather that all earnings are distributed. This point may not seem intuitive; nevertheless, it is important. It is another example of the magic of compound interest, where, over time, the earnings on earnings become more important than the earnings themselves.

---

[15] For example, assume a public company is expected to grow earnings at 30% for five years then at 20% for the next five years, and then at 10% for the following 50 years. The equivalent terminal value is reached assuming a constant growth in earnings of 12.4% for 60 years. Note, however, that this calculation is not value-weighted to reflect the much earlier realization of cash flows under the first scenario. Further, the 30% earnings growth in the near-term does not reflect "core" earnings growth alone since it is likely that no dividends are expected to be paid during this period.

While the distinction between the core business and the cumulative impact of reinvestment decisions may seem artificial, it is essential to understanding the nature of value creation. The DCF model can be used to examine both the core business and reinvestment decisions to facilitate this understanding. To do so, we will now focus on *future values*, rather than the *present values* that are the result of the DCF model as presented in Figure 1-2. But this is logical – without the expectation of future value, there is no present value. We use the same valuation example in Figure 1-2:[16]

Figure 1-4 takes the DCF model used in Figure 1-2 and focuses on expected future values, consistent with the discussion of the enterprise as being comprised of two components. Note the difference between Figure 1-4 and Figure 1-2. In Figure 1-2, all cash flows were *distributed* and investors achieved a return equal to the discount rate. In this case, the cash flows are reinvested in the business *and* they are reinvested at the discount rate of 20%. The future value of the core business is determined based on calculating expected value at the end of each year, given the next year's cash flow expectations, the discount rate of 20%, and expected growth rate in (core) earnings of 10%, or g_e.

Several observations about the future value analysis of Figure 1-4 help our understanding of the value creation process:

- The expected future value of the core business is $16.1 million, which is identical to the terminal value calculation in the DCF model in Figure 1-2. The terminal value comprises 65% of expected future value, just as the present value of the terminal value provided 65% of present value.

- The expected future value of reinvestments of cash flow is $8.8 million, or 35% of expected future value at the end of five years. The present value of the expected future value of reinvestments is precisely equal to the present value of expected interim cash flows, or $3.5 million (from Figure 1-2).

---

[16] Note two things about this example. First, we have used capital letters to denote expected growth in earnings (G_e) and growth in value (G_v) as well as the discount rate (R). We tend to do this when we move from the purely theoretical discussion to practical application. Second, it is explicitly assumed that earnings on reinvested cash flows earn a return of R, the discount rate.

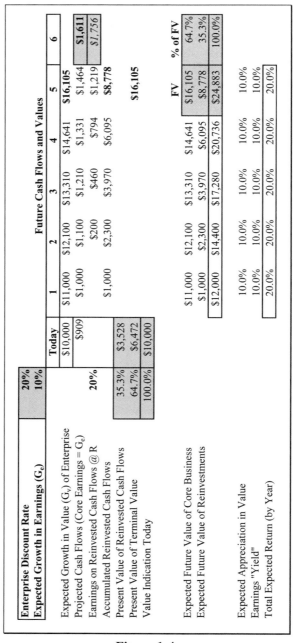

Enterprise Discount Rate	20%							
Expected Growth in Earnings (G$_e$)	10%							
				Future Cash Flows and Values				
		Today	1	2	3	4	5	6
Expected Growth in Value (G$_v$) of Enterprise		$10,000	$11,000	$12,100	$13,310	$14,641	**$16,105**	
Projected Cash Flows (Core Earnings = G$_e$)		$909	$1,000	$1,100	$1,210	$1,331	$1,464	**$1,611**
Earnings on Reinvested Cash Flows @ R	20%			$200	$460	$794	$1,219	*$1,756*
Accumulated Reinvested Cash Flows			$1,000	$2,300	$3,970	$6,095	$8,778	
Present Value of Reinvested Cash Flows	35.3%	$3,528						
Present Value of Terminal Value	64.7%	$6,472				$16,105		
Value Indication Today	100.0%	$10,000						
							FV	% of FV
Expected Future Value of Core Business			$11,000	$12,100	$13,310	$14,641	$16,105	64.7%
Expected Future Value of Reinvestments			$1,000	$2,300	$3,970	$6,095	$8,778	35.3%
			$12,000	$14,400	$17,280	$20,736	$24,883	100.0%
Expected Appreciation in Value			10.0%	10.0%	10.0%	10.0%	10.0%	
Earnings "Yield"			10.0%	10.0%	10.0%	10.0%	10.0%	
Total Expected Return (by Year)			20.0%	20.0%	20.0%	20.0%	20.0%	

Figure 1-4

- All reinvestments are assumed to provide a return equal to the discount rate of 20%. The compounding effect of these reinvestments has significant influence on the conclusion of value. How important is the reinvestment decision? If this company could grow core earnings at 10% and reinvested all cash flows at a net rate of 5% in cash and liquid securities for the first five years, rather than 20%, the value of the business would fall to $9.2 million from $10 million. This is true even assuming that the terminal value is calculated based on the higher reinvestment assumption (i.e., of reinvesting from the terminal year forward at the discount rate). We will investigate the impact of this issue on the value of enterprises and minority interests in those enterprises in later chapters.

- The expected return from an investment in this company is 20% per year over the forecasted five-year holding period. The expected return has two sources, the expected growth in value of the core business (10% per year based on g_e) and the "earnings yield" that is reinvested in the business, which is equivalent to 10% in this case (or r of 20% minus g_e of 10%). Note in Figure 1-4 that the forecasted cash flows for Year 6 are $1.611 million and that the *earnings on reinvested cash flows* are $1.756 million.

In Chart 1-1, we can see the growing importance of reinvestments in terms of expected future value for a 10-year forecast. Chart 1-1 continues to use the base example valuation but carries the discrete forecast period to 10 years:

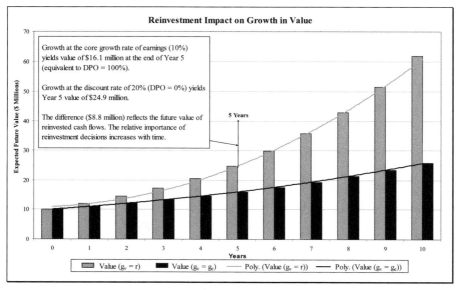

Chart 1-1

Chart 1-1 illustrates the magic of compound interest in the form of expected future values of a business. The expected growth in core value of the enterprise, the bottom area of the chart, is based on the expected growth of core earnings, or 10%. As a result, this base value grows from $10 million today to $16.1 million in five years. The compounding effect of reinvestment decisions is shown in the upper area of the chart. The upper boundary of the chart provides the cumulative effect of the growth of the core business and reinvestment decisions. Expected future value grows to $24.9 million after five years, aided by $8.8 million of future value of reinvested cash flows. The relative importance of reinvestment decisions is magnified with the passage of time, as can be seen as the forecast is extended to 10 years above.

To further highlight the importance of reinvestment decisions on value, note in the upper right portion of Figure 1-5 where the analysis is carried forward for a sixth year. At that point, the "earnings on earnings" from reinvestment exceed the projected core level of earnings.

It should be clear from the discussion above that the core growth rate of earnings is one driver in the determination of expected future value (and therefore, present value). In the present case, g_e is 10%. If all reinvested earnings are invested to yield r, the discount rate of 20%, then the expected total return in the example is 20%. The cumulative impact of reinvestment of cash flows raises the total return embodied within the business from 10% (based on g_e) to 20%, or r.[17]

The (present) value of the business in the example is $10 million (PV). The (future) value of the business at the end of five years will be $24.9 million (FV), which is the sum of the value of the core business growing at g_e and the accumulated value of all reinvestments, which have been made at r. As noted earlier, the compound return over the period is 20%. Said another way, the *expected growth in value* (g_v) is equal to r, the discount rate of 20%.

The consistency of the conclusions regarding present value and future value are derived directly from the nature of the DCF model. By now, it should be clear that g_e and g_v are different concepts. The inherent growth potential of the core business enterprise is reflected in g_e. The impact of reinvestment decisions regarding retained and reinvested cash flows adds to the growth of value of the enterprise above the level of g_e. To summarize:

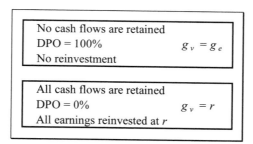

Figure 1-5

g_v will equal or exceed g_e and be less than or equal to r, depending upon the assumptions regarding DPO (the dividend payout ratio) used in the DCF model. In summary:

g_e is less than or equal to g_v which is less than or equal to r

---

[17] Of course, the same return would be earned by shareholders if all earnings were distributed to them and the business did not grow beyond its core earnings.

And finally, it should be clear from the foregoing discussion that the g of the $(r\text{-}g)$ term of the generalized Gordon Model of Equations 6 relates to g_e and not to g_v.

Two important observations have been made thus far:

1. The Gordon Model is equivalent to a discounted future cash flow analysis with certain simplifying assumptions, namely, (a) earnings grow at a constant rate into perpetuity and (b) all earnings are either distributed to shareholders or, if retained by the company, reinvested at the discount rate.

2. The expected growth in core earnings of an enterprise (g_e from Equation 1-6) is a distinct concept from the expected growth in value of an enterprise, or g_v. The expected growth in core earnings is a function of the markets in which a company operates, the quality of its management, the strength of the economy, inflation, long-term productivity enhancements, and other variables. The expected growth in value is a function of the expected dividend and reinvestment policy of the enterprise and the risk of the enterprise (as manifest in the required return), in addition to the expected growth in core earnings.

We can view the Gordon Model as a summary formulation for the valuation of public and private securities. It is a shorthand way of expressing key relationships between expected earnings (expected cash flow), expected growth of those cash flows, and risk. Of course, the Gordon Model is also a way of expressing two-stage discounted cash flow models (Equation 1-5) or the basic discounted cash flow model (Equation 1-4). Reinvested earnings, if successfully deployed at the discount rate, accelerate the growth in value, g_v, toward the discount rate, r. If all earnings are retained, and successfully reinvested at the discount rate, then the expected growth rate in value becomes the discount rate.

Core Earnings Growth (g_e) vs. Analysts' Expected Earnings Growth ($g*$)

In this section, we focus specifically on the relationship between expected growth in core earnings and the expected growth in reported earnings in the public securities markets that we call *analysts' g*, or $g*$. The Gordon Model represents the formula for determining the present value of a growing perpetuity. In other words, it is a mathematical relationship akin to the formula for determining the present value of an annuity.

As mentioned previously, the Gordon Model is also referred to as the Gordon Dividend Discount Model. In the context of a publicly traded stock, we can specify the Gordon Model as follows:

$$P_0 = \frac{D_1}{r - g_d}$$

Equation 1-13

The price of a publicly traded stock today reflects the present value of all expected future dividends. Ignoring for a moment the possibility of share repurchases by the company, the receipt of dividends represents the only return the shareholders, as a group, will receive from ownership of the stock – other than a sale of stock in the public market, where all expected future dividends are continuously capitalized in the market price. We derive the price/earnings multiple by dividing both sides of the equation by earnings for the coming year (E_1).

$$P_0/E_1 = \frac{D_1/E_1}{r - g_d}$$

Equation 1-14

Recognize that the expression (D_1/E_1) is the dividend payout ratio, or DPO.

$$P_0/E_1 = \frac{DPO}{r - g_d}$$

Equation 1-15

Now, assume that DPO equals 100%, or 1.0. Therefore, the P/E of Equation 1-15 is ($1 / (r - g)$). This should clarify that valuation analysts, who typically derive earnings multiples as ($1/(r - g)$), are making an implied assumption that all earnings of the company will be distributed, i.e., that the DPO = 100%.

We know it is a rare public company that distributes all of its earnings to shareholders. Therefore, it is important to understand the relationship between the expected earnings growth rates discussed by public securities analysts, the dividend payout ratios of public companies, and the expected earnings growth rates that analysts apply in the derivation of valuation multiples for closely held companies.

Assume the hypothetical company described in Figure 1-1 is publicly traded. As shown in Figure 1-1, an earnings multiple of 10.0x is appropriate, given the discount rate and core earnings growth assumptions. Assume further that the consensus estimate of analysts is that the company's reported earnings will grow at an annual rate of 17.5%. Does this imply that the company is undervalued with an earnings multiple of 10.0x? Not necessarily.

Why? Assume the company is expected to pay out approximately 25% of earnings as dividends. As shown in Figure 1-3, the retention (and subsequent reinvestment) of earnings fuels incremental earnings growth beyond that of the core earnings stream. The public securities analyst is concerned with growth in reported earnings, which includes both core and reinvested earnings. According to the dividend discount model introduced in Equations 1-6 through 1-8 and 1-15, the estimated 17.5% growth in reported earnings is consistent with the earnings multiple of 10.0x and the dividend payout ratio of 25%. Note that the g in Equation 1-6 is g^*. In Equation 1-16, these values are substituted from Equation 1-15.

$$10.0 = \frac{25\%}{20\% - 17.5\%}$$

Equation 1-16

Note that if there is a constant DPO, then $g_d = g^*$. If the valuation analyst had relied upon the $(1/(r - g))$ framework for determining the earnings multiple, consideration of the growth in reported earnings rather than core earnings would result in a material overvaluation of the company (Equation 1-17).

$$40.0 = \frac{1}{20\% - 17.5\%}$$

Equation 1-17

We can see then that an important and predictable relationship exists among the growth in core earnings, the dividend payout ratio, and the expected growth in reported earnings. This analysis assumes a constant dividend payout ratio (or its complement, a constant earnings retention ratio), so the reported growth in earnings will be equal to the growth rate of the cash flow based on a given level of retention.

We can now work with the Gordon Model equation to develop the following relationship between the expected growth rate of (core) earnings and the expected growth rate in cash flow (and, with a constant dividend payout ratio, the expected growth rate in reported earnings) in the series of equations labeled Equation 1-18.

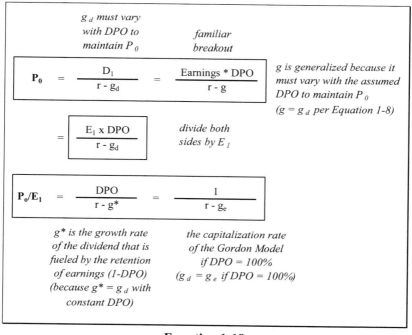

Equation 1-18

These equations can be further developed to illustrate the growth in core earnings of a company (g_e) according to the following relationships (where $g*$ equals growth in reported earnings) in Equation 1-19.[18]

$$g_e = \frac{g* - r\,(1\text{-DPO})}{DPO}$$

Equation 1-19

Conversely:

$$g* = r\,(1\text{-DPO}) + g_e DPO$$

Equation 1-20

The relationship among these variables at various dividend payout ratios and assuming $r = 20\%$ is developed in Figure 1-6:

	Required Return	*20.0%*
Dividend Payout Ratio	Growth in Core Earnings (g_e)	Growth in Reported Earnings ($g*$)
0%	10.0%	20.0%
10%	10.0%	19.0%
20%	10.0%	18.0%
40%	10.0%	16.0%
60%	10.0%	14.0%
80%	10.0%	12.0%
100%	10.0%	10.0%

Figure 1-6

---

[18]   Those like me who are algebraically impaired can believe that Equations 1-19 and 1-20 are derivable as shown.   Intuitively, the relationships make sense, and a practical example below will illustrate the results.

As the results in Figure 1-6 indicate, the expected growth in core earnings (g_e) is equal to that of reported earnings (g^*) only when the dividend payout ratio is 100%, in other words, when there are no expected earnings from reinvested cash flows. The Figure also indicates that, for a given level of core earnings growth, reported earnings growth is inversely related to the dividend payout ratio.

Therefore, we have seen that the growth in reported earnings estimated by public securities analysts is conceptually distinct from the core earnings growth rate. As our example has illustrated, failure to understand the relationship between these growth rates can result in significant overvaluation of a business. Put more simply, investors do not pay for earnings both as they are created (core earnings) and as the earnings subsequently generate returns after being reinvested by the company (earnings on reinvestment). Investors will only pay for a given dollar of earnings once. If an analyst relies on an estimate of growth in reported earnings, the valuation analysis should be based on cash flows actually received by the investor (a dividend discount model, rather than a single period income capitalization model based on earnings).[19]

NET INCOME VS. NET CASH FLOW

In the preceding section, we made what to some might appear to be an artificial distinction between the core growth in earnings and the reported growth in earnings. However, the distinction is critical to understanding the valuation principles embedded in the Gordon Model and the discounted cash flow model.

Multiple *g*'s and One *r* for the Gordon Model

Equation 1-21 illustrates four equalities using the algebraic framework of the Gordon Model. Three critical insights should be drawn from these equations.

$$V_0 = \frac{\text{Earnings}}{r - g_e} = \frac{D_1}{r - g_d} = \frac{\text{Earnings} * \text{DPO}}{r - g_d} = \frac{CF_1}{r - g_{cf}}$$

Equation 1-21

---

[19] If a single period income capitalization model is used, it should be appropriately adjusted for the dividend payout ratio (which would be complicated if the DPO is not expected to be constant over time).

For illustration, consider Earnings to be (net) Earnings. Net earnings are earnings net of depreciation and taxes, with no reinvestment of cash flows into the business. Net earnings can be equated with the earnings of the core business.

V_0 is constant. We show multiple expressions that are indicative of the same value for an enterprise. Now consider the following:

- *Insight 1.* The portion of (net) Earnings capitalized *varies* based on dividend payout (or earnings retention) policy. Differences between Earnings and expected cash flow (CF_1) are the result of differences in dividend payout policies.

- *Insight 2.* The expected growth rate, g, *varies* with the earnings measure employed (i.e., with DPO changes). This should be apparent, because earnings paid out cannot be retained to finance future growth.

- *Insight 3.* r, the discount rate *remains unchanged* with the degree of earnings retention or distribution.

We have shown that there are multiple g's involved in single period capitalization models:

- g_e is the growth in core earnings. It is associated with the first identity, which capitalizes (net) Earnings.

- g_d is the expected growth rate in the dividend associated with a particular dividend, D_1.

- And g_{cf} is the expected growth rate in cash flow associated with a particular dividend payout policy, which is to say, with a particular earnings retention or reinvestment policy.

In other words, as the portion of net earnings that is capitalized changes, g must change to retain the equality of V_0.

Now focus on the fact that r did not change in any of the equations. r is the discount rate applicable to expected (net) Earnings, to the expected dividend next period, to the (net) Earnings subject to any particular dividend payout policy, and to the expected net cash flow of the enterprise. We have a symbolic answer to the frequently asked question: "Does r relate to net income or to net cash flow?" Clearly the answer is yes. We now explore the implications of this observation.

Focus Again on g_e – the Long-Term Expected Growth Rate in Earnings

Although they were just stated above, the assumptions defining g_e bear repeating. g_e is a constant, long-term growth of net earnings available to a business that distributes all reported earnings each year. This implies that this level of growth occurs within the following parameters:

- Capital expenditures are assumed equal to depreciation. To the extent that current capital expenditures are more productive than the machinery or equipment that they replace, some growth can occur.

- Inflationary price increases are achieved to the extent they are achievable over time.

- Productivity enhancements are also captured to the extent available over time.

- Incremental working capital requirements are assumed to be negligible, with incremental assets being financed by incremental liabilities.

g_e is the long-term expected growth rate of the net earnings of a business. If it were not so, there would be some "automatic" level of reinvestment for which there would be no incremental return. Recall that the owners of businesses have the opportunity to make one of four decisions each period:

- Distribute all cash flows or earnings to the owners; or,

- Retain all cash flows or earnings in the business and reinvest them; or,

- Distribute a portion of cash flows and retain (reinvest) the rest; or,

- Repurchase shares (which, for our purposes, is analogous to a distribution).

Logically, there is no reason to retain earnings if there are no reinvestment opportunities. Reinvestment implies incremental return, or an acceleration of growth from the level of g_e towards r, the discount rate. Recall, investors always demand returns equal to the discount rate, r. That return can come in the form of current return or yield and from capital appreciation, which is fueled by reinvestment of net earnings.

Focus Again on $g*$ and the Long-Term Growth Rate in Cash Flow

If g_e is the long-term growth in the net earnings of an enterprise, what is $g*$? In Equation 1-21, we note that the g of the Gordon Model framework changes with dividend payout policy. This is to be expected, since funds that are not reinvested provide current returns and are not available to finance future growth. In Figure 1-4, we showed that $g*$, which was characterized as the growth in reported earnings, was different than g_e because of differences in the dividend payout ratio.

$g*$ is the expected growth in both reported earnings and net cash flow (assuming a constant dividend payout ratio). Consider this observation in the context of the appraisers' typical definition of net cash flow, which is defined as:

Net Income (after taxes)

+   Noncash Charges (depreciation and amortization and, possibly, deferred taxes)
-   Net Capital Expenditures (new purchases of fixed assets less disposals)
+/- Incremental Changes in Working Capital
+/- Net Changes in Long-Term Debt (or, perhaps, total debt, depending on capital structure)

=   **Net (Free) Cash Flow**

It is not necessarily obvious from examining the definition above, but the difference between Net Income (*Earnings* from Equation 1-21) and Net (Free) Cash Flow (CF_1 from Equation 1-21) is the firm's dividend payout policy. In a growing firm, net cash flow is usually less than net income as earnings are reinvested to finance that growth. The net cash flow (CF_1) is assumed to be distributable, while the difference between net income and net cash flow, the net reinvestment, is retained in the firm to finance growth.

We now see that $g*$, which was developed above conceptually as the *analysts' g*, or the expected growth in reported earnings, is also the expected growth rate in net cash flow under the assumption of a constant dividend payout policy.

The Relationship Between Net Income and Net Cash Flow

Figure 1-6 presented one way of illustrating the relationship between net income and net cash flow in terms of expected growth rates. There we say that the expected growth rate in reported earnings (net cash flow) increases as the dividend payout ratio is reduced, i.e., as earnings are retained to finance growth. However, a picture is often worth the proverbial thousand words.

Chart 1-2 shows the long-term relationship between net income (*Earnings*) and net cash flow (CF_1) in graphical form as two "strategies" are illustrated. The first strategy distributes 100% of earnings and the second distributes only 80%, retaining 20% to finance future growth. Investors are assumed to be indifferent to the two strategies. The first provides a higher current return and lower expected growth. The second provides a lower current yield, but higher expected capital appreciation.

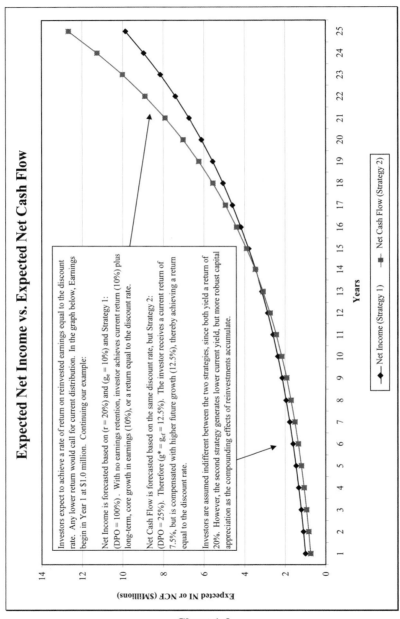

Expected Net Income vs. Expected Net Cash Flow

Investors expect to achieve a rate of return on reinvested earnings equal to the discount rate. Any lower return would call for current distribution. In the graph below, Earnings begin in Year 1 at $1.0 million. Continuing our example:

Net Income is forecasted based on (r = 20%) and (g_e = 10%) and Strategy 1: (DPO = 100%). With no earnings retention, investor achieves current return (10%) plus long-term, core growth in earnings (10%), or a return equal to the discount rate.

Net Cash Flow is forecasted based on the same discount rate, but Strategy 2: (DPO = 25%). Therefore (g^* = g_{cf} = 12.5%). The investor receives a current return of 7.5%, but is compensated with higher future growth (12.5%), thereby achieving a return equal to the discount rate.

Investors are assumed indifferent between the two strategies, since both yield a return of 20%. However, the second strategy generates lower current yield, but more robust capital appreciation as the compounding effects of reinvestments accumulate.

Chart 1-2

Does *r* Relate to Net Income or to Net Cash Flow?

In 1989, I wrote an article introducing the Adjusted Capital Asset Pricing Model (ACAPM), which presented a methodology for building up discount rates based on the Capital Asset Pricing Model (CAPM).[20] While some appraisers had been using similar techniques for some time, to the best of our knowledge, the 1989 article was the first written presentation of the build-up method using the CAPM. Appraisers were (and remain) somewhat divided regarding the applicability of build-up method discount rates to the net income or the net cash flow of enterprises.

From a practical viewpoint, analysts at Mercer Capital often capitalized (and still do) net income estimates, rather than net cash flow estimates because we have consistently achieved reasonable results in doing so. Other appraisers, in making the case that net cash flow is the appropriate measure for capitalization, have argued the following [with current comments in parentheticals]:

- For growing companies, net cash flow is generally less than net income. This point was made based on the definition of net cash flow that we examined above:

  Net Income (after taxes)

  \+ Noncash Charges (depreciation and amortization and possibly, deferred taxes)
  \- Net Capital Expenditures (new purchases of fixed assets less disposals)
  +/- Incremental Changes in Working Capital
  +/- Net Changes in Long-Term Debt (or, perhaps, total debt, depending on capital structure)

  = **Net Free Cash Flow**

  [Note, however, that if Net Cash Flow is less than Net Income, those who make this argument are implicitly assuming that a portion of earnings is being retained (i.e., that DPO < 100%).]

---

[20] Z. Christopher Mercer, "The Adjusted Capital Asset Pricing Model for Developing Capitalization Rates: An Extension of Previous 'Build-Up' Methodologies Based Upon the Capital Asset Pricing Model," *Business Valuation Review*, Vol. 8, No. 4 (1989): pp. 147-156. The concepts in this 1989 article form the foundation for the discussion of discount rates in Chapter 6.

- If one discount rate and growth rate are developed and used to capitalize both net income and an estimate of net cash flow, the former capitalized value will exceed the latter capitalized value. [This argument assumes the existence of multiple r's without logical or theoretical proof.]

- Ibbotson and others say, based on the fact that the returns used in the Ibbotson data series are *net cash flow to investors* (i.e., dividends plus capital appreciation), that the appropriate income measure to capitalize (or to discount) is therefore *the net cash flow of enterprises*. [This is reasonable if the returns include the full range of net cash flows, DPO=0% to DPO=100%.]

- If the above are true, it would follow that if the ACAPM (build-up) discount rate is used to capitalize net income, rather than net cash flow, an *adjustment factor* must be employed to convert the net cash flow discount rate to one applicable to net income.

So this line of reasoning suggested that there must be an adjustment factor for r. But no one could determine what it should be, except in a general range of 2% to 6% or so. In light of these comments, I wrote an article in 1990 with the title "Adjusting Capitalization Rates for Differences Between Net Income and Net Free Cash Flow."[21] While the title of the article mentions adjusting *capitalization rates*, the article actually developed an adjustment factor to adjust build-up *discount rates* (based on the Adjusted Capital Asset Pricing Model), i.e., the subject of the 1989 article noted above (and the subject of Chapter 6). The adjustment factor was then used across a range of expected growth assumptions to determine the impact on capitalization rates.

The 1990 article suggested that it was appropriate to apply the ACAPM discount rate to the net income (or the net cash flow) of enterprises. It also developed a way to estimate the mathematical adjustment factor that showed, under relevant ranges of assumptions regarding earnings retention (dividend payout) policies, that the factor would be fairly small. It further concluded that the magnitude of any adjustment factor applicable to r was within the range of judgments made routinely by appraisers regarding discount rates and capitalization rates. These judgments include the choice of Treasury rates, the selection of arithmetic means or geometric mean returns (or something in between), and the estimation of size premiums and other company-specific risk premiums.

---

[21]   Z. Christopher Mercer, "Adjusting Capitalization Rates for Differences Between Net Income and Net Free Cash Flow," *Business Valuation Review*, Vol. 11, No. 4 (1992): p. 201.

As it turns out, I believe I was right in 1990, but for the wrong reasons. The analysis above suggests that there is no adjustment factor for r, but rather, any adjustments in capitalizations of earnings relate to dividend payout policies and their accompanying impact on the expected growth of cash flows. In Equation 1-20 (and repeated in Equation 1-22), we developed the means to convert an estimate of g_e into g^*, or the expected growth rate in net cash flow given a particular r and DPO:

$$g^* = r(1-DPO) + g_e DPO$$

Equation 1-22

We have calculated a range of implied g^*s and the related adjustment factors (relative to g_e) in Figure 1-7, given our recurring example of a discount rate of 20% and expected growth in earnings of 10%.

						Dividend Payout Ratios						
r	20.0%	100.0%	97.5%	95.0%	92.5%	90.0%	87.5%	85.0%	82.5%	80.0%	77.5%	75.0%
						Implied Earnings Retention Ratios						
			2.5%	5.0%	7.5%	10.0%	12.5%	15.0%	17.5%	20.0%	22.5%	25.0%
g	10.0%	g_e				g^* = Expected Growth Rates Applicable to Net Cash Flow						
		10.0%	10.3%	10.5%	10.8%	11.0%	11.3%	11.5%	11.8%	12.0%	12.3%	12.5%
						Adjustment Factor for g (g^* - g_e)						
			0.3%	0.5%	0.8%	1.0%	1.3%	1.5%	1.8%	2.0%	2.3%	2.5%

Figure 1-7

As with the estimation of the mistaken adjustment factor relative to r in the 1990 article, we find that the adjustment factors over the relevant *long-term* range of dividend payout ratios, which would be applicable to single-period income capitalization methods, are relatively small.[22] However, this analysis does suggest that appraisers need to focus more clearly on the expected growth rates used when applying the Gordon Model.

---

[22] The calculated adjustment factors tend to increase in size as the capitalization rate, or the difference between r and g increases (as the implied multiples of earnings/cash flows decreases). Alternatively, the calculated adjustment factors tend to decrease as r - g decreases and the capitalization rate increases.

Further Analysis Regarding Net Income vs. Net Cash Flow

It appears to be a widely held thought among appraisers that build-up discount rates and those developed using the Adjusted Capital Asset Pricing Model are applicable to the *net cash flow* of enterprises. In fact, a leading textbook addresses the issue of net income versus net cash flow as follows:

> 501.10　　Both of the methods mentioned above [either guideline company or build-up] result in a discount rate for *net cash flow*, which is the benefit stream used in the discounted cash flow method. However, another common benefit stream that may be appropriate is *net earnings*. This benefit stream is used in the capitalized net earnings method. Whatever benefit stream is selected (net income or net earnings), the corresponding discount rate or cap rate must be stated in that same manner. For example, a net cash flow discount rate should not be used to discount net earnings. Instead, a separate net earnings discount rate must be developed, or the benefit stream should be adjusted to net cash flow. [23] [emphasis in original]

The Fishman text quoted above then discusses two methods to convert net cash flow discount rates to net income discount rates (at pages 5-8 to 5-10). The first method is based on judgmental comparisons to a rule of thumb range of 3% to 6%. The second method is based on the procedures outlined in my 1990 article quoted above (which also appeared in *Valuing Financial Institutions*, my first book). The Fishman text provides a step-by-step procedure (based on my article) for converting a net cash flow discount rate (using the build-up method or the ACAPM method) to one applicable to net income. The discussion in the Fishman text is in the context that relates specifically to single-period income capitalization methods. The same methodology is discussed in the fourth edition of Pratt's *Valuing a Business*.[24]

---

[23]　Jay E. Fishman, Shannon P. Pratt, J. Clifford Griffith, and D. Keith Wilson, *Guide to Business Valuations* 14th ed. (Fort Worth, TX: Practitioners Publishing Company, 2004), p. 5-6. For convenience, we refer to this as the Fishman text.

[24]　Shannon P. Pratt, Robert F. Reilly, and Robert P. Schweihs, *Valuing a Business: The Analysis and Appraisal of Closely Held Companies*, 4th ed. (New York, NY: McGraw-Hill, 2000), pp. 151-201.

It should be clear from the discussion in this chapter, however, that the market's discount rate does not change as a result of changes in dividend policy or with changes in earnings retention decisions. Market-derived discount rates apply to enterprise cash flows. This is true whether they are derived directly from guideline company analysis or indirectly using build-up methods.

Chapter 6 addresses the issue further, noting that Dr. Shannon Pratt reiterates the point that build-up and CAPM-related discount rates are applicable to net cash flow. That discussion is based solely on comments from Ibbotson Associates.

Now, let us look at a very practical example. Figure 1-8 displays a two-stage valuation model to value the net income and/or net cash flows of a public (or private) company. The first stage covers Years 1-10 and the second stage relates to the terminal value. As indicated, the model provides a value indication of a company where the discount rate is 16.0%, and expected growth in earnings (near-term and thereafter) is 6.0% per year. This is, effectively, the same example used earlier in this chapter.

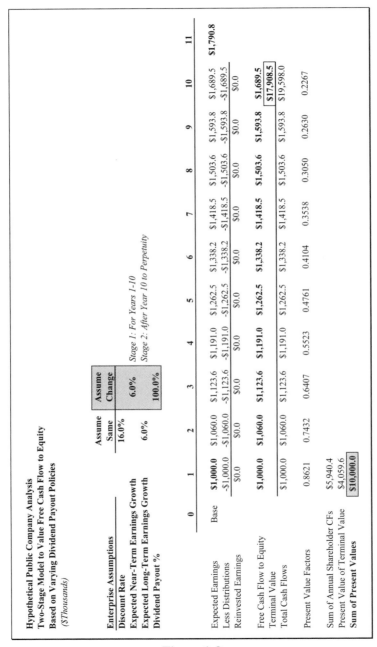

Hypothetical Public Company Analysis
Two-Stage Model to Value Free Cash Flow to Equity
Based on Varying Dividend Payout Policies
($Thousands)

Enterprise Assumptions	Assume Same	Assume Change
Discount Rate	16.0%	
Expected Near-Term Earnings Growth	6.0%	6.0%
Expected Long-Term Earnings Growth	6.0%	
Dividend Payout %		100.0%

Stage 1: For Years 1-10
Stage 2: After Year 10 to Perpetuity

	0	1	2	3	4	5	6	7	8	9	10	11
Expected Earnings	Base	**$1,000.0**	$1,060.0	$1,123.6	$1,191.0	$1,262.5	$1,338.2	$1,418.5	$1,503.6	$1,593.8	$1,689.5	**$1,790.8**
Less Distributions		-$1,000.0	-$1,060.0	-$1,123.6	-$1,191.0	-$1,262.5	-$1,338.2	-$1,418.5	-$1,503.6	-$1,593.8	-$1,689.5	
Reinvested Earnings		$0.0	$0.0	$0.0	$0.0	$0.0	$0.0	$0.0	$0.0	$0.0	$0.0	
Free Cash Flow to Equity		**$1,000.0**	**$1,060.0**	**$1,123.6**	**$1,191.0**	**$1,262.5**	**$1,338.2**	**$1,418.5**	**$1,503.6**	**$1,593.8**	**$1,689.5**	
Terminal Value											**$17,908.5**	
Total Cash Flows		$1,000.0	$1,060.0	$1,123.6	$1,191.0	$1,262.5	$1,338.2	$1,418.5	$1,503.6	$1,593.8	$19,598.0	
Present Value Factors		0.8621	0.7432	0.6407	0.5523	0.4761	0.4104	0.3538	0.3050	0.2630	0.2267	

Sum of Annual Shareholder CFs	$5,940.4
Present Value of Terminal Value	$4,059.6
Sum of Present Values	**$10,000.0**

Figure 1-8

The value of the indicated enterprise is $10.0 Million. Note that the identical conclusion is reached by the application of the Gordon Model ($1,000/(16%-6%)). The purpose of this illustration is to show clearly that all earnings are being paid out, and that earnings are growing based on the long-term g_e, or 6.0%.

In Figure 1-9, we show the results of running this model under three other assumptions regarding dividend payout, 50%, 25%, and 0%. This analysis makes clear all the calculations implied in the earlier discussion surrounding Figure 1-6.

In the two-stage model, there is a relationship between the dividend payout policy and the ability of the enterprise to grow during the Stage 1 period of the first 10 years. If DPO = 100%, the enterprise can grow at its long-term, core earnings rate (g_e) of 6.0%. At the other extreme, if DPO= 0%, and all earnings are reinvested, the business can grow earnings (and value) at 16.0%, or at r, the discount rate (assuming reinvestment at the discount rate). And with dividend payouts in between, near-term earnings growth is accelerated from the core rate of 6.0% towards the discount rate (again, assuming reinvestment at r).

This analysis should make clear, even before discussing discount rates in more depth in Chapter 6, that the discount rate of the discounted cash flow model and the Gordon Model *relates both to the net income and the net cash flow* of business enterprises. Distribution policy does not change the discount rate, as implied by the quote from the Fishman text (and reference to the Pratt text). Rather, distribution policy (and the implied reinvestment policy) impacts expected growth in earnings, cash flows, and value.

Summary of Free Cash Flow to Equity Model
for Four Different Assumptions re Dividend Payout Policy
($Thousands)

Assumptions/Results	DPO #1	DPO #2	DPO #3	DPO #4	
Discount Rate	16.0%	16.0%	16.0%	16.0%	Only difference is DPO policy -- otherwise companies exactly identical
Expected Near-Term Earnings Growth	6.0%	11.0%	13.5%	16.0%	Increasing reinvestment fuels near-term growth of earnings
Expected Long-Term Earnings Growth	6.0%	6.0%	6.0%	6.0%	The second stage calls for 6% long-term growth in all cases
Dividend Payout %	100.0%	50.0%	25.0%	0.0%	Assume four different levels of constant free cash flow to equity holders
Year 1 Expected Net Income	$1,000.0	$1,000.0	$1,000.0	$1,000.0	
Indicated Value	$10,000.0	$10,000.0	$10,000.0	$10,000.0	Dividend policy should not impact enterprise value
Year 11 Net Income	$1,790.8	$2,839.4	$3,547.8	$4,411.4	The "cost" of a current, higher payout is lower expected future earnings
Terminal Value	$17,908.0	$28,394.0	$35,478.0	$44,114.0	and lower expected terminal values
Present Value of Dividends	$5,940.4	$3,563.5	$1,957.7	$0.0	As the DPO % decreases, the shareholder returns are shifted to
Present Value of Terminal Value	$4,059.6	$6,436.5	$8,042.3	$10,000.0	the future
Portion of Expected Value as Terminal Value	40.6%	64.4%	80.4%	100.0%	

Model Discounts/Capitalizes

		DPO #1	DPO #2	DPO #3	DPO #4	
	Near-Term (Years 1-10)	Net Income	FCF	FCF	Nothing	As varies the DPO %, which is synonymous with varying the ratio of Net Cash Flow to Net Income the model discounts Free Cash Flow during the interim periods and Net Income for the Terminal Value. The discount rate does not change.
The Gordon Model	Terminal Value	Net Income	Net Income	Net Income	Net Income	

Figure 1-9

In practical application, these observations suggest at least the following:

- When applying single-period income capitalization methods, it is entirely appropriate to estimate ongoing (normalized) earning power based on the net income of an enterprise, and then to capitalize that earning power using a build-up discount rate or one developed using the Adjusted Capital Asset Pricing Model.

- When using the discounted cash flow model, the appropriate earnings measure to discount during a discrete forecast period would be the net (free) cash flow of the business. This net free cash flow would be that level of cash flow available to shareholders after all capital expenditures, working capital requirements, debt service retirements, and the like. When developing the terminal value, it would then be appropriate to capitalize the expected net income of the enterprise, growing at its core, long-term growth rate. We will comment further on this issue in Chapter 6.

We expect these findings to be somewhat controversial with many appraisers. However, they are, in reality, no different than what we have suggested since 1989 – albeit now with much more refined logic.

PRACTICAL OBSERVATIONS FROM THE VERY BASICS OF VALUE

This chapter thus far has explored the discounted cash flow model and the Gordon Model in detail. Hopefully, readers will have gained fresh perspective into both models. Truthfully, we were employing both models for many years before gaining the insight necessary to write the chapter. We conclude with a number of observations regarding the DCF method in light of the discussion above and assuming a basic understanding of valuation approaches and methods. At this point it is helpful to place our discussion of the DCF and the Gordon Model into the context of everyday valuation practice.

There are three basic approaches to valuation. Within the basic approaches, there are numerous valuation methods, and within various methods, appraisers apply appropriate valuation procedures. Definitions for each of the three valuation approaches can be found in the most current *Business Valuation Standards* of the American Society of Appraisers, but they can be described generally as follows:

- *Cost Approach.* The cost approach considers the cost to reproduce or replace the service capability of assets. In business valuation, methods under the cost approach are usually asset-based methods.

- *Income Approach.* Under the income approach, measures of income are discounted to the present or are capitalized. The discounted cash flow method is a method under the income approach, as is the single-period income capitalization method represented by the Gordon Model. The two-stage DCF model represented by Equation 1-5 incorporates both the DCF method (for the PVICF) and the single-period income capitalization (for the PVTV).

- *Market Approach.* The market approach compares valuation measures for a subject company with valuation metrics taken from the markets – either the public securities markets, the market for similar companies, or even the market for the securities of the subject (public or private) company. Typical valuation methods under the market approach are the guideline (public) company method and the guideline transactions method.

This book outlines the Integrated Theory of Business Valuation. However, theory must be applied in everyday practice. At this point, it will be helpful to make several observations about the discounted cash flow method, lest the theory be misused or misunderstood.

An examination of Equation 1-5 and experience lead to a number of important observations about the discounted cash flow method.

- *The projected earnings are important.* While this observation may seem obvious, the projected earnings must be reasonable for the subject company. What does this mean? It means that the projection for the interim period must make sense in the context of a company's past (if it has one), the market within which the company operates, the performance of similar companies, the capabilities of management, other logical benchmarks, and common sense. Excel^{TM} will forecast anything, depending on the inputs to a spreadsheet. It is up to the appraiser to make logical and reasonable assumptions when forecasting cash flow.

- *The interim period of the forecast is a matter of appraiser's judgment.* If income is stable and growing at a fairly constant rate, a single-period income capitalization method may be appropriate. The DCF method is most helpful when the expected cash flows over the next year or two (or three or four or more) are significantly different from those that may be expected after a finite period of growth, decline, recovery, or stabilization. Appraisers may forecast for any relevant period, although most forecasts are in the range of three to 10 years, with five years being the most common.

- *r, the discount rate, should be appropriate to the measure of cash flow selected.* This chapter on the very basics of valuation is conceptual and does not address the development of the discount rate, which will be treated in Chapter 6. But note that the measure of cash flow can vary from Net Earnings (DPO = 100%) to Net Cash Flow (DPO < 100%), while the discount rate does not change. All cash flows considered thus far have been net (after-tax) cash flows. If pre-tax cash flows are considered, the discount rate should be adjusted appropriately.

- *The terminal value estimation is critical.* In a typical five-year DCF forecast, the terminal value will account for 60% to 80% or more of the total present value for the method. Obviously, the development of the terminal value is important.

  - Other things being equal, the higher the discount rate, r, the lower will be the terminal value (and the indication of value for the method), and the terminal value will account for a lower portion of the total present value.

  - Other things being equal, the higher the expected growth rate, g (i.e., the long-term expected growth in g core earnings, or g_e), used in the terminal value calculation, the higher will be the terminal value, and it will account for a larger portion of the total present value. This should be apparent, because $1 / (r - g)$ develops the multiple (capitalization factor) to be applied to the terminal cash flow, and the higher the g, the higher the multiple.

- In theory, the g in the terminal value should not be very high – and most appraisers use long-term g's in the range of 3% or 4% up to 8% or 10% on the high side. Double digit long-term g's are typically considered unusual, since the implied earnings growth into perpetuity becomes astounding over time. Further, higher g's almost certainly include the effect of reinvestment rather than growth in core earnings.

- While this book will scarcely address the r to be used in a DCF forecast based on the total capital of an enterprise, i.e., the weighted average cost of capital (WACC), it should be obvious that the terminal value determination is even more sensitive to the selection of g in such scenarios than for forecasts of cash flows to equity holders.

- *Not all appraisers use the Gordon Model to develop the terminal value.* In practice, many appraisers (and market participants) use market-based methods to develop the terminal value multiple. Current market multiples (of net income, pre-tax income, EBITDA, debt-free net income, or others, as appropriate to the selected cash flow measure) are often applied to the forecasted cash flow in Year f, the last year of the discrete forecast, or to the Year f + 1. Some appraisers have suggested that this method is "wrong" because it mixes an income approach method (DCF for the finite forecast) and a market approach method (usually guideline company methods). It is unclear to me why such a mixing is necessarily wrong. Given this procedure's widespread use and utility in developing reasonable indications of value using the DCF method, it should not be considered unusual or incorrect – provided that reasonable multiples from the public marketplace (or the market for transactions) are selected.[25] But "reasonable multiples" from the public marketplace today may not be reasonable for application five to 10 years from now, particularly if the industry is in a very rapid growth phase and growth is expected to slow down in a few years.

---

[25] This point about the reliability of "mixing" approaches is further substantiated by common practice. If the Gordon Model is used to develop a terminal multiple, the very first test of the reasonableness of the derived multiple is to test it in the context of current public market multiples. For example, an appraiser used $1 / (r\text{-}g)$ to develop a terminal multiple of 20.0x debt-free net income in a subject company's DCF method. The credibility of that multiple will be supported if the median debt-free net income multiple for his guideline public group is in the range of 18x to 22x or so. However, its credibility might be questioned if the range of similar multiples in his guideline group was from 10x to 14x.

- *What projections should be used?* This observation is the corollary to the statement that the cash flow forecast is important. In many cases, the management of a subject enterprise will provide a forecast (or forecasts) of expected future performance. Appraisers using such forecasts are obligated to test their reasonableness and to develop discount rates that are reasonably reflective of the risks of achieving the forecasted results. In the absence of management forecasts, appraisers must take care to develop forecasts that make sense in the context of a company's history, its outlook and the capabilities of its management, as well as in the context of its market and industry. For example, I recently reviewed a valuation report in which the appraiser projected rapid growth in earnings (in this case, EBITDA, or earnings before interest, taxes, depreciation, and amortization) that reflected margins for the terminal year in excess of any public company in its industry. In this case, the appraiser failed to show calculations of EBITDA margins in his report for either the subject company or for the selected guideline public companies. This appraiser then failed to calculate the EBITDA multiple implied by his DCF conclusion, which was 80% higher than the EBITDA multiple employed in his guideline transactions method in the same report. Projections used in the DCF method should be reasonable.

The discounted cash flow method is an excellent tool for appraisers. However, its use is neither appropriate nor necessary in every appraisal. Some appraisers seem to believe that the DCF method provides "ultimate truth" – whatever that is. It does not. It can be used directly to provide reasonable valuation indications and, like other valuation methods, it can be misused. The DCF method can also be used effectively to test the reasonableness of other valuation methods or conclusions.

CONCLUSION

The "very basics of value" are not so basic. This chapter has analyzed the discounted cash flow model and the Gordon Model in considerable detail. Hopefully, we have provided fresh insights and a growing understanding of these two tools that appraisers often use without a full appreciate of their implications.

The "very basics of value" form the foundation for the Integrated Theory of Business Valuation introduced in Chapter 3. Before proceeding to the Integrated Theory, however, we examine certain fundamental principles of the world of value that are important to understanding how the "very basics of value" are used for investing and financial decision-making in the real world, as well as in the hypothetical world of fair market value.

Chapter 2

Organizing Principles of the "World of Value"

INTRODUCTION

During the formative years of my business valuation career, I gradually became aware that six underlying financial, economic, logical, and psychological principles provide a solid basis for looking at what we can call the "world of value." Let us refer to these as the *organizing principles of business valuation,* because the integration of the principles provides a logical and consistent framework within which to examine business valuation questions and issues. These principles also provide the qualitative framework within which to discuss the Integrated Theory of Business Valuation. This chapter is reflective of my continuing journey to understand the world of value and is written in a more personal tone that the other chapters in the book.

COMMON QUESTIONS

1. Where does the generalized valuation model: Value = Earnings x Multiple come from?

2. How can business appraisers test the reasonableness of their valuation assumptions and conclusions?

THE WORLD OF VALUE

The "world of value" consists of all the various markets in which valuation and investment decisions are made by real investors, whether individuals, companies, institutions or governments. This world includes, but is certainly not limited to, the public stock and bond markets, the private placement markets for debt and equity securities, and the market participation reflected by the investment decisions of individuals, corporations, institutions, and governments.

The world of value is the real world. If appraisers develop a solid understanding of the world of value, they are more likely to be able to develop reasonable valuation conclusions under the standards of value appropriate for valuation assignments, including fair market value, fair value, investment value, and others. So we begin with a general, noninstitutionally oriented, discussion of the world of value.

GRAPES OF VALUE

Six organizing principles of the world of value have been identified, and the six give rise to a seventh. The acronym, GRAPES, provides a convenient word to help arrange and remember the first six organizing principles. So, with a tribute to John Steinbeck, GRAPES are called the "Grapes of Value."

G	Growth
R	Risk/Reward
A	Alternative Investments
P	Present Value
E	Expectational
S	Sane, Rational, and Consistent

The seventh principal embodies the characteristics of the six elements of GRAPES – *knowledge*. The element of knowledge is the proverbial basket that holds the GRAPES of Value.

The world of value is fascinating. The organizing principles lay the groundwork for the Integrated Theory of Business Valuation, which will be introduced shortly. In the meantime, the organizing principles provide a basis for addressing nearly every business valuation issue. They are descriptive of the underlying behavior of public securities markets, which form the (direct or indirect) comparative basis for the valuation of most businesses and business interests.

The principles also provide a framework for testing the rationality or reasonableness of valuation positions advanced by appraisers. I have used these principles actively for many years, both as an organizing tool for valuation thinking and as a review tool for work performed by Mercer Capital and other firms.

CLARITY COMES SLOWLY

The following section relates to my first valuation client and a business relationship that lasted almost fifteen years. It represents an element of self-indulgence, although I do believe it highlights the process of grappling with valuation issues and growing in the process. Readers can skip it or read it without loss of continuity.

Lessons Learned from First Valuation Client

My business valuation career began officially in late 1978, when I was hired as the bank stock analyst by Morgan Keegan & Company, Inc., then, a small New York Stock Exchange member investment banking firm. No one there was doing appraisals, so I volunteered to take over that small segment of the firm's business, as well as the bank research function. As luck would have it, I sold a business valuation engagement within a few days of being hired, and then had to provide the service. I searched everywhere at the firm for a book on business valuation – to no avail.

Fortunately, my former boss, the CFO at First Tennessee National Corporation, gave me the only book he had. It was written by two partners of what was then Price Waterhouse & Co., and had been published in 1971.[26]

---

[26] George D. McCarthy and Robert E Healy, *Valuing a Company: Practices and Procedures* (New York: The Roland Press Company, 1971).

Unfortunately, after reading the book in its entirety, I did not have the foggiest idea of what a business valuation was or how to perform one. In fairness to the authors, the book was filled with useful information about the public markets, securities regulation, and accounting issues. However, it did little to solve my immediate problem, which was to provide the annual appraisal for Plumley Rubber Company.[27]

So I did what any rational person would do under the circumstances. I located every written appraisal report I could find, read them all, and played a game of "monkey see, monkey do." The first two reports I wrote on Plumley Rubber Company ("Plumley") have been lost. However, I have file copies beginning with 1980, the third year of Morgan Keegan's assignment with the company. Plumley obtained an annual appraisal in connection with a non-qualified Employee Retirement and Savings Plan. The appraisals were used as the basis for employee stock purchases and for repurchases of shares from departing employees, so they provided the basis for the pricing of transactions each year. The company and its employees took these appraisals seriously.

A brief walk down memory lane may be instructive. In fairness to myself and to Morgan Keegan, my comments about the Plumley reports are made from today's perspective and with today's experience. The quality of the reports at the time exceeded that of the best appraisals I was aware of in the late 1970s and early 1980s. So we walk:

---

[27] As a matter of policy, Mercer Capital does not disclose client names without specific permission. Mr. Harold Plumley was my first business appraisal client. When I left Morgan Keegan in 1982 and formed Mercer Capital, Morgan Keegan declined to continue to provide Mr. Plumley's annual appraisal, so he became one of Mercer Capital's first clients. We valued the company every year until 1995, the year in which it was sold. Mr. Mike Plumley, son of the founder, and then chairman of Plumley Companies, made a presentation at the Advanced Business Valuation Conference of the American Society of Appraisers in 1996. During that presentation, he discussed, among other things, the value to the Plumley family and to the company of having an annual appraisal over a period of nearly 20 years.

- *Fiscal 1978.* Somehow, I wrote a valuation report and valued Plumley Rubber Company. As it turns out, Morgan Keegan's appraisal was the second appraisal of Plumley that year – Mr. Plumley had been having another firm provide an annual appraisal for several years. When I called to discuss a reappraisal for fiscal 1979, Mr. Plumley told me that Morgan Keegan had the job going forward. I was, of course, ecstatic, and thanked him for the business. Mr. Plumley asked me if I wanted to know why we had gotten the business exclusively for future years. Then he said something I have never forgotten, "Chris, when I read your report, I recognized my company." May we all remember the advice embodied in Mr. Plumley's comment!

- *Fiscal 1980.* The report consisted of 12 pages of text and four pages of exhibits. The financial analysis was decent and on point. The comparable company analysis reflected a reasonable understanding of public markets and the need to make relevant comparisons between the subject company and the guideline group. However, it is apparent that I had little concept of what a marketability discount was, and little objective information to support one. The report reads: "In addition, we have considered the lack of marketability of the minority interests being valued. In each of the previous reports we have arrived at a discount to the average price/earnings multiple, considering all factors, of between 20-25 percent." That was the conclusion, and that was the extent of the discussion of the marketability discount. However, it is apparent from the surrounding text that the 20% to 25% discount also related to fundamental differences between Plumley Rubber Company and the comparable public companies. The conclusion seems reasonable based on a reading of the report and the information included in it. However, clarity was lacking on some important issues.

- *Fiscal 1981.* The report grew to 15 pages of text and five pages of exhibits, and the financial analysis was lengthened. We added a statement of independence, and information on the qualifications of the firm and the appraisers. We also added an appendix listing contingent and limiting conditions. The fundamental/marketability discount remained nebulously specified in the 20% to 25% range. Still not so good on these important issues.

- *Fiscal 1982.* The business relationship shifted to Mercer Capital in early calendar 1983, when the annual appraisal for fiscal year 1982 was prepared. The guideline company analysis was more thorough, and we (I) developed the appropriate multiple by focusing on specific companies in a broader group. In effect, without using the term, we applied a *fundamental discount* to the group's median and average multiples.[28] For the first time, there is a section entitled *Minority Discount.* In that section, we actually discussed the concept of lack of marketability and applied a 20% *discount for lack of marketability.* So it was late 1982 or early 1983 before I focused specifically and solely on the issue of the marketability discount. There is no reference to benchmark pre-IPO or restricted studies, but the brief discussion indicates that the selected discount was mitigated by the company's long-standing policy of repurchasing shares (at appraised values) from departing or terminated employees who had obtained stock under the employee savings and investment program. Some progress. We distinguished between fundamental issues relating to the value of the enterprise and issues related to the value of the shareholders' minority interests.

- *Fiscal 1983.* Report not in the file.

- *Fiscal 1984.* This report was issued in February 1985, and demonstrates considerable evolution in report structure and content. The report consisted of 25 pages of text and eight pages of exhibits. The fiscal 1984 report contained three features that remain, to this date, part of "the way things are done" at Mercer Capital. More progress:

  - *Fundamental Adjustments.* In a section labeled *Adjustments to the Base Capitalization Rate,* we developed a 15% fundamental discount based primarily on differences in leverage and growth between Plumley and the comparable public companies. That was pretty good. However, we confused this concept with an additional 10% discount relating to the fact that our subject paid no dividends and all but one of the comparables paid regular dividends. This clearly (now) should have been considered as an element influencing the marketability discount. So clarity began to come only slowly.

---

[28] We now refer to fundamental *adjustments* relative to public guideline groups because subsequent experience has proven that such adjustments can be positive or negative.

- *Marketability Discount.* There is a section entitled *Adjustments for Lack of Marketability.* Since this book will discuss the concept of the marketability discount at great length in future chapters, I thought it would be instructive to quote this early discussion of the marketability discount in its entirety:

  The valuation of shares in stock in closely held corporations typically warrants large discounts (up to 50%) for lack of marketability and control. An interest in a public company can readily be sold at or near its quoted price. Shares in closely held corporations are not easily sold due to the lack of a public market.

  In our opinion, a valuation discount of approximately 10% is necessary to reflect the net impact of the lack of marketability and control for the minority interest nature of the Company's shares under the definition of fair market value cited above.

  The marketability discount considers the Company's recent "market making" activities will continue for the near future. The assumption is made based upon specific conversations with management about plans to continue purchasing stock at currently appraised values. Apart from these considerations, the marketability discount would be higher. The 10% discount is the same as used in our valuation report for the fiscal year ending October 31, 1983.

Except for the confusion between marketability and (lack of) control, we were on the right track with the marketability discount. We likely had Shannon Pratt's first edition of *Valuing a Business* by 1984, therefore the reference to marketability discounts of up to 50%.[29] And it was refreshing to see that I did not *always* fall into the trap of thinking that all marketability discounts had to be around 35%, plus or minus a bit (not to suggest that we did not frequently fall into that trap in the early years).

- *Reasonableness and Reconciliation of Value Conclusions.* The fiscal 1984 report provided a brief discussion of the reasonableness of its conclusion in light of relative comparisons with the guideline group of public companies. And since this was a recurring client, the report provided a table that compared the key components of the 1984 valuation with those of the 1983 appraisal. For example, the table included adjusted earnings, the base price/earnings multiples, the selected fundamental discounts, the adjusted price/earnings multiples, the initial valuation conclusions, the number of shares outstanding, the initial per share valuations, the marketability discount, and the conclusions of value. The concluded fair market value per share rose 17.5%, and the table showed, and the text discussed, the components of the net change.

---

[29] Pratt, *Valuing a Business*, 1st ed. I met a former librarian for Willamette Management Associates at a CFA review course in May 1984. I cannot remember if we already had a copy of Shannon Pratt's first edition (1981) of *Valuing a Business*, but if we did not, I am sure that we purchased it shortly thereafter. We exchanged information on the valuation of bank core deposits (which we knew something about), and I was introduced to Shannon Pratt on the telephone. In the summer of 1985, I had dinner with Shannon and Millie Pratt for the first time. They were attending the ASA International Conference in Orlando, and I drove from a client location in Florida to meet them.

Shannon shared a good deal of his knowledge about business valuation and the business of business valuation with me that night. At that time, Mercer Capital's business was split about evenly between business appraisal and bank consulting. By late 1985, Ken Patton, my friend and business partner since 1984, and I decided that the future of our company would be in business appraisal and not bank consulting. By 1987, we were out of the bank consulting business and had become a business appraisal shop with perhaps eight employees. I credit Shannon with helping us see the potential for the business of business appraisal. I recall that I bought dinner that night. The advice has definitely been worth the price of dinner, even inflation-adjusted since 1985! Thankfully, there have been many conference meetings and dinners with Shannon over the last nearly 20 years.

The appraisal reports for Plumley companies continued to reflect the growth of our knowledge and understanding of business valuation until 1995, when the company was sold. The point of the memory walk through fiscal 1984 (early 1985) is to show that we were grappling with the key valuation issues from the start. As our understanding of the organizing principles evolved, that understanding has been reflected in Mercer Capital's work products and in our writing and speaking.

THE ORGANIZING PRINCIPLES

Others have surely discussed the meaning and implications of the organizing principles. I make no claim of originality here, other than in using them as a means of describing and discussing the valuation world. In the following sections, we will discuss each of the organizing principles. At the conclusion of the chapter we will see that, while each principle is separate, it is their integration that provides for solid understanding of valuation issues.

G – the Principle of GROWTH and Time

We live in a growing world. Change and growth are an integral part of nature, economies, and the business world. Investors look at the world, the economy, and individual businesses with an underlying assumption that growth will occur. Implicitly, growth occurs over time, so we call this the Principle of Growth and Time. There can, of course, be negative aspects to economic, industrial or business growth. But we live in an economic world where growth is viewed, on balance, as good.

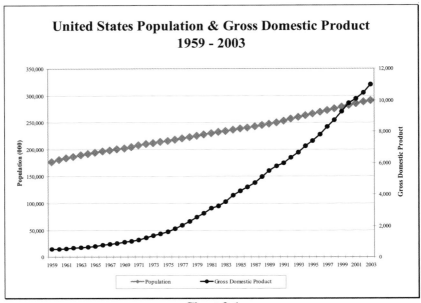

Chart 2-1

Charts 2-1 and 2-2 illustrate that the population of the United States has grown steadily over the last 40 years. Longer term analyses would show similar trends. Gross Domestic Product has grown more rapidly than population, fueled by inflation and productivity growth. Chart 2-2 reflects the Industrial Production Index, published by the Federal Reserve Bank of St. Louis. Economic growth over this period has contributed to growth in value for Corporate America, as shown by the growth in the Dow Jones Industrial Index and the S&P 500 Index in Chart 2-3.

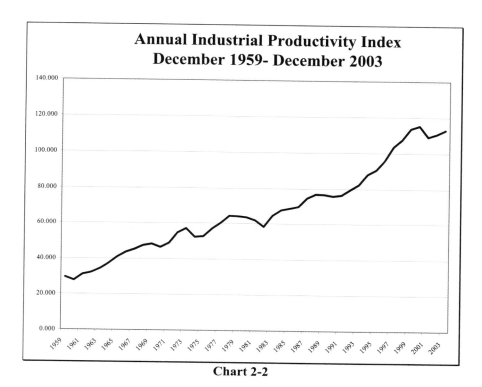

**Annual Industrial Productivity Index
December 1959- December 2003**

Chart 2-2

Other things being equal, a growing business is more valuable than a similar business that is not growing. Other things being equal, a business that is growing more rapidly than another similar business is more valuable than the slower-growing entity. The Growth Principle suggests, in nonmathematical terms, that there is an underlying relationship over time between growth and value. That relationship is indirectly reflected in Chart 2-3, which tracks the Dow Jones and S&P 500 for the last 50-plus years. Both indices have shown substantial growth in value over the charted period, as well as for longer periods not shown.

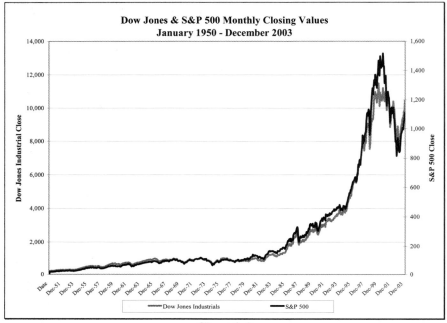

Chart 2-3

As appraisers address valuation questions, we need to focus on relevant aspects of growth, ranging from the world economy, to the national economy, to the regional economy, to a local economy, to a particular industry, to a particular company, or to the facts and circumstances influencing the ownership of a particular business interest. As Chart 2-3 illustrates, while the long-term trend in market valuation is rising, the rise is punctuated by reversals, or decreases in valuation.

The Principle of Growth and Time is often linked, as we will see, to the Principle of Expectation and to the Present Value Principle. But they are not the same principles.

R – the Principle of RISK and REWARD

Life is full of risks and rewards. In the context of life, there is a relationship between risk and reward that has been known for many centuries – long before the development of modern financial and valuation theory.

This relationship is evidenced by the Biblical "Parable of the Talents" (Matthew 25:14-30). In this New Testament parable, there are three servants who, upon the departure of their master, are given stewardship responsibility for resources. One steward receives five talents (currency units), another two talents, and the third, one talent.

The first servant invests the five talents and grows the master's stake. The second servant invests the two talents and similarly grows the master's stake. The third steward is fearful of loss and buries his talent until the master's return.

When, the master returns, the first servant renders his report and tells the master of his gain. The second servant reports similarly. And the third steward gives the original talent back to the master. The master is pleased with the work of the first two servants. But the third servant, who was not a good steward, is rebuked. The master takes away the talent and gives it to the first steward, who had handled his responsibilities well.

The "Parable of the Talents" is summarized here, not to make a theological statement (if, indeed I could), but to illustrate that the concept of the relationship between risk and reward has been in existence for thousands of years.

The Principle of Risk and Reward can be summed up in the words of an immortal unknown: "No risk, no blue chips!" This principle is integrated within the Present Value Principle via the factor known as the discount rate, or required rate of return. It is also embodied, implicitly or explicitly, when we employ the Principle of Alternative Investments.

The Principle of Risk and Reward suggests that an investor considering two possible investments, with one clearly riskier than the other, will require a greater expected reward for the riskier investment. If it were not so, there would be no incentive to purchase the riskier investment.

The bottom line of the Principle of Risk and Reward is that the markets require higher expected returns from riskier investments. This principle is rather obviously related to the Principle of Expectations.

A – the Principle of ALTERNATIVE Investments

We live in an alternative investment world. The Principle of Alternative Investments suggests that investments are made in the context of choices between or among competing alternatives. When investors make investment decisions, there are almost always choices that must be made.

The Principle of Alternative Investments lies at the heart of business valuation theory and practice. For example, many valuations of private companies begin with the development of a valuation indication at the marketable minority interest level of value, which is also called "as-if-freely-traded." In other words, appraisers develop hypothetical indications of value in the process of appraising private companies.[30] From the derived marketable minority interest values, appraisers may adjust their initial conclusions by the application of appropriate control premiums (if appropriate to achieve a controlling interest value) or marketability discounts (to achieve a nonmarketable minority interest value).

When Revenue Ruling 59-60 directs appraisers to make comparisons of a subject enterprise with the securities of similar companies with active public markets, the Principle of Alternative Investments is being invoked. The public securities markets are massive and active and provide liquid investment alternatives to investments in many privately owned businesses. Business appraisers need to have a thorough, working knowledge of these markets in order to provide realistic appraisals of private business interests.

By combining the organizing principles, we can begin to describe the workings of the world of value. For example, by combining aspects of the Principle of Risk and Reward and the Principle of Alternative Investments, investors make asset allocation decisions regarding their investments. In the public securities markets investors ask questions like: "Should we buy FEDEX or UPS stock?" "Should we buy large cap or small cap stocks?" "Should we buy stocks or bonds or real estate?"

---

[30] Note that this is completely different from rendering a hypothetical appraisal, which is made based on facts not in evidence. See *Principles of Appraisal Practice and Code of Ethics* (Washington, D.C.: The Appraisal Foundation, 1994). The overlap of terms is unfortunate.

The Principle of Alternative Investments suggests that there are many competing, alternative investments. The mirror suggestion is that there are many alternative investors, who may look at investments in different ways. This realization is causing appraisers to focus more frequently on who the typical buyers are for particular assets. For example, it is now generally recognized that there are different types of buyers for companies, including financial buyers and strategic or synergistic buyers. Strategic or synergistic buyers can often pay more for companies than can financial buyers who may be substantially dependent upon a company's existing cash flows for returns. Decisions by appraisers regarding who constitutes the "typical buyer" for an asset can significantly impact their conclusions of value.

The Principle of Alternative Investments also suggests the concept of opportunity costs. When resources are deployed to acquire one asset, they are not available to purchase another. When business assets are lost, destroyed or diminished in value, appraisers and economic experts employ the organizing principles to estimate the magnitude of alleged damages.

The point of this discussion of the Principle of Alternative Investments is that the principle requires (or assumes) that business appraisers be familiar with the public securities markets and capable of making reasonable comparisons between the public and private markets and drawing reasonable valuation inferences.

P – the PRESENT Value Principle

Stated in its simplest form, the Present Value Principle says that a dollar today is worth more than a dollar tomorrow. Alternatively, a dollar tomorrow is worth less than a dollar today. Present value is really an intuitive concept that even children understand. Ask any child whether it is better to get a toy today or to get the same toy next week! Or to have a piece of candy now or after finishing his or her dinner!

When we talk about present value, we really talk about four aspects of investments:

- *Investments (in equities) are expected to grow in value* (or have lower risk for fixed income investments). Recall the Principle of Growth.

- *Investments have cash flow characteristics that must be understood.* Appraisers must understand the nature of the cash flows of a business over time, and the fact that the cash flows of the business may differ materially from the cash flows available to its (minority) shareholders. And the cash flows may occur over time.

- *Investments have duration.* They exist over time. We forego consumption today (or make a choice among competing alternatives) in order to gain the benefit of the investment over its duration.

- *Investments have different risk characteristics.* Risk is the great leveling force in the world of present value via investors' required rates of return, or discount rates.

The Present Value Principle enables us to compare investments of differing durations, growth expectations, cash flows, and risks. Present value calculations enable us to express the present value of different investments in terms of dollars today and, therefore, provide a means to make investment or valuation decisions. Alternatively, we sometimes compare investments based on their expected values at dates in the future.

The generalized valuation model based on the Gordon Model was developed and discussed at length in Chapter 1.[31] The generalized model is summarized as:

$$\text{VALUE} = \text{Earnings}/(\,r - g\,)$$

$$= \text{Earnings} \times \text{Multiple}$$

This generalized model reflects a single-period income capitalization valuation method commonly employed by business appraisers. The appropriate earnings (cash flow) might be the net income, the pre-tax earnings, or some measure of cash flow expected to be achieved and from which income can grow. The discount rate is developed by comparisons with relevant alternative investments, and the expected growth rate of the cash flow is estimated by the appraiser. VALUE in the equation above represents the present value of all expected future cash flows of an enterprise, which are assumed to be growing at a constant rate (g). Present value is determined by discounting all those future cash flows to the present at the appropriate discount rate (r). This method derives an identical conclusion of value to a discounted cash flow method under the same assumptions.

---

[31]   See Chapter 1 for a much more detailed discussion of the Gordon Model and the DCF method.

Normally, we use the Gordon Model (or the DCF method) to solve for the value of a business. However, the Principle of Present Value can also be used to facilitate comparing alternative investments. If we can estimate the future cash flows from a business (or a business strategy or investment), and we know what that business or strategy or investment costs today, we can solve for the implied internal rate of return. If we calculate the implied internal rates of return from similar investments and hold other risk factors constant, the investment with the higher internal rate of return is the preferable investment.

Whether an appraiser solves the DCF equation for its value conclusions, or whether a CFO of a company makes comparisons of investments based on their relative internal rates of return, different aspects of the same principle are being considered.

The purpose of this brief discussion is to illustrate that we live in a present value world. Business appraisers must be intimately familiar with present value concepts and be able to articulate valuation facts and circumstances in a present value context.

E – the Principle of EXPECTATIONS

Today's value is a function of tomorrow's expected cash flows, not yesterday's performance. This is a simple but often overlooked aspect of valuation.

Appraisers routinely examine a company's historical performance and develop estimates of earning power based on that history. The earnings that are capitalized may be a simple average of recent years' earnings, or a weighted average of those earnings. In the alternative, an appraiser might capitalize the current year's earnings or the annualization of a partial year of earnings, or a specific forecast of expected earnings for next year might be made. The purpose of all historical analysis, however, is to develop reasonable expectations for the future of a business.

History is the window through which appraisers look at the future. We should never forget, however, that visibility is not the same through all windows. Some windows have been cleaned recently and provide a good picture, others are shaded, tinted or dirty. And the view through some windows is just blocked. Appraisers must make reasonable judgments about the expected future performance of subject companies. And those judgments can often be tested or evaluated in light of a company's recent history.

A sidebar to this brief discussion of the role of expectations in valuation relates to the use of *unrealistic* expectations. One of the most frequent problems seen in valuation reports today is the use of projected earnings that bear little or no resemblance to those of the past. These projections often lack any explanation of how the rose-colored glasses, through which they view a business, reflect realistic expectations for the future of a business. The projection phenomenon just described is so common that it has been given a name – "hockey-stick projections."

In a recent deposition, I was asked how a bank with currently low earnings could possibly meet the projections found in bank management's own current capital plan for the next five years. The deposing attorney accused me of unrealistically relying on the capital plan, which was prepared by his client for regulatory review in the normal course of business. How could any bank possibly achieve the results of such a "hockey-stick" set of projections?

I referred the attorney to the exhibit in our report that compared the previous five years' performance with the earnings and returns of the capital plan. There, it was clear that the projected returns (on assets and equity) were within the levels achieved by the bank in the previous few years, and below the current level of the bank's peer group. The Principle of Expectation says that value today is a function of expectations for future performance – and the expectations we used were in line with past performance, management's stated plans, management's business plan, and the performance of similar banks.

Appraisers should remember that every going concern business valuation reflects, implicitly or explicitly, a projection of expected future performance. If the expectations imbedded in the valuation are not realistic, the valuation's conclusions will be flawed.

The Gordon Model could not be clearer about the expectational nature of valuation. Nevertheless, the Principle of Expectations is one of the most difficult for beginning (and even experienced) appraisers to embrace in practice, particularly those with limited public securities market backgrounds.

The efficient market hypothesis suggests that, in general, the markets incorporate information that is known about a company (that forms the basis for future expectations regarding its performance) into its stock price today. This information is considered, of course, in the context of expectations regarding the company's industry and economic conditions. In other words, the market evaluates the expected future performance in light of the consensus estimate of riskiness for a security and moves the price of a stock to the level that equates that expected performance with its expected riskiness.

The Principle of Expectations suggests that participants in the world of value must deal with uncertainty. After all, we cannot know the future until it happens, and then it is not the future.

Sometimes expectations are bipolar. Either A will occur or B will occur. If A occurs, one level of pricing for a company is suggested. If B occurs, an entirely different level of pricing is indicated. Investors deal with the potential for bipolar (or multiple) future outcomes using various forms of probability analysis. In appropriate circumstances, appraisers may need to use probability analysis, as well.

Consider the following example: a real-world investor plans to invest in a company that expects to engage in an initial public offering (IPO) within a year or so. The stock is currently illiquid and is burdened by a right of first refusal flowing to the shareholders and the company. If the IPO does occur as expected, there will likely be a substantial boost in the overall value of the company. The shares under consideration would be marketable in that case, so there would be potential for a significant gain.

However, if the IPO does not occur, growth prospects will be significantly lower than if it had (because the expected capital infusion will not occur). And the investor knows that one of the reasons that companies do not go public is because their emerging performance does not meet expectations. If the company does not have the IPO, the investor faces a potentially lengthy holding period before other opportunities for liquidity arise. In this case, the stock would be worth much less than if the IPO had occurred.

What does the investor do in this world of value we live in? He or she makes an informed judgment ("best guess") about the probabilities of the favorable and unfavorable outcomes. A decision is made at a value above the no-IPO scenario level, but considerably below the IPO scenario. Why? *Because investors tend to be risk-averse, and, according to the Principle of Risk and Reward, may charge a high, even a very high, price for that uncertainty.*

The investor in our hypothetical example makes a decision based on his probability-adjusted expected return, writes a check, and moves on. Either A (the IPO) or B (getting stuck) will occur, and the ultimate return on the investment will be determined over time.

Unlike the investor described above, who will take his licks or count his rewards based on the negotiated price, the business appraiser must write a report. In situations like this, the report's conclusion is almost certain to be wrong at a point in the future with the benefit of hindsight. If the company goes public, the conclusion of value may appear low in relationship to the ultimate IPO price. If the IPO is unsuccessful, the report's conclusion, which considered favorable aspects related to that potential, will appear to have been too high.[32]

Business appraisers facing similar valuation situations must attempt to mirror the thinking of investors in the world of value and must reach conclusions and document them. We must solve valuation problems by exercising the appropriate organizing principles if our conclusions are to have credibility and the potential to withstand critical scrutiny after the uncertainties about the future have been resolved by the passage of time.

S – the Principle of SANITY (and Rationality and Consistency)

The Principle of Sanity might have been that of Rationality had another "R" fit into the acronym of GRAPES. But sanity will do.

When I speak to appraisers about the nature of the public securities markets, many are quick to explain to me the many (apparent or real) exceptions to sane, rational, or consistent investment behavior. However, while the exceptions are always interesting, what we are discussing is the underlying rationality of the markets operating as a whole.

Many an unthinking investor has been taken to the proverbial cleaners by the investment pitch that "seemed almost too good to be true." It probably was too good to be true. Lying beneath the surface of this comment are implicit comparisons with alternative investments that are sane, rational, or consistent with normal expectations.

---

[32]   Note that these observations are true even if the earlier report provided both favorable and unfavorable scenarios and probability weighted them.

Other appraisers are quick to point out that the markets sometimes behave abnormally or, seemingly, irrationally. I am using the comments of appraisers to illustrate that too many of us get caught up in the exceptions and miss the big picture that is played out in the public securities markets. If we can understand the underlying rationality or sanity of the markets, we then have a basis to explain or to try to understand the apparent exceptions.

The Principle of Sanity should be applied to appraisers as well as markets. Revenue Ruling 59-60, in the paragraph prior to the enumeration of the eight factors that are listed in nearly every appraisal report, suggests that appraisers employ three additional factors – common sense, informed judgment, and reasonableness. We call the eight factors the "Basic Eight" factors of valuation. We call the less well-known factors from Revenue Ruling 59-60 the "Critical Three" factors of valuation.

The Principle of Sanity suggests that appraisers need to study the markets they use as valuation reference points (comparables or guidelines). It also suggests that valuation conclusions should be sane, rational, consistent, and reasonable.

We employ tests of reasonableness in Mercer Capital valuation reports to compare our conclusions with relevant alternative investments or to explain why we believe our conclusions are reasonable. Other appraisers call the same process that of using sanity checks. Readers of appraisal reports should expect such proof of the sanity of the conclusions found in those reports as well as at key steps along the way as critical valuation decisions are made.

THE BASKET FOR GRAPES: THE PRINCIPLE OF KNOWLEDGE

The organizing principles provide an excellent framework within which to think about the world of value. Business value is determined by investors "out there" who either have or are seeking information about their potential investments. The various bits of information that are gathered are part of a mosaic. When the pieces are put together in an organized fashion, they form the knowledge that is necessary for decision-making about investments and their future performance in the face of uncertainty.

From the viewpoint of business appraisers, the GRAPES of Value provide a number of avenues along which to seek and obtain the knowledge necessary to develop and support, and later to defend, valuation conclusions.

Knowledge is gained by employing one or more or all of the GRAPES of Value. The objective of every business valuation should be to provide well-developed, well-reasoned, and well-written conclusions of value upon which clients and other intended users can rely for their intended purposes. If meeting that objective can be likened to creating a fine wine, then the GRAPES of Value are the ingredients: If employed in the right proportions for the right amount of time, a fine wine can develop; if not employed properly, vinegar may be the result.

To carry this analogy to its logical conclusion, knowledge is the full basket of GRAPES that enable the business appraiser to turn facts, circumstances, and bits of information that may seem disjointed and unrelated, into appropriate valuation judgments and reasonable valuation conclusions.

CONCLUDING COMMENTS

The importance of the Organizing Principles of Business Valuation, summarized by GRAPES, lies in their integrated consideration by appraisers. We offer a few thoughts in conclusion:

> **G-rowth**. Examine the outlook for the future of the business, i.e., for its earnings and cash flows.

> **R-isk/Reward.** Examine the history and nature of a business to discern its particular risk characteristics. These characteristics are used in the overall assessment of riskiness, which impacts value through the discount rate (r) selected.

> **A-lternative Investments**. Compare subject private companies to publicly traded securities or other similar investments because they represent realistic alternative investments for hypothetical buyers of private companies or to the valuation metrics from change of control transactions.

> **P-resent Value.** The common denominator for comparing alternative or competing investments is found in present value analysis. Value for a *business* today is, conceptually, the present value of the expected future cash flows of the enterprise discounted to the present at an appropriate discount rate. Value for an *illiquid interest in a business* is, conceptually, the expected future cash flows attributable to the interest (in the context of an overall enterprise valuation) discounted to the present at an appropriate discount rate.

E-xpectations. The market price for securities in companies is based on expected future benefits. The baseline valuation question is not: "What have you done for me in the past?" Nor is it even: "What can I expect that you will do for me today?" Valuation is forward-looking or expectational. "What can I expect for you to do for me tomorrow?"

S-anity. There is an underlying sanity, rationality, and consistency to the public markets that is sometimes difficult to discern. Appraisers who focus on exceptions in the marketplace rather than on underlying logic and rationality are prone to major swings of overvaluation or undervaluation.

And, **Knowledge.** It should be clear that decisions in the world of value are made based on knowledge available about various investments.

Appraisers who have a grasp on the organizing principles, or the GRAPES of Value, have a leg up in the process of developing reasonable valuation conclusions. Attorneys and other advisors to business owners who use the GRAPES of Value as a framework in which to discuss valuation questions can get to bottom-line issues more rapidly and effectively.

The importance of understanding the organizing principles of business valuation and being able to employ them in appraisal assignments should become clearer as this book progresses. The Integrated Theory of Business Valuation presented in the next chapter relies heavily on these principles.

As noted at the outset of this chapter, we have been discussing the world of value thus far. We have made only passing references to fair market value and no mention of any other standards of value. The world of value is where value is created. Value-based decisions get made there every day in the stock markets, the bond markets, and in the investment decision-making processes of many thousands of businesses and millions of investors. After introducing what is referred to in this book as the Integrated Theory of Business Valuation, we will discuss the hypothetical world of fair market value in which appraisers must make many of their valuation decisions.

Appendix 2-A

THE PRINCIPLES
CRYSTALLIZE

I did not consciously articulate the organizing principles during the 1980s, but they were firmly established in my thinking by the time my earliest articles on business valuation were published in 1988 and 1989:

- "Not So Random Thoughts Regarding the Business of Business Appraisal," *Business Valuation Review,* June 1988, pp. 62-63. This article was written in response to an earlier article by John Emory, ASA (who prepares the Emory Restricted Stock Studies). It was quoted in a speech shortly thereafter marking me as a "friend" of using the public markets as benchmarks in the valuation of private companies. Guilty as charged. [33] It was also in this article that I suggested that appraisers review their historical work to provide a benchmark for comparison regarding the extent of their work's improvement over time. This article is reproduced as Appendix 2-B to this chapter. [34]

- "Issues in Recurring Valuations: Methodological Comparisons from Year to-Year," A Letter to the Editor to the *Business Valuation Review,* December 1988, pp. 171-173. In this article, I suggested that appraisers need to be consistent and rational in valuing companies from year to year, and that significant changes in methodologies need to be explained. We realized the importance of this procedure as a result of clients like Plumley Rubber Company and our growing list of ESOP and planning clients, all of whom had to be valued each year (or so).

---

[33] The label works if we consider both direct and indirect comparisons to the public markets. Reasonable groups of guideline companies simply cannot be developed as a basis for valuing many private companies.

[34] I was asked to update the "not so random thoughts" for the American Society of Appraisers in early 2004. The current comments are also reproduced as part of Appendix 2-B.

- "The Adjusted Capital Asset Pricing Model for Developing Capitalization Rates: An Extension of Previous 'Build-Up' Methodologies Based Upon the Capital Asset Pricing Model," *Business Valuation Review,* December 1989, pp. 147-156. This last article, which we call the ACAPM article, provided the first clear, published articulation of the use of the Capital Asset Pricing Model to develop capitalization rates for valuing private companies. This article introduced the concept of the *fundamental adjustment* and provided an analytical method for estimating its magnitude based on differences in risk and expected growth between subject enterprises and guideline companies. All of the organizing principles were present in the ACAPM article, either implicitly or explicitly.

Appendix 2-B

Not So Random Thoughts Regarding The Business Of Business Appraisal[35]

Z. Christopher Mercer, ASA, CFA

- **There is no such thing as a "simple" valuation**.

- Business Rule No. 1: Prepare an engagement letter for client acceptance for every valuation assignment specifying what is being valued, the as of date, the purpose of the appraisal, and the fee arrangement.

- Business Rule No. 2: Reread Business Rule No. 1 until it is second nature.

- There is no such thing as "the value" of anything. Valuation is a "range" concept tied to another concept, that of "reasonableness." **Experience will probably tend to narrow your personal concept of "reasonable range."**

- If you start with reasonable facts and make reasonable assumptions or assertions along the way, chances are your conclusions will be perceived as reasonable.

- The public marketplace provides many objective "markets" as reference points for appraisals of closely held companies. A well-crafted valuation conclusion will sit reasonably in relationship to one, or preferably, several of these markers.

- Summarize your valuation conclusions for related businesses over time. As your business grows, your internal data base will become your "conscience" and an automatic test of reasonableness for many situations.

- When you draft any appraisal report, keep in mind that in a litigation situation, every word you write is fodder for cross examination.

---

[35] Z. Christopher Mercer, "Not So Random Thoughts Regarding the Business of Business Appraisal," *Business Valuation Review*, Vol. 7, No. 7 (1988): pp. 62-63.

- **Caveat. Do not play the "compromise" game** by preparing an opinion that is higher or lower than you can reasonably justify. Courts are increasingly getting out of the "averaging" game and are selecting the more convincing appraisal conclusion. The average of two unreasonable opinions will not necessarily yield a reasonable result.

- **Corollary. Beware of walking too far out on a limb. If it doesn't break of its own accord, someone will invariably saw it off at the trunk.**

- The more complex your valuation rationale, the less likely those who count (judges, juries, clients, IRS agents, etc.) will understand, and the more likely you will be challenged and unable to successfully support your conclusions.

- Most trial attorneys do not stop cross examination soon enough. Use this flaw to your advantage by being well prepared and ready to establish and reestablish the overall reasonableness of your conclusions at every opportunity.

- **Never be intimidated by a cross-examination attorney.** Most good attorneys will craft their questions to require "yes" or "no" answers that will seemingly damage your case. **You always have the right to explain your answer.** Don't worry about the uncomfortable "yes" or "no" response. Make your points with a clearly stated and reasonable explanation.

- ESOP appraisals are far more complex than many appraisers seem to believe. Be sure you understand the complete situation, the entire transaction, and its implications before issuing a valuation opinion.

- When dealing with controlling shareholders who are selling to an ESOP, remember the difference between a minority appraisal and a control appraisal and know which one is appropriate for the circumstance.

- Remember, when you value a company for an ESOP the first time, you will have to value it the next year and the next year and the next year. It is a professional challenge to maintain reasonableness, consistency, objectivity, and clients over time.

- Beware of the appraiser who boasts of how many tax-related appraisals he has defended. The objective in a tax appraisal should be quiet acceptance by the IRS.

- In spite of admonitions to the contrary, **clients almost always tell you what they want the answer to be.** Sometimes they are overt, and other times they are subtle. **Sometimes they are reasonable.** In spite of this, your valuation conclusions must be your own. You cannot satisfy every client and retain your independence. **How you deal with the issue, and the reasonableness of your approach, will determine if you retain your independence, the client, or both.**

- **The best definition of "independence" is having many clients, no one of which accounts for a significant portion of you business.**

- Re-read Revenue Ruling 59-60 from time to time. You may be surprised at what it says.

- When valuing financial institutions, never confuse the bank and the bank holding company.

- **Make it a regular practice to go back and reread our older appraisals if you need and occasional object lesson in humility.**

Mr. Mercer is President of Mercer Capital Management, Inc., of Memphis, Tennessee. He holds the Senior Member designation in business valuation from the American Society of Appraisers and serves on the ASA's International Board of Examiners.

NOT SO RANDOM THOUGHTS ON THE BUSINESS OF BUSINESS APPRAISAL 2004 EDITION[36]

Z. Christopher Mercer, ASA, CFA

John Emory and I captured our "not so random thoughts" on the business of business valuation in 1988. For those who have entered the field in the last few years, picture our world in 1988:

- The use of personal computers was in its infancy. We had them, but they were not very robust. Mercer Capital had one computer with a hard drive – a Compaq luggable machine with a 5 MB hard drive, which we thought was huge!

- Networks in most appraisal shops were of the "tennis shoe" kind – save onto a floppy disk and take it to another machine – you know, the really floppy, floppy disks!

- Fax machines were not omnipresent. This was the year of Federal Express' big failure with ZapMail, a same day service using facsimile transmission between FedEx locations and the delivery capabilities in local markets. So the proliferation of "fax it to me" was just beginning.

- The Internet did not exist, at least commercially, and neither did e-mail.

- The Business Valuation Standards of the ASA did not exist, and USPAP had little, if any, impact on business appraisal.

- The "levels of value" chart had not yet been published although the concepts were generally known.

---

[36]   Z. Christopher Mercer, "Not So Random Thoughts on the Business of Business Appraisal," *ASA BV E Letter,* Issue 8-15, April 14, 2004.

- There was great confusion regarding how to develop capitalization rates using so-called build-up methods or the Adjusted Capital Asset Pricing Model.

It is now 2004, nearly 16 years later, and things have certainly changed. Let's discuss a few current "not so random thoughts" through the lens of over 25 years of experience.

- Professional standards are here to stay. Maintain your personal, current copies of the *Uniform Standards of Professional Appraisal Practice* and the *Business Valuation Standards* and *Principles of Appraisal Practice and Code of Ethics* of the American Society of Appraisers. Remember to:

  - Read these documents frequently.

  - Evaluate your personal work and the relevant work products of your firm in light of these standards.

  - Prepare in advance for the day that your work is subjected to detailed examination based on its compliance with these standards.

- Remember that everything you do (or do not do) in your professional career builds your professional reputation over time. There are no shortcuts on the road to professional success.

- Professional growth is all about learning and that cannot be accomplished when you are in your comfort zone doing things the same way "because that's the way we've always done them."

- Computers are wonderful; however, they will never do your thinking for you.

- Begin every valuation assignment with a detailed spreadsheet analysis of the company's historical performance. As a former boss instilled in me long ago: "You have to talk to the numbers until the numbers talk to you." Ask questions raised by the changes you see. Do not stop until you understand how things have worked. Your appraisals are forecasts of how things will or may work in the future. A company's past provides a window into the present that enables appraisers to anticipate its future. If the window is dirty, or worse yet, broken, the future may be cloudy indeed.

- Some appraisers love litigation and others hate it. Others love to hate it and still others hate to love it. Regardless, if you stay in the business for some length of time you will likely end up testifying in deposition and/or trial related to your work, the reports of others, or on valuation or damages issues. Always be in the process of getting ready.

- Nearly every valuation conclusion is highly sensitive to one or more of the assumptions made in its determination. *This is a fact of life.* Appraisers need to be keenly aware of these sensitivities and may need to alert readers of their reports at appropriate points. Tests of the sensitivity of conclusions to changes in assumptions can be helpful as can proving the reasonableness of assumptions in light of available economic and valuation evidence.

- Differences in appraisal conclusions almost always relate to differences in one or more of a limited number of assumptions. When you are making those key assumptions in your appraisals, be sure of your facts and rationale at each point along the way.

- Never bury a calculating number in a cell. Always show all calculating numbers so they can be checked.

- In 1988, I wrote that courts are getting out of the business of "splitting the baby," or averaging the conclusions of opposing experts. I think I was wrong.

- Judging from what has been written about appraisers in many court decisions, I believe that many judges hold our profession in low regard. The job of the expert in a valuation matter is to provide his or her independent rationale and conclusions. It often seems that judges assume at the outset that the appraisers are advancing the positions of their respective sides. Maybe that is why there are so many "split babies."

- Benchmark analysis based on using the averages of restricted stock studies or pre-IPO studies is dead in the Tax Court – as it should be. Comparisons to the average of a study or attempts to use a very limited database of restricted stock transactions stretching over many years will yield appropriate marketability discounts only by chance and that is simply not good enough.

- Appraisers need to place similar effort, energy, and intellect into valuing illiquid *interests* of enterprises as they do with valuing the enterprises themselves.

- Post-valuation date information is often misused by appraisers and by courts. Given a valuation date, the "future" becomes clearer and clearer with the passage of time. Mercer's Law states: "If post-valuation date information will corroborate my valuation conclusions, it will not be admitted into evidence; however, if is not corroborative, it will be admitted!" That makes it all the more important to provide well-reasoned, well-written, and reasonable valuation opinions every time based on what is known or reasonably knowable at the valuation date.

- E-mail is wonderful. However, here is a good rule to follow: Never write anything in an e-mail that you do not mind explaining under hostile circumstances at a future date.

- One of the toughest things we have to deal with in the business appraisal arena is *ambiguity*. Things are seldom as certain as many would like them to be. How we deal with this ambiguity reflects on the credibility of our work.

- If your assignment calls for rendering an independent opinion of value, then do just that. Clients have problems, and that is why they hire us. But the moment you lose your independence in a matter, you make the client's problem your own and lose the credibility to help resolve it.

The business of business appraisal has been intellectually stimulating, challenging, and rewarding over the last 25-plus years. I have high expectations for an even brighter future.

– Z. Christopher Mercer, ASA, CFA
is CEO of Mercer Capital. He is the author of
Quantifying Marketability Discounts, and has
contributed several previous articles to the *Business
Valuation Review*. He served on the Business Valuation
Committee for six years, and was Vice Chairman of the
International Board of Examiners for business valuation
for three years. In addition, Mr. Mercer served on the
Standards Sub-Committee of the Business Valuation
Committee for more than 10 years.

Chapter 3

The Integrated Theory
of Business Valuation

INTRODUCTION

In this chapter, we introduce the Integrated Theory of Business Valuation, or the Integrated Theory. Simply stated, the Integrated Theory of Business Valuation allows business appraisers to account for all the cashflows of an enterprise, whether at the level of the enterprise or by examining the portions of enterprise cash flows attributable to specific interests of those enterprises. It does this by harmonizing the Gordon Model (and implicitly, the discounted cash flow model) with the levels of value concept with which we are all familiar.

More specifically, the Integrated Theory of Business Valuation employs the Gordon Model and explains each level of value in the context of financial and valuation theory as well as why value might differ from level to level. In addition, the Integrated Theory defines the conceptual adjustments relating the various levels of value to each other (control premiums and minority interest discounts and marketability discounts) in terms of the discounted cash flow analysis summarized by the Gordon Model. Importantly, however, the Integrated Theory also describes the conditions necessary for the relevant valuation premiums or discounts to exist.

COMMON QUESTIONS

Not every question posed below is answered (or addressed) in this chapter. However, the framework for addressing the questions is established here in Chapter 3.

1.   What is the source of value of an *interest* in a business enterprise?

2.   If a minority interest is worth less than its pro rata share of an enterprise, what are the sources of this diminution in value?

3. What are the theoretical reasons for the existence of a control premium?

4. In the context of fair market value, should control premiums be applied "automatically" in developing controlling interest value indications?

   a. If a control premium is applied, what types of data from the marketplace should be used to estimate it?

   b. To what earnings base should it be applied, if applicable?

   c. How can the reasonableness of control premiums be tested?

   d. Are control premiums economic drivers or merely valuation results?

5. What factors give rise to "financial control premiums"?

6. What factors give rise to "strategic control premiums"?

7. When applying the DCF method, should appraisers apply control premiums when developing controlling interest values? If so, why? And where?

8. What does the term *marketable minority* level of value mean in the context of public security values?

9. When valuing minority interests of private companies, should appraisers normalize earnings?

   a. If yes, what kinds of normalizing adjustments should be made?

   b. What is the objective of making normalizing adjustments?

10. When using guideline public company multiples, should appraisers apply control premiums to resulting "marketable minority" value indications?

11. What are the theoretical reasons for the existence of minority interest discounts?

12. Should appraisers rely on *Mergerstat Review* and other control premium studies to determine the magnitude of control premiums applicable to "marketable minority" value indications?

13. Should those same control premium studies be used to estimate minority interest discounts for operating companies?

14. Is the often lower value of minority interests (relative to pro rata enterprise values) a function of the "lack of power" of minority shareholders?

   a. Do minority shareholders of public enterprises have any more "power" in terms of voting rights or ability to control management than do shareholders of private enterprises?

    b.   Is the "lack of power" of minority investments in private enterprises more akin to a lack of liquidity (inability to sell at will) than to the ability to exercise control over a business?

15. Are marketability discounts applicable to 100% controlling interests of companies?

16. What are the economic factors that give rise to the marketability discount?

17. Using the levels of value framework, can the following phenomena be explained or described?

    a.   The existence of control premiums when public companies sell.

    b.   Most public companies do not sell in any given period.

    c.   Illiquid minority interests often sell for less than their pro rata share of enterprise value.

    d.   Private companies often sell for less than public company multiples in their industries.

    e.   Private companies often sell at lower relative valuations than public companies in their industries.

    f.   A public stock may sometimes sell for higher prices than the entire company is worth.

    g.   Strategic buyers may pay more than financial buyers for the same company.

    h.   Financial buyers may compete with strategic buyers and win.

18. What are the similarities and differences between a restricted stock discount when public companies issue restricted shares at prices less than their market prices and marketability discounts applicable to minority interests of private companies?

19. What assumptions are necessary to value illiquid interests in private enterprises that do *not* pay dividends?

20. What assumptions are necessary to value illiquid interests in private enterprises that *do* pay dividends?

21. What is the relationship between the standard of value of fair market value and the strategic control level of value?

22. In valuing illiquid interests of private businesses, why do appraisers normally begin with appraisals at the marketability minority level of value?

23. Why is the concept of the expected holding period an integral element in the valuation of illiquid minority interests of enterprises?

24. What is the relationship between the discount rates of minority shareholders of business enterprises and the discount rates of the enterprises themselves?

25. Do guideline public company multiples yield marketable minority or controlling interest level of value indications?

THE GORDON MODEL

In Chapter 1, we provided background information on the Gordon Model. This model is a single-period income capitalization model and is reflective of the way that securities are valued in the public markets. The Gordon Model is shown again as a beginning point for a discussion of the Integrated Theory of Business Valuation.

$$V_0 = \frac{CF_1}{r - g_e}$$

Equation 3-1

The basic formulation of the Gordon Model can be interpreted as follows. Value today is equal to next period's (year's) expected cash flow (income measure) divided by (or capitalized by) a firm's discount rate less the expected (constant) growth rate of the measure of cash flow in the numerator. As we have previously shown, this formula is a summary of the discounted cash flow (future earnings) method of valuation under the following assumptions:

- The expected cash flows are growing at the constant rate of g, and

- All cash flows are reinvested in the firm at the discount rate, r (or are otherwise distributed to shareholders).

Appraisers have been using the basic Gordon Model for many years. Some appraisers suggest that the appropriate measure of earnings (CF) to use is *net cash flow to equity*, which is usually defined as follows:[37]

Net Income

+   Depreciation/Amortization

+/- Net Changes in Working Capital

+/- Net Changes in Interest Bearing Debt

-   Capital Expenditures

=   **Net Cash Flow to Equity**

Other appraisers suggest that the appropriate measure of cash flow is net income. While over the long run, net income and net cash flow will be approximately equal, there can be significant differences over any short period of time. For a growing company, net cash flow, as defined above, will normally be less than net income because of working capital requirements of growth and investment in capital expenditures necessary to support growth. As the discussion in Chapter 1 should have made clear, the appropriate measure of cash flow is a range of flows from net income to net cash flow, depending on the assumed level of the dividend payout ratio (DPO). If DPO = 100%, then the appropriate flow is that of net income. If, however, DPO < 100%, then the earnings retention rate is greater than zero, and the appropriate flow to measure is that of net cash flow. Typically, a single period income capitalization method, the Gordon Model, and the generalized valuation model developed from it, assumes DPO = 100%.

It should be clear that the discounted cash flow model as summarized by the Gordon Model is sufficiently well known and well accepted to provide the basis for the Integrated Theory of Business Valuation.

---

[37] The net cash flow or cash flow addressed in this chapter is the net cash flow to equity holders.

EARLY VIEWS OF THE LEVELS OF VALUE

The so-called levels of value chart first appeared in the valuation literature some time around 1990.[38] However, the general concepts embodied in the chart were known by appraisers (and courts) prior to that time. To date, virtually all discussions regarding levels of value in the valuation literature have been very general, lacking any compelling logic or rational in terms of the factors giving rise to value differences at each level.

The early levels of value chart showed three conceptual levels. The chart is so important to an understanding of valuation concepts that analysts at Mercer Capital have included it in virtually every valuation report since about 1992. While we will examine the chart in the context of the Integrated Theory, it is useful to understand that it has been in use for many years.

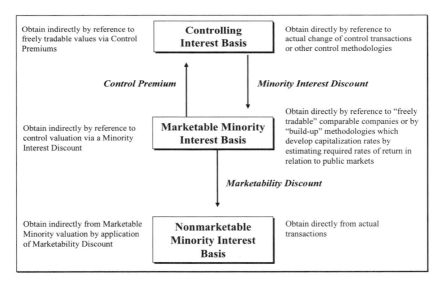

---

[38] Z. Christopher Mercer, "Do Public Company (Minority) Transactions Yield Controlling Interest or Minority Interest Pricing Data?," *Business Valuation Review* Vol. 9, No. 4 (1990). This article was written in response to an insightful article by Eric W. Nath, published earlier that year. See Eric W. Nath, "Control Premiums and Minority Interest Discounts in Private Companies," *Business Valuation Review*, Vol. 9, No. 2 (1990). See also James H. Zukin, *Financial Valuation: Business and Business Interests* (New York: Maxwell MacMillan, 1990), p. 2-3. While the concepts of the levels of value had been around for some time prior to 1990, to the best of our knowledge, the levels of value chart was not published until the Mercer article in 1990 and in the Zukin text that same year. See the further discussion at the beginning of Chapter 10.

We, like most appraisers, assumed the existence of the conceptual adjustments to value known as the Control Premium, the Minority Interest Discount, and the Marketability Discount. We relied on market evidence provided from control premium studies to help ascertain the magnitude of Control Premiums (and Minority Interest Discounts). And we relied on certain benchmark studies, the so-called Pre-IPO Studies and the Restricted Stock Studies as the basis for estimating the magnitude of Marketability Discounts. Such reliance contributed to a failure to understand the basis for the premiums and discounts being estimated.[39]

The purpose of this chapter is the integration of the Gordon Model, as a basic statement of how the markets value companies, and the conceptual framework of the levels of value. In other words, this chapter introduces the Integrated Theory of Business Valuation. The Integrated Theory:

- Explains each level of value in the context of the Gordon Model.

- Uses the components of the Gordon Model to define the conceptual adjustments between the levels of value, e.g., the Control Premium (and its inverse, the Minority Interest Discount) and the Marketability Discount.

- Explains why the resulting integrated valuation model is illustrative of pricing behavior in the marketplace for public securities (the Marketable Minority level), the market for entire companies (the Controlling Interest level(s) of value), and the markets for illiquid, minority interests of private enterprises (the Nonmarketable Minority Level of Value).

With these objectives in mind, we proceed with the development of the Integrated Theory of Business Valuation.

---

[39] By the early 1990s, we became increasingly uncomfortable with the prevailing methodologies for developing marketability discounts. The Quantitative Marketability Discount Model, which is based on our early development of the Integrated Theory, was introduced in speeches beginning in 1994 and in a book in 1997. See Z. Christopher Mercer, *Quantifying Marketability Discounts* (Memphis: Peabody Publishing, LP, 1997). The various studies mentioned in this paragraph are summarized in Chapters 1-3 of that book.

THE MARKETABLE MINORITY INTEREST LEVEL OF VALUE

It is generally accepted that the Gordon Model provides a shorthand representation of the value of public securities at the marketable minority interest level of value. For privately owned enterprises, it is indicative of the same level, i.e., the "as-if-freely-traded" level. In developing the Integrated Theory, we discuss the Gordon Model in the context of the levels of value to understand how they relate to each other. To do so, we introduce a symbolic notation to designate which elements of the model relate to each level of value. Equation 3-2 introduces the conceptual math of the benchmark level of value – the marketable minority value.

$$V_{mm} = \frac{CF_{e(mm)}}{R_{mm} - G_{mm}} \quad \text{or} \quad \frac{CF}{R - G}$$

Equation 3-2

The marketable minority level of value was just described as the "benchmark level of value." It is so described because it is the level to which control premiums are added to achieve controlling interest indications of value. It is also the level from which marketability discounts are subtracted to reach the nonmarketable minority level of value. As we will see, the Integrated Theory affirms that the marketable minority level of value is the appropriate benchmark from which to compare the other levels.

Equation 3-2 is defined as follows:

- V_{mm} is the equity value of a public security at the marketable minority level of value (mm), and the value of a privately owned security at the same level, i.e., as-if-freely-traded. This is the benchmark, observable value for public securities. The as-if-freely-traded value for private enterprises is a *hypothetical* value. It does not exist by definition for illiquid interests of private enterprises since there are no active, public markets for the shares. Appraisers develop indications of value at the marketable minority level as a first step in determining other levels of value. Such indications of value are developed either by direct reference to the public securities markets (using the Guideline Company Valuation

Method)[40], or indirectly, using the Adjusted Capital Asset Pricing Model (or other build-up methods based on the Capital Asset Pricing Model).[41]

- $CF_{e(mm)}$ is equal to the expected cash flow (earning power) of the (public or as-if-public) enterprise at the marketable minority level for the next period. The marketable minority level of cash flow is assumed to be "normalized" for unusual or non-recurring events and to have an expense structure that is market-based, at least in terms of owner/key shareholder compensation.[42] Public companies attempt to keep the investment community focused on their "normalized" earnings. Many public companies, for example, disclose *pro forma earnings*, or earnings after adjusting for unusual or nonrecurring (and sometimes not so non-recurring) items. A more detailed discussion of the importance of normalizing earnings in developing marketable minority value indications is found in Chapter 4. The need to adjust for unusual or non-recurring items is intuitively apparent. In Chapter 4, we discuss the other frequent type of normalizing adjustments – adjusting owner and/or officer compensation to market levels. At this point accept this assumption and then consider the more detailed treatment in Chapter 4.

- R_{mm} is a public company's discount rate, or the discount rate at the marketable minority level of value. While it is not directly observable, it can be inferred from public pricing or estimated using the Capital Asset Pricing Model or other models. For private companies, R_{mm} is most often estimated using one of several build-up approaches.[43]

---

[40] See "SBVS-1 The Guideline Company Method," *ASA Business Valuation Standards* (Washington, D.C.: The Appraisal Foundation, 2002), p. 31.

[41] See Chapter 6.

[42] If it were not so, there would be potential for excess returns through the acquisition of public companies and the realization of normalized earnings. The 1990 Nath article (see Footnote 2) makes this point clearly.

[43] Z. Christopher Mercer, "The Adjusted Capital Asset Pricing Model for Developing Capitalization Rates: An Extension of Previous 'Build-Up' Methodologies Based Upon the Capital Asset Pricing Model," *Business Valuation Review*, Vol. 8, No. 4 (1989): pp. 147-156. Some writers make a distinction between the ACAPM and the *build-up* method, which is identical to the ACAPM under the assumption that beta is equal to 1.0. This distinction is artificial since it should be apparent that the build-up method is based on the Capital Asset Pricing Model, just as is the ACAPM. See the more detailed discussion of discount rates in Chapter 6.

- G_{mm} is the expected growth rate of *core earnings* for the public security under the assumption that all earnings are distributed to shareholders (or g_e from Chapter 1). As shown previously, it is the compounding effect of reinvested earnings that enables a company to grow its *reported earnings (and value)* at rates (g^* from Chapter 1) in excess of its *underlying core earnings growth rate.* For reasons discussed in Chapter 1, G_{mm} is not equal to the expected growth rate of earnings published by stock analysts for public companies. The *analysts' g* (g^*) includes the compounding effect of the reinvestment of cash flows on the expected growth of earnings.

At this point, we can begin to connect the mathematics of valuation theory with the conceptual levels of value chart. The marketable minority level of value is the conceptual value from which other levels of value are derived. Figure 3-1 presents the conceptual math of the marketable minority level of value.

	Conceptual Math	Relationships	Value Implications
Marketable Minority Value	$\dfrac{CF_{e(mm)}}{R_{mm} - G_{mm}}$	$G_v = R_{mm}$	V_{mm}

Figure 3-1

We define the marketable minority level of value as an *enterprise level* of value. We do so because $CF_{e(mm)}$ is defined as the *cash flow of the enterprise.* All the shareholders of a publicly traded enterprise, controlling or minority, share the benefit of 100% of its cash flows (as they are capitalized in the public stock markets every day). The importance of this definition will become clear as the remaining mathematical relationships of the conceptual levels of value are built.

We build the Integrated Theory from the base found in Figure 3-1 (and the in-depth discussion of the discounted cash flow model and the Gordon Model in Chapter 1).

- First, the conceptual math is illustrated. In Figure 3-1, that math is the familiar Gordon Model. We will develop the conceptual math for the other levels of value as the chapter progresses.

- The next column is labeled Relationships. Here we see that the expected growth in value, G_v, is equal to the discount rate, R_{mm}. We will follow the progression of relationships between expected cash flows, risk, and growth as we develop the other levels of value.

- The final column is labeled Value Implications. In Figure 3-1, the conceptual math yields the marketable minority value. The value implications of the other levels of value will be explored in relationship to V_{mm} in this column.

The marketable minority level of value is that level *to which* appraisers have almost automatically applied control premiums to develop controlling interest indications of value. It is also the level *from which* appraisers have subtracted marketability discounts to derive indications of value at the nonmarketable minority level of value. The control premium and the marketability discount are conceptual adjustments enabling appraisers to relate the marketable minority level of value with the controlling interest level (control premium) and the nonmarketable minority level (marketability discount). The minority interest discount also relates the controlling interest and marketable minority levels.

As pointed out clearly by Pratt, Reilly, Schweihs and others, no valuation premium or discount has meaning unless we understand the base to which it is applied.[44] *The marketable minority value is the base level of value for the enterprise in the Integrated Theory of Business Valuation.*

A review of the valuation literature until the latter part of the 1990s yields little insight into the theoretical basis for applying the well-known conceptual premiums and discounts. Practically, appraisers applied control premiums because they were observable in the marketplace in which public companies changed control. And marketability discounts were applied because it was observed that restricted stocks of public companies traded at prices lower than their freely traded counterparts. Only in recent years have appraisers begun to understand and to articulate *why* control premiums and restricted stock discounts

---

[44]   Shannon P. Pratt, Robert F. Reilly, and Robert P. Schweihs, *Valuing a Business: The Analysis and Appraisal of Closely Held Companies*, 4th ed. (New York, NY: McGraw-Hill, 2000).

Shannon P. Pratt, Robert F. Reilly, and Robert P. Schweihs, *Valuing a Business: The Analysis and Appraisal of Closely Held Companies*, 3rd ed. (Chicago, IL: Irwin Professional Publishing, 1996).

Shannon P. Pratt, *Valuing a Business: The Analysis and Appraisal of Closely Held Companies*, 2nd ed. (Homewood, IL: Dow Jones-Irwin, 1988).

Shannon P. Pratt, *Valuing a Business: The Analysis and Appraisal of Closely Held Companies*, 1st ed. (Homewood, IL: Dow Jones-Irwin, 1981).

Z. Christopher Mercer, "Valuation Overview," *Valuing Financial Institutions* (Homewood, IL: Business One Irwin, 1992), pp. 193-206.

exist, and consequently, to understand the theoretical basis for their existence. The Integrated Theory presented in the remainder of this chapter explains the *why* behind the generally accepted valuation premiums and discounts.

THE CONTROL LEVELS OF VALUE

There is a growing understanding that there are at least two conceptual levels of value above the marketable minority level:

- *Financial Control.* The first level describes what a financial buyer is able (and perhaps willing) to pay for control of a business. Financial buyers acquire companies based on their ability to extract reasonable (to them) rates of return through the acquisition of companies, often on a leveraged basis.

- *Strategic Control.* The second control level is referred to as the strategic, or synergistic, level of value. Strategic buyers can (and do) pay more for companies than financial buyers because they expect to realize synergies from acquisitions (e.g., perhaps through eliminating duplicate expenses or achieving cross-selling benefits) that increase future cash flows.[45]

This growing understanding, supported by evidence from change-of-control transaction data, has led to conceptual levels of value charts with four, rather than three, levels. A general comparison of the two charts is shown in Figure 3-2. Further refinements of the comparison follow at Figure 3-4.

---

[45] Steven D. Garber, "Control vs. Acquisition Premiums: Is There a Difference?" (Presentation at the American Society of Appraisers International Appraisal Conference, Maui, HI, June 23, 1998).

Z. Christopher Mercer, "A Brief Review of Control Premiums and Minority Interest Discounts," *The Journal of Business Valuation*, (Toronto: Carswell Thomas, 1997), pp. 365-387.

M. Mark Lee, "Premiums and Discounts for the Valuation of Closely Held Companies: The Need for Specific Economic Analysis," *Shannon Pratt's Business Valuation Update*, August 2001.

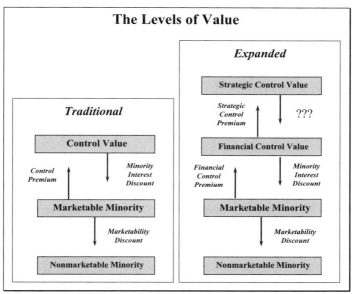

Figure 3-2

The left side of Figure 3-2 presents the traditional, three-level chart showing the conceptual premium and discounts that enable appraisers to relate the three levels to each other. The right side of the Figure presents the expanded, four-level chart. Note that the "financial control premium" on the right and the "control premium" on the left are the equivalent conceptual premiums.[46] As a result, the minority interest discounts shown on the left and right sides of Figure 3-2 are the same conceptual discount. We have called the conceptual premium relating the financial control value with the strategic control value the "strategic control

---

[46] This flows from the general belief that fair market value is a financial concept based on the hypothetical negotiations of hypothetical willing buyers, and that the "strategic control premium" is reflective of the consideration of specific buyers who benefit from particular synergies or strategies. The strategic control level of value might become the appropriate level for fair market value if the *typical buyers* are strategic buyers. This situation existed during much of the 1990s in the banking industry and in numerous other consolidating industries.

premium."[47] Now note that no name is provided for the conceptual discount that would eliminate the strategic control premium relative to the financial control value. Further, note that this conceptual discount *is not the minority interest discount* relating the financial control value with the marketable minority level of value.

As we move up from the marketable minority level to the levels of financial control and strategic control, we see that it is possible that a controlling shareholder may make adjustments to expected cash flows based on the expected ability to run an enterprise better (financial control) or differently (strategic control). Such adjustments would be *control adjustments* and could have the impact of increasing value if such adjustments would normally be negotiated between hypothetical (or real) buyers and sellers. In other words, from a conceptual viewpoint, *control adjustments* are those that, if appropriate, increase enterprise cash flow *above that of the (normalized) marketable minority level*. As Figure 3-2 indicates in a conceptual sense, the value of the expected cash flows of the enterprise from the viewpoint of either a financial control buyer or a strategic control buyer may be greater than the value of the normalized expected cash flow of the enterprise.

Careful review of the control premium data (Pratt/Reilly/Schweihs would suggest "acquisition premium") available to appraisers indicates they generally result from transactions motivated by strategic or synergistic considerations. Consequently, the available control premium data is more generally reflective of

---

[47]   Shannon P. Pratt, Robert F. Reilly, and Robert P. Schweihs, *Valuing a Business: The Analysis and Appraisal of Closely Held Companies*, 4th ed (New York, NY: McGraw-Hill, 2000). calls the strategic control premium "strategic acquisition premium" in their chart. They state, regarding the chart:

> The diagram presented in Exhibit 15-1 reflects the value influence of the ownership characteristics of control versus the noncontrolling stockholder's situation as discussed in Chapter 16. This schematic usually would represent the *fair market value standard of value* on a *going-concern basis premise of value*. In some cases, there may be yet another layer of value, which may reflect synergies with certain third-party buyers (as examples of: (1) reducing combined overhead by the consolidation of operations or (2) raising prices by reducing competition). There is not yet a widely used term for this additional layer of price premium over fair market, going-concern value. However, this price premium -- when combined with the ownership control premium -- is sometimes called an *acquisition premium*. The standard of value reflecting these synergies usually would be considered *investment value*. This is because it reflects the *value to a particular buyer*, generally referred to as the *synergistic buyer*, rather than value to the hypothetical willing buyer. This "hypothetical" typical willing buyer acquires the subject company strictly because of its financial merits, and is generally referred to as a *financial buyer*. (emphasis in original)

the *combination of the financial control premium and the strategic control premium* (see Figure 3-2).[48] Our expanded conceptual understanding leads to the following observations:[49]

- Use of available control premium studies as a basis for inferring minority interest discounts in a fair market value context is not conceptually correct, except where strategic buyers are the norm.

- Such use would tend to *overstate* the magnitude of minority interest discounts.

- When applied to financial control values, such discounts would not yield marketable minority interest levels of value, but rather something below that level (with no clear conceptual definition).

- And finally, the application of a "standard" marketability discount to that lower (and conceptually undefined) value would tend to *understate* the value of illiquid interests of private enterprises.

THE FINANCIAL CONTROL LEVEL OF VALUE

With this conceptual backdrop, we can examine the controlling interest levels of value. Equation 3-3 introduces the conceptual math of the first control level of value – *the financial control value*. Equation 3-3 introduces notation that will be used as we discuss the levels of value in the context of The Integrated Theory. Each symbol is defined below.

$$V_{e(c,f)} = \frac{CF_{e(c,f)}}{[\,R_f - (G_{mm} + G_f)\,]}$$

Equation 3-3

---

[48] *Mergerstat/Shannon Pratt's Control Premium Study.* This study is available in print versions and on-line at www.BVMarketData.com.

[49] While others have concluded that strategic control premiums may overstate value in the context of developing financial control values, these observations follow the implications to their logical conclusions. The Garber, Mercer, and Lee articles cited above reach this same conclusion, as does the following article.

Z. Christopher Mercer, "Understanding and Quantifying Control Premiums: The Value of Control vs. Synergies or Strategic Advantages," *The Journal of Business Valuation*, (Toronto: Carswell Thomas, 1999), pp. 31-54.

As with the marketable minority level of value, the terms found in Equation 3-3 are defined as follows:

- $V_{e(c,f)}$ is the value of the equity of an enterprise from the viewpoint of financial purchasers of the entire enterprise (control) who do not have the expected benefits of synergies or strategic intent that could further increase value relative to the marketable minority value. Traditionally, appraisers have developed the financial control level of value in two ways: 1) directly, by comparisons with change of control transactions of similar businesses (the guideline company changes of control method); and 2) indirectly, by the application of control premiums to indications of value at the marketable minority level of value.

- $CF_{e(c,f)}$ is equal to the cash flow of the enterprise from the viewpoint of the financial control buyer. The first step in developing $CF_{e(c,f)}$ is to derive $CF_{e(mm)}$ by normalizing the earnings stream as described in Chapter 4. Note that the normalization of earnings is not a "control" process, but one of equating private company earnings to their as-if-public equivalent.[50] The second step involves judgments regarding the ability of a control buyer to *improve* the earnings stream beyond the normalization process. This could involve the ability of a specific buyer to improve the existing operations or to run the target company better. However, unless there are competing financial buyers, a single buyer would likely be unwilling to share the benefit of all expected cash flow improvement with the seller. In the real world, there would be a negotiation to determine the extent of such sharing.[51]

- R_f is the discount rate of the universe of financial buyers. In the real world, R_f may be identical to R_{mm}, as other writers have observed.[52] While market forces will tend to equate R_f and R_{mm}, R_f is specified separately to allow for differences. ($R_f < R_{mm}$) recognizes that financial

---

[50] The issue of normalizing earnings will be discussed at more length in Chapter 4, However, it should be clear that normalization is an integral part of public securities pricing. It is not uncommon to find companies with well above-peer group price/earnings multiples based on trailing 12-month earnings, yet with near average multiples of forward (next-year's) earnings. Commonly, investigation reveals an unusual, non-recurring item in the most recent period that the market is "normalizing" and pricing based on the expectation of more normal earnings next year.

[51] Note that the negotiation between buyers and sellers affects the purchase price and not the expected after-acquisition cash flows. This observation suggest that observed takeover premiums do not reflect the expected total change in cash flow, but only that portion that is negotiated and shared with sellers.

[52] Shannon P. Pratt, *Cost of Capital* (New York: John Wiley, 1998), pp. 111-112.

control buyers may bid up prices in competition with other financial or strategic buyers. This can explain why certain buyers may bid prices above their valuation. They do so by consciously lowering R_f in favor of a deal. Alternatively, $(R_f > R_{mm})$ recognizes that the value of an enterprise to financial control buyers may be less than the freely traded value. In the public markets, this result could occur, for example, when speculative trading pushes a stock's price above financial control values. In the context of various control premium studies, this specification of R_f helps explain the existence of *negative* control premiums in acquisitions, or acquisition prices below the before-announcement trading price of targets.

- $(G_{mm} + G_f)$ is the expected growth rate of earnings for the financial control buyer. The first factor is the same G_{mm} found at the marketable minority level. The second factor (G_f) is the increment in the growth rate of earnings that a financial control buyer expects to generate. The second factor might not be relevant in determining the value of an enterprise for two reasons: 1) the universe of buyers may not expect such an increment in growth; and 2) a specific buyer who can accelerate growth may not share that expected benefit in a negotiation.[53] Nevertheless, this component of expected growth needs to be specified in order to understand market behavior. Financial control buyers might expect to augment growth by better managing the relationship between the growth of revenue and expenses, more productive use of facilities, better processes, and the like.

We now have a conceptual model describing the value of the equity of an enterprise at the financial control level. That model is based on the conceptual model for value at the marketable minority level, which is based on the Gordon Model. The relationship between the two levels of value is shown in Figure 3-3.

---

[53] Multiple financial buyers in an auction process may end up competing with each other such that the seller gains all or most of the growth benefit from the second-highest estimate of G_r.

	Conceptual Math	Relationships	Value Implications
Financial Control Value	$\dfrac{CF_{e(c,f)}}{R_f - [G_{mm} + G_f]}$	$CF_{e(c,f)} \geq CF_{e(mm)}$ $G_f \geq 0$ $R_f = R_{mm}$ (+/- a little)	$V_{e(c,f)} \geq V_{mm}$
Marketable Minority Value	$\dfrac{CF_{e(mm)}}{R_{mm} - G_{mm}}$	$G_v = R_{mm}$	V_{mm}

Figure 3-3

The conceptual differences in value at the marketable minority and financial control levels of value can be discerned by examining Figure 3-3. This analysis is important because it illustrates that control premiums (or other conceptual adjustments) are not automatic, but are based on expected differences in cash flows, risk, and/or growth. Based on Figure 3-3, the financial control value would exceed the marketable minority value if, all other things being equal, one or more of the following conditions were true:

- $CF_{e(c,f)}$ *is greater than* $CF_{e(mm)}$. This would be true if the buyer of the enterprise could be expected to improve the operations of the enterprise (and would share that expected benefit with the seller). Note that $CF_{e(c,f)}$ will not exceed $CF_{e(mm)}$ because of above-market salaries paid to owners of a business. Adjustments of that nature were required to arrive at $CF_{e(mm)}$.[54]

- G_f *is greater than zero.* If the financial control buyer expects to be able to augment the future growth of cash flows (and will share that benefit with the seller), then $V_{e(c,f)}$ can exceed V_{mm}, other things being equal.

- R_f *is noticeably less than* R_{mm}. Conceptually, R_f could be less than or exceed R_{mm}. Either condition could be true for a specific buyer; however, it is likely that market forces would tend to force the relevant universe of buyers to accept R_{mm} as the appropriate discount rate. The specification of R_f does provide an explanation for financial control

---

[54] Many appraisers still insist that in valuing minority interests of private companies, no adjustments should be made for above-market owner salaries or perquisites "because the minority shareholder lacks the power to change the cash flows." I hope that the discussion thus far, the upcoming discussion of the minority interest discount and Chapter 4's treatment of normalizing adjustments will eliminate this misconception.

premiums that might be paid for enterprises based on competition between private equity funds. Such funds have the capacity to bid up prices by accepting lower returns on individual deals.[55]

- Note that the financial buyer does not need to assume both higher expected cash flows and enhanced growth prospects for $V_{e(c,f)}$ to exceed $V_{e(mm)}$. It is quite possible that lower, near-term cash flows resulting from expected investments can augment expected growth enough to achieve higher present values. The same could be true for an adjustment in R_f. For financial control value to exceed marketability minority enterprise value, it is only necessary that the net of the above adjustments be positive to value.

The point of this analysis is that the financial control premium, as represented by value in excess of marketable minority value in Figure 3-3, is not automatic based on this conceptual analysis. Sellers have a history of earnings (appropriately adjusted) that provides the basis for future cash flow expectations. Buyers have benefit of that history and may have their own perceptions of greater future cash flows. Any differential in value is the function of negotiations between buyers and sellers of enterprises. The conceptual analysis of the Integrated Theory does not predict financial control value, but provides a vocabulary to describe the rational economic behavior of market participants.

---

[55] In fact, financial buyers have been shown to compete with strategic buyers in a recent study. See "Control Premium Study Shows Decline in Market Multiples," *Shannon Pratt's Business Valuation Update*, October 2001, pp. 6-7.

Financial Control Premium

At this point, the control premium that a financial control buyer might pay (CP_f) can be specified in relationship to the value of a business at the marketable minority level, but is based on differences (from the marketable minority level) in expected cash flow, risk and/or growth.

$$CP_f = \frac{V_{e(c,f)} - V_{e(mm)}}{V_{e(mm)}}$$

$$CP_f = \frac{\dfrac{CF_{e(c,f)}}{R_f - [G_{mm} + G_f]} - \dfrac{CF_{e(mm)}}{R_{mm} - G_{mm}}}{\dfrac{CF_{e(mm)}}{R_{mm} - G_{mm}}}$$

Equation 3-4

Conceptually, the control premium of a financial control buyer reflects the difference in value between the financial control and the marketable minority levels. This is shown symbolically in the upper equation of Equation 3-4. The lower equation substitutes the conceptual notation for each level of value (see Figure 3-3). Several important observations about the relationship between value at the marketable minority level and financial control levels of value can now be made.

Unless the financial control buyer expects to:

- Increase cash flows relative to normalized cash flows of the enterprise; and/or,

- Increase expected growth of cash flows of the enterprise, (and in either case), share that expected benefit with hypothetical sellers); and/or,

- *Decrease* the discount rate relative to R_{mm} (which most observers would consider unlikely);

- Achieve combination of expected cash flows, risk and growth, the net of which yields a positive result; and,

- Be willing to share all of a portion of the expected value-benefits of the above; *then*

  - $V_{e(c,f)}$ will be the same as V_{mm}.

  - The financial control premium of the financial control buyer will be zero.

  - Financial control value for the financial control buyer will be the same as the freely traded, marketable minority value to the seller.

  - Guideline public company multiples applied to normalized earnings of privately owned enterprises will yield financial control values, or values very close to this level. This will be true, of course, only if the public multiples are properly adjusted for fundamental differences in expectations (primarily for risk and growth) between the guideline public companies and the subject private enterprises. The concept of the fundamental adjustment and its role in the Integrated Theory is discussed in Chapter 5.

It should be clear that the concept of a financial control premium is a range concept. The financial control premium that might be paid for a particular enterprise will vary with potential buyers based on their unique circumstances. In fact, unless one or more of the above conditions hold true, the financial control premium may well be zero.

We have come a long way since Eric Nath made his then-revolutionary observation in 1990 suggesting that the public market multiples of guideline companies yielded controlling interest values.[56] Suffice it to say that many appraisers thought this observation was nothing short of heresy. I was in that group![57] The Integrated Theory reconciles Nath's position of control multiples coming from the public markets if the financial control premium is zero.

---

[56] Eric W. Nath, "Control Premiums and Minority Interest Discounts in Private Companies," *Business Valuation Review*, Vol. 9, No. 2 (1990): pp. 39-46.

[57] Z. Christopher Mercer, "Do Public Company (Minority) Transactions Yield Controlling Interest or Minority Interest Pricing Data?," *Business Valuation Review*, Vol. 9, No. 4 (1990): pp. 123-126. In this article, I charged to the defense of public multiples providing marketable minority value indications. Nath's view is reconciled with the Integrated Theory under the assumption that no value-enhancing factors are available to the financial control buyer, and the financial control premium is therefore zero. I did not recognize this potential for reconciliation in 1990.

We have defined $V_{e(c,f)}$ from the viewpoint of financial control buyers. $V_{e(c,f)}$ sets the upper boundary for negotiation of price with sellers (unless a particular buyer is willing to lower R_f). The greater the positive differences between $V_{e(c,f)}$ and $V_{e(mm)}$, the greater the potential for transactions. Nath's observation was that, given the relatively low number of acquisitions in any year relative to total public companies, the difference, in most instances, must be zero (or not large enough to warrant the interest of financial buyers). This reconciliation suggests that public market pricing could reflect both marketable minority and financial control pricing. A more detailed discussion of these issues is found in Chapter 10. Suffice it to say that there is a growing consensus among appraisers that there is a difference between financial and strategic control values, and a growing recognition that, to the extent they exist, financial control premiums are likely small.

Prerogatives of Control (Introduction to the Minority Interest Discount)

We now turn our attention to the corollary implications of the analysis of the financial control premium. The *minority interest discount* necessary to adjust a financial control value to a marketable minority value in an operating company may be zero, or quite small. This conclusion follows from the conceptual discussion surrounding Figure 3-2 and from the conceptual math of the Integrated Theory.

The difficulties of dealing with these issues absent an Integrated Theory can be illustrated by examining the discussion of control and noncontrol in the most recent edition of Pratt/Reilly/Schweihs. Many appraisers have cited the list of prerogatives of control found in each of the Pratt/Reilly/Schweihs books (and other books) as the reason for the application of a substantial minority interest discount.[58] The prerogatives of control include the ability to unilaterally:

1. Appoint or change operational management

2. Appoint or change members of the board of directors

3. Determine management compensation and perquisites

4. Set operational and strategic policy and change the course of the business

---

[58]   Shannon P. Pratt, Robert F. Reilly, and Robert P. Schweihs, *Valuing a Business*, 4th ed (New York: McGraw-Hill, 2000), pp. 347-348. The list is growing with succeeding editions.

5. Acquire, lease, or liquidate business assets, including plant, property, and equipment

6. Select suppliers, vendors, and subcontractors with whom to do business and award contracts

7. Negotiate and consummate mergers and acquisitions

8. Liquidate, dissolve, sell out, or recapitalize the company

9. Sell or acquire treasury shares

10. Register the company's equity securities for an initial or secondary public offering

11. Register the company's debt securities for an initial or secondary public offering

12. Declare and pay cash and/or stock dividends

13. Change the articles of incorporation or bylaws

14. Set one's own compensation (and perquisites) and the compensation (and perquisites) of, related-party employees

15. Select joint venturers and enter into joint venture and partnership agreements

16. Decide what products and/or services to offer and how to price those products or services

17. Decide what markets and locations to serve, to enter into, and to discontinue serving

18. Decide which customer categories to market to and which not to market to

19. Enter into inbound and outbound license or sharing agreements regarding intellectual properties

20. Block any or all of the above actions

In short, the prerogatives of control indicate that the controlling shareholder is empowered with the rights and responsibilities to run a business enterprise for the benefit of the controlling shareholder. Appraisers (and courts) have long thought that control buyers pay control premiums for the prerogatives of control listed above. The Pratt/Reilly/Schweihs text concludes the presentation of this list, which first appears in Chapter 15, "Control and Acquisition Premiums," with:

From the above list, it is apparent that the owner of a controlling interest in a business enterprise enjoys some very valuable rights that the owner of a noncontrolling ownership interest does not enjoy.[59]

The authors present two levels of value charts at the same point in the text. The first chart is the three-level one used for several years by Pratt/Reilly/Schweihs in editions of *Valuing a Business* and in other Pratt publications. The second is a reproduction of the right portion of Figure 3-2.[60] This is important because it is clear from the charts that the control premium being discussed by Pratt/Reilly/Schweihs is the same conceptual premium as the financial control premium indicated in Figure 3-2.

We will see shortly that the statement quoted above may be true as it relates to a controlling owner of a private company and a minority (noncontrolling) shareholder in the same company. It is likely not true (or is not relevant) as it relates to the managements and boards of directors of well-run public companies and the corresponding minority shareholders of their publicly traded stocks.

The prerogatives of control list are repeated in the next chapter of Pratt/Reilly/Schweihs, "Discounts for Lack of Control." Following the second list, we read:[61]

As the equity holder enjoys fewer and fewer of these elements of ownership control, his or her position changes from absolute control to relative control to lack of control to absolute lack of control. Along this spectrum: (1) The control premium begins to decrease, (2) then becomes zero, and finally (3) changes to a lack of control discount.

A careful reading of this conclusion in connection with a visual inspection of Figure 3-2 indicates that it is conceptually incorrect. The control premium referred to measures the value differential between the marketable minority value and the financial control value. If the aforementioned prerogatives of control give rise to this differential, then the decrement to value associated with absence of these prerogatives can be no greater than the financial control premium. As the

---

59   Ibid, p. 349.

60   Ibid, p. 347. Citing Jay E. Fishman, Shannon P. Pratt, *Guide to Business Valuations*, 10th ed. (Fort Worth, TX: Practitioners Publishing Company, 2000). Also, at p. 348, citing Z. Christopher Mercer, "Understanding and Quantifying Control Premiums: The Value of Control vs. Synergies of Strategic Advantages," *The Journal of Business Valuation* (Toronto: Carswell Thomson, 1999), p. 51.

61   Ibid, p. 366.

control premium falls to zero, for whatever reason, we are back at the marketable minority level of value. If the conceptual levels of value represented by the two charts found in Pratt/Reilly/Schweihs are a valid representation of economic and financial reality, any further decrement in value below the marketable minority level must result from factors other than the prerogatives of control.

The further reduction in value described in (3) in the quote above, where there is a change to a lack of control discount, is actually the decrement in value known as the marketability discount. Under this interpretation, the ownership interest of a noncontrolling shareholder of a private enterprise may have a lower value than either the hypothetical, marketable minority value or the financial control value.

The conceptual name for this value is the nonmarketable minority (level of) value. The freely traded (marketable minority) value is the base to which the control premium is applied. If there is a positive value to the prerogative of control, then the control premium should not be negative.[62] The conceptual model outlined by Pratt/Reilly/Schweihs breaks down at this point.[63] The lack of control discount in (3) above must be the marketability discount.

A careful examination of the conceptual math shown in Figure 3-4 reveals no component related to the aforementioned prerogatives of control. What, then, is a control buyer paying for? Assume that R_f is equal to R_{mm} for purposes of the following attempt to address this critical question. We observe from Figure 3-4, which defines the control premium of a financial control buyer:

- The financial control premium is created by any differential in cash flow that the control buyer is willing to price into a deal and any expectation for increased growth in those cash flows.

- In other words, the conceptual model suggests that a control buyer would pay a financial control price based only on the expectation of greater future cash flows than expected at the marketable minority level.

---

[62] We have observed that entire companies are sometimes worth less than their indicated, freely-traded values. If present, this difference could be termed a (negative) control premium. In fact, many of the observations of control premiums in the marketplace as captured in available data sources are *negative* control premiums. Consideration of control premiums without including the negative premiums tends to overstate the magnitude of "typical" premiums, and therefore of minority interest discounts estimated using them. These points are well made in the earlier citations to Mercer and Garber.

[63] This breaking down is likely the result of an editing oversight rather than a misunderstanding of the conceptual model.

- The prerogatives of control are *assumed* in the valuation process of control buyers. What good are an enterprise's cash flows without the ability to exercise control over them? The prerogatives of control accompany the transfer of control in purchase transactions.[64]

  For example, when the equity of a company is sold it is assumed that the operating assets and liabilities will be acquired. It is further assumed that any intangible assets related to the enterprise, including goodwill, will also be acquired. *Among the intangible assets to be acquired are the prerogatives of control.* Such prerogatives are granted by the combination of the charter, by-laws, articles of incorporation, other relevant agreements and contracts, and stock ownership. If a control premium is paid, it is paid for the right to run the enterprise differently to achieve enhanced cash flow or accelerated growth. The price is paid for the expected cash flow and not for the naked right, or prerogative.

- There is no specific portion of the value of an enterprise that should be allocated to the prerogatives of control.

It can therefore be concluded that the control premium, to the extent it is observed, is *not* the price paid for the prerogatives of control. Rather, it is the negotiated price paid for control of the cash flows of an enterprise in cases where the buyer expects to augment those cash flows (relative to the marketable minority level of cash flow) through the operation of the business.

We have observed thus far that unless the control buyer can expect to achieve augmented levels and growth of cash flows, the financial control premium could be zero, or at least, quite small. The reason is simple: If it were not so, if a substantial premium were paid with no expectation of augmented cash flows, then the control buyer would have to accept a substantially lower than market return.

---

[64] Anyone receiving dividends from minority investments can attest to the fact that it is nice to receive them and have no control. However, no rational purchaser would pay a control price for an enterprise without receiving the right to determine when dividends are to be paid – or not.

The Minority Interest Discount

The conceptual difference between the financial control value and the marketable minority value is the financial control premium (see Figure 3-2). If that premium is zero (or quite small), as observed above, it is also true that the minority interest (or lack of control) discount is quite small.[65] Several observations about the relationships between the marketable minority and financial control levels of value are summarized below:

- Minority shareholders of public companies lack control, which is vested with managements and boards of directors. Yet we have observed (practically as with Nath, and conceptually with the Integrated Theory) that the marketable minority value and the control financial value may be equal or very close to each other for most public companies. Again, if it were not so, there would be strong financial incentive for the takeover of many public companies. Absent such a level of activity, it is reasonable to assume that the marketable minority and financial control values for most public companies must be equivalent or reasonably close to each other.

- The implication of this line of reasoning is that there is no (or very little) discount for lack of control considered in the pricing of public securities. This makes sense because investors in the public markets are not investing to gain control – they invest in companies and assume that managements will run them in the best interests of the shareholders. If it were not so, the shareholders would exercise the control they do have – selling their shares and putting downward pressure on market prices, creating opportunities for takeovers by financial buyers.

- Further, observe that at the marketable minority level all the cash flows of public enterprises are assumed to be distributed to the shareholders in dividends or reinvested in the enterprises at their discount rates. There is no pricing penalty because minority shareholders do not control or have direct access to enterprise cash flows. This is true because minority shareholders have access to the benefit of the market's capitalization of all expected future cash flows in the current market price. At any time, a minority shareholder in a public enterprise can place a sale order and achieve current market value in three days.

---

[65]   "Definitions," *Business Valuation Standards* (Washington, D.C.: The Appraisal Foundation, 2001), pp. 21-27. This lack of control discount, unlike the term used in (3) above in the quote from Pratt/Reilly/Schweihs, is theoretically consistent with eliminating a financial control premium.

- Conceptually, this suggests that the mechanism of the public securities markets eliminates most, if not all, of any discount for lack of control of cash flows for minority shareholders.

- The logical inference is that unless there are cash flow-driven differences between the enterprise's financial control value and its marketable minority value, there will be no (or very little) minority interest discount.[66]

The analysis suggests that use of the terms "lack of control discount" and "minority interest discount" may not be descriptive of the economic factors and issues that they are being used to describe. Rather than attempting to introduce new vocabulary at this point, we proceed with efforts to understand what the existing terms mean.

The financial control premium was defined in Figure 3-4. The related minority interest discount from the financial control value (MID_F) is defined as indicated at the top of Equation 3-5.

$$MID_F = \left[1 - \frac{1}{1 + CP_f}\right]$$

$$MID_F = \left(1 - \left[\frac{1}{1 + \left[\dfrac{V_{e(c,f)} - V_{e(mm)}}{V_{e(mm)}}\right]}\right]\right)$$

Equation 3-5

---

[66] The capital structure of an enterprise may include voting and nonvoting stock. If the vote is perceived to decrease risk somewhat relative to the nonvoting shares, voting shares may trade at a small premium to nonvoting shares. Stated alternatively, nonvoting shares may trade at a small discount to voting shares.

Examination of the bottom portion of Equation 3-5 indicates that the minority interest discount will exist only if the typical control financial buyer can expect to augment cash flows from properly normalized cash flows at the marketable minority level.[67]

Market discipline causes most public companies to be run in reasonable fashion, with cash flows being optimized and either reinvested or distributed to achieve appropriate returns to shareholders. If it were not so, as Nath observed in 1990, there would be incentive for financial buyers to acquire underperforming companies and there would be considerably more merger and acquisition activity than was observed in the markets then or now.

The conceptual analysis thus far suggests that the appearance of Figure 3-2 should be modified to reflect the conceptual relationship between the financial control and marketable minority levels.

---

[67] These observations are made in relationship to operating companies. Their relevance for asset holding entities needs to be addressed further. The logic of the Integrated Theory suggests that there is no reason for minority interest discounts related to asset holding entities to be at great magnitude. In practice, we have used minority interest discounts in the range of 0% to 15% for several years when valuing asset holding entities. The issue of minority interest discounts seldom arises when valuing operating companies, since most valuation methods, other than comparisons and guideline transactions of whole companies, yield marketable minority level indications of value.

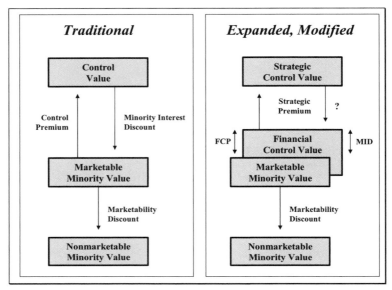

Figure 3-4

The expanded, modified chart shows the much closer correspondence between the financial control and marketable minority levels of value suggested by the conceptual discussion and by the math of the levels of value.

The conceptual strategic control value will be developed to round out the enterprise levels before proceeding to the shareholder level represented by the nonmarketable minority value. However, a critical observation flows from the expanded, modified levels of value chart at the right side of Figure 3-4:

Assuming the conceptual analysis thus far is correct, the source of what can be large differences between enterprise values (financial control or marketable minority) and the shareholder level, nonmarketable minority value is entirely (or at least substantially) found in the conceptual discount known as the marketability discount. The analysis thus far has eliminated the minority interest discount as a source of this value differential.

The analysis of the relationship between the financial control value and the marketable minority value can be recapped as follows:

• Value at the marketable minority level of value presumes that enterprise cash flows are normalized. If it were not so, market pressures would force such a process to occur, and/or takeovers would occur.

- Unless the financial control buyer will price an expectation for greater cash flows (level or expected growth) than the normalized earnings of an enterprise, there is no conceptual reason for there to be a distinction in value between the financial control and marketable minority levels.

- The financial control premium is *not* a payment to reflect the value of the so-called prerogatives of control. Those prerogatives are vested with managements and directorates of public entities, and are presumed vested for purposes of deriving private company values at the marketable (as-if-freely-traded) minority level of value.

- The minority interest discount is *not* a discount to reflect the absence of the so-called prerogatives of control. Lack of control on the part of minority shareholders is presumed in pricing at the marketable minority level.

- Application of strategic acquisition premiums may overstate value in the context of fair market value.

- Use of strategic acquisition control premium data to infer minority interest discounts from financial control values will tend to overstate the magnitude of minority interest discounts.[68]

- The need to understand the conceptual nature of the marketability discount and the causes of often-observed large differences between marketable minority values and the values of illiquid securities of private (or public) enterprises is critical.

Thus far, the marketable minority and financial control levels of value have been examined, and we have drawn inferences about the other levels. This Integrated Theory of Business Valuation is beginning to take shape and has raised questions about the value relationships reflected in the traditional three-level chart found in Figure 3-2, calling for a modification as found in Figure 3-4.

---

[68] Of course, if the strategic controlling interest value is developed by referencing strategic control acquisitions, then the elimination of such strategic premiums (from the strategic control level of value) would be appropriate. See Figure 3-4.

STRATEGIC CONTROL LEVEL OF VALUE

Equation 3-6 introduces the conceptual math of the second control level of value
– *the strategic control value.*

$$V_{e(c,s)} = \frac{CF_{e(c,s)}}{[\,R_s - (G_{mm} + G_s)\,]}$$

Equation 3-6

As with the other levels, we define the terms in Equation 3-6.

- $V_{e(c,s)}$ is defined as the value of the equity of an enterprise from the viewpoint of buyers of the entire enterprise (control) when considering the expected benefit of synergies or strategic intent that could increase value relative to the financial control value (and the marketable minority value). This level is called the *strategic control* level of value. As noted in the quote from Pratt/Reilly/Schweihs above, the concept of strategic control value relates to value as perceived by *particular buyers*, rather than the *typical buyers* in the fair market value context. As such, $V_{e(c,s)}$ is generally more akin to a concept of *investment value* rather than fair market value.

- $CF_{e(c,s)}$ is equal to the cash flow of the enterprise from the viewpoint of a strategic control buyer(s). As with $CF_{e(c,f)}$, the first step in developing $CF_{e(c,s)}$ is to normalize earnings to derive $CF_{e(mm)}$. Additional adjustments may then be made to reflect:

  - Improvements that typical financial buyers might expect to make by running the company better (to derive $CF_{e(c,f)}$);

  - Concrete expectations of synergies (e.g., from eliminating overlapping functions or positions); and/or,

  - Strategic benefits (e.g., from selling more of a purchaser's products through the target's existing distribution chain).

  In other words, in addition to expectations of running a company better (optimal management), strategic control buyers may take into consideration benefits expected by running the company *differently.*[69]

---

[69]   These terms are addressed in more detail in Chapter 4.

- R_s is the discount rate of potential strategic (or synergistic) buyers. R_s can be lower than R_{mm} or R_f for at least two reasons. First many strategic buyers are considerably larger in size than the smaller public and private companies that they may desire to acquire. As such their equity cost of capital may be lower than the discount rates appropriate for their smaller targets.[70] Second a strategic acquirer of similar size may expect business risk to decrease as the result of a strategic combination, and may therefore consider an R_s lower than its expected discount rate absent the acquisition.

- $(G_{mm} + G_s)$ is the expected growth rate of earnings for the strategic control buyer. The first factor is the same G_{mm} found at the marketable minority level. The second factor is the increment in the growth rate that a strategic control buyer may expect to create. In other words, expected synergies can impact both the level of cash flow ($CF_{e(c,f)}$) and the growth of those cash flows ($G_{mm} + G_s$).

The conceptual model now incorporates the value of the equity of an enterprise at the strategic control level. It builds on the base created by the other two enterprise levels, marketable minority and financial control. The relationship between the three enterprise levels of value is illustrated in Figure 3-5.

---

[70] Whether strategic buyers should give benefit to their lower cost of capital in strategic acquisitions is a separate question. However, if the market consists of numerous, competing strategic buyers some or all of that benefit may get reflected in value to selling companies.

	Conceptual Math	Relationships	Value Implications
Strategic Control Value	$$\frac{CF_{e(c,s)}}{R_s - [G_{mm} + G_s]}$$	$CF_{e(c,s)} \geq CF_{e(c,f)}$ $G_s \geq 0$ $R_s \leq R_{mm}$	$V_{e(c,s)} \geq V_{e(c,f)}$
Financial Control Value	$$\frac{CF_{e(c,f)}}{R_f - [G_{mm} + G_f]}$$	$CF_{e(c,f)} \geq CF_{e(mm)}$ $G_f \geq 0$ $R_f = R_{mm}$ (+/- a little)	$V_{e(c,f)} \geq V_{mm}$
Marketable Minority Value	$$\frac{CF_{e(mm)}}{R_{mm} - G_{mm}}$$	$G_v = R_{mm}$	V_{mm}

Figure 3-5

The strategic control value can be greater than the financial control value if one or more of the following conditions holds:

- $CF_{e(c,s)}$ *is greater than* $CF_{e(c,f)}$ *(and greater than* $CF_{e(mm)}$*).* This would be true if a strategic purchaser of an enterprise expects synergies or strategic benefits unavailable to the financial control buyer. A lone strategic buyer, for example, has no incentive to pay any more than $1 more (or just enough more to get the deal) than the highest price offered by a financial buyer.[71] In other words, there may be a considerable difference in what a particular strategic buyer is *able* to pay and what he is *willing* to pay in an acquisition.

- G_s *is greater than zero.* If a strategic control buyer expects to augment the future growth of cash flows (and will share that benefit with the hypothetical seller), then value can be augmented above the financial control or marketable minority levels.

---

[71] Mr. Gilbert A Matthews, ASA, currently of Sutter Securities, Inc. and for many years an investment banker with Bear, Stearns & Co., made this observation years ago. Its relevance in the context of fair market value determinations should now be clear based on this conceptual analysis.

- R_s is less than R_f or R_{mm}. If a strategic buyer considers its own discount rate (cost of capital), which may be lower than that of a target, in pricing an acquisition, strategic control value can be greater than at the other enterprise levels. It is also possible that financial buyers may sometimes act like strategic buyers (e.g., when they have multiple investments in an industry) or they may elect to pay a strategic price (i.e., accept a lower return) in order to stay in the game.

- Just as with the financial control buyer, it is the net result of expectations regarding augmented cash flow, expected growth and the discount rate considered that determine willingness to negotiate prices above the marketable minority or financial control levels.

Critical Insight for Appraisers. If a strategic control buyer is willing to consider expected cash flow enhancements (either one-time increases in level and/or increases in growth from that new level *and* its own lower discount rate (or cost of capital)) in pricing an acquisition, $V_{e(s,c)}$ can be substantially higher than V_{mm} or $V_{e(c,f)}$. If multiple strategic buyers are seeking the same (public or private) business, then strategic value is more likely to be achieved by that seller, and pricing can sometimes seem almost irrational.[72]

Critical Insights for Corporate Finance Professionals, Managements, and Boards. Corporate finance professionals, managements, and boards of directors of acquisitive companies responsible for the pricing of acquisitions should take note of these observations. Finance theory suggests that the appropriate discount rate is that of the *investment*, rather than the *investor*. Strategic purchasers who substitute their own discount rates (R_s) (or cost of capital) for the discount rates of acquisition targets (R_{mm} or R_f) may be overpricing their acquisitions relative to the risks assumed. This overpricing will be even more certain if expected strategic and/or synergistic cash flow benefits are considered in the discounted cash flow (or market multiple) acquisition valuation models through adjustments either to the level or the expected growth of a target's cash flows. In such case there would be no incremental reward for accepting all of the operational and execution risks of achieving the hoped-for economies. Since execution is not a flawless concept, diminished shareholder returns may be the result.

---

[72] I have often said in speeches that there are *three* kinds of buyers of businesses: financial buyers, strategic buyers, and irrational buyers. What every seller wants to find is an irrational buyer. Unfortunately, when they are really needed, they are hard to find. However, fair market value is a rational concept, not an irrational one. Appraisers need to keep these concepts in mind when determining fair market value at the financial control level.

In other words, strategic buyers should use their own discount rates (R_s) only in competition with other strategic buyers and for their own, unique and strategic reasons. To begin pricing of acquisitions at the strategic level of pricing is to shift current benefit to sellers and to take on future execution risks without compensation.

Strategic Control Premium

The control premium that a strategic control buyer might pay (CP_s) in relationship to the value of a business at the marketable minority level can now be specified. We specify the premium in this way because there is no observable market for financial control values (other than if public companies are trading at their financial control values).[73] Note that this premium would include any financial control premium available from financial buyers. CP_s is specified in Equation 3-7.

$$CP_s = \frac{V_{e(c,s)} - V_{e(mm)}}{V_{e(mm)}}$$

$$CP_s = \frac{\dfrac{CF_{e(c,s)}}{R_s - [G_{mm} + G_s]} - \dfrac{CF_{e(mm)}}{R_{mm} - G_{mm}}}{\dfrac{CF_{e(mm)}}{R_{mm} - G_{mm}}}$$

Equation 3-7

The control premium of a strategic buyer is the difference in value at the strategic control level and the marketable minority level in relationship to the marketable minority value. As measured, it would include any financial control premium that resulted from assumptions regarding performance improvements at a company. The strategic control premium is shown symbolically in the upper equation of Equation 3-7. The lower equation substitutes the symbolic definitions for each conceptual value into the upper equation.

---

[73] We can observe the net pricing of private companies in the acquisition markets; however, the marketable minority base is not observable, and therefore the extent of any control premium cannot be observed directly.

Several important observations about the relationship between value at the marketable minority and financial control levels and at the strategic control level can now be made. Unless a strategic buyer is willing to consider the potential for enhanced cash flows (level of flows and/ or growth rate) or the fact that R_s might be lower than R_{mm}:

- $V_{e(c,s)}$ will be the same as V_{mm} (or the same as $V_{e(c,f)}$ if the strategic buyer does not expect to be able to enhance cash flows from the normalized, marketable minority level).

- Observed strategic control values, then, are not automatic, but are the result of negotiations between sellers and one or more strategic purchasers.

- Strategic control values will likely be received in transactions only if: 1) there is a single, motivated strategic buyer who is willing to share the expected synergistic or strategic benefits with a seller; 2) there are multiple strategic buyers who will compete in a bidding process; or 3) elements of motivation or irrationality enter into the bidding process.[74]

- The marketable minority value is the base from which strategic control values would be negotiated. This statement is true for publicly traded companies. Private company values tend to be negotiated directly, since there is no observable, freely traded value for closely held companies. These principles would be embedded within negotiated values in private transactions.

---

[74] Note that a target seller who is not motivated to sell may be able to extract some or all of the potential strategic control premium if there is only a single strategic buyer – if that buyer is motivated.

Having developed the strategic control premium, the discount that would eliminate it from strategic control value can be briefly discussed. Refer to the right side of Figure 3-2 and note the question mark between the strategic control and financial control levels. We have already observed that the question mark is not the minority interest discount, which relates the financial control and marketable minority levels. However, the question mark discount would include or subsume the minority interest discount.[75] It might represent the minority interest discount if strategic transactions are the norm for an industry. Rather than attempting to give this question mark discount a name at this time, we leave it for further consideration by appraisers in specific valuation situations.

ENTERPRISE LEVELS VS. THE SHAREHOLDER LEVEL OF VALUE

Thus far, the enterprise levels of value – marketable minority, financial control, and strategic control – have been addressed. These conceptual levels are called enterprise levels because each is determined on the basis of (potentially) differing market perceptions and valuations of the cash flows of the enterprise. A critical assumption of the Gordon Model is that value is a function of the expected cash flows of the enterprise, all of which are available for distribution or for reinvestment.

The fourth conceptual level of value is the nonmarketable minority level. As opposed to an enterprise level of value, this level is referred to as the *shareholder* level of value. Value to a *shareholder* is determined based on the expectation of cash flows (or future benefits) *to the shareholder*. This is an important point, and the distinction is, unfortunately, lost by many observers.

---

[75] This is true based on the realization that the control premium reflected in the traditional levels of value was a strategic control premium. The empirical evidence supporting the traditional control premium related primarily to strategic control transactions.

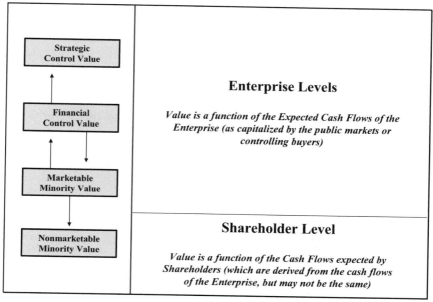

Figure 3-6

For years, appraisers have called the conceptual difference between the marketable minority and nonmarketable minority levels of value the *marketability discount*. An alternative name for this concept is the *discount for lack of marketability*.[76] There is more to this discount than the mere absence of marketability, so it makes little sense to argue over which is the preferable term.

---

[76] "Definitions," *Business Valuation Standards* (Washington, D.C.: The Appraisal Foundation, 2001), pp. 21-27. The marketability discount is defined as "an amount or percentage deducted from the value of an ownership interest to reflect the relative absence of marketability."

We recently wrote an article discussing the logical basis for the marketability discount. It focused on the distinction between enterprise and shareholder values and a portion is excerpted here:[77]

> There is almost unanimous agreement in the valuation profession that the value of a business, at the marketable minority level, where most valuations originate, is the present value of the expected future benefits to be generated by the business, discounted to the present at an appropriate, risk-adjusted discount rate. In other words, the value of a business depends on the expected cash flows of the business (including their expected future growth), and the risk of generating those cash flows (manifested in the discount rate).
>
> Likewise, a nonmarketable minority interest in a business is a financial asset whose value must derive from the same factors determining the value of the business: expected cash flows (including their expected future growth), and the risk of generating those cash flows (as manifested in the discount rate).
>
> - The expected cash flows to the holder of a nonmarketable minority business interest have as their source the cash flows generated by the business. The cash flows received by the nonmarketable minority investor may be less than, or equal to, but may be no greater than the cash flows generated by the business.
>
> - Since the expected cash flows generated by the business are the source of the nonmarketable minority investor's cash flows, the risks faced by the nonmarketable minority investor encompass the risk of the business generating those cash flows, as well as incremental risks arising from the illiquidity of the investment. Therefore, the embodiment of risk for valuation purposes, the relevant discount rate, must for nonmarketable investors be greater than or equal to, but cannot be less than, the discount rate applicable to the valuation of the business.
>
> - From the standpoint of the nonmarketable minority investor, this confluence of circumstances (he may not receive all the cash flows of the business, and he faces additional risks not borne by the business) leads to the inevitable conclusions that his nonmarketable interest is worth less than (or possibly the same as) his pro rata share

---

[77] Z. Christopher Mercer and Travis W. Harms, "Marketability Discount Analysis at a Fork in the Road," *Business Valuation Review*, Vol. 20, No. 4 (2001): pp. 21-22.

of the business. The difference in value is the "amount or percentage" from the definition of the marketability discount quoted above.

- The preceding discussion should make clear the logical and theoretical basis for the existence of a disparity between the value of illiquid business interests and the value of the corresponding business. Without any reference to empirical observation, the fact of marketability discounts is undeniable. Given any two investments, if it is known that one has both less cash flow (and corresponding growth) expectations *and* greater risk, its value will be lower than its counterpart.

The stage is now set to discuss the nonmarketable minority level of value and the marketability discount that separates it from the marketable minority level of value.

THE NONMARKETABLE MINORITY LEVEL OF VALUE

Equation 3-8 introduces the conceptual math of the shareholder level of value, which corresponds to the nonmarketable minority level of value.

$$V_{sh} = \frac{CF_{sh}}{R_{hp} - G_v}$$

Equation 3-8

As with the other levels of value, the terms in the conceptual definition of value at the nonmarketable minority level are defined:

- V_{sh} is the value of an equity interest of an enterprise that lacks an active market for its shares – with value considered from the viewpoint of the holder (or purchaser) of that interest. Appraisers typically develop indications of value at this level by subtracting a marketability discount from a marketable minority interest value. In the case of asset holding entities, appraisers often begin with a net asset value (deemed to be the financial control level) and then subtract minority interest and marketability discounts in sequence. Appraisers also examine transactions in the stock of companies without public markets as another means of developing indications of value at the nonmarketable minority level for their shares.

- **CF_{sh}** is equal to the portion of the cash flow to equity of an enterprise expected to be received pro rata by the shareholders of the enterprise. Consistent with the discounted future benefits method, CF_{sh} represents both interim cash flows (expected dividends or distributions) and any expected terminal value upon ultimate sale of an equity interest.[78]

- **R_{hp}** is the discount rate of the minority investor in a nonmarketable equity security for the expected duration of the holding period, or the *required holding period return*. The concept of holding period risks is discussed in more detail in the context of the Quantitative Marketability Discount Model (QMDM) in Chapter 7. However, as noted above, logic suggests that R_{hp} will be equal to or greater than R_{mm}. This required return can be stated symbolically as in Equation 3-9, where HPP is the indicated *holding period premium*. Note that if HPP is equal to zero, and there are no holding period risks, as with a publicly traded security where liquidity can be achieved immediately, then R_{hp} is equal to R_{mm}.

$$\mathbf{R_{hp}} = R_{mm} + HPP$$

Equation 3-9

- **G_v** is the *expected growth rate in value* of the enterprise, which will yield the terminal value of the enterprise at the end of the expected holding period for the investment. In the earlier chapter on the basics of the discounted cash flow method, we learned that for a non-dividend paying, publicly traded security, the expected growth rate in value is equal to R_{mm}. If there is leakage of cash flow from the enterprise (e.g., as through the payment of above-market compensation to a controlling shareholder), then G_v will be less than R_{mm}. The same result will occur if a company's expected reinvestment rate is less than its discount rate (e.g., as with the accumulation of low-yielding cash assets, vacation

---

[78] CF_{sh} is a symbolic notation to describe all expected interim cash flows and any expected terminal value at the end of the holding period for the investment. In other words, Equation 3-8 cannot be literally used to determine the value of a nonmarketable minority business interest.

homes, or other assets providing no yield or a yield less than the discount rate).[79]

Enterprise valuation is a perpetuity concept. Value today is the present value of all expected cash flows attributable to an enterprise discounted to the present at an appropriate discount rate. Shareholder valuation is a finite concept. Investments are made with finite expected holding periods, even if such holding periods are not precisely knowable at the time investments are made. The expected growth in value is the means of estimating the exit value of an illiquid investment at a future date or range of future dates.

Assuming no dividends, an expected growth in value of 6% (from whatever source), an expected holding period of precisely 10 years, a discount rate of 20%, and a marketable minority value of $1.00 per share, we can illustrate the present value (and the implied marketability discount) for an investment graphically.

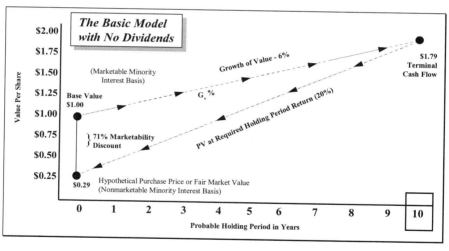

This graph was used to illustrate the derivation of the marketability discount in Chapter 8 of *Quantifying Marketability Discounts*.

---

[79] For a more in-depth discussion of this issue, see Z. Christopher Mercer and Travis W. Harms, "Marketability Discount Analysis at a Fork in the Road," *Business Valuation Review*, Vol. 20, No. 4 (2001): pp. 21-22.

We now have a conceptual model to describe the value of the equity of an enterprise at the nonmarketable minority level. The model anticipates that the appraiser will develop an indication of value at the marketable minority level. In so doing, there will be a thorough understanding of the expected cash flows, their expected growth, and their risks. Based on this analysis, the appraiser can then consider the expected benefits to be derived by the minority shareholder of the enterprise. These relationships are shown symbolically in Figure 3-7.

	Conceptual Math	Relationships	Value Implications
Marketable Minority Value	$\dfrac{CF_{e(mm)}}{R_{mm} - G_{mm}}$	$G_v = R_{mm}$	V_{mm}
Nonmarketable Minority Value	$\dfrac{CF_{sh}}{R_{hp} - G_v}$	$CF_{sh} \leq CF_{e(mm)}$ $G_v \leq G_{mm}$ $R_{hp} \geq R_{mm}$	$V_{sh} \leq V_{mm}$

Figure 3-7

Examining the components of Figure 3-7, we can discuss the conceptual differences in value between the marketable minority and nonmarketable minority levels of value. The nonmarketable minority value, i.e., V_{sh}, or value to the shareholder, will be less than V_{mm} if holding the other variables constant, one or more of the following conditions holds:

- CF_{sh} *is less than* $CF_{e(mm)}$. The expected cash flow of a shareholder will be less than the expected cash flows of the enterprise if the cash flows are reinvested in the business or paid out on a non-pro rata basis to certain shareholders, as with "leakage" to a controlling shareholder/group.[80]

- G_v *is less than* R_{mm}. The expected growth rate in value reflects the combined effect of the expected growth rate of core earnings, or the G of

---

[80] Recall that the benchmark marketability minority value is determined under the assumption that all cash flows are paid out to shareholders pro rata or reinvested in the enterprise to achieve a return equal to the discount rate. After this determination is made, the appraiser then estimates CF_{sh}, which may be less than or substantially less than the cash flow of the enterprise ($CF_{e(mm)}$).

the Gordon Model, and the reinvestment of those cash flows into the enterprise. If the reinvestment rate is equal to the discount rate, then, as shown in Chapter 6, G_v will be equal to the discount rate, or R_{mm}. To the extent that cash flows are not reinvested in the enterprise or that they are reinvested suboptimally (at rates less than the discount rate), then G_v will be less than R_{mm}.[81] To the extent G_v is less than R_{mm}, the expected terminal value at the end of any holding period is reduced, resulting in a lower value today.

- R_{hp} *is greater than* R_{mm}. Few observers question that the owner of an illiquid asset bears greater risk than the owner of an otherwise identical asset with an active, public market.[82] We have given a name to the compensation necessary for an investor to accept this incremental risk – the holding period premium, or HPP. HPP is comprised of numerous factors, including the potential for a long and indeterminate holding period and many other risks that flow from this holding period or from the factual situation in any valuation. Other things being equal, greater risk implies lower value.

The circumstances under which the nonmarketable minority value will be less than the marketable minority value are now clear. The marketability discount, which is the name given to this net differential in value, can now be examined.

---

[81]   Note that the expectation of suboptimal reinvestment, and the accompanying lowering of expected growth in value impacts both controlling and noncontrolling shareholders. The difference between the two situations is that the controlling shareholder can change the reinvestment and/or distribution policies in order to maximize value while the noncontrolling shareholder cannot make those changes. Said another way, the value, today, of a business to a controlling shareholder can exceed the value of the expected business plan.

[82]   This should have been obvious to appraisers years ago (me included) based on the restricted stock studies and their observed discounts on average. If the restricted shares were identical in all respects save restrictions (for a period of time) under Rule 144, the only reason for discounts to market prices of freely traded shares relates to perceived incremental risk.

THE MARKETABILITY DISCOUNT

The marketability discount (MD) that investors might demand when purchasing illiquid interests of enterprises that do not have active public markets for their shares can now be specified.

$$MD = 1 - \frac{V_{sh}}{V_{mm}}$$

$$MD = 1 - \left(\frac{\dfrac{CF_{sh}}{R_{hp} - G_v}}{\dfrac{CF_{e(mm)}}{R_{mm} - G_{mm}}} \right)$$

Equation 3-10

Conceptually, the first equation of Equation 3-10 illustrates that if the shareholder level value (V_{sh}) is equal to the marketable minority value (V_{mm}) there will be no marketability discount. To the extent that any of the three factors outlined in the previous section are present, there will be a marketability discount.

Frequently, holders of illiquid securities of private enterprises are faced with expectations that include all three of these factors:

1. Cash flow to the shareholder (CF_{sh}) less than that of the enterprise ($CF_{e(mm)}$);

2. Expected growth in value less than the discount rate; and,

3. Incremental risks associated with illiquidity during the expected holding period.

In such cases, the marketability discounts that are appropriate relative to the marketable minority value can be quite large. In other cases, however, as with fully distributing entities, or in cases where the expected growth rate in value is relatively high and holding period risks are not large, the appropriate marketability discounts can be quite small.

Conceptually, no portion of the marketability discount is the result of a subtraction in value because of the prerogatives of control. The economic penalty of the marketability discount is explained in terms of divergences between the expected cash flows of the enterprise and those to shareholders, expected growth in value less than the underlying discount rate, and holding period risk in excess of the risks associated with the enterprise.

Note that the minority investor in a public company has no more direct control over the enterprise than does the minority investor in a private company. However, as previously noted, the public minority shareholder does have an element of *personal control* that the private minority shareholder lacks. He has the ability to obtain cash for his investment in three days through the public securities markets at the marketable minority level (present value of all expected cash flows of the enterprise).

NO MARKETABILITY DISCOUNT APPLICABLE TO CONTROLLING INTERESTS OF COMPANIES

Theoretical Basis

Some appraisers have attempted to define a discount applicable to controlling interests of companies. This discount is often called a "marketability discount" or a "discount for lack of marketability for controlling ownership interests."

An examination of the conceptual relationships of the three enterprise levels of value in Figure 3-5 suggests that such a discount does not exist. Examination of the conceptual math for each enterprise level indicates that value is a function of expected cash flow, risk and expected growth. If an appraiser adequately measures expected cash flow and the risks and growth of those cash flows, the result is an enterprise value.[83]

The argument for the nonexistence of a marketability discount applicable to controlling interests is simple and elegant. If business value is determined based on expected cash flows, expected growth of those cash flows, and the riskiness of those cash flows, then proper consideration of these factors determines such value. We defined enterprise value in Chapter 1 as the present value of all expected future benefits of the enterprise discounted to the present at an appropriate discount rate. Once we have determined value based on these factors, what additional factors remain to require a discount from this value? None, according to the Integrated Theory.

Counter Arguments

The "discount for lack of marketability for controlling ownership interests" is discussed in Pratt/Reilly/Schweihs.[84] The text discusses this discount in the context of decisions of the U.S. Tax Court, where, it is observed that the court has recognized discounts for lack of marketability for controlling ownership interests in several cases, of which one is cited:[85]

---

[83]   See *Quantifying Marketability Discounts* (Memphis, TN, Peabody Publishing, LP, 1997), Chapter 11, 'Marketability Discounts and the Controlling Interest Level of Value.' This chapter primarily consisted of a reprint of a previous article: Z. Christopher Mercer, 'Should 'Marketability Discounts' be Applied to Controlling Interests of Private Companies?' *Business Valuation Review*, June 1994, pp. 55-65. These articles elaborated on a position taken in *Valuing Financial Institutions* (at p. 205), published in 1992, which concluded:

> In any event, appraisers applying 'marketability discounts' to controlling interest values should be clear as to the objective basis for their discounts or run the danger of having their discounts (and their valuation conclusions) considered illogical and/or arbitrary.

[84]   Pratt, Reilly, and Schweihs, *Valuing a Business*, 4th ed., previously cited, pp. 411-414.

[85]   Ibid, p. 412, quoting *Estate of Woodbury G. Andrews*, 79 T.C. 938 (1982).

Even controlling shares in a nonpublic corporation suffer from lack of marketability because of the absence of a ready private placement market and the fact that flotation costs would have to be incurred if the corporation were to publicly offer its stock.

In my opinion, an opinion of the Tax Court, which was based on the economic evidence provided to it relative to a specific case, does not provide economic evidence for appraisers. It is the job of appraisers to instruct the Tax Court (or any court) on valuation issues, and not the reverse.

Pratt/Reilly/Schweihs then suggest that controlling interests are typically liquidated by consummating initial public offerings or in private sales of entire companies or controlling interests. First, it is rare if the owner(s) of a private company can effect an IPO and sell a controlling interest of the business to the public, so this reference point is not particularly helpful.

Pratt/Reilly/Schweihs also suggest that there are five "transactional considerations" faced by owners of closely held businesses desiring to sell their controlling interests:[86] Each consideration is presented below followed by appropriate comments.

1. *Uncertain time horizon to complete the offering or sale.* This suggestion is analogous to considering a holding period for the liquidation of a controlling interest. The first problem is that the controlling shareholder enjoys the ability to direct and to distribute enterprise cash flows during any period of sale.[87] Further, for there to be a discount from the otherwise determined controlling interest price level, appraisers would have to assume that the risks of the holding period exceeded the discount rate of the enterprise which just determined the base value which would be discounted. If the discount rate was properly specified, there is no basis for a discount for lack of marketability for controlling ownership interests.

---

[86]   Ibid, p. 413.

[87]   We recognize that when deals get down to the letter of intent or definitive agreement stages, the controlling owners may agree, for the short time to expected closing, not to make distributions and to run the business in the "ordinary course of business" or with pre-agreement with the buyer regarding taking specified management actions. Such periods of restriction typically come at the very end of the holding period during which enterprises are marketed, are typical of the way deals are done, and seem unlikely to give rise to a "discount for lack of marketability for controlling ownership interests."

2. *Cost to prepare for and execute the offering or sale.* These costs include auditing and accounting fees, legal costs, administrative costs, and transaction costs. Such costs impact the proceeds of a sale of an enterprise and not its value. Some appraisers have advanced the further argument that the marketability discount for controlling interests relates to the costs of getting a company "ready for sale." In other words, a company that is not ready for sale (needs audited financial statements, consulting to improve operations, capital expenditures to enhance productivity, and the like) could be discounted for its lack of marketability. This argument falls short, as well, because a company that is not "ready for sale" is, well, not ready for sale, and it is not worth as much as one that is ready. Why? Because it has lower cash flows and lower growth potential for those cash flows, and perhaps, higher attendant risks.

3. *Risks concerning eventual sale price.* These risks relate to market uncertainties regarding pricing, which definitely influence value. But they do not give rise to discounts from some hypothetical, higher price which cannot be observed or even explained. Discount rates or earnings multiples for controlling interest appraisals are based on the very same market evidence which reflects uncertainty. So further discounting might be perceived as "double-dipping."

4. *Noncash and deferred transaction proceeds.* The text notes that some deals have deferred payments, or other noncash elements. These elements do not give rise to discounts from some higher value, but simply recognize, in terms of their then present values, the actual value of transactions.

5. *Inability to hypothecate.* It is suggested that controlling interests in closely held businesses may not be good bank collateral, and that, during the holding period for sale, an owner may not be able to borrow funds for liquidity needs. The suggestion may or not be true, depending on the particular enterprises under consideration, but the issue was dealt with in the discussion of the holding period while an enterprise is marketed in number (1.) above.

Cynics could argue that the only reason there is no marketability discount for controlling interests in the Integrated Theory is because we have not drawn boxes for them on the levels of value chart. However, as should be clear from the preceding discussion regarding the marketable minority, control financial and strategic control levels of value, each box is defined in terms of risk, expected cash flows and their expected growth. There are no boxes for marketability discounts for controlling interests because the risks, expected cash flows and their expected growth have already been accounted for.

In the Pratt/Reilly/Schweihs text, the levels of value charts provided also show no "boxes" for the nonmarketable control or illiquid control values suggested in the discussion above.[88] The first levels of value chart presented in the text, which is quoted from Fishman, Pratt, et al., *Guide to Business Valuations,* 10th ed., indicates the following:

> Control shares in a privately held company may also be subject to some discount for lack of marketability, but usually not nearly as much as minority shares.

There is no theoretical justification or explanation for the discount for lack of marketability for controlling ownership interests in Pratt/Reilly/Schweihs. The explanations for the discount fall short, and there is no evidence or guidance as to how to determine its magnitude. Finally, the base value from which the discount for lack of marketability for controlling ownership interest is not specified.

No discount or premium can be specified unless the valuation base from which it is taken or to which it is applied is defined. The "marketable controlling interest" base value, from which a discount for lack of marketability for controlling ownership interests would be taken has not been defined. Therefore, the discount itself has not been specified. Appraisers should apply such a discount only with caution – and then they should be prepared to justify the reasons for the discount and why it is applicable to the base value from which it is taken. Readers are referred to the further discussion of this subject in Chapter 5.

---

[88]   Ibid, pp. 347-348.

THE INTEGRATED THEORY OF BUSINESS VALUATION

The four conceptual levels of equity value for a business, a business ownership interest, or equity security of a business observed by appraisers have now been examined in depth. Figure 3-8 incorporates all four levels into a single chart to present the conceptual math of the levels of value and summarizes the Integrated Theory of Business Valuation.

	Conceptual Math	Relationships	Value Implications
Strategic Control Value	$\dfrac{CF_{e(c,s)}}{R_s - [G_{mm} + G_s]}$	$CF_{e(c,s)} \geq CF_{e(c,f)}$ $G_s \geq 0$ $R_s \leq R_{mm}$	$V_{e(c,s)} \geq V_{e(c,f)}$
Financial Control Value	$\dfrac{CF_{e(c,f)}}{R_f - [G_{mm} + G_f]}$	$CF_{e(c,f)} \geq CF_{e(mm)}$ $G_f \geq 0$ $R_f = R_{mm}$ (+/- a little)	$V_{e(c,f)} \geq V_{mm}$
Marketable Minority Value	$\dfrac{CF_{e(mm)}}{R_{mm} - G_{mm}}$	$G_v = R_{mm}$	V_{mm}
Nonmarketable Minority Value	$\dfrac{CF_{sh}}{R_{hp} - G_v}$	$CF_{sh} \leq CF_{e(mm)}$ $G_v \leq G_{mm}$ $R_{hp} \geq R_{mm}$	$V_{sh} \leq V_{mm}$

Figure 3-8

The Integrated Theory has accomplished several objectives:

- Explained each level of value in the context of financial and valuation theory.

- Explained why value differs from level to level in financial and economic terms.

- Defined the conceptual adjustments relating the various levels of value in terms of that theory, i.e., in terms of discounted cash flow analysis summarized by the Gordon Model. Specifically, the financial control premium and the related minority interest discount, the strategic control premium, and the marketability discount have been defined in financial and economic terms.

- Explained why the integrated model is illustrative of pricing behavior observed in public and nonpublic markets for equity interests.

- Provided an increased level of understanding of the value of control and, conversely, the economic consequences of lack of control. Specifically, it should now be clear that an illiquid minority interest in a business is not worth less than its actual or hypothetical marketable minority value because of any lack of control, except over the timing of exit (which does not relate to a lack of control over the enterprise, but to a lack of control over the timing and conditions of exit, which is the very essence of illiquidity).

- Provided an economic explanation for Eric Nath's observation in 1990 that the public market pricing of securities offers, at least in many instances, a controlling interest level of pricing. The Integrated Theory does not confirm his original premise that from the public/control price appraisers should take both a minority interest and marketability discount to arrive at the nonmarketable minority level of value (unless, as observed above, the minority interest discount is zero). When public company earnings are reasonably optimized, there is no incentive for financial buyers to exert control over them to achieve greater earnings and value (and the implied minority interest discount is equal to zero). In this case, our conceptual analysis suggests that only one discount is appropriate – the marketability discount.

CONCLUSIONS

The Integrated Theory of Business Valuation presented in this chapter is valuable to business appraisers for several important reasons:

1. An Integrated Theory of Business Valuation addressing each of the levels of value has been presented for the first time. This theory is consistent with observed pricing behavior in the public markets and provides a framework within which to discuss the appraisal of privately held companies and interests therein.

2. The Integrated Theory does not relate to any particular standard of value, for example, fair market value, fair value, or investment value. Rather, it enables the appraiser to understand the nature of the valuation process in the context of any standard of value.

3. The Integrated Theory should cause appraisers to focus more clearly on the relationships between financial control value and marketable minority value.

4. The Integrated Theory raises significant questions about and objections to the use of control premium data to estimate minority interest discounts.

5. The Integrated Theory explains the relationship between the marketable minority and nonmarketable minority levels of value in financial and economic terms.

6. The Quantitative Marketability Discount Model has scarcely been mentioned in this chapter. However, the analysis of the nonmarketable minority level of value provides the economic and financial rationale for quantitative, rate of return analysis (of which the QMDM is one example) to determine marketability discounts.

7. The Integrated Theory of Business Valuation undermines the conceptual rationale for another discount frequently used by appraisers – a marketability discount applicable to controlling interests of companies. There is no conceptual basis for a marketability discount applicable to controlling interests of companies. Financial control and strategic control values should be determined based on the economic factors outlined above. If an enterprise has particular risks that might not be applicable to a hypothetical, freely traded security, those risks should be estimated in terms of the impact on its discount rate or expected returns – and ultimately, to the multiples applied to earnings.

Appendix 3-A

ACQUISITION PRICING FOR CFOS
IN USING THE INTEGRATED THEORY
(Why Many Acquisitions Do Not Enhance Shareholder Value)

The Situation

A hypothetical public company ("Company") made an acquisition of a smaller company in its industry ("Target"). This exercise recreates the internal analysis and discussion leading to the final price paid.

1. Target's capital structure was similar to that of Company's. The acquisition was a cash purchase of the stock of Target. Therefore, the objective of the exercise is to develop estimates of Target's equity value for purposes of the acquisition. To the best of the CFO's knowledge, there were no other *strategic purchasers* bidding for Target, so the bidding competitors, if any, were *financial purchasers*.

2. Target had *normalized* net earnings of $1,000 (as discussed in Chapter 4). The concepts of this exercise are scalable, so a representative, round-number is used for illustration. Staff of Operations at Company (supporting the acquisition) normalized the earnings of Target, adding back excess owner compensation (over and above her expected, ongoing salary post-acquisition). In addition, adjustments for non-recurring items were made. Company's CFO agreed that these normalizing adjustments were reasonable.

3. Finance Staff developed an equity discount rate of 15% *for Target*, based on its particular risks. Company's equity discount rate component of its cost of capital was 13%, so this estimate made sense to the CFO.

4. Finance Staff also estimated that Target's earnings could reasonably grow at the rate of about 7% for the foreseeable future based on historical performance and discussions with Operations Staff. There was actually a detailed, discounted cash flow model, but this single-point estimate was used to illustrate value using the Gordon Model.

Based on these assumptions, the Finance Staff prepared an initial valuation for Target as follows. The valuation is at the marketable minority (V_{mm}) level in terms of the levels of value discussed in Chapter 3.

$$V_{mm} = \frac{CF}{R_{mm} - G_{mm}} \qquad \begin{array}{lcl} CF & = & \$1,000 \\ R_{mm} & = & 15\% \\ G_{mm} & = & 7\% \end{array}$$

$$V_{mm} = \frac{\$1,000}{15\% - 7\%} = \boxed{\$12,500}$$

The result of $12,500, reflecting a multiple of 12.5x net earnings (about 7.5x pre-tax earnings), was the base valuation from which the CFO planned to assess all bids suggested by Operations Staff. Company was currently trading at 22x next year's earnings, so a successful acquisition at this level would clearly be accretive to earnings.

Bidding Analysis

Finance Staff held discussions with Operations Staff about the adjustments that competing financial buyers might consider reasonable for Target. It appears that there were potential efficiencies because Target's operating margin was a bit lower than industry norms. Financial buyers (and Company) might therefore reasonably consider that earnings could be increased by $50, or 5%. In addition, the Operations Staff suggests that earnings growth could likely be enhanced by 1% or so if management were a bit more aggressive.

As result of these discussions, Finance Staff valued Target at the financial control Level (V_f) of value.

$$V_f = \frac{CF + \Delta CF_f}{R_{mm} - (G_{mm} + \Delta G_f)}$$

$$CF_f = (CF + \Delta CF_f)$$
$$G_f = (G_{mm} + \Delta G_f)$$

CF	$=$	$1,000$
R_{mm}	$=$	15%
G_{mm}	$=$	7%
ΔCF_f	$=$	50
ΔG_f	$=$	1%

$$V_f = \frac{\$1,000 + \$50}{15\% - (7\% + 1\%)} = \boxed{\$15,000}$$

Using the same Gordon Model analysis as with the marketable minority value, adjusting cash flow for the $50 (5%) increment and expected growth for the 1% increment, the financial control value is $15,000, or 20% higher than the initial valuation. That price reflects a multiple of 15x normalized net earnings for Target, and 14.3x earnings adjusted for the potential better margins.

This did not mean, however, that other financial buyers would automatically offer prices in the range of $15,000 for Target's equity. After all, that value is dependent on their ability to operate Target better than present management, and they would have to accept all execution risk if that price was paid. So Finance Staff had developed a negotiating range of $12,500 to $15,000 for the equity of Target. Given Company's position as a strategic purchaser, CFO was comfortable with pricing within this range, and he knew that paying at even the top-end range would provide for an accretive transaction.

Based on the above analysis, which was provided to Operations Staff, the CFO informally approved a bidding range up to $15,000 for Target's equity.

Operations' Strategic Considerations

The CFO did not hear anything from Operations Staff for some time, but then was informed that the deal for Target had been struck at $24,000. Realizing that he did not have decision-making authority in the matter, he was nevertheless upset and perplexed. He went to the COO to discuss the rationale for the purchase price.

When they met, the COO handed him a valuation analysis performed by Operations Staff. That analysis mirrored the earlier analysis prepared by Finance Staff, but valued Target at the strategic control level. As the CFO reviewed the analysis, he saw that it had been based on the earlier analysis, but made the following additional assumptions:

1. As a strategic buyer, Company could expand sales through new channels, therefore increasing potential earnings and cash flow by another $50, raising expected earnings to the level of $1,100 (from the normalized level of $1,000 and the financial control level of $1,050).

2. In addition, Operations Staff had assumed that earnings growth could be expanded by another 1% (because of growth into new channels), to 9% per year.

3. Finally, Operations Staff, knowing that Company's cost of equity was 13.0%, used that discount rate as the cost of equity for Target,

As a result of these assumptions, the valuation prepared by Operations Staff was considerably higher, and valued Target at $27,500, or more than double the marketable minority value and nearly double the financial control value.

$$CF_s = (CF + \Delta CF_f + \Delta CF_s)$$
$$G_s = (G + \Delta G_f + \Delta G_s)$$

$$V_s = \frac{CF + \Delta CF_f + \Delta CF_s}{R_s - (G_{mm} + \Delta G_f + \Delta G_s)}$$

CF	= $1,000
G_{mm}	= 7%
ΔCF_f	= $50
ΔG_f	= 1%
ΔCF_s	= $50
R_s	= 13%
ΔG_s	= 1%

$$V_s = \frac{\$1,000 + \$50 + \$50}{13\% - (7\% + 1\% + 1\%)} = \boxed{\$27,500}$$

The COO was proud of his accomplishment. He observed that at $24,000, he had negotiated a price some 13% below what Target was worth to Company. He then mentioned the following additional factors as supporting the pricing decision:

1. The deal should earn the Company's cost of equity capital. And Company's return would be even better if additional enhancements, not included in the valuation, were achieved.

2. A price of $24,000 represented a multiple of 21.8x expected earnings, so the multiple paid was right in line with Company's multiple of 22x.

3. This was truly a strategic fit for Company and it should enhance the public markets' impression of the stock.

CFO Reprise

Back at his office, the CFO bemoaned the fact that the CEO did not require better coordination between Operations and Finance. While he hoped that the acquisition of Target would be successful and he saw that if it were, it could have some benefits for Company. However, he knew that in this situation, Company had substantially overpaid for the acquisition. He made the following observations about the deal.

- With normalized net earnings of $1,000 and pro forma earnings of $1,100:

  - Company accepted all of the execution risks involved in achieving the improvement.

  - The price/earnings multiple based on normalized earnings is 24x, which exceeds the multiple of Company's stock in the market.

- With normalized expected earnings growth of 7% and pro forma earnings growth of 9%, Company accepted all of the execution risks involved in achieving the increase.

- By basing the pricing on Company's 13% cost of equity, rather than on the Target's discount rate of 15%, Company had no "risk cushion" to absorb integration problems or failures to achieve objectives.

- No one on Operations Staff was responsible for achieving the projected revenue and growth synergies. In fact, unless he asked Finance Staff to do a follow-up analysis in the future, which was particularly difficult, there would be no operational accountability for the assumptions used to establish the purchase price for Target.

- The Company had just overpaid substantially in terms of market value for Target, with the Company bidding against itself in the process.

But life goes on …

Chapter 4

Adjustments to Income Statements:

Normalizing and Control Adjustments

INTRODUCTION

The Integrated Theory in Chapter 3 explained the levels of value on a conceptual basis beginning with the Gordon Model and the discounted cash flow model. Recall the generalized valuation model that flows from the Gordon Model.

Value = Earnings x Multiple

The conceptual model of the Integrated Theory and the generalized valuation model suggest that value indications should be developed by selecting appropriate indications of earning power and multiplying (capitalizing) by an appropriate multiple. It follows that appraisers may need to consider potential adjustments for both earnings and the multiple in order to develop appropriate indications of value.

- *Normalizing Adjustments.* This chapter will now address adjustments to the earnings of the generalized valuation model. Normalizing adjustments adjust private company earnings to public company equivalency in order to correspond with (public equivalent) multiples developed from comparisons with guideline companies. The combination of enterprise earnings that are appropriately normalized with valuation multiples that have been adjusted for fundamental differences (between a private company and a guideline group) yields a marketable minority indication of value (as-if-freely-traded).

- *Control Adjustments.* This chapter will also address adjustments to the earnings of the generalized valuation model that relate to the other enterprise levels of value, namely, the controlling interest and the strategic levels of value. A fundamental assumption flowing from the Integrated Theory is that the discount rate flowing from the public markets (directly or indirectly) applicable to individual private companies should remain the same for the various enterprise levels of value. Control adjustments therefore allow for the derivation of earnings appropriate to the control levels of value.

- *Fundamental Adjustments.* Discussed in Chapter 5, fundamental adjustments adjust the level of the levels of value for individual private companies in relationship to the typical (median or average) multiples of guideline company groups. Fundamental adjustments account for differences in risk and expected growth for private companies relative to selected groups of guideline companies. Fundamental adjustments help appraisers select appropriate valuation multiples and are applicable to the multiple of the generalized valuation model.

This chapter and the next are therefore key to an understanding of the Integrated Theory as it is applied in valuation practice.

COMMON QUESTIONS

1. What are the differences between *normalizing adjustments* to the earnings stream and *control adjustments*?

2. In the context of fair market value, should control premiums be applied "automatically" in developing controlling interest value indications?

   a. If a control premium is applied, what types of data from the marketplace should be used to estimate it?

   b. To what earnings base should they be applied, if applicable?

   c. How can the reasonableness of control premiums be tested?

   d. Are control premiums economic drivers or merely valuation results?

3. When applying the DCF method, should appraisers apply control premiums when developing controlling interest values? If so, why? And where?

4. What is the reason for making normalizing adjustments?

5. What does the term "marketable minority" level of value mean in the context of public security values?

6. When valuing minority interests of private companies, should appraisers normalize earnings?

   a. If yes, what kinds of normalizing adjustments should be made?

   b. What is the objective of making normalizing adjustments?

7. When using guideline public company multiples, should appraisers apply control premiums to resulting "marketable minority" value indications?

8. Should appraisers rely on *Mergerstat/Shannon Pratt's Control Premium Study* and other control premium studies to determine the magnitude of control premiums applicable to "marketable minority" value indications?

9. Should those same control premium studies be used to estimate minority interest discounts for operating companies?

10. Should those same control premium studies be used to estimate minority interest discounts for asset holding entities?

11. In valuing illiquid interests of private businesses, why do appraisers normally begin with appraisals at the marketability minority level of value?

THE INTEGRATED THEORY AND INCOME STATEMENT ADJUSTMENTS

In the conceptual development of the Integrated Theory in Chapter 3, we began with the Gordon Model and developed algebraic expressions for each of the various levels of value. The basic expression of the Gordon Model, which is used to provide a summary expression of how the securities markets value publicly traded stocks, is reproduced in Figure 4-1 as is the conceptual math representing the marketable minority level of value.

	Conceptual Math	Relationships	Value Implications
Marketable Minority Value	$\dfrac{CF_{e(mm)}}{R_{mm} - G_{mm}}$	$G_v = R_{mm}$	V_{mm}
Nonmarketable Minority Value	$\dfrac{CF_{sh}}{R_{hp} - G_v}$	$CF_{sh} \leq CF_{e(mm)}$ $G_v \leq G_{mm}$ $R_{hp} \geq R_{mm}$	$V_{sh} \leq V_{mm}$

Figure 4-1

Cash flow of the enterprise at the marketable minority level is represented by $CF_{e(mm)}$. This level of cash flow is assumed to be "normalized" for publicly traded securities, at least on average. If it were not so, and there were, for example, excessive compensation or other discretionary expenditures of an ongoing, egregious nature, there would be pressure from shareholders (or potential acquirers) for the earnings stream to be normalized.

The summary expression for the nonmarketable minority level of value is reproduced at the bottom of the Figure above. As noted in the "Relationships" column, cash flow to shareholders (CF_{sh}) may be less than or equal to, but not greater than, the cash flow of the enterprise (at the marketable minority level). This should not be surprising. As we saw in Chapter 3, where the components of diminution in value from the marketable minority level to the nonmarketable minority level were summarized, there are four basic reasons for lower nonmarketable minority values:

1. Agency costs, or the extent of non-pro rata distributions to selected shareholders. This is often referred to as "leakage" to controlling shareholders. Agency costs would also include excess perquisites and other discretionary expenditures.

2. Suboptimal reinvestment policy, or the extent to which expected reinvestment policy calls for a return lower than that embedded in the enterprise discount rate.

3. Required holding period returns (R_{hp}) in excess of the enterprise equity discount rate (R_{mm}).

4. Finally, it is possible to misspecify the expected growth rate in value for the QMDM, in which case that misspecification would also be part of the discount.

The last three items above have nothing to do with the current enterprise income statement. So we will focus on the first item, or agency costs. It should be clear that such costs would be normalized in determining enterprise value. If cash flows are so normalized, they will be equal to expected enterprise cash flows except for the existence of nonrecurring items in historical earnings that should be eliminated in the process of developing future cash flow expectations. Both agency costs and nonrecurring items would fall into the category of *normalizing adjustments*.

The Integrated Theory as it relates to the four levels of value is reproduced as Figure 4-2.

	Conceptual Math	Relationships	Value Implications
Strategic Control Value	$\dfrac{CF_{e(c,s)}}{R_s - [G_{mm} + G_s]}$	$CF_{e(c,s)} \geq CF_{e(c,f)}$ $G_s \geq 0$ $R_s \leq R_{mm}$	$V_{e(c,s)} \geq V_{e(c,f)}$
Financial Control Value	$\dfrac{CF_{e(c,f)}}{R_f - [G_{mm} + G_f]}$	$CF_{e(c,f)} \geq CF_{e(mm)}$ $G_f \geq 0$ $R_f = R_{mm}$ (+/- a little)	$V_{e(c,f)} \geq V_{mm}$
Marketable Minority Value	$\dfrac{CF_{e(mm)}}{R_{mm} - G_{mm}}$	$G_v = R_{mm}$	V_{mm}
Nonmarketable Minority Value	$\dfrac{CF_{sh}}{R_{hp} - G_v}$	$CF_{sh} \leq CF_{e(mm)}$ $G_v \leq R_{mm}$ $R_{hp} \geq R_{mm}$	$V_{sh} \leq V_{mm}$

Figure 4-2

As we move up the levels of value chart from the marketable minority level to the levels of financial control and strategic control, we see that it is possible that a controlling shareholder *may* make adjustments to expected cash flows based on the expected ability to run an enterprise better (financial control) or differently (strategic control). Such adjustments would be *control adjustments*, and could have the impact of increasing value if such adjustments would normally be negotiated between buyers and sellers. In other words, from a conceptual viewpoint, *control adjustments* are those that, if appropriate, increase enterprise cash flow *above that of the (normalized) marketable minority level*. As the conceptual chart indicates, the cash flow of the enterprise from the viewpoint of either a financial control buyer or a strategic control buyer *may* be greater than the normalized cash flow of the enterprise.

TWO TYPES OF INCOME STATEMENT ADJUSTMENTS

Having described the general nature of normalizing adjustments and control adjustments in the context of the Integrated Theory, we can now focus more keenly on these adjustments and the potential impact they can have in the determination of value.

- With normalizing adjustments, we attempt to adjust private company earnings to a reasonably well-run, public company equivalent basis. Normalizing adjustments can be further divided into two types to facilitate discussion and understanding. Normalizing adjustments are *not* control adjustments.

- Control adjustments adjust private company earnings 1) for the economies or the efficiencies of the *typical financial buyer*; and 2) for synergies or strategies of *particular buyers*. Control adjustments can therefore also be divided into two types.

This nomenclature for income statement adjustments is fairly new.[89] Many appraisers do not yet make distinctions between normalizing and control adjustments or between types of normalizing and control adjustments. Vocabulary such as presented in this chapter is not essential to understanding the issues with income statement adjustments. It is, however, helpful in clarifying the nature and reasons for income statement adjustments.

INCOME STATEMENT ADJUSTMENTS AND THE RELEVANT DISCOUNT RATE

The importance of distinguishing between types of income statement adjustments becomes apparent when we discuss the discount rates applicable to derived earnings. It should be fairly obvious that the discount rate or capitalization rate applied to any measure of earnings must be appropriately developed for that measure, whether net income, pre-tax income, debt free pre-tax income or another level of the income statement. The ACAPM (and CAPM, or build-up) discount rates discussed here are generally considered as applicable to either the net income or net cash flows of business enterprises.

There has also been considerable discussion in recent years regarding whether discounted future earnings or discounted cash flow valuation models develop minority interest or controlling interest indications of value. The two major trains of thought are as follows:

1.   The ACAPM discount rate is applicable to the net income (or net cash flow) of a business enterprise. This discount rate is generally believed to develop value indications at the marketable minority interest level of value. Therefore, the value indication from discounted future cash flow or earnings valuations is a minority interest, marketable conclusion. As a result, it would be proper to apply a control premium to this value indication if a controlling interest conclusion is called for in an appraisal.

---

[89]   I have been using this vocabulary in speeches and articles since the latter 1990s. It received first publication in Pratt's *Cost of Capital* (1st ed.), which was published in 1998 (previously cited) in an appendix I wrote dealing with developing discount rates using the Wiley *ValuSource Pro* Software.

2. Appraisers often make so-called controlling interest adjustments in developing their projections for DFE or DCF methods. If the income stream is "control adjusted," the resulting valuation indication is at the controlling interest level. As a result, no additional control premium would be appropriate, and a minority interest discount might be applied to derive a marketable minority value indication.

These two viewpoints have been debated among appraisers for years. Depending on the adjustments made, either approach might yield similar results. However the issue has been a source of confusion, and the debate has found a forum in the Tax Court. A number of recent appraisals have been scrutinized over the very issue of whether or not a DCF model is a minority interest or a controlling interest valuation. Pursuant to the first argument, the text in my appendix to Pratt's *Cost of Capital* reads:

> Buyers of companies might appear to have different discount rates than hypothetical investors at the marketable minority interest level. According to the latter argument, there is only one discount rate and it is the same for appraisers at the marketable minority interest level and for acquirers at the controlling interest level. According to the former argument, one would add an appropriate control premium to the DCF/DFE valuation method to arrive at a controlling interest level of value. According to the latter argument, a control premium might not be appropriate. As is often the case, the truth may lie somewhere in between. To begin to resolve the controversy, we can divide the so-called controlling interest adjustments into their two primary components.[90]

The appendix proceeds to discuss normalizing adjustments and control adjustments because they have an impact on the cash flow capitalized. Pratt and others, including me, have suggested that in DCF methods, the value of control is generally developed by adjusting the numerator, i.e., the cash flows. That this is well understood should be clear from the following quote from Pratt's *Cost of Capital*:

---

[90] Shannon P. Pratt, *Cost of Capital*, 2nd ed. (Hoboken, NJ: John Wiley & Sons, Inc., 2002), p. 269. As noted above, this was first published in the first edition of *Cost of Capital*.

The discount rate is meant to represent the underlying risk of a particular industry or line of business. There may be instances in which a majority shareholder can acquire a company and improve its cash flows, but that would not necessarily have an impact on the general risk level of the cash flows generated by that company.

In applying the income approach to valuation, adjustments for minority or controlling interest value should be made to the projected cash flows of the subject company instead of to the discount rate. Adjusting the expected cash flows better measures the potential impact a controlling party may have while not overstating or understating the actual risk associated with a particular line of business.[91]

While the quote from Pratt comes from a chapter dealing with discount rates, it should be clear that he is stating that *control adjustments* would be made to the marketable minority level of cash flows. If such adjustments are made, the indicated value would rise above the marketable minority level towards the controlling interest levels on the conceptual chart.

A clear focus on normalizing versus control adjustments in the context of the Integrated Theory of Business Valuation should bring clarity to this issue.

NORMALIZING ADJUSTMENTS TO THE INCOME STATEMENT

Normalizing adjustments adjust the income statement of a private company to show the prospective purchaser the return from normal operations of the business and reveal a "public equivalent" income stream. If such adjustments were not made, something other than a freely traded value indication of value would be developed by capitalizing the derived earnings stream. For appraisers using benchmark analysis, this would be disastrous, since the restricted stock studies were based on freely traded stock prices.[92]

---

[91] Ibid, pp. 127-128.

[92] In other words, the value indication derived from the use of non-normalized earnings for a private company and the application of a marketability discount derived from freely traded transactional bases would yield something other than a nonmarketable minority value indication. Because the earnings capitalized were not normalized, and a "normal" marketability discount was applied, the indicated value conclusion would likely be *below* that of the nonmarketable minority level.

Keep in mind the integration of levels of value in the Integrated Theory. In creating a public equivalent for a private company, it need not have all of the characteristics required to engage in an IPO for this model to be relevant. Another name given to the marketable minority level of value is as-if-freely-traded. This terminology emphasizes that earnings are being normalized to where they would be as if the company were public. This framework does not require that a company be public or even that it have the potential to become public.

A new vocabulary is needed to clarify the nature of normalizing income statement adjustments. As noted earlier, there are two types of normalizing adjustments. Being very original, we call them Type 1 and Type 2.

- *Type 1 Normalizing Adjustments.* These are adjustments that eliminate one-time gains or losses, other unusual items, non-recurring business elements, expenses of non-operating assets, and the like. Every appraiser employs such income statement adjustments in the process of adjusting (normalizing) historical income statements. Regardless of the name given to them, there is virtually universal acceptance that Type 1 Normalizing Adjustments are appropriate for consideration.

- *Type 2 Normalizing Adjustments.* These are adjustments that normalize officer/owner compensation and other discretionary expenses that would not exist in a reasonably well-run, publicly traded company. Type 2 Normalizing Adjustments should not be confused with control adjustments or Type 1 Normalizing Adjustments.

Normalizing adjustments reveal the income stream available to the controlling interest buyer who will gain control over the income stream and who may be able to do other things with that income stream. They also reveal the income stream that is the source of potential value for the buyer of minority interests.

Appraisers should not be confused by the fact that minority shareholders of private companies lack the control to make normalizing adjustments. Some have argued that because minority shareholders lack control to change things like excess owner compensation, normalizing adjustments should not be made in minority interest appraisals. This position is simply incorrect.[93] Minority shareholders of public companies lack control as well. The difference is they expect normalized operations and they expect management to perform. If management of a public company does not perform, if egregious salaries are paid, or if expenses are not reasonably managed, minority shareholders of the public company tend to walk. They take their money some place else. And the price of the poorly run public company normally reflects this lack of investor interest.

Shareholders of nonmarketable minority interests often lack this ability to "take my money and run." These considerations have no impact on the value of the enterprise. Rather, they lower the value of the interest in the enterprise in relationship to its pro rata share of enterprise value. This diminution of value must be considered separately from, but in conjunction with, the valuation of the enterprise.

Normalize or Not?

Let me illustrate with an example I have used in many speeches. First, I pose the following example:

> Consider an investment in a partnership. The relevant interest is a 1% limited partnership interest, so there are no elements of control. The partnership pays $100 per unit per year in annual distributions and is certain to be liquidated in exactly five years.

I then ask how much those in the audience would pay for the interest. The responses are universally the same. Appraisers want to know, for example, what is in the partnership and how much it is worth today. They want to know if it is appreciating, and at what rate. They ask these questions because without answers to them, one does not have sufficient information to make an intelligent investment decision.

Yet many appraisers suggest that Type 2 Normalizing Adjustments are "control" adjustments and believe they should not be made in minority interest appraisals. It should be clear that they put readers of their reports in exactly the same position as the investors for my partnership unit – i.e., lacking sufficient information to make an intelligent investment decision. In other words, if Type 2 Normalizing Adjustments are not made, readers of reports (and hypothetical investors) do not know the value of the underlying enterprise or its ability to grow into the future. Absent that information, rational investment decisions cannot be made (in addition to the level of value issue noted in this chapter).

---

[93]   See the more detailed discussion regarding the Integrated Theory in Chapter 3.

NORMALIZING ADJUSTMENTS ILLUSTRATED

While some appraisers still disagree regarding Type 2 Normalizing Adjustments, the logic of this presentation, in conjunction with the conceptual discussions both above and in Chapter 3, is compelling. Consider a concrete example and relate it to the Levels of Value Chart.

In Figure 4-3, ABC, Inc. is a $10 million-sales company reporting operating profit of $300,000.

ABC, Inc. Normalizing Adjustments ($000's)		Normalizing Adjustments		
		Type 1	Type 2	
		Non-Recurring	Normalize to	
	Reported	Items	Public Equivalent	Normalized
Sales	$10,000	$0	$0	$10,000
COGS	$5,800	$0	$0	$5,800
Gross Profit	$4,200	$0	$0	$4,200
Litigation Settlement	$200	($200)	$0	$0
Selling (Cousin Joe)	$800	$0	($100)	$700
G&A (Cousin Al)	$1,600	$0	($100)	$1,500
Owner Comp (Big Daddy)	$900	$0	($600)	$300
Chalet (Big Daddy's Vacation Home)	$400	$0	($200)	$200
	$3,900	($200)	($1,000)	$2,700
Operating Profit	$300			$1,500
Operating Margin (No debt)	3.0%			15.0%

Figure 4-3

Assume that we are appraising ABC and are now considering normalizing adjustments. There is one Type 1, or unusual, non-recurring normalizing adjustment to be made in this particular appraisal. There are also several Type 2 normalizing adjustments that relate to the owner and the controlling shareholder of the business.

- *Type 1 Normalizing Adjustment (Non-Recurring Items):*

  - The company settled a lawsuit regarding damages when one of its vehicles was in an accident. The settlement, inclusive of attorneys' fees, was $200,000 in the most recent year. Expenses associated with the lawsuit are eliminated from operating expenses.

- *Type 2 Normalizing Adjustments (Agency Costs and Other Discretionary Expenses):*

  - Our examination of selling expenses reveals that Cousin Joe is on the payroll at $100,000 per year and he is not doing anything for the good of the business. An adjustment is clearly called for regarding Cousin Joe. His compensation must be eliminated in order to see the "as-if-freely-traded" income stream.

  - In the Administrative Department, Cousin Al comes to work every day, but it is clear that the department is being run by someone else and that Cousin Al is not productive. We adjust by removing his $100,000 salary.

  - Big Daddy takes a substantial salary out of the business. Based on a salary survey, earnings should be adjusted by $600,000 for his excess compensation to lower the expense to a normal, market level of compensation.

  - Finally Big Daddy owns a chalet, which costs the company about $400,000 a year. Expenses associated with Big Daddy's vacation home are adjusted accordingly.

Summing the Type 1 and Type 2 adjustments, a total of $1.2 million of adjustments to operating expenses have been identified. These adjustments raise the adjusted operating profit to the level expected were this company publicly traded (even though it likely never will be!). The adjusted (normalized) operating margin of 15%, and adjusted earnings are stated "as if freely traded." [94]

Before proceeding to examine control adjustments, we should carry the discussion of normalizing adjustments a step further in order to address any lingering concerns. Some appraisers will still want to say that Type 2 Normalizing Adjustments are really control adjustments and that they should not be made when valuing minority interests.

---

[94] Note that this appraisal process would not ignore the valuation impact of the agency costs associated with Big Daddy and his family if the objective were a nonmarketable minority value indication. The economic impact of the excess compensation not accruing to all shareholders would substantially impact the expected growth in value of the business and the dividend policy (key assumptions of the Quantitative Marketability Discount Model). The risks of illiquidity over an appropriate expected holding period would also be considered.

Why, they may ask, should we not value the minority interest directly and forego making Type 2 Normalizing Adjustments? Let's be explicit. If we do not make these adjustments:

- The earnings stream that would be valued would not be "public equivalent" in nature.

- Discount rate based on build-up (CAPM) or a guideline company analysis would not be appropriate and the resulting value indication would not be at the marketable minority level.

- Marketability discounts referencing restricted stock and pre-IPO transactions involving public companies would be inappropriate if needed Type 2 Normalizing Adjustments are not made. The various restricted stock and pre-IPO studies are based on marketable minority value bases and the resulting, non-normalized base would not be at the marketable minority level.

- There would be an implicit assumption that the shareholder would never realize his or her pro rata share of the value of the enterprise. In the alternative, there would be no basis to estimate what that future terminal value might be. There would be no basis, for example, to estimate the expected growth in value of the enterprise over any relevant expected holding period, since that base, marketable minority value is not specified.

The bottom line is that, absent making Type 2 Normalizing Adjustments (when appropriate of course), an appraiser is not able to specify that his or her conclusion is at the nonmarketable minority level of value, which is typically the objective of minority interest appraisals. The bottom, bottom line is that appraisers who do not make Type 2 Normalizing Adjustments in the process of reaching value conclusions at the nonmarketable minority level have neither the appropriate theoretical nor practical bases for their conclusions

CONTROL ADJUSTMENTS TO THE INCOME STATEMENT

We suggested above that there are two types of controlling interest adjustments to the income statement. Control shareholders have control over the cash flows of a business. Prospective purchasers of control anticipate the same benefit. They tend to look at the earnings stream of a company and ask: How can we change the earning stream to our advantage?

ABC, Inc. Control Adjustments ($000's)	*As if Publicly Traded*	*Financial Control*		*Strategic Control*	
		Type 1 Control	**As Adjusted Type 1**	*Type 2 Control*	**As Adjusted Type 2**
	Normalized				
Sales	$10,000	*$0*	$10,000	*$0*	$10,000
COGS	$5,800	*$0*	$5,800	*($200)*	$5,600
Gross Profit	$4,200	*$0*	$4,200	*$200*	$4,400
Litigation Settlement	$0	*$0*	$0	*$0*	$0
Selling	$700	*($150)*	$550	*$0*	$550
G&A	$1,500	*$0*	$1,500	*($250)*	$1,250
Owner Comp	$300	*$0*	$300	*$0*	$300
Chalet	$200	*$0*	$200	*$0*	$200
	$2,700	*($150)*	$2,550	*($250)*	$2,300
Operating Profit	$1,500		$1,650		$2,100
Operating Margin (No debt)	15.0%		16.5%		21.0%

Figure 4-4

The two types of control adjustments (named just as creatively as normalized adjustments) are:

- *Type 1 Control Adjustments.* This first type of control adjustment corresponds with the financial control level of value. Type 1 Control Adjustments enable appraisers to adjust private company earnings for the economies or efficiencies available to the typical financial buyer (which may not be present in a private company at the time of appraisal), and not present on the as if freely traded basis.

  Prospective financial control buyers may consider adjustments that can improve the normalized earnings stream. As noted above, these

"Ready for Sale" and Adjustments

Should appraisers consider possible financial restructurings as part of the earnings normalization process? This question is raised by the distribution between the Type 2 Normalizing Adjustment related to Cousin Al and the potential reorganization of the Administrative Department treated here as a Type 1 Control Adjustment.

This question is tantamount to asking whether a company that is "ready for sale," and operating efficiently with reasonable margins, is worth more than one that is not ready for sale? Logically, the company that is ready should be worth more. Clearly, if ABC, Inc.'s earnings already reflected the potential reorganization, normalized earnings would be $150,000 higher than adjusted in Figure 4-3. And those earnings would be capitalized and reflected in as-if-freely-traded value.

The potential reorganization is treated in Figure 4-4 as a Type 1 Control Adjustment because it represents only potential value to the shareholders of ABC, Inc. *If* competing financial buyers recognize this potential *and if* they bid the price up to share all or part of the capitalized benefit, *then* that benefit may be reflected in a higher financial control value. Otherwise the appropriate valuation of ABC, Inc. should reflect only the normalizing adjustments. ABC, Inc. is not "ready for sale," and its value should reflect that fact.

adjustments may occur from financial economies of better management, which may also impact the expected growth rate of adjusted earnings.

The thought process behind Type 1 Control Adjustments is the consideration that typical buyers *could run a company better* than the existing owners and/or the level of public equivalent earnings. We live in an expectational world. If a prospective purchaser reasonably believes that a particular change can be implemented, he may be willing to pay for all or part of that expectation. If there are other purchasers with similar expectations, market value may be bid up to include a sharing of some or all of that benefit with the seller. The Type 1 Control Adjustment may be the result of expected financial economies from better management or more rapid growth from more aggressive management.[95]

For example, ABC, Inc. reports selling costs of $700,000, or 7% of sales. It is well known in its industry that selling costs should run on the order of 5.5% of sales, so there is a potential benefit of $150,000 from a reorganization or restructuring of the selling process. Financial and/or strategic buyers would realize this based on limited due diligence and might consider adjusting the income statement for such expected benefits. It should be clear that

---

[95] Type 1 Control Adjustments might be reflected in a negotiation or in an appraisal at the controlling interest level if the indicated economies or growth prospects are generally available to multiple buyers and competition forces their sharing by the winning bidder with the seller.

such a reorganization involving selling costs would be a Type 1 Control Adjustment. That reorganization could increase earning power by as much as $150,000, and that adjustment is made in Figure 4-4.

ABC's earnings were previously normalized using Type 1 and Type 2 Normalizing Adjustments and reported earnings were raised from $300,000 to $1,500,000 in the process. The operating margin was increased from 3.0% to 15.0%. With the consideration of Type 1 Control Adjustments, expected operating income is further increased by $150,000 to $1,650,000, or to 16.5%. As it turns out, ABC, Inc. is actually a very profitable company and can likely be more profitable under control of new buyers.

Assume that the prospective buyer is a financial buyer. By employing Type 1 Control Adjustments, such a buyer could improve earnings potential by another $150,000 with the potential reorganization of the Administrative Department (in addition to eliminating Cousin Al, already considered a Type 2 Normalizing Adjustment). So this Type 1 Control Adjustment would raise the earning potential from $1,500,000 to $1,650,000 with the operating margin rising to 16.5%.

- *Type 2 Control Adjustments.* These types of control adjustments reflect changes that can *alter* the normalized earnings stream. Strategic buyers may consider potential benefits from several sources, including synergies from consolidating general and administrative expenses, lower costs of goods sold through volume purchasing, benefits from horizontal or vertical integration, the ability to achieve lower financing costs, and others. Essentially strategic buyers do not normally contemplate operating acquired businesses as independent firms, but rely on elements of consolidation with other business costs and/or revenue opportunities. Strategic buyers may also seek beachheads in an industry, thinking it cheaper to "pay up" than to build from scratch. Other considerations include the preemption of other competitors from obtaining a certain "space."

With ABC, Inc., one or more strategic buyers might reasonably believe that their larger purchasing volumes could lower cost of goods sold by $200,000, and that a consolidation of general and administrative expenses could eliminate an additional $250,000 of expenses.   So the strategic buyer is looking not at $300,000 of reported earnings for ABC, Inc., not at $1,500,000 as normalized, not at $1,650,000 as adjusted for Type 1 Control, but potentially at $2,100,000, as adjusted for Type 2 Control as shown in Figure 4-4.

We have now developed four separate and distinct measures of operating income for ABC, Inc. ranging from $300,000 to $2,100,000.   The implication of these differences is discussed as we examine the potential value impact of earnings adjustments.

POTENTIAL VALUE IMPACT OF EARNINGS ADJUSTMENTS

Income statement adjustments are critically important in providing estimates of earnings for capitalization using methods under either the income or market approaches to valuation, as well as for providing a base level of earnings from which to forecast when using discounted future benefits methods.

Appraiser judgment is obviously required in the assessment of potential income statement adjustments.   Hopefully, the vocabulary and analysis of this chapter, together with the previous conceptual discussion of the Integrated Theory, have highlighted the importance of income statement adjustments and the judgments made in developing them.

Types of Income Statement Adjustments and Levels of Value

	As Reported	"Public Equivalent" Normalized	Financial Control	Strategic Control
Operating Income	$300,000	$300,000	$1,500,000	$1,650,000
Net Adjustments	*none*	*$1,200,000*	*$150,000*	*$450,000*
Adjusted Operating Income	$300,000	$1,500,000	$1,650,000	$2,100,000
Implied Operating Margins	*3.00%*	*15.00%*	*16.50%*	*21.00%*
Types of Adjustments Considered	*None*	*Type 1 Normalizing Type 2 Normalizing*	*Type 1 Control*	*Type 2 Control*
Assumed Multiple of Operating Income *(No Debt; Discount Rate Remains Unchanged)*	**5.0**	**5.0**	**5.0**	**5.0**
Implied Value Indications	$1,500,000	$7,500,000	$8,250,000	$10,500,000
Implied Level of Value	*unknown*	*Marketable Minority*	*Financial Control*	*Strategic Control*
Implied Differences Over/Under "Public Equivalent"	*-80.0%*	*"Public Equivalent"*	*10.0% "Financial Control" Premium*	*40.0% "Strategic Control" Premium*
Implied Multiples of "Public Equivalent" Normalized	*1.00x*	*5.00x*	*5.50x*	*7.0x*

Figure 4-5

Figure 4-5 examines each of the measures of ABC, Inc.'s operating income thus far. The adjustments are summarized and then capitalized using a common, pre-tax multiple of 5.0x. As discussed earlier, we assume that the enterprise discount rate does not change across categories of investors (and we are implicitly assuming a common outlook for expected growth in earnings).

Figure 4-6 begins with the Implied Value Indications of Figure 4-5. Enterprise-level value indications are developed, the respective levels of value are identified, and each value indication is compared to the "Public Equivalent" (normalized) indication. Marketability discounts are applied to the reporting and normalized (marketable minority) value indications. Implied premiums to the normalized, marketable minority value indication are computed for all indications. Finally, the Figure includes explanatory commentary to focus the reader on important differences and distinctions.

Types of Income Statement Adjustments and Levels of Value

	As Reported	"Public Equivalent" Normalized	Financial Control	Strategic Control
Implied Value Indications				
Implied Level of Value	$1,500,000 *unknown*	$7,500,000 *Marketable Minority*	$8,250,000 *Financial Control*	$10,500,000 *Strategic Control*
Implied Differences Over/Under Normalized	-80.0%	*"Public Equivalent"*	10.0% *"Financial Control" Premium*	40.0% *"Strategic Control" Premium*
Implied Multiples of Normalized	1.00x	5.00x	5.50x	7.0x
Assumed Marketability Discount	35.00% *"Typical Benchmark"*	60.00% *Based on QMDM*		
Nonmarketable Minority Indications	$975,000	$3,000,000		
Implied Multiples of "Public Equivalent" Normalized	0.65x	2.0x		
Comments	Clearly unreliable Masks underlying value of enterprise Crux of the problem is the failure to consider appropriate normalizing adjustments	Large marketability discount reflects the agency costs (i.e., foregone cash flows to minority shareholders) of Big Al and time to expected liquidity	Analysis provides logical explanation for a fairly wide range of observed control premiums as well as for the attractiveness of finding competing strategic buyers when a company is being sold. Absent a market with competing strategic buyers, there would appear to be little rationale for large control premiums over normalized (marketable minority) levels of value.	

Figure 4-6

We make the following observations from the Figures 4-5 and 4-6:

- If the objective of an appraisal is to achieve an indication at the nonmarketable minority level of value, appraisers who fail to normalize in situations similar to the above have little chance to develop a reasonable indication of value. In the present case, the capitalization of reported operating income yields a result that is 20% of the appropriate nonmarketable minority value ($1,500,000 vs. $7,500,000).

- The application of typical marketability discounts based on benchmark analysis only exacerbates the problem noted above.

- The normalized, public-equivalent income stream includes Type 1 Normalizing Adjustment related to the litigation and all of the Type 2 Normalizing Adjustments related to Big Al, his family, and his chalet. If these adjustments were not made, there would be no appropriate indication of the value of the enterprise at the marketable minority level.

- The example illustrates that it is quite possible for different buyers and types of buyers to see different income potential – to them – when examining the same company.

- It is important to distinguish between the types of adjustments in order to understand the level of the income stream being developed. For example, if it is unlikely that there are any strategic buyers for a particular company, it would seem inappropriate to consider Type 2 Control Adjustments in a valuation. To do so would overstate value.

- A corollary to the above is that the blind application of a so-called typical control premium of 40% or so to a normalized income stream would tend to overvalue a company in situations where no competition among strategic buyers is expected for the property.

- Wide variations in value indications can result between appraisers at the nonmarketable minority level based on assumptions made regarding the normalization process.

- Wide variations in value indications can result between appraisers at the control level based on assumptions made regarding the applicability of Type 1 or Type 2 Control Adjustments.

- By implication, it would be inappropriate to apply a control premium to a value indication that considers Type 1 or Type 2 Control Adjustments – such a premium is already embedded in the capitalized value.

- The application of a control premium in cases where no control adjustments are made to the forecasted earnings stream is equivalent to assuming the existence of benefits that, in the case of fair market value, typical buyers would be willing to pay for.

- For example, the strategic control value of $10,500,000 could be developed as indicated in the Figure or by applying a 40% control premium to the marketable minority value of $7,500,000. In both cases, there is an assumption that a total of $600,000 in combined Type 1 and Type 2 Control Adjustments is available, including $400,000 of savings in operating expenses and a $200 reduction in cost of goods sold.

- By way of further implication, it should be clear that when using discounted future benefits methods:

  - No control premium would be applicable to value indications developed based on forecasts that included Type 1 or Type 2 Control Adjustments.

  - If the forecast does not include control adjustments to income, it may be appropriate to consider the application of *an appropriate* control premium. However, that premium should relate to the expectation of benefits that buyers would pay for – else, it could lead to overvaluation.

THE NATURE OF CONTROL PREMIUMS

Control Premiums and Fair Market Value

Combining the practical analysis of this chapter with the conceptual analysis of the Integrated Theory in Chapter 3, it is appropriate to address several questions about the nature of control premiums that might be used by business appraisers. Unless otherwise indicated, the questions are asked in the context of developing controlling interest value indications under the standard of fair market value.

- Are the typical buyers for an entity financial buyers?

  - The appraiser may need to evaluate the market for similar enterprises to ascertain the nature of the so-called *typical buyers* in a fair market value determination.

  - Financial buyers *may* believe they can improve the earnings stream.

- They *may* reflect this potential in pricing.

- They *may* share some of the potential benefit in the negotiation of firm value.

- They *may* pay a financial premium to enterprise value before consideration of the benefits they bring to the table.

- If there are no expected improvements, there may be little or no premium to the normalized value (i.e., to the marketable minority value developed using normalized cash flows).

- The bottom line is that control premiums are not automatic. Appraisers must make appropriate judgments in the context of fair market value appraisals.

- Is the typical buyer a synergistic buyer?

  - Again, the appraiser may need to evaluate the market for similar enterprises to ascertain the nature of typical buyers.

  - Synergistic buyers may believe they can alter and improve the earnings stream.

  - They may reflect this potential in pricing.

  - They may share some of this benefit in negotiation, particularly if there are other synergistic buyers who may be in competition for the same property.

  - Synergistic buyers may pay a premium in excess of that available to typical financial buyers, however, as previously noted, a rational synergistic buyer will willingly pay no more than a conceptual dollar more than the highest rational financial premium – or than the price that the next most capable synergistic buyer would rationally pay.

    - Consideration of synergistic buyers may be irrelevant in the context of fair market value determinations. For example, if there are no synergistic buyers in a particular market, it would likely not be appropriate to consider a control premium based on synergistic cash flows. Alternatively, if the likely buyers are synergistic, for example, in consolidating industries, it may be appropriate to consider potential synergistic benefits in the context of a fair market value determination. Once again, appraisers must make appropriate judgments in the context of their overall analysis of a subject enterprise and the likely market for their subject enterprises.

- What accounts for control premiums?

  ▪ Premiums over marketable minority value may be paid in the process of acquiring control over enterprise cash flows.

  ▪ An acquiring company's desire to "get a deal done" can cause a price offered to increase a larger premium. If this occurs, there may be elements of compulsion involved in establishing the price.

  ▪ Irrational buyers can pay any price that they can afford to pay.

  ▪ The first element above relates to fair market value determinations; however, elements of compulsion and irrationality should not be considered in fair market value determinations according to the very definition of fair market value.

Control Premiums: Valuation Results, Not Value Drivers

At this point, it is appropriate to recall the conceptual discussion of control premiums in the context of this practical discussion of adjustments to the earnings stream. A control premium (CP) is observed when a public company is acquired at a price in excess if its before-announcement, freely traded price. The announced acquisition price of a public enterprise, or control value (CV) can be shown as a function of its marketable minority, or unaffected public price before the announcement (MMV) as:

$$CV = MMV * (1 + CP)$$

Prior to the announcement, we could observe that the market value price of an entity reflected a given multiple of normalized earnings (or $Earnings_n$):

$$MMV = Earnings_n * M$$

Economically, MMV is a function of capitalized Earnings (which is a shorthand for the discounted present value of all future cash flows). Therefore, an announced control price can be described as:

$$CV = (Earnings_n * M) * (1 + CP)$$

However, the control value can also be expressed in terms of the economics that drive controlling interest transactions. As we have seen conceptually in Chapter 3 and in practical terms in this chapter, control values are driven by *economic earning power from the viewpoint of prospective acquirers*. Economic earning power for a purchaser is the level of earnings expected post-acquisition based on economies or synergies available to that purchaser ($Earnings_c$). Therefore, the announced control value can also be expressed, from the viewpoint of the acquirer, as:

$$CV = Earnings_c * M$$

The two derived expressions for control value can now be equated as follows:

$$(Earnings_n * M) * (1 + CP) = Earnings_c * M$$

At this stage, it is clear that the control premium is an observation from the marketplace that equates two economic expressions of value, the public market price on the left side of the equation and the announced acquisition price on the right. Observed control premiums are not value drivers – they reflect the result of underlying economic and financial factors. This analysis makes it clear that appraisers should be very careful in applying control premiums in valuations, and particularly large control premiums. And since the control premium is the observed link between normalized enterprise cash flows for a public entity and the expected cash flows available to acquirers, it should further be clear that we should not apply control premiums without also examining the underlying multiples of earnings that were paid in acquisitions (or the implied multiples of the earnings of subject enterprises represented by resulting value implications).

Finally, if we assume that the acquirer's discount rate (embedded in M) is the same as the market discount rate for the public company, the relationship can be simplified to the following:

$$Earnings_n * (1 + CP) = Earnings_c$$

This expression suggests that observed control premiums represent the benefit of the increment in expected earnings of a public enterprise that is to be received by selling shareholders. (See Appendix 4-A.)

CONCLUSION

This chapter amplifies concepts discussed in the Integrated Theory of Business Valuation from a practical viewpoint. We have been making many of these points in articles and speeches since the mid-1990s. We are not suggesting in this chapter that appraisers who do not use the vocabulary for income statement adjustments are wrong. We are suggesting, however, that the same vocabulary regarding Type 1 and Type 2 Normalizing Adjustments and Type 1 and Type 2 Control Adjustments can help appraisers clarify the impact of valuation adjustments on their conclusions. This vocabulary also clarifies the level of value that a particular valuation method yields.

In the next chapter we address another type of valuation adjustment, the fundamental adjustment that may be appropriate when using guideline public company or guideline transactions as the basis for developing capitalization factors using the guideline company method(s).

Appendix 4-A

A WAR STORY

I was asked recently to review a valuation prepared by another firm. While multiple methods were employed in the appraisal, two are relevant for this story, the guideline transactions method (using sales of similar companies as a basis for developing a capitalization factor), and the guideline company method. Since the appraisal was on a controlling interest basis, the appraiser developed a marketable minority value indication using the guideline company method and applied a control premium.

The subject company's industry was in a consolidation phase and there was considerable acquisition activity of both private and public companies. In this industry, the focus was on the multiples of EBITDA paid in acquisitions. The appraiser's research indicated many acquisitions of similar companies in recent years – nearly one hundred. Over the entire time period leading to the valuation date, the average and median multiples paid for companies was on the order of 11x EBITDA, which was the approximate multiple used by the appraiser in the guideline transaction method.

A marketable minority value was developed for the guideline company method. Interestingly, the multiple of normalized EBITDA implied by this indication was about 10.5x. The appraiser next reviewed control premium data found in *Mergerstat Control Premium Study*. Two transactions were identified involving similar companies, and the observed control premiums were on the order of 100% each. Based on a discussion of a short paragraph or so, the appraiser concluded that a range of control premiums of 75% to 90% was appropriate. Since the difference was split, a control premium of 82.5% was actually applied.

The result of the guideline company method was substantially higher than other indications of value in the valuation. In fact, it reflected a multiple of over 19x EBITDA (i.e., 10.5 x (1 + 82.5%)). Recall that the median and average multiples of EBITDA in the many transactions examined in the guideline transactions method was about 11x. The appraiser should have attempted to reconcile the difference between 19x and 11x but, unfortunately, did not.

As it turns out, the two acquisitions examined from *Mergerstat Control Premium Study* were reflected among the transactions examined for the guideline transactions method. The EBITDA multiples recorded for these two transactions were 10.5x and 11.2x, respectively. There was no justification for a value indication at 19x EBITDA, and the report lost credibility because of its failure to reflect an understanding of the economics of pricing in the subject company's industry.

Appraisers who understand the Integrated Theory and its practical applications as illustrated in this chapter will not make such embarrassing mistakes.

Chapter 5

Fundamental Adjustments to Market Capitalization Rates

INTRODUCTION

Thus far, we have discussed two types of valuation adjustments used by appraisers:

- Conceptual Adjustments (Chapter 3)
  - Control premiums
  - Minority interest discounts
  - Marketability discounts

- Adjustments to the Earnings Stream (Chapter 4)
  - Normalizing adjustments (Type 1 and Type 2)
  - Control adjustments (Type 1 and Type 2)

An understanding of conceptual adjustments is critical to the Integrated Theory. We have seen the integration of controlling interest and minority interest valuation issues in the context of enterprise cash flows. And we have defined the major conceptual adjustments (the marketability discount, the financial control premium, etc.) in the context of enterprise valuation using the Gordon model and discounted cash flow. Value at the enterprise level is a function of enterprise cash flows. Value at the level of the shareholder is a function of the portion of enterprise cash flows expected to be received by shareholders.

It was equally important to develop an understanding of the important adjustments that are made to the income stream in the process of conducting an appraisal – and why and when certain adjustments are appropriate or not. We learned, for example, that *not making* normalizing adjustments in *minority interest* appraisals is inconsistent with the Integrated Theory.

We now need to consider a third category of valuation adjustments, *fundamental adjustments*. This term is used to describe a category of adjustments employed by appraisers in the application of the guideline company method. I first posed the question about the necessity for fundamental adjustments in the 1989 ACAPM article cited numerous times in this book. In that article, I used the term *fundamental discount*. In *Valuing Financial Institutions* published in 1992, we framed the issue as follows:

> Business and bank appraisers face a difficult task in developing capitalization rates in situations where they are unable to identify a comparable group of public companies to use as a foundation. The ACAPM model provides some assistance in this regard.

> But the analyst sometimes faces an equally imponderable task in assessing where, relative to a public comparable group, to "price" the earnings of a valuation subject. The analytical question is straightforward: How can the analyst justify a significant discount to the P/E multiples derived from public comparables even when it seems obvious that the subject should command a considerably lower multiple?

> While a public company comparable group provides an objective basis for comparing a subject company's results, either with measures of the group average (such as the mean or median) or with regard to the performance of specific companies in the group, appraisers often end up applying what amounts to a large judgmental discount to the comparable group average (e.g., …"on the order of 50 percent based on our detailed analysis") to obtain a correct (i.e., more reasonable and realistic) valuation multiple to be applied to the subject company.[96]

Interestingly, both in the ACAPM article and in *Valuing Financial Institutions*, we referred to fundamental adjustments as *fundamental discounts*. Along the way, however, we learned that private companies can compare both favorably and unfavorably with groups of guideline companies, so we began using the term *fundamental adjustments*.

---

[96] Z. Christopher Mercer, "Minority Interest Valuation Methodologies," *Valuing Financial Institutions* (Homewood, IL: Business One Irwin, 1992), p. 235.

COMMON QUESTIONS

1. Fundamental adjustments allow the business appraiser to relate public guideline multiples to the valuation of private enterprises. How should appraisers determine and apply fundamental adjustments?

2. What are the differences in fundamental adjustments applied to equity versus total capital valuation metrics?

3. In valuing illiquid interests of private businesses, why do appraisers normally begin with appraisals at the marketability minority level of value?

THE GRAPES OF VALUE REVIEWED

A brief review of the GRAPES of Value is appropriate as we begin to address the concept of fundamental adjustments. We begin with A (*alternative investment world*) because of its direct correlation with the guideline company method. While the examples in the following discussion apply to the guideline (public company) method, the considerations raised are applicable to guideline transactions involving entire companies, to guideline transactions involving restricted shares of public companies, or any other relevant comparisons of private enterprises with market transactions.

A – The world of value is an *alternative investment* world. We value private enterprises and interests in private enterprises *in relationship to alternative investments*. In using the guideline company method, we look, for example, at groups of similar (or comparable) publicly traded companies to develop valuation metrics for application to private enterprises.

G – The world of value is a *growth* world. Investors purchase equity securities with the expectation that the underlying enterprises will grow and that their investments will grow in value. This suggests that it would be important, when comparing private enterprises with groups of guideline public companies, to examine the underlying growth prospects for each.

R – The world of value is a world in which *risk* is both charged for and rewarded. This would suggest that in making comparisons with guideline companies, appraisers should account for differences in the relative riskiness of subject enterprises and the guideline groups.

P – The world of value is a *present value* world. To the extent that one investment is riskier than another, the impact of that greater risk dampens the present value of expected future cash flows, and therefore, value.

E – The world of value is an *expectational* world. If it is important to understand the growth prospects of both guideline public companies and private enterprises with which they are being compared, it is also important to examine the impact on value of *differences in expectations*.

S – The world of value is a *sane and rational* world. While pockets of seeming irrationality may always exist in the public markets, on balance, the markets operate on a rational basis. It is often incumbent on the analyst to decipher the underlying rationale reflected in market transactions.

The seventh principle in the GRAPES of value is *knowledge*, which is the basket within which appraisers can hold their symbolic grapes. This review frames the following discussion of fundamental adjustments employed when developing valuation metrics (multiples) for private enterprises based on comparisons with public companies (or other guideline transactions).

A CONCEPTUAL OVERVIEW OF FUNDAMENTAL ADJUSTMENTS

In Chapter 3, we illustrated that the levels of value can be shown conceptually using the Gordon Model. The symbolic representation of the markets' valuation of a public company was described as:

$$V = \frac{CF}{r - g}$$

Equation 5-1

Conceptually, when we examine price/earnings *multiples* from guideline public companies, we are seeing the result of the capitalization of expected future cash flows or earnings based on each company's r and expected g. Using the market approach, analysts often examine market multiples directly and do not attempt to derive either r or g specifically. There is an implicit assumption that reported public company earnings are normalized.[97] In some cases, the analyst may actually make normalizing adjustments to individual public companies before calculating earnings multiples.

When valuing a private company, its normalized cash flows are capitalized based on the appropriate discount rate for that private enterprise *(R)* and its expected growth in core earnings *(G)*. Conceptually, we define the value of a private enterprise as:

$$V_{PVT} = \frac{CF}{R - G}$$

Equation 5-2

The normalized cash flows of the private company (i.e., the result of adjusting for unusual or nonrecurring items and items like excess owner compensation) are capitalized at the appropriate rate for the enterprise based on its risk profile and growth expectations. This construct works well with direct capitalization (income methods) if the analyst appropriately assesses risk and growth expectations, either with a single period capitalization of earnings or using the discounted cash flow method. In other words, if the discount rate (built-up using the Adjusted Capital Asset Pricing Model) and expected growth of cash flows are appropriately estimated, reasonable valuation indications can be developed.

Risk Differentials Cause Fundamental Adjustments

However, when comparisons are made between a subject private company and public guideline companies, the objective is to compare a subject private company in appropriate ways to ascertain the appropriate discount rate or capitalization rate. Conceptually, this analysis must allow for the following range of comparisons of discount rates.

---

[97] Recall that even if there are unusual or non-recurring items in the most current (twelve months) earnings of a public company, the public markets tend to accomplish the normalization process described in Chapter 4 based on the capitalization of *next year's* earnings.

$$R_{pvt} > = < R_{mm}$$

Equation 5-3

Quite often, it is the case that the subject private company is riskier than the public companies with which it is being compared. For example, it may be smaller, have key person risks, customer concentrations, or other risks not present in most or all of the selected guideline companies. Skeptical readers might suggest that the selected guideline companies were not sufficiently comparable to the private enterprise for use. However, by common practice, and judicial and client expectation, if there are publicly traded companies somewhat similar to the subject, even if somewhat larger, they will need to be considered for their valuation implications.

As discussed at length in Chapter 6 regarding the Adjusted Capital Asset Pricing Model, it is common practice when using income methods to "build up" a discount rate. Analysts routinely add a small stock premium to the base, CAPM-determined market premium to account for the greater riskiness of small companies relative to large capitalization stocks, or specify a more refined size premium based on historical rate of return data. In addition, analysts routinely estimate a specific company risk premium for private enterprises, which is added to the other components of the ACAPM or build-up discount rate.

Implicitly, analysts adjust public market return data (from Ibbotson Associates or other sources) used to develop public company return expectations to account for risks related to size and other factors. In other words, they are making *fundamental adjustments* in the development of discount rates. In so doing, analysts develop credible valuation indications for the subject enterprises.

Now, consider making direct comparisons between a subject enterprise and valuation metrics obtained from a guideline public group. Assume that the subject enterprise is riskier than the public companies used for comparison. Other things being equal (like expected growth in earnings), the direct application of guideline public multiples to the subject private enterprise would result in an *overvaluation* of the private enterprise.

Why? Because the cash flows are normalized to public equivalent basis and growth expectations are comparable. However, the lower r from the public group was applied to the normalized cash flows of the private enterprise – and the higher (relative) risk of the private enterprise was not captured.

Expected Growth Differentials Cause Fundamental Adjustments

Now, consider that the growth expectations for the subject private enterprise may be the same, greater than, or less than the growth expectations embedded in the public company multiples.

$$G_{pvt} > = < G_{mm}$$

Equation 5-4

Quite often (indeed, more often), it is the case that the *realistic growth expectations* for the subject private enterprise are less than the *growth expectations* embedded in public market pricing.[98] Familiarity with public markets is crucial when examining relative growth expectations between private and public companies.

- For private companies, examination of historical growth may provide the best evidence relating to future growth expectations, although "hockey stick" projections are seen quite often in private company appraisals. The question in such cases is: "How realistic are the forecasted results in light of history and what is happening at the private enterprise?"

- For a public company, examination of historical growth may provide little indication *of the expectations for future growth* embedded in its stock price. "Hope springs (almost) eternal" in the public markets, and analysts' estimates of future growth may be considerably higher than an examination of past results would indicate.[99]

---

[98] Analysts may compare the *historical* growth patterns of a subject private company with public guideline companies and find similarity in levels and/or patterns. Under such circumstances, it could be tempting to apply median or typical public multiples to the private company. This can result in error, however, if the growth expectations embedded in current public market pricing are significantly different than the past and higher than the expectations for the subject private company. Remember the E of the GRAPES – the world of value is an *expectational* world. The text addresses also addresses this issue.

[99] If public guideline companies are priced based, for example, on a long-term G_e of 10%, and the appropriate G_e for a subject private company is only 6%, is it appropriate to apply the higher, public multiples directly to the private company without adjustment? Hopefully this question is answered in the following discussion.

In direct capitalization methods, analysts typically make estimates of expected future growth to convert their ACAPM or build-up discount rates into capitalization rates. Growth expectations are normally based on historical analysis and realistic expectations for future growth of earnings or cash flows. Based on personal experience, discussions with hundreds of appraisers and reviews of hundreds of appraisal reports, it is fair to say that the typical G_e, or expected growth is less than 10%. When discrete earnings forecasts are made, this observation is also true when direct capitalizations are used to develop terminal value indications.[100]

However, the effective, long-term G_e embedded in the pricing of public companies is often 10% or a bit more. Appraisers who recognize this fact (when true) and who use lower expected growth in income methods implicitly reflect fundamental adjustments in the resulting indications of value.

Other things being equal (like risk), if valuation metrics from guideline public companies are applied directly to cash flows of private enterprises in cases where the *growth expectations* for the public companies exceed those of subject private enterprises, overvaluation will result. (The opposite result would be true if the private company's growth expectations exceeded those of the publics.) Therefore, analysts should consider whether a *fundamental adjustment* is appropriate relative to guideline company multiples, or overvaluation (or undervaluation) will result.

Why? Because the cash flows are normalized to public equivalent basis and risks are comparable in this example. However, the higher G_e from the public group was applied to the normalized cash flows of the private enterprise – and more future cash flow than is realistically available is capitalized.

---

[100] There are occasional exceptions to these statements in exceptional circumstances or when overly optimistic expectations are used.

Fundamental Adjustments by Another Name

Most appraisers, even those who have never employed the term "fundamental adjustment" have employed the same concept in appraisals. In fact, any appraiser who has selected guideline company multiples other than the median (or perhaps, the average), whether above or below, has implicitly applied the concept of the fundamental adjustment. Based on comparisons between private companies and guideline groups of companies, appraisers often select multiples above or below the measures of central tendency for the public groups. In so doing, they are no less applying the concept of the fundamental adjustment than others who make explicit determinations of the adjustments such as will be discussed in the remainder of this chapter.

The next section provides practical examples of applying fundamental adjustments using a quantitative methodology and consciously selecting valuation parameters other than the median (or average) of a guideline company group for application to private company earnings or cash flows.

PRACTICAL TECHNIQUES FOR DEVELOPING FUNDAMENTAL ADJUSTMENTS

Quantifying Fundamental Adjustments (from the Median of Mean) Using the ACAPM

Consider two companies, Publico and Privateco. Both are in the same industry, so there is no issue of business comparability between the two. Privateco is somewhat smaller than Publico, has issues with customer concentration and with key person dependency on the majority shareholder. Using these two companies, and the broader guideline group within which Publico falls, we can observe and understand the nature of fundamental adjustments and the necessity for considering such adjustments when using the guideline company method.

Compare Publico and Privateco

Publico is trading with a relatively liquid market for a small capitalization company. Based on its expected earnings growth, its current share price represents a price/earnings multiple of 17.0x, as seen at Line 6 in Figure 5-1. We can reverse-engineer this multiple to develop the base equity discount rate for Publico. The capitalization rate (R - G_e) is 5.9% (Line 5). Assume that we determined (through a separate analysis) that the long-term earnings growth expectation is 9.6% (Line 4). The sum of the capitalization rate and the expected growth rate (G_e) is equal to the equity discount rate (R) of 15.5% (Line 3). Since we are observing actual market pricing, there is no incremental, specific company risk to consider (Line 2), the equity discount rate can be considered to be the base discount rate for use as we consider the value of Privateco (Line 1).

Compare Publico with Privateco
Derive Publico Discount Rate and Adjust for Privateco

Line	Capitalization Rate Components	Publico	Privateco	
1	Base Discount Rate (R)	15.5%	15.5%	Derived for Publico
2	Specific Company Risk (SCR)	0.0%	2.0%	Greater risks
3	Equity Discount Rate (R)	15.5%	17.5%	
4	Expected Growth (G_e)	-9.6%	-7.0%	Slower growth expectations
5	Capitalization Rate (R - G_e)	5.9%	10.5%	
6	P/E Multiple 1 / (R - G_e)	17.0	9.5	Lower implied P/E for Privateco
		Observed Multiple		
7	**Effective Fundamental Adjustment**		**-44.0%**	

Figure 5-1

Relative to Publico, it is clear that Privateco bears risks not present in Publico. There are key person and customer concentration risks that must be considered. Assume that an appropriate premium for these risks is 2.0% (Line 2). The resulting discount rate for Privateco is therefore 17.5% (Line 3). Based on a detailed historical analysis and consideration for its outlook, it is concluded that the appropriate earnings growth expectation (G_e) for Privateco is 7.0% (Line 4), or somewhat lower than for Publico. The resulting capitalization rate of 10.5% and the corresponding price/earnings multiple of 9.5x are shown on Lines 5 and 6.

The appropriate price/earnings multiple for Privateco is clearly lower than that observed for Publico. The difference between the two price/earnings multiples can be described as the fundamental adjustment necessary to apply to the observed multiple of Publico in order to develop an appropriate indication of value for Privateco. The fundamental adjustment based on this analysis is -44%.

We have just used the income approach to validate a valuation adjustment that is necessary in many applications of the market approach to valuation.

Our fundamental analyses of both Publico and Privateco indicate that Privateco is both riskier and expected to grow at a slower rate in the future. Appraisers presented with this example will have to adjust the 17.0x multiple observed for Publico in some fashion if an appropriate indication of value for Privateco is to be obtained.

In practice, appraisers make adjustments like the one necessary to value Privateco in several ways:

- Select multiples from guideline company groups for application to private company earnings measures based on the median or the average multiples of the group, i.e., based on some measure of central tendency.

- Omit obvious outlier multiples (very high or very low) and select a multiple based on an adjusted median or average.

- From a range of multiples for a particular earnings measure, select a multiple for one company that is most appropriate in the appraiser's judgment.

- From a range of multiples for a particular earnings measure, select a multiple that the appraiser thinks is most appropriate.

Make no mistake. Any appraiser applying a guideline company multiple much different than the measures of central tendency for a group to the earnings of a private enterprise has applied a fundamental adjustment relative to the group. The question is not whether appraisers use fundamental adjustments. We do. The questions are how we determine their magnitude and justify them in appraisals.

Problems arise when using the guideline company method if the subject of an appraisal is riskier than the guideline group of companies, prompting a downward adjustment to the observed multiples. Problems also arise if the expected growth for the subject private company is significantly less than the growth expectations embedded in the market prices to the public guideline companies.

In such cases, the selection of a median or average multiple would clearly be incorrect and would tend to overvalue a subject enterprise. The selection of a multiple from a single guideline company is also risky in such circumstances, although such a selection could result in a reasonable indication of value. The selection of a multiple within the range is also potentially dangerous. The selection can appear to come out of thin air, and may be subject to criticism as a result, absent a compelling rationale.

Estimate Long-Term Growth for Public Group

The 1989 ACAPM article suggested using a version of the method outlined in the comparison of Publico and Privateco as a means of quantifying the necessary fundamental adjustments in many applications of the guideline company method. The CAPM can be used to estimate public company discount rates. The model can also be used to estimate the long-term G_e embedded in public market pricing.[101]

Estimate Long-Term Growth Rate of Public Guideline Group
Publico Represents the Median of a Guideline Company Group

Line	Guideline (Public) Company Growth Analysis			Sources/Comments
1	Long-Term Government Bond Yield-to-Maturity		4.9%	As of March 2003
2	Ibbotson Common Stock Premium	6.2%		Per Mercer Capital analysis
3	x Industry Beta	1.2		
4	Beta-Adjusted Common Stock Premium	7.4%		
5	+ Ibbotson Small Stock Premium	3.2%		Per Mercer Capital analysis
6	= Total Equity Premium		10.6%	
7	Industry Discount Rate (required rate of return)		15.5%	
8	- Industry P/E and Resulting Cap Rate (1 / P/E)	17.0	5.9%	Based on median guideline p/e
9	= Implied Long-Term Growth Rate for Public Companies		9.6%	

Figure 5-2

We estimated the discount rate for Publico as 15.5% in Figure 5-2. If we know the discount rate and the market capitalization rate (or price/earnings multiples) we can estimate the expected growth rate embedded in the public market pricing. Assume now that there are several other public companies in Publico's industry that are suitable for inclusion in the guideline public group for Privateco. Assume further, for purposes of this illustration, that Publico's market multiples represent the median of the broader group.

---

[101] The model may be used to estimate either parameter, but not both simultaneously for a given public company.

Given the estimated discount rate (15.5% on Line 7 directly above) and the market-observed capitalization rate of 5.9% (based on the p/e of 17.0x) on Line 8, we can estimate the expected long-term growth rate for the (median) group. That is 9.6% as indicated on Line 9.

Because we are examining pricing that includes all the risks of the public companies, there is no need for further consideration of specific company risk for the guideline group. As for Publico above, the specific company risk is equal to zero.

Determine a Fundamental Adjustment Using ACAPM

Figure 5-3 presents the ACAPM summary build-up for the median company of a guideline public group and for Privateco for ease of reference. Then, in four steps, a methodology is presented to develop a fundamental adjustment for Privateco.

Determine a Fundamental Adjustment
Use the ACAPM to Narrow the Range of Judgment
Privateco in Relationship to Guideline Company Group

Line	Subject Company Analysis	Medians for Public Group	Privateco ACAPM Build-up	Step 1 Set Risk = Privateco GROWTH = Public	Step 2 Set G = Privateco RISK = Public	Step 3 GROWTH = Privateco RISK = Privateco
1	Long-Term Government Bond Yield-to-Maturity	4.9%	4.9%	4.9%	4.9%	4.9%
2	+ Total Equity Premium (Line 6 above)	10.6%	10.6%	10.6%	10.6%	10.6%
3	+ Specific Company Risk Premium	0.0%	2.0%	2.0%	0.0%	2.0%
4	= Discount Rate (required rate of return)	15.5%	17.5%	17.5%	15.5%	17.5%
5	- Growth Rate Estimates	-9.6%	-7.0%	-9.6%	-7.0%	-7.0%
6	= Implied Capitalization Rates	5.9%	10.5%	7.9%	8.5%	10.5%
7	Implied P/E Multiples	17.0	9.5	12.7	11.8	9.5
8	*Implied Adjustment from Guideline Median P/E*	na		*-25.4%*	*-30.8%*	*-44.0%*

9   Step 4: Selected Fundamental Adjustment   -35.0%

Figure 5-3

Step 1   Using the discount rate for Privateco, which includes 2.0% of company-specific risk factors, substitute the expected G_e for the public group into the build-up of a capitalization factor. Implicitly, analysts using this procedure are comparing a subject private company with their perception of the group of public companies from which the market data was derived. In this case, Privateco is considered somewhat riskier than the broad group of smaller capitalization stocks from which Ibbotson Associates and others develop return data. Given the discount rate for Privateco of 17.5% (Line 4, Step 1), the expected growth for the guideline public group of 9.6% is substituted for the 7.0% expected growth for Privateco (on Line 5). The result is a capitalization rate of 7.9% (Line 6) and a price/earnings multiple of 12.7x (Line 7), which represents a discount of 25.4% relative to the median public multiple of 17.0x. Stated another way, relative to the median of the guideline group, the consideration of 2.0% of incremental risk for Privateco would justify a -25.4% fundamental adjustment to the median public multiple.

Step 2   Using the discount rate for the guideline group, i.e., excluding Privateco's specific risk premium, and setting the expected growth at the 7.0% level for Privateco (Lines 4 and 5), we develop a capitalization rate of 8.5% (Line 6) and a resulting price/earnings multiple of 11.8x (Line 7). Considering only slower growth expectations relative to the guideline group median would justify a -30.8% fundamental adjustment.

Step 3   Now, consider the effects of Privateco's slower expected growth and its higher riskiness. Step 3 replicates the 44.0% discount initially found in the first chart in this series.

Step 4   The first three steps have created a range of potential fundamental adjustments, from -25.4% (based on extra risk), to -30.8% (based on slower expected growth), to the largest of -44.0% (based on extra risk and slower expected growth). In Step 4, the analyst must reach a conclusion for the appropriate fundamental adjustment. Obviously, there is a difference between a -25% and a -44% adjustment. It is rare in valuation when a set of calculations provides such a precise result that the need for judgment is eliminated. What the calculations in Steps 1-3 have accomplished is to establish a reasonable range for the appropriate fundamental adjustment. The analyst must reach a conclusion within this range based on other quantitative comparisons, qualitative comparisons, and, ultimately, judgment.   In this case, a 35% fundamental discount was selected, which is approximately the midpoint of the indicated range.[102]

By employing the ACAPM to analyze the potential impact of risk and growth differentials on valuation multiples, the analyst can develop confidence making the judgments necessary when the guideline company method is used.   This method provides a framework within which to adjust public company multiples for private company valuations.   While the example illustrated a fundamental discount, there can be cases where similar analysis would suggest application of a fundamental premium.

It is important to note that, since the ACAPM or build-up discount rate is applicable to the net income or net cash flow of business enterprises, the fundamental adjustments developed with this methodology relate to equity, rather than total capital multiples.

Application of the Fundamental Adjustment

We have demonstrated that the fundamental adjustment is a function of the combination of relative differences in risk and expected growth between a subject company and a selected group of public guideline companies.   We have also developed a model for estimating the fundamental adjustment for (market value of) equity multiples.

---

[102]   It could be argued that if the appraiser believes in both the estimates of higher risk and slower growth, the concluded fundamental discount should be the highest estimate considering both, or -44%. However, the objective of the analysis is to price a private company "as-if-freely-traded", or close to how the analyst believes the public markets would price that firm if public. The judgments required for this analysis should allow some discretion within a calculated range of potential adjustments.

However, appraisers often derive total capital multiples when using guideline groups. Logically, the fundamental adjustment for total capital multiples might be different than that for equity multiples. The presence of leverage influences the appropriate adjustment to total capital multiples. While it can be shown that a fundamental adjustment based on equity multiples bears a predictable relationship to that appropriate for total capital multiples, appraisers at Mercer Capital have developed a presentation of the fundamental adjustment for total capital measures that applies the fundamental adjustment to derived equity values. Both equity and total capital measures are illustrated in Figure 5-4, where a fundamental discount of 35% has been applied to total capital (left of the dotted line) and equity measures (right of the line) for a hypothetical company.

Application of Fundamental Adjustments to Total Capital and Equity Value Indications

	Derivation of Value	Market Value of Total Capital to			Price to Net Income (Market Value of Equity/NI)	
		Sales	EBITDA	EBIT	Ongoing/Tr 12	Current FY
1	Appropriate Earnings or Performance Measure	$100,000,000	$15,000,000	$10,500,000	$6,500,000	$8,200,000
2	x Guideline Company Capitalization Factor	1.25	8.10	11.15	16.00	13.50
3	= Capitalized Value: Total Capital	$125,000,000	$121,500,000	$117,075,000	$104,000,000	$110,700,000
4	- Interest Bearing Debt (Operational)	(18,000,000)	(18,000,000)	(18,000,000)		
5	= Capitalized Value: Total Common Equity	$107,000,000	$103,500,000	$99,075,000	$104,000,000	$110,700,000
6	- Fundamental Adjustment **-35.0%**	(37,450,000)	(36,225,000)	(34,676,250)	(36,400,000)	(38,745,000)
7	= Adjusted Guideline Company Capitalized Value	$69,550,000	$67,275,000	$64,398,750	$67,600,000	$71,955,000
	INDICATED VALUES:	*Rounded to:*				
8	GUIDELINE COMPANY METHOD	*$10,000*				
		$69,550,000	$67,280,000	$64,400,000	$67,600,000	$71,960,000
9	Concluded Multiples Based on Derived Equity Value	0.876	5.685	7.848	10.400	8.776
10	Effective Fundamental Adjustment to the Guideline Median	-30.0%	-29.8%	-29.6%	-35.0%	-35.0%
11	Adjustment Factor (Equity to Total Capital)	-14.4%	-14.8%	-15.4%		

- (Market Value of Equity Before Fundamental Adjustment / Market Value of Total Capital) (Line 5 / Line 3)

Figure 5-4

Note that for the total capital indications, the fundamental adjustment has been considered at Line 6, and is applied to the implied market values of total capital less applicable debt (Line 5), or the derived equity values for each measure. Note also that the fundamental adjustment is applied directly to the implied equity value indications for the equity measures to the right of the dotted line.

Adjusting Equity-Based Fundamental Adjustments for Total Capital Methods

This presentation is used to avoid the error that would occur if the equity-based fundamental adjustment were applied to total capital measures. For example, in Figure 5-4, in the market value of total capital to sales column (the left-most column), Line 9 calculates the implied multiple of total capital to sales based on the conclusion equity value found on Line 8. A multiple of 0.88x sales would yield an equity value of $69.55 million. This multiple represents a 30% discount to the guideline median multiple of 1.25x sales (Line 10), not a -35% fundamental adjustment, a difference of about 14% (30% / 35% - 1).[103]

---

[103] It turns out that the conversion factor is easily determined. Line 11 calculates the adjustment factor (AF) necessary to convert an equity-based fundamental adjustment (FAE) to a total capital basis. In this case, the adjustment factor is -14.4%. Symbolically, the fundamental adjustment for total capital (FATC) can be represented as follows (where market value of debt is MVD and market value of total capital is MVTC):

$$FATC = FAE + AF \times FAE$$
$$AF = - (MVD / MVTC)$$

AF is the necessary adjustment factor to convert an equity-derived fundamental adjustment to one appropriate for total capital. Using the example in the sales column above, we can substitute terms:

$$AF = - (- Line\ 4 / Line\ 3)$$
$$= - (-\$18,000,000) / \$125,000,000)$$
$$= - (.144)$$
$$= -.144$$

Now, substituting into the equation for AF, we confirm the calculations in the table and the rationale for differences in total capital and equity-based fundamental adjustments:

$$FATC = 35.0\% + (-.144 \times 35.0\%)$$
$$= 35.0\% - 5.0\%$$
$$= 30.0\%$$

This analysis is presented in the context of Figure 5-4. A more generalized algebraic expression is undoubtedly available; however, it is beyond the scope of this brief discussion. We can make several observations about the adjustment factor:

- It is constant over the range of fundamental discounts once the guideline multiple (for a given indication) is fixed and the debt level is fixed. Note, however, that while the percentage adjustment factor is fixed, the actual difference between the total capital adjustment factor and the equity adjustment factor rises as the absolute value of the equity fundamental adjustment increases.

- Other things being equal, the adjustment factor rises in absolute value as the amount of debt is increased.

- For a fixed level of debt, the adjustment factor is lower (less negative) the higher the level of the base guideline multiples. This is because a higher multiple raises the market value of total capital, thereby lowering the portion of total capital represented by debt.

While it is important to understand the nature of the adjustment factor, it is simpler to apply the equity-based adjustment factor to equity indications developed.

Using a Factor Other Than the Median or Mean to Determine the Fundamental Adjustment

Quite often, based on size differences, less favorable growth outlooks, lower margins or unfavorable financial comparisons, an appraiser may believe that a private company should be valued at a discount to the measures of central tendency of a selected guideline group. The procedure outlined above using the Adjusted Capital Asset Pricing Model provided one objective way to narrow the range of consideration for fundamental adjustments. Appraisers using the guideline company method make subjective and objective comparisons between subject companies and the selected guideline companies. In so doing, they may prefer another procedure for adjusting from the median, or typical multiples for a guideline group.

One way to accomplish this would be to select a statistical measure other than the median as the base multiple. For example, an appraiser might, based on comparisons of revenues, growth, margins, leverage, or other factors, conclude that a private company should most appropriately be compared with a specific portion of the entire guideline group, for example, the lower half of the group's multiples, rather than the entire group. This would be tantamount to making an additional screen to the guideline company group by eliminating multiples above the median or mean and focusing on the lower half of multiples in the group.[104]

Assume for purposes of illustration that an appraiser has determined that his subject company should be compared, based on his overall analysis, with the lower half of multiples for his guideline group than with the entire group. Two possible (related) techniques are illustrated in Figure 5-5 to select multiples for application to the subject private company. The techniques implicitly determine effective fundamental adjustments from the public group's overall median.

In Figure 5-5, a guideline group of six public companies was selected based on a thorough and detailed screening of the public markets. The six companies were deemed by the appraiser as reasonably comparable with the subject company in terms of business lines, size, and other operating and financial characteristics. The median and average multiples of total capital to revenues was 0.43x and 0.39x. The comparable multiples of EBITDA were 8.69x and 9.19x. In reviewing the guideline company multiples relative to the subject private company, the analyst was concerned that the above-median multiples could provide an inappropriate upward bias to his conclusion.

Technique #1 below illustrates the selection of the first quartile of multiples as the appropriate multiple for consideration in this particular example.

- The first quartile is that observation in a sample above which 75% of the observations lie and below which 25% of the observations lie.

- The median total capital to sales and to EBITDA were 0.43x and 8.69x, respectively. The respective first quartile multiples were 0.28x (revenues) and 7.51x (EBITDA). In this case, the analyst selected the first quartile multiples as appropriate for application to the subject private company.

---

[104] This same technique could obviously be used to focus on the multiples above the median (or average) of a guideline public company group.

Is the selection of the first quartile the functional equivalent of determining a fundamental discount relative to the median of the group? Clearly so, as indicated in Figure 5-5. The first quartile total capital to sales multiple represents a -35% fundamental adjustment relative to the median of the group. The total capital to EBITDA multiple represents a fundamental adjustment of -14% relative to the median of the group.[105]

Guideline Companies	Sample Company Guideline Multiples	
	Revenues	EBITDA
	0.53	14.69
Multiples from Six Selected Guideline	0.53	10.21
Companies Arranged in Descending	0.52	9.67
Order for Ease of Visual Inspection	0.34	7.72
	0.26	7.44
	0.13	5.40
Median Multiples	**0.43**	**8.69**
Average Multiples	**0.39**	**9.19**
1. First Quartile Analysis		
Calculate First Quartiles	**0.28**	**7.51**
Implied Adjustment from Overall Medians	*-35%*	*-14%*
Implied Adjustment from Overall Averages	*-27%*	*-18%*
2. Lower Half Average Analysis		
	0.53	*14.69*
Upper Half for Perspective	*0.53*	*10.21*
	0.52	*9.67*
Averages (for Top of Lower Half Range)	**0.39**	**9.19**
	0.34	7.72
Lower Half of Multiples (Including Average)	0.26	7.44
	0.13	5.40
Averages of Lower Half	**0.28**	**7.44**
Implied Adjustment from Overall Medians	*-35%*	*-14%*
Implied Adjustment from Overall Averages	*-28%*	*-19%*

Figure 5-5

---

[105]   It might be asked why there is a difference between the two implied fundamental adjustments.   This result can occur because decisions have been made based on medians and first quartiles of individual multiples, rather individual companies.   In practice, this kind of result is not unusual. For example, an individual public company may be the median observation by one measure and above – or below – median for other valuation multiples.

Technique #2 focuses on a lower half average analysis and is a variation on Technique #1. In the example, the analyst focuses on the lower half of observations. The average multiples are included as if they were observations in the middle portion of Technique #2 in order to allow for the impact of the above-average observations, which are shown for perspective in the Figure. The average of the lower half of the range is 0.28x for total capital to revenue, which represents a -35% fundamental adjustment below the median. The average of the lower half range is 7.44x for total capital to EBITDA, which is a -14% fundamental adjustment below the median. Similar calculations are made for comparisons with sample averages in the Figure.

Note again that the adjustments for each parameter vary between valuation multiples, unlike when a single fundamental adjustment was applied to equity value indications using the ACAPM technique above. Either method is, I believe, credible and justifiable (and not unusual) in the context of judgments made in appraisal assignments – if the adjustments are based on the facts and circumstances and are reasonable.

Conceptual Illustrations of Fundamental Adjustments

The concept of the fundamental adjustment can be illustrated in the context of the levels of value, and, therefore, in the context of the Integrated Theory. As noted above, fundamental adjustments can be either positive, which would indicate that a subject private company has more favorable valuation characteristics than a guideline group, or negative, where the opposite holds true.

Fundamental adjustments relative to the marketable minority level of value can be depicted as follows:

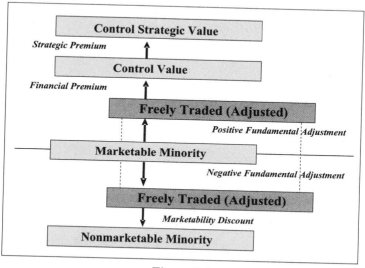

Figure 5-6

Conceptually, if guideline transactions of controlling interests form the basis for valuation comparisons, fundamental adjustments can be considered relative to those transactions, which yield value indications at the controlling interest level(s).

The following discussion, which compares a guideline public group with a series of private companies will help illustrate the significance the fundamental adjustment accomplishes in an appraisal.

Since application of a fundamental adjustment based on public market multiples provides a marketable minority, or "as-if-freely-tradable" indication of value, the other levels of value for the private company would tend to move with the adjustment. The adjustments below therefore illustrate that the levels of value for private companies are shifted relative to the public guideline groups.

Median Pricing. The analyst "prices" a private company by selecting appropriate multiples based on fundamental comparisons with the guideline information. In this case, the application of median multiples would achieve realistic valuation indications for the subject private company.

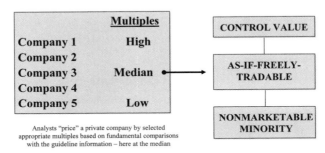

Figure 5-7

Above Median Pricing. High performing private companies may be priced at the high end of the guideline company range. In Figure 5-8, the subject private company is an excellent performer, and its fundamentals suggest that it should be priced above median levels for the guideline group.

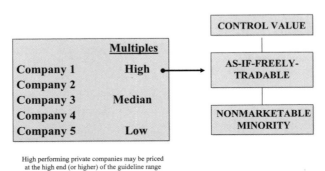

Figure 5-8

Below Median Pricing. Sometimes it is the case that fundamental comparisons between a guideline group of public companies and a private company will indicate that a private's performance and expectations fall short of that of the public group. This could be a result of higher risk or an outlook for slower growth or both. The example above regarding pricing at the first quartile illustrates this concept.

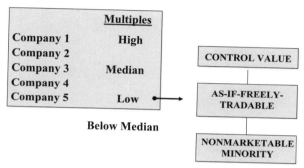

Figure 5-9

Below the Range of Guideline Multiples. In some cases, it is quite possible that comparisons of a private company with selected guideline companies suggest pricing below the range of pricing for the public group. While some would argue that the group might not be sufficiently comparable to the private company for appropriate comparison, such situations do arise. In such cases, the selected pricing multiples should be below the range of the public multiples.

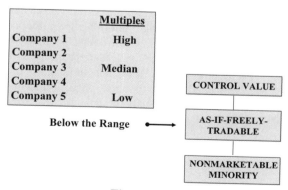

Figure 5-10

Figure 5-11 summarizes the comparisons we have just seen, depicting all four situations on a single chart. Private companies are priced above median, at the median, below the median, and below the range of the public guideline multiples.

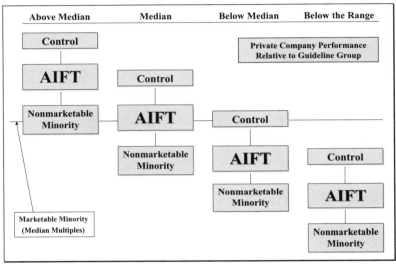

Figure 5-11

It should be clear that the decision to make fundamental adjustments is important in the valuation process when comparisons with public guideline groups are being made. In effect, fundamental adjustments adjust the level of the levels of value for private companies. The horizontal line indicates the marketable minority level of pricing indicated by median (or average) multiples for guideline public groups. The application of a fundamental adjustment, whether positive or negative, shifts the "levels of value" for a private company to its appropriate position relative to the public group. From this shifted level, the application of an appropriate marketability discount will yield an appropriate conclusion at the nonmarketable minority level. Similarly, if it is appropriate to adjust the as-if-freely-traded value by a control premium, an appropriate control value indication will result only if the private company "levels of value" is shifted to its appropriate level by the application of a fundamental adjustment.

The Double-Dipping Argument

Fundamental adjustments are made based on differences in risk and expected growth. Differences in margin performance, revenue per employee, etc. already are reflected in earnings or cash flow. Such differences would normally be priced by applying unadjusted multiples, particularly if risk and expected growth are considered identical.

For example, assume that the median margin of EBITDA to sales is 15% for a public guideline group, and that the median EBITDA multiple is 10x. The implied multiple of total capital to sales is therefore 150% (15% x 10). If a company with similar risk and growth prospects has an EBITDA margin of 10%, the implied total capital to sales multiple is 100% if the median multiple is applied (10% x 10). The valuation penalty of lower earnings is already present without considering a fundamental adjustment. Applying a fundamental adjustment for lower profit margins would add another penalty and, therefore, could be described as double-dipping.

The potential for potential double-dipping can be alleviated by appropriate screening of public guideline companies for similar performance characteristics as the subject.

Analysts should always test the reasonableness of valuation conclusions by making appropriate comparisons with their selected guideline group. It is often the case that individual adjustments can be questioned, but that the ultimate conclusion may be quite reasonable in relationship to the selected guideline group.

"MARKETABILITY DISCOUNTS" FOR CONTROLLING INTERESTS?

Some appraisers have applied marketability discounts to controlling interests of companies. We saw in Chapter 3 that there is no conceptual basis for a marketability discount at the enterprise level. By way of brief review, it is the present value of expected future cash flows that generate enterprise value. If control over (and the cash flows) are being transferred, there is no basis for discounting those flows for their lack of marketability. Such discounting is an incorrect application of the concept of the marketability discount applicable to minority interests.

When appraisers resort to the use of a so-called "marketability discount" applicable to a controlling interest, it is quite likely that they are using such a discount in place of the more theoretically appropriate fundamental adjustment. When faced with value indications that are obviously too high, most appraisers will attempt to resolve the discrepancy in some fashion to reach a reasonable result. I made this observation in the 1989 ACAPM article and repeat it now – in words and in a picture.

Figure 5-12 illustrates how two different appraisers arrived at the same controlling interest value.

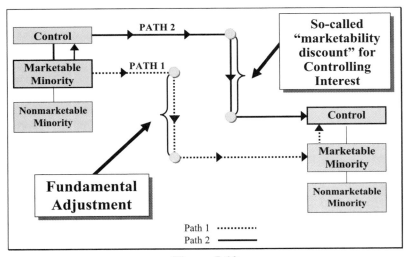

Figure 5-12

Figure 5-12 is interesting and illustrates two possible paths to the "right" controlling interest value for a private company. The first path begins with a public guideline company analysis in the left portion of the Figure. Median public multiples are developed (marketable minority) and a fundamental adjustment (a discount) is applied. The effect of the fundamental adjustment is to lower the levels of value for the private company to their as-if-freely-traded, or marketable minority level, on the right. A small control premium is added (based on appropriate analysis, of course), and the "right" value is achieved.

The second path begins with the same guideline company analysis and a marketable minority value is developed on the left side of the Figure. A control premium is added, reaching a control value, still on the left part of the Figure. The appraiser following this path realizes from common sense and experience that the resulting value is simply too high. He then applies a sizable "marketability discount" to the left side of the Figure – which is the "right" answer.

Path 1 is consistent with the Integrated Theory. Value is based on the present value of expected cash flows at an appropriate discount rate. Path 2 is inconsistent with the Integrated Theory. There is no theoretical justification for the selected "marketability discount," and there is no market evidence to support it.

Reasonable appraisal practice calls for the application of appropriate adjustments that can be justified both theoretically and in practice. Appraisers should consider this discussion, together with the theoretical considerations raised in Chapter 3 before blindly applying "marketability discounts" in controlling interest appraisals.

I am a bit less dogmatic than in years past that there cannot be taints on the marketability of private companies. Mercer Capital represented a bank holding company beginning in 1997. We solicited competitive bids and a satisfactory letter of intent was signed. Before the definitive agreement could be signed, a lawsuit was filed against the bank holding company. While it was essentially frivolous, the suit carried a $10 million claim against the company. As result of the suit, the planned merger was not completed. The suit progressed until early 2002, when it appeared that the magnitude of any resolution would be quite small. Discussions were held with a logical strategic buyer who stated that they would be able to isolate the impact of the litigation in pricing. When it became apparent that this would not be possible, we recommended to the company's board that negotiations cease until the suit was resolved.

Some months later, the lawsuit was settled at nominal cost. Negotiations were reinitiated with the strategic buyer and a deal was signed at favorable pricing. The sale closed in late March, 2003, some six years after we initially marketed the bank. During the intervening period, the company was essentially unmarketable. The good news is that management ran the bank exceedingly well during the period of "unmarketability." Substantial growth occurred and a growing dividend was paid. If an appraisal on a controlling interest basis had been necessary during this period, the taint on marketability resulting from the litigation would have to have been considered in some fashion. However, references to restricted stock studies would not have been a satisfactory means of assessing the value impact of the lawsuit.

Dr. Shannon Pratt was kind enough to review this book prior to its publication. I am extremely grateful for his review. He wrote a comment regarding the marketability discount applicable to controlling interests and approved of my including it in the text. The comment appears in the nearby sidebar.

Most of the factors raised by Dr. Pratt in the sidebar were addressed in the theoretical discussion of marketability discounts applicable to controlling interests in Chapter 3, including the issues of costs to sell (which impact proceeds, not value) and readiness to sell (which definitely influences value in terms of cash flows and their expected growth and risk).

> **Shannon Pratt Responds: Marketability Discounts Applicable to Controlling Interests**
>
> "The marketability discount applicable to controlling interests has something to do with the company not being ready for sale. In other words, Grandma is still on the payroll, the equipment has not been cleaned and shined, the accounting statements are not in shape for a buyer to see them credibly, there may be some unresolved lawsuits or questions with some of the contracts with suppliers or customers, there may be some legal work – and all of this takes management time, elapsed time, and the cost of lawyers and accountants and probably other advisors to accomplish. These are the bases on which I quantify the DLOM for controlling interests, at least partially. There may be other reasons. For example, the company may be so unique that it would be hard to find a buyer. Call them what you like, I'm sure that you agree that these are real problems of many companies and you would probably choose to call them by some other name rather than lumping them under the marketability discount, but that is just a semantic argument."

There may be unusual circumstances such as with the bank in litigation mentioned above, but such circumstances should be treated by appraisers for what they are.

In any event, we continue to caution appraisers against using the concept of a "marketability discount" applicable to controlling interests.

THE LITERATURE REGARDING FUNDAMENTAL ADJUSTMENTS

As previously discussed, we introduced the concept of fundamental adjustments in the 1989 ACAPM article and in *Valuing Financial Institutions* in 1992. I have also discussed the concept in many speeches over the years since then. The third edition of *Valuing a Business* contained a brief, conceptual discussion of the concept, although the term fundamental adjustment was not used. The

Pratt/Reilly/Schweihs text provides an example illustrating how to adjust for differences in expected growth and risk.

> We will continue with the example where the guideline company indicated price/cash flow multiple is 8, resulting in a capitalization rate for cash flow of 12.5 percent. Let us assume the comparative risk analysis leads us to conclude the discount rate for the subject company would be five percentage points higher than for the guideline companies, which would bring the capitalization rate to 17.5 percent (12.5 + 5.0 = 17.5). On the other hand, let us assume our smaller, riskier company had two percentage points higher infinitely sustainable long-term growth prospects than the guideline companies. This offsetting factor would bring the capitalization rate back town to 15.5 percent (17.5 − 2.0 = 15.5). This, then, equates to a valuation multiple of 6.5 (1 / 15.5 = 6.5).[106]

Given that the adjusted valuation multiple above is 6.5x and the beginning guideline multiple is 8.0x, the Pratt/Reilly/Schweihs analysis implies that a fundamental discount of 19% is appropriate in their example. Unfortunately, this analysis does not appear in the fourth edition of *Valuing a Business.*

Richard Goeldner, ASA has also focused on the concept of fundamental adjustments. His material on this subject includes the following:

- Goeldner, "Bridging the Gap Between Public and Private Market Multiples," *Business Valuation Review*, September 1998. Goeldner cites the 1989 ACAPM article and *Valuing Financial Institutions* and provides an algebraic and graphic analysis of equity-based fundamental adjustments.

- Goeldner, "Adjusting Market Multiples of Public Guideline Companies for the Closely Held Business," a paper presented at the 18th Annual Advanced Business Valuation Conference of the American Society of Appraisers, October 1999. In this paper, Goeldner made an initial attempt to address the fundamental adjustment in the context of total capital appraisals.

---

[106] Shannon P. Pratt, Robert F. Reilly, and Robert P. Schweihs, *Valuing a Business: The Analysis and Appraisal of Closely Held Companies*, 3rd ed. (Chicago, IL: Irwin Professional Publishing, 1996), pp. 225-226.

There is need for more investigation, thought, and analysis regarding fundamental adjustments in the application of the guideline company method. However, it should be clear that the concept exists and that consideration of fundamental adjustments is an integral part of the guideline company method.

CONCLUSION

We can summarize the discussion of fundamental adjustments with the following observations.

- Fundamental adjustments are used to account for observed differences between subject private companies and the guideline companies with which they are being compared.

- The need for fundamental adjustments arises because of differences in size, risk profile, performance, or growth expectations.

- Fundamental adjustments can be positive or negative.

- Fundamental adjustments are applicable to marketable minority multiples when using the guideline company method.

- Fundamental adjustments may be applicable to controlling interest guideline multiples.

- Fundamental adjustments can be sizeable. Appraisers need to develop methods and techniques for identifying the need for, and then justifying, the application of fundamental adjustments in the appraisal process.

- A failure to consider fundamental differences between valuation subjects and selected guideline groups of companies can result in material undervaluation or overvaluation.

- Appraisers who make selections of multiples within the range (or outside the range) of guideline company multiples – which includes virtually every appraiser based on queries at dozens of conferences – are embracing the concept of the fundamental adjustment.

In conclusion, we hope that the methods presented in this chapter will assist appraisers as they attempt to quantify and to justify fundamental adjustments relative to guideline company multiples. Finally, we hope that this chapter on fundamental adjustments will prompt further consideration and reflection on this issue by others in the appraisal profession.

Chapter 6

The Adjusted Capital Asset Pricing Model

INTRODUCTION

We have discussed the Gordon Model, the levels of value, and business earnings and cash flow from the viewpoint of both business enterprises (CF_e) and their shareholders (CF_{sh}). And we have discussed the importance of expectations for the growth of those cash flows (G_e) and of the expected growth in value (G_v).

This chapter focuses on the discount rate, *r*, or in practical application, R. We consider the remaining element of the Gordon Model, R, in the context of the Adjusted Capital Asset Pricing Model (ACAPM). The ACAPM provides an analytical framework within which to develop equity discount rates for the valuation of private (or public) company income streams. This framework was first introduced in *Business Valuation Review in* 1989.[107] We wrote further about the ACAPM in *Valuing Financial Institutions* in 1992, and again, in *Quantifying Marketability Discounts* in 1997.[108] As will become clear, the ACAPM is the name we have given to what others call the "build-up method" and/or Capital Asset Pricing Model (CAPM) related methods for developing discount rates and capitalization rates for business valuation applications.

---

[107] Z. Christopher Mercer, 'The Adjusted Capital Asset Pricing Model for Developing Capitalization Rates: An Extension of Previous 'Build-Up' Methodologies Based Upon the Capital Asset Pricing Model,' *Business Valuation Review*, Vol. 8, No. 4 (1989): pp. 147-156.

[108] Z. Christopher Mercer, *Valuing Financial Institutions*, (Homewood, IL: Business One Irwin, 1992), pp. 228-241, and *Quantifying Marketability Discounts* (Memphis, TN: Peabody Publishing, LP, 1997), pp. 260-267.

The logic of the Integrated Theory, together with market dynamics, suggests that the remaining element of the Gordon Model, the discount rate, would be the same or similar for business enterprises at the marketable minority and control (financial and strategic) levels of value. This can be seen in the expanded levels of value chart from Chapter 3. The Integrated Theory allows for the potential that strategic buyers may price enterprise valuations based on their own discount rates, rather than on the discount rate of the investment. However, as discussed earlier, strategic buyers should value acquisitions based on their own discount rates (considering $R_s < R_{mm}$) only in competition with other strategic buyers and for their own, unique and strategic reasons.

Figure 6-1 recaps the conceptual math of the Integrated Theory in order to place our discussion of the Adjusted Capital Asset Pricing Model into proper perspective.

	Conceptual Math	Relationships	Value Implications
Strategic Control Value	$\dfrac{CF_{e(c,s)}}{R_s - [G_{mm} + G_s]}$	$CF_{e(c,s)} \geq CF_{e(c,f)}$ $G_s \geq 0$ $R_s \leq R_{mm}$	$V_{e(c,s)} \geq V_{e(c,f)}$
Financial Control Value	$\dfrac{CF_{e(c,f)}}{R_f - [G_{mm} + G_f]}$	$CF_{e(c,f)} \geq CF_{e(mm)}$ $G_f \geq 0$ $R_f = R_{mm}$ (+/- a little)	$V_{e(c,f)} \geq V_{mm}$
Marketable Minority Value	$\dfrac{CF_{e(mm)}}{R_{mm} - G_{mm}}$	$G_v = R_{mm}$	V_{mm}
Nonmarketable Minority Value	$\dfrac{CF_{sh}}{R_{hp} - G_v}$	$CF_{sh} \leq CF_{e(mm)}$ $G_v \leq G_{mm}$ $R_{hp} \geq R_{mm}$	$V_{sh} \leq V_{mm}$

Figure 6-1

This chapter assumes a basic knowledge of the Capital Asset Pricing Model and the build-up method and is designed to address practical concerns and issues in discount rate and capitalization rate development. Some of the more popular theoretical issues and controversies are rendered moot in the face of the actual practice of discount rate development, where the range of judgment can be broad, indeed. For this reason, a section addressing Judgment and Reasonableness and the ACAPM is included following the discussion of the ACAPM itself.

COMMON QUESTIONS

1. When applying the DCF method, is the appropriate measure of benefits for discounting supposed to be net income or net cash flow?

2. How can business appraisers test the reasonableness of their valuation assumptions and conclusions?

3. When capitalizing net income versus net cash flow, should adjustment factors to r, the discount rate, be applied?

THE ADJUSTED CAPITAL ASSET PRICING MODEL

The Adjusted Capital Asset Pricing Model combines elements of the build up or summation methodologies, which have commonly been used to derive earnings capitalization rates for closely held securities, with those of the Capital Asset Pricing Model. The CAPM was first developed by W. F. Sharpe in a seminal article that introduced a theoretical framework now widely used in the valuation of publicly traded securities.[109]

---

[109] W. F. Sharpe, "Capital Asset Prices: A Theory of Market Equilibrium Under Conditions of Risk," *Journal of Finance*, Vol. 19 (1964): pp. 425-442.

Historical Evolution of ACAPM

Until the latter 1980s, published build-up methodologies attempted to develop capitalization rates for closely held companies by adding together the components of the required rate of return for a particular situation.[110] These methods, referred to as "summation methodologies," typically used four components of a required rate of return to develop capitalization rates:

1. A "risk-free" rate of return (usually measured by a U.S. Treasury bond of appropriate maturity).

2. An "equity premium" over the risk-free rate determined by examining the public market for equity securities in general.

3. A specific company risk premium (which could include what some appraisers refer to as a "size premium") based upon the analyst's examination in each particular valuation situation; and, possibly,

4. An estimate of expected inflation (to eliminate the inflation rate expectation embedded in the risk-free rate).

The early summation methods did not include specific consideration of expected nominal earnings growth, but they were the precursors of the buildup method currently used by many appraisers, which reduces the discount rate by a fifth factor, the expected nominal growth of earnings, in the development of capitalization rates.

It should be clear that both the early summation methods (#1 to #4 above) and the build-up method (#1 to #3, less expected growth of earnings) were based, at least in part, on the Capital Asset Pricing Model.

---

[110] The summation methods and early build-up methods are discussed in: Z. Christopher Mercer, "The Adjusted Capital Asset Pricing Model for Developing Capitalization Rates: An Extension of Previous 'Build-Up' Methodologies Based Upon the Capital Asset Pricing Model," *Business Valuation Review*, Vol. 8, No. 4 (1989): pp. 147-156.

Overview of the Capital Asset Pricing Model (CAPM)

The Capital Asset Pricing Model was offered as an explanation of the relationship between risk and expected returns in the public markets. The essence of the CAPM is expressed in the expected return for an individual security, as seen in Equation 6-1:

$$ER_i = RFR + beta_i(MR - RFR)$$

Equation 6-1

In this equation:

1. ER_i is the expected return on an equity security$_i$.

2. **RFR** is the risk-free rate.

3. *beta$_i$* is a measure of the systematic (or non-diversifiable) risk of a particular publicly traded security, considering both the correlation and volatility of the subject security relative to the broader market (the S&P 500, for example). In other words, *beta* attempts to measure the riskiness of a particular public security in relationship to the broader market.

4. **MR** is the expected return on an investment in the market portfolio (the S&P 500 is often used as a proxy), or the expected return of the market.

5. **(MR - RFR)** is the expected premium in return from an investment in the market portfolio over and above the risk-free rate.

According to the security market line equation (discussed in every basic finance text), the expected return on any security is proportional to its systematic risk. In other words, as systematic risk (*beta*) increases, the expected return (the risk-free rate plus the product of *beta* and the market premium) also increases.

That portion of the security's volatility which is not related to market movements is called *unsystematic risk*. In theory, unsystematic risk can be diversified away by holding a sufficiently large number of assets whose returns are not perfectly correlated with each other. In other words, the *alphas* in a diversified portfolio will sum to zero, with unexpected favorable events in some securities offsetting unexpected unfavorable events in others.[111] CAPM, therefore, considers only that portion of a security's volatility that can be correlated with the volatility of the market.

Sensitivity to the market is called *systematic risk* and is measured in the CAPM by *beta*. A *beta* of 1.0 for a security means that a given percentage change in the return on the market is expected to correspond with the same percentage change in the return for the security. For a security with a *beta* of less than 1.0, expected changes in the return will be less volatile than those of the market. For example, the value of a given stock with a *beta* of 0.80 might be expected to rise or fall only 0.8% when the overall market rises or falls by 1.0%.[112]

As with any theoretical model, there are several underlying assumptions of the CAPM. These are summarized in most any finance text and include:[113]

1. Investors are interested in maximizing terminal wealth over identical time horizons.

2. Investors are risk averse. They seek to hold diversified portfolios of securities (so that unsystematic risk can be diversified away).

3. Borrowing and lending costs are identical, and investors can borrow or lend at the risk-free rate of interest.

4. There are no investor-related taxes and no transactions costs.

5. Investor expectations are homogeneous with respect to the markets.

6. All assets are perfectly divisible and salable in perfectly liquid markets.

7. Investors are price-takers, and their market activities are assumed not to be able to influence the market prices of securities.

---

[111]   Note that the CAPM equation expresses the *expected return* for the subject security. The *actual return* in any given period will, of course, differ from the expected return due to unforeseeable factors. This difference, known as *alpha*, may be positive, negative, or zero.

[112]   This discussion should not be interpreted to suggest that company-specific risks do not exist for individual public securities. They do. Nor should it be interpreted to suggest that investors in public securities do not care about these risks. They do. The theory of diversification, for which there are logical and mathematical proofs, suggests that in a properly diversified portfolio of publicly traded stocks (in a reasonably efficient market), the adverse consequences of bad things happening to certain stocks in the portfolio will, on balance, be offset buy good things happening to others, leaving the investor with the beta-adjusted expected return of the portfolio.

[113]   Investment, corporate finance and valuation texts too numerous to cite contain discussions of the underlying assumptions of the CAPM.

Clearly, not all of the CAPM assumptions hold when investors are considering purchasing or selling interests of closely held companies. Time horizons differ, portfolios may not be diversified, borrowing costs can be substantial, and investor taxes and transaction costs are real elements of consideration. Investor expectations are not homogeneous, and no markets exist for the shares of most closely held businesses. Finally, investors may or may not be able to dictate price in real transactions. Nevertheless, the CAPM has been used as a basis for developing discount rates and capitalization rates for closely held businesses and business interests for many years.

This review of the CAPM suggests that there are at least three basic issues that must be addressed in using the model to develop discount rates, and, specifically, capitalization rates for use in the valuation of non-public business enterprises.

- *Growth.* The CAPM develops a discount rate, not a capitalization rate. Growth (or G, as discussed in the context of the Gordon Model) is not directly observable in the CAPM discount rate (nor should it be). It must be separately developed.

- *Specific Risk.* CAPM assumes a diversified portfolio of investments such that unsystematic (or company-specific) risks are diversified away. When valuing the equity of closely held companies, it may not be possible to diversify away the specific risks of ownership. Indeed, one of the purposes of the appraisal process is to identify and quantify the impact on value of those risks.

- *beta.* Appraisers must come to grips with the use of *beta* in practical application. One way that appraisers have dealt with the concept of *beta* is to assume that it is 1.0x when building up discount rates. Since this assumption is not always appropriate, the use of *beta* must be carefully considered.

Developing the Adjusted Capital Asset Pricing Model

The ACAPM replaces the summation method's estimate of inflation with an estimate of future earnings growth for a subject company, expressed in nominal terms in order to include expected inflation. The ACAPM also borrows the *beta* statistic from the original Capital Asset Pricing Model in the form of an estimated industry *beta* (when there is a well-developed market for companies in the subject company's industry) in order to reflect the risk of the subject company's industry relative to the overall market.

The CAPM assumes, in effect, that specific (unsystematic) risk associated with any given stock is eliminated through the diversification of an investor's portfolio. The restrictive assumption of adequate diversification is unrealistic when considering investments in closely held companies. For owners of controlling interests of closely held businesses, their interests typically account for major, undiversified portions of their wealth. This lack of diversification cannot normally be remedied by selling interests (the larger interest cannot be subdivided into smaller, minority pieces without diminishing their values, and there is no ready market for the interests) and diversifying. In addition, purchasers of such controlling interests will consider such specific risks, regardless of their degree of diversification elsewhere.

Similarly, both buyers and sellers of illiquid minority interests acknowledge the impact of non-diversifiable risks even if they are otherwise diversified in their portfolios.

In the practical application of the ACAPM, the neutral assumption of a *beta* of 1.0 is often made. Some writers attempt to distinguish between using build-up methods with no beta (which is an effective assumption of using a beta of 1.0) and the CAPM-related discount rate, where beta statistics different from 1.0 may be applied. This method is sometimes referred to as simply the build-up method. The inference is that the closely held stock has the same expected volatility as the market index used in deriving the market equity premium over the risk-free rate.[114] This assumption of beta being 1.0 is quite reasonable in appropriate circumstances.

---

[114] I do not have a problem with anyone making a distinction between a straightforward build-up method and a CAPM-related build-up. But we should all recognize that both have the same source and that the only difference between the two is the implicit assumption in the former that *beta* equals 1.0x.

Jay E. Fishman, Shannon P. Pratt, J. Clifford Griffith and D. Keith Wilson, *Guide to Business Valuations*, 14th ed. (Fort Worth, TX: Practitioners Publishing Company, 2004) Volume 1, Chapter 5.

Shannon P. Pratt, *Cost of Capital: Estimation and Applications*, 2nd ed. (Hoboken, NJ: John Wiley & Sons, 2002) Chapters 8-9.

Shannon P. Pratt, Robert F. Reilly, and Robert P. Schweihs, *Valuing a Business: The Analysis and Appraisal of Closely Held Companies*, 4th ed. (New York, NY: McGraw-Hill, 2000) Chapter 9.

The application of a *beta* of other than 1.0 in valuing the stock of a closely held company under the ACAPM can be considered when there is a reasonable group of guideline public companies with historically stable and closely correlated *beta*s from which to derive a meaningful industry average *beta*. In the alternative, the appraiser may determine an appropriate beta through analysis of one or more industry groups.

The ACAPM discount rate, R_{ACAPM}, is developed from the theoretical base of the CAPM and practical experience. R_{ACAPM} is presented symbolically in Equation 6-2, with the symbolic notation discussed below:[115]

$$R_{ACAPM} = RFR + \textit{beta} \times (LSP - RFR) + SSP + SCR$$

Systematic Risks	*Unsystematic Risks.* The
The CAPM Expected Return from Equation 6-1	non-diversifiable risks of private company ownership in excess of CAPM measure of unsystematic risk

Equation 6-2

The terms in Equation 6-2 are defined briefly here and in more detail below:

1. R_{ACAPM} is the ACAPM discount rate.

2. **RFR** is the same risk-free rate considered above in the introduction of the CAPM.

3. ***beta*** is the relevant beta statistic applicable for the particular private company being valued.

4. **LSP** is the historical return of larger capitalization stocks in the public market place. It is analogous to MR, or the return of the market, above.

---

[115] The following equation should clarify that the build up method and the ACAPM are conceptually the same:

$$R_{Buildup} = RFR + (1.0) \times (LSP-RFR) + SSP + SCR$$

The build up method is precisely the ACAPM method under the assumption of *beta* equal to 1.0x.

5. **SSP** is the small stock premium, or, historically, the average return of smaller capitalization stocks followed by Ibbotson Associates.

6. **SCR** is any additional specific company risks associated with an investment in a closely held enterprise.

The sum of SSP and SCR includes all the risks (in addition to those of CAPM) associated with a private enterprise. As far as we can tell from historical research, the first, published discussion of the concept of SSP was prepared by Roger J. Grabowski, ASA.[116] The Grabowski text suggested two analytical approaches for developing equity discount rates.

The first method began with an average stock portfolio return of 16% to 18% (in the example) and added increments of return for the example company's "small financial size," for it being a "one product company," and for the "risk in potential decline in needlepoint." By way of perspective, the example valuation date was 1983 and long-term Treasuries were yielding 10%. The text also indicated: "Stockholders of an average diversified stock portfolio expect to receive approximately a 16% to 18% equity return."

The second method was based on CAPM using the following formula:

$$k = R_f + beta(R_m - R_f) + a$$

R_f is the risk-free rate, *beta* is the beta coefficient for the stock, and R_m is the return on a representative market index. The *a* is the stock's *alpha* factor, or "the premium for risk specific to a single stock or industry." In other words, Grabowski's *a* factor was the sum of SSP and SCR in Equation 6-2.

These methods were clearly better stated than any other source we have seen prior to 1989. I wish I had seen this publication in the 1980s. It would have helped clarify our thinking on discount rates and capitalization rate development. The Grabowski paper is the clearest pre-1990 exposition of moving toward an Adjusted Capital Asset Pricing Model we have seen.

---

[116] Grabowski, Roger J. (developer), *Closely Held Corporations Valuation* (1984: Steven C. Dilley's Tax Workshops, Inc.), pp. 81-83.

Recent research regarding SSP indicates that the size effect suggested by the Small Stock Premium can be further refined. This research is at least partially cited below. At this point, however, we note that an appraiser could have properly specified the sum of SSP and SCR based on knowledge, experience and judgment, before the availability of such research. If more current research suggests that the appropriate size premium is less than (or greater than) the Ibbotson Small Stock Premium, the implication is that the appraiser would have to increase (or decrease) SCR in order to achieve reasonable appraisal results. Available research sets the framework for the exercise of judgment.[117]

Prior to research refining the magnitude of the size premium, there was no direct market evidence directly supporting the magnitude of SCR. Subsequent to the publication of this research, there is still no direct market evidence directly supporting the magnitude of SCR. So whether a generalized small stock premium or a more refined size premium is used, the appraiser must still estimate SCR in the context of the base discount rate employed. Recall the frequent guidance of Shannon Pratt and others (including me): *no premium or discount has meaning unless the base to which it is applied is specified.* Appraisers who refuse to recognize the impact of the size base (SSP) on the discount rate (R_{ACAPM}) may find themselves in the unenviable position of being theoretically correct but absolutely wrong.

The ACAPM "builds" a capitalization rate for application to closely held businesses based on the theoretical base of CAPM and practical experience. The equation specifying the ACAPM for a particular closely held security when using the S&P 500 as the indicator of "the market" is shown in Equations 6-3 and 6-4:

$$CR_{ACAPM} = R_{ACAPM} - G_e$$

Equation 6-3

---

[117] A cynic might comment here that it seems as if the hypothetical appraiser of this paragraph already knew the answer, so why go to the bother of building up the discount rate – just specify it straight away. The measured response to this observation is that appraisers do not make valuation judgments in a vacuum. On the one hand, we observe historical rates of return as used in the build-up of the Adjusted Capital Asset Pricing Model. On the other hand, we observe transactional values in the marketplace for enterprises. Real world market evidence, then, provides a check regarding the reasonableness of selected small company (SSP) and/or specific company risks (SCR).

$$CR_{ACAPM} = \underbrace{RFR + beta \ x \ (LSP - RFR) + SSP + SCR} - G_e$$

The ACAPM Discount Rate

Equation 6-4

Ongoing Earning Power and Theoretical/Practical Comments

Equation 6-4 is used to develop the ACAPM capitalization rate, or CR_{ACAPM}, which is then used to convert an estimate of earning power into an indication of value. In other words, dividing an estimate of earning power by a capitalization rate develops a value indication (Value = Earnings / Capitalization Rate). As we have previously seen, the formula of Value = Earnings / Capitalization Rate (functionally equivalent to the generalized valuation model of Value = Earnings x Multiple) is a derivation of the Gordon Model.

Finance texts often include the mathematical proof that the present value of a perpetual (no growth) income stream is Value = [Dividend / k], where k is an appropriate required rate of return for a dividend income stream. It can be further proven that if the income stream is growing at a constant percentage rate, the formula reduces to the Gordon Model, where Value = [Dividend x (1+g)] / (k-g), where g is the constant percentage growth rate to be applied to the initial dividend. If the income stream is changed to an estimate of earnings (DPO = 100%), this basic formula becomes: Value = [Earnings x (1+g)] / (R-g), where R is a required rate of return appropriate for the selected earnings stream.

Theory and practice can sometimes seem to diverge. When this happens, it is important for the appraiser to understand both the theory and the practice in order to achieve reasonable valuation results:

- The theory cited above calls for capitalization of *next year's earnings* (or dividends). However, in practice, many appraisers use ACAPM capitalization rates for application to their current estimate of earning power or weighted averages of historical and/or expected earnings.

- At Mercer Capital, we refer to the earnings measure selected for capitalization with the ACAPM capitalization rate as *ongoing earning power*. Earnings are normalized for unusual and/or non-recurring items and for discretionary expenses quite often associated with controlling shareholders. Then, depending on the pattern of adjusted historical earnings and, perhaps, the near-term outlook for the future, earnings for various periods are weighted to derive a weighted average of earnings, which is referred to as ongoing earning power.

- The *g* in the formula above is a long-term earnings growth rate and may bear little resemblance to the actual projection of next year's income if, indeed, a projection exists at all. In the valuation of many closely held companies, particularly smaller ones where no forecasts are available, the analyst may be more comfortable capitalizing an earning power estimate based on historical earnings (as reflective of future earning power).

- Theoretical purists sometimes disagree with this practical simplification of earnings capitalization methodologies. Not inflating earnings by next year's *g*, which, other things being equal, provides lower indications of value and could be considered to be an element of conservatism sorely needed in many valuations.[118]

- The alternative assumption is that the analyst, grounded in his or her earnings estimate, assumes that it is applicable to next year, from which level earnings are assumed to grow at the assumed long-term growth rate of *g*. This is an important point and deserves amplification. The single period income capitalization method is a summary discounted cash flow method (as discussed at length in Chapter 1). In employing such a method, the appraiser must specify the base level of earnings or cash flow that is to be capitalized *and* the expected growth rate of those cash flows. In so doing, he or she may intentionally specify a base level of earnings other than $[E \times (1 + g)]$ as more appropriate in applying a shorthand DCF method. For example, an appraiser may specify pre-tax earnings (another equity-based earnings stream) or total capital earnings stream like earnings before interest and taxes (EBIT) or earnings before interest, taxes, depreciation, and amortization (EBITDA).

---

[118] An "element of conservatism" is meant to relate to the *valuation process* generally and not to any particular valuation conclusion. I had to make this point in a trial a number of years ago when a cross-examining attorney attempted to criticize my use of the ACAPM method by suggesting that from the point of view of his client, who desired a higher valuation conclusion, my methodology was anything but conservative.

- The generalized valuation model (the Gordon Model) assumes that all earnings are distributed to shareholders, or DPO = 100%. This is another reason that the *g* used in the ACAPM capitalization rate should be a long-term growth rate.

- A final point should be made. When using the ACAPM as a single-period income capitalization method, it is entirely appropriate to capitalize the net earnings of business enterprises. Net cash flow, if less than net earnings, presumes a level of reinvestment that is fueling growth of earnings above G_e.

Suffice it to say that in practice, many analysts use estimates of earning power based on the last year (or trailing 12 months), or averages or weighted averages of recent years' (and expected) earnings in the application of single-period income capitalizations under the Income Approach. And many analysts quite reasonably apply the ACAPM capitalization rate to the net earnings of business enterprises. However used, appraisers should explain the ultimate reasonableness of their conclusions when employing the ACAPM in the context of alternative investments, market multiples, or implied returns.

THE COMPONENTS OF THE ACAPM

Having specified the Adjusted Capital Asset Pricing Model and discussed its historical development and practical issues raised by its use, it is appropriate to examine the components of the model in some detail. Repeating Equation 6-4, the components of the ACAPM capitalization rate include:

$$CR_{ACAPM} = \underbrace{RFR + beta \times (LSP - RFR) + SSP + SCR}_{\text{The ACAPM Discount Rate}} - G_e$$

1. CR_{ACAPM} is the capitalization rate derived from application of the ACAPM. Note that if G is excluded from the equation, we have the ACAPM discount rate that can be used to discount discretely forecasted earnings or cash flows to the present.

2. **RFR** is a risk-free rate. This rate is typically the risk-free rate available in the marketplace at or about the valuation date. An intermediate or long-term Treasury yield is most often used as a measure of the base opportunity cost of a long-term investment in a closely held business. However, as will be discussed below, some analysts have suggested using a shorter-term Treasury rate in actual practice. Many analysts assume that the appropriate risk-free rate is the long-term (20-year) Treasury yield (to maturity). Others argue for a composite long-term Treasury yield. For purposes of this discussion, RFR is a long-term risk-free rate considered appropriate by the analyst.

3. *beta* is an appropriate industry *beta*, if available. Otherwise it is often assumed to be 1.0, or "the risk of the market." *beta* is applied to the excess return of the market (and not to the small stock return.)[119,120] This latter assumption (of beta = 1.0) is particularly used in the valuation of small businesses or in cases where no group of sufficiently comparable public companies is identified. In such cases, there may be no objective basis to estimate beta. However, analysts dealing with diverse industry groups may find that utilization of an industry beta (or a related industry beta, if a directly related group is not available) can be helpful in adjusting capitalization factors for certain industries with known lower- or higher-than-market risk profiles.

4. **LSP** is the historical premium over the risk-free return attributable to investments in larger capitalization stocks. It is the same return indicated by (MR-RFR) above in the CAPM. This return measure is most frequently developed by business appraisers based on analysis of historical rate-of-return data provided by Ibbotson Associates.[121] In the terminology supplied by Ibbotson Associates, LSP is the long-term premium return of the S&P 500 as a measure of the broader market (i.e., the large stock premium) over the long-term return from Treasuries.

---

[119] The 1989 ACAPM article was less than clear on this point. Thankfully, it is possible to grapple with issues, to learn in the process, and to grow professionally.

[120] No effort is made in this chapter to address the academic questions related to whether *beta* is dead or alive. For purposes of valuing closely held businesses, *beta* is very much alive. Business appraisers and market participants rely on this conceptual measure of volatility of returns in making valuation decisions every day. And they achieve reasonable results in the process.

[121] *Stocks, Bonds, Bills, and Inflation: 200x Yearbook* (Chicago: Ibbotson Associates, 200x). This is an annual book that provides historical rate-of-return information for investments over the period from 1926 to the current year.

Returns are based upon analysis of the monthly or annual returns of each series for the period 1926-200x, or for selected sub-periods.[122] In the current valuation editions, Ibbotson Associates refers to this premium as the "equity risk premium." In the current 'market results' editions, this equity premium is referred to as being derived from 'large company stocks.'[123]

In the *SBBI 2004 Yearbook* on page 31 for example, there is a chart titled "Basic Series: Summary Statistics of Annual Total Returns from 1926 to 2003."[124] The LSP would be calculated (based on the arithmetic mean) by taking the large company stock arithmetic mean return of 12.4% and subtracting the arithmetic mean long-term government bond return of 5.8%. This yields an "equity risk premium" or an LSP of 6.6%. This compares with a LSP of 5.0% if calculated based on the geometric mean returns (10.4% minus 5.4%). The LSP based on a rolling average of multi-year holding periods (1926-2001) (cited below with Julius and Copeland) of 6.0% often turns out to be fairly close to the average of the geometric mean and arithmetic mean premiums (but will certainly be between the two). The issue of using the arithmetic or geometric mean returns in the ACAPM is reserved for the discussion below regarding the sensitivity of the model to assumptions made by analysts. In terms of recommendation, analysts at Mercer Capital have employed an analysis based on rolling averages of multi-year holding periods since the mid-1990s.

5. **SSP** is the historical premium over the large stock premium attributable to investments in smaller capitalization stocks (the small stock premium). This premium reflects the fact that, on average, smaller capitalization (higher risk) stocks have yielded a premium in returns over the larger capitalization (lower risk) stocks represented by the S&P 500 Index. If the subject of the valuation is quite large it may be appropriate to use only the LSP in developing a capitalization factor using the ACAPM. When *beta* is assumed to be 1.0 and a smaller company is being valued,

---

[122] In current editions of the *Yearbook*, Ibbotson Associates refers to the return of large capitalization stocks (the S&P 500 stocks) as the *large stock premium*. In earlier editions, the term *common stock premium* was used.

[123] *Stocks, Bonds, Bills, and Inflation: Valuation Edition 2001 Yearbook* (Chicago: Ibbotson Associates, 2001), and *Stocks, Bonds, Bills, and Inflation: 2001 Yearbook Market Results for 1926-2000* (Chicago: Ibbotson Associates, 2001).

[124] *Stocks, Bonds, Bills, and Inflation: 2004 Yearbook* (Chicago: Ibbotson Associates, 2004), p. 33.

the small stock premium over Treasuries may be used as a single premium, comprising the sum of (LSP + SSP).

SSP can be calculated as above with LSP by reference to *SBBI 2004 Yearbook* on page 33. As employed in the ACAPM, SSP is the excess return of smaller capitalization stocks, or the historical average (arithmetic, geometric, or rolling average) returns of smaller capitalization stocks over the average returns of large capitalization stocks. So we can calculate the arithmetic mean SSP by subtracting the historical average market return (12.4%) from the small capitalization company return (17.5%), which is 5.1%. Similarly, the geometric mean SSP can be calculated (12.7% - 10.4%) as 2.3%. The corresponding multi-year rolling average return is 3.0%.

As in many areas of valuation, there has been considerable research and analysis on the issue of risk premia related to the size of companies being valued. It is not our intent to discuss or analyze this size-related information in detail, but to make appraisers aware of the growing research on the issue. Beginning with the *SBBI 1993 Yearbook*, Ibbotson Associates published a table showing decile portfolios of the New York Stock Exchange indicating the relative market capitalizations of the various deciles as well as the identification and market capitalization of the largest company in each decile.[125] Ibbotson Associates has provided increasing information about the impact of firm size and returns in subsequent issues of the *Yearbook*. In the most recent editions, Ibbotson Associates has broken the tenth decile into deciles 10a and 10b, for further delineation of the size effect.[126]

Roger J. Grabowski, ASA and David W. King, CFA, currently with Standard & Poors Corporate Value Consulting, have extended the concept of size analysis by segregating the New York Stock Exchange into 25 size categories. After screening for companies with established histories by sales, publicly traded for five years, positive EBITDA and book value, and ratios of debt to total capital on a market value basis of less than 80%, the remainder of actively traded stocks are placed into

---

[125] *Stocks, Bonds, Bills, and Inflation: 1993 Yearbook* (Chicago: Ibbotson Associates, 1993), and subsequent editions.

[126] The size effect as measured by Ibbotson Associates is based on market capitalization alone. This measure is subject to criticism of circularity. Do firms have small market capitalizations because they are small in an absolute sense or because they may be poor performers? The answer is, of course, yes.

these 25 size categories, including a category for high financial risk companies. Grabowski and King considered several measures of size in addition to market capitalization, including the five-year average operating margin, return on equity, market value and book value of equity, sales and assets. Versions of this study have been presented at a number of appraisal conferences, and the study is available for sale.[127]

Pratt's *Cost of Capital* (2nd ed.) provides a discussion of the "size effect" and provides citations to available studies.[128] This Pratt text also provides a summary of the Grabowski and King study as part of its Chapter 11.

As noted earlier, SSP and SCR must both be estimated in developing ACAPM discount rates. Suppose we know the following:

$$SSP + SCR = 5.0\%$$

Appraiser #1 estimates this portion of the discount rate as:

$$SSP\ (3.0\%) + SCR\ (2.0\%) = 5.0\%$$

Appraiser #2 uses a refined size estimate reflecting the general range of market capitalization of the subject company as:

$$Size\ (1.5\%) + SCR\ (3.5\%) = 5.0\%$$

---

[127] See the *2004 S&P Corporate Value Consulting/Risk Premium Report*, now updated through December 2003. This study is available at www.ibbotson.com at the Cost of Capital Center. The first article was: Roger J. Grabowski and David W. King, "New Evidence on Equity Returns and Company Risk," *Business Valuation Review*, Vol. 18, No. 3 (1999): pp. 112-130. A subsequent article provided a revision to the first analysis. See Roger Grabowski and David King, "New Evidence on Equity Returns and Company Risk: A Revision," *Business Valuation Review*, Vol. 19, No. 1 (2000): pp. 32-43. When originally published, Grabowski and King were with PriceWaterhouseCoopers. Roger Grabowski and David King, "Equity Risk Premium," *Valuation Strategies*, September/October 2003, pp. 4-11.

[128] Shannon P. Pratt, *Cost of Capital Estimation and Applications*, 2nd ed. (New York: John Wiley & Sons, Inc., 2002). See especially Chapter 11, "Size Effect," p. 90.

Both achieved an appropriate result; however Appraisers #1 and #2 estimated SCR from a different base. Further refinements regarding the size premium as it relates to enterprises of differing sizes will make it crucial for appraisers to focus carefully on SCR and ultimately, on proving the reasonableness of their conclusions. It should be apparent that the indicated refinement in the size effect above should have no impact on the ultimate discount rate, but rather reflects an allocation of a total premium between the two categories (SSP and SCR).

6. **SCR** is the cumulative amount of incremental risk over and above risk not previously captured with the LSP and the SSP that is appropriate for the valuation subject. The selection of this risk premium (or the accumulation of risk factors that comprise SCR) is an abstract concept. Conceptually, a specific company is being compared indirectly with a universe of relatively small public companies. Direct comparative data on this universe of stocks are not available, so the analyst must be able to conceptualize the risk profile of the selected universe.[129] One of the factors often cited by appraisers in selecting a specific risk premium is the small size of a subject entity in relationship to the basket of public companies with which it is implicitly being compared. In fact, the size-related research reflects an effort to help appraisers quantify this aspect of specific company risk. So appraisers who use information from the highest deciles in Ibbotson's data, or the smallest of the categories from Grabowski and King must be careful not to overestimate (or underestimate) SCR.

The specific risk factors enumerated in the 1989 ACAPM article included key personnel issues (or lack of management capability or depth), absolute size, financial structure (leverage), diversifications (related to products, geography, or customers), earnings (margins, stability and predictability), and other risks associated with a particular company. For multi-million-dollar companies that have been in business for several years, the total SCR for all comparisons may run as low as zero (or even less than zero) to as high as 8-10% or more. SCR may be even less than zero for closely held businesses that are larger than the smaller capitalization stocks considered in the development of SSP, but smaller than the large capitalization stocks in the broad market. Further research on size may help appraisers specify this factor.

---

[129] SCR premiums in enterprise valuations are analogous to investor-specific risk premiums that must be estimated when valuing shareholder-level cash flows.

The selection of the total SCR for a specific valuation assignment requires experience, common sense, and judgment in the context of a detailed analysis of the subject company, as well as a general working knowledge of the public securities markets.

The ACAPM Discount Rate.   The components of the ACAPM capitalization rate to this point yield the ACAPM discount rate. Many appraisers use the ACAPM discount rate (or build-up rates or CAPM-related rates) in discounted cash flow analysis or as a step in developing the weighted average cost of capital (WACC) for total capital (debt-free) valuation methods.

7. G_e is the estimated long-term growth rate for the subject company's earnings. ACAPM expresses growth in nominal terms. The implied growth forecast is expressed in terms of annual percentage growth and should be reasonably achievable for at least the next five to 10 years or more. In theory, of course, G_e is a perpetuity assumption; however, in practice the expected G_e might be realistically higher for a discrete forecast period of up to 10 years or so and then lower thereafter.

Having said this, in practice, analysts seldom use G_e assumptions in excess of 10% in single period income capitalization.[130] If near-term growth is expected to be relatively high and then followed by slower growth, it is possible to use a two (or more) stage analysis to develop G_e. Assume, for example, that the analyst forecasts that earnings will grow at about 15% per year for the next five years and then would grow at 6% for the next 40 years (as an estimate of perpetuity). The blended growth rate for this 45 year period is 7.0%.[131] As noted in earlier chapters, this blended G_e would not reflect the higher level of cash flows in the first five years (relative to constant growth at 7.0%), but that is the nature of single-income capitalization methods. Issues like this in valuation are one good reason that analysts often employ more than one valuation method in arriving at their valuation conclusions. Note also that the G_e

---

[130]   Because of the general sensitivity of single period income capitalizations to changes in G, it is often a topic of debate in litigated matters.

[131]   Note that this is the arithmetic average return for 45 years, or

$$\frac{(5 \times 15\%) + (6 \times 40\%)}{45}$$

This technique may be useful for single-period income capitalizations, but would tend to overstate growth if used to develop the terminal value in a DCF method.

of the ACAPM is related to the analyst's estimate of ongoing earning power $(G_e \leq G_v \leq R)$.

As noted earlier, G_e is, at least theoretically, a perpetuity concept. Some appraisers insist that G_e should be sustainable for periods of 20 years or more. Conceptually, both SCR and G_e should relate to a company under normal operating circumstances. If the analyst overestimates a company's growth potential and uses a high G_e, he or she has likely invoked a corollary and offsetting increase in the specific company risk factors. While it may be difficult or impossible to measure, there is a relationship between SCR and G_e, particularly at higher than normal levels of forecasted growth. Practically speaking, when the ACAPM is used in a single-period income capitalization method, the analyst may consider a G that is sustainable for five or 10 years and when there is an appropriate consideration of specific company risk. And recall the earlier discussion that G_e in application is almost always of single-digit (%) magnitude.

There are practical ways to confirm that the overall methodology is reasonably employed. For example, if an appraiser uses a high G_e and low SCR and develops a conclusion of value that would suggest that a company is worth 10 times EBITDA (if reverse-engineered to make the calculation), and companies routinely sell in an industry for 5-6x EBITDA, something is obviously wrong. Again, experience and familiarity with actual market data are essential to the development of reasonable capitalization rates.

Given these considerations, the Adjusted Capital Asset Pricing Model develops a capitalization rate based upon the analyst's review of the subject company, including its specific risk characteristics (SCR) and core earnings growth prospects (G_e), as well as an analysis of its industry risk profile relative to the market (*beta*). And the ACAPM discount rates or capitalization rates relate to the analyst's estimate of ongoing earning power, which may differ from the most current year's earnings or a specific forecast for next year's earnings.

THE ACAPM CAPITALIZATION RATE AND SENSITIVITY

The ACAPM differs from CAPM in that it attempts to develop a specific capitalization rate for a private company rather than to develop an expected total return for a publicly traded security in the context of a diversified portfolio of investments. The expected return given in the Capital Asset Pricing Model is the internal rate of return resulting from the price of the security and the future cash flows it is expected to generate. The capitalization rate derived in the ACAPM is applied to expected earning power, rather than to a series of estimated future cash flows, and thus must include an adjustment for expected earnings growth (which is an implicit forecast of future earnings or cash flows).

The ACAPM capitalization rate is converted to a price earnings multiple using Equation 6-5:

$$\text{Price/Earnings Multiple (P/E)} = 1 \,/\, \text{Capitalization Rate (CR}_{\text{ACAPM}})$$

Equation 6-5

The resulting price/earnings multiple can then be used to capitalize the analyst's estimate of ongoing net income or net cash flow using Equation 6-6:

$$\text{Value} = \text{P/E} \; \text{x} \; \text{Earnings}$$

Equation 6-6

Many appraisers seem to think of the ACAPM (or build-up methods) in a one-dimensional context. They develop a capitalization rate (or multiple) and apply it to the estimate of earning power to achieve an indication of value.

The ACAPM equation provides a broad range of price/earnings ratios under varying assumptions regarding specific company risk (SCR) and expected growth (G) for any set of assumptions with respect to RFR, LSP, SSP and *beta*. For example, we can test the sensitivity of the ACAPM capitalization factors in an example. Consider the following ACAPM capitalization rate, which we can stipulate is "valuation truth" for purposes of the following examples:

```
Adjusted Capital Asset Pricing Model
Example Capitalization Rate - Stipulated

Component                                        Term
Risk Free Rate                         5.00%     RFR
Large Stock Premium        6.0%
beta                    x    1.0                 beta
beta-adjusted LSP                      6.00%     LSP
Small Stock Premium                    3.00%     SSP
Specific Company Risk                  2.00%     SCR
                                      16.00%     R
Less: Expected Gₑ                     -6.0%      Gₑ
ACAPM Capitalization Rate             10.00%     CR
ACAPM Net Multiple (P/E)               10.0      1/CR
```

Figure 6-2

By stipulation, the capitalization rate of 10.0% derived above is 'correct' and the implied price/earnings multiple of 10.0x is appropriate. Quite often, appraisers view such a derivation of a capitalization rate as a one-dimensional exercise. However, this multiple should be viewed in the context of a matrix of multiples derived by varying the relevant assumptions. In the example below, the assumptions regarding expected growth and specific company risk are varied. The range of resulting price/earnings multiples is calculated in the top portion of Figure 6-3:

ACAPM Multiples Under Given Assumptions					
Specific Company Risk (SCR)					
	0.0%	1.0%	**2.0%**	3.0%	4.0%
G 3.0%	9.1	8.3	7.7	7.1	6.7
R 4.0%	10.0	9.1	8.3	7.7	7.1
O 5.0%	11.1	10.0	9.1	8.3	7.7
W **6.0%**	12.5	11.1	10.0	9.1	8.3
T 7.0%	14.3	12.5	11.1	10.0	9.1
H 8.0%	16.7	14.3	12.5	11.1	10.0
9.0%	20.0	16.7	14.3	12.5	11.1

% Difference from Agreed Indication					
Specific Company Risk (SCR)					
	0.0%	1.0%	**2.0%**	3.0%	4.0%
G 3.0%	-9.1%	-16.7%	7.7%	-28.6%	-33.3%
R 4.0%	0.0%	-9.1%	8.3%	-23.1%	-28.6%
O 5.0%	11.1%	0.0%	9.1%	-16.7%	-23.1%
W **6.0%**	25.0%	11.1%	0.0%	-9.1%	-16.7%
T 7.0%	42.9%	25.0%	11.1%	0.0%	-9.1%
H 8.0%	66.7%	42.9%	12.5%	11.1%	0.0%
9.0%	100.0%	66.7%	14.3%	25.0%	11.1%

Figure 6-3

With a stipulated multiple of 10.0x, the upper portion of the table indicates a range of multiples of 8.3x to 12.5x based on varying the specific risk and growth assumptions by no more than (+ or -) 1%. The lower portion of the table calculates the percentage changes from the 10.0x multiple. These range from *negative* 16.7% to positive 25.0%.

The point of this example is that seemingly small changes in estimates for SCR or G_e can generate surprisingly large changes and percentage changes in the derived multiples (and therefore, value indications derived using the derived multiples). This is a fact of life in valuation.

It is clear that there can be a considerable difference in indicated capitalization factors (and indicated values) with what might seem to be rather small differences in critical assumptions regarding specific company risk and expected growth. Note that if growth is higher and SCR is lower, the differential compounds on the high side. Similarly, if risk is over-estimated and growth is under-estimated, the differential compounds on the low side.[132]

For these reasons, we have always suggested that appraisers "prove" the reasonableness of their valuation conclusions by comparisons with market multiples, transaction multiples, or other appeals to common sense.

LEVEL OF VALUE AND EARNINGS STREAM

The capitalization rate developed using the ACAPM is applied to a subject company's estimated ongoing net earning power to develop a minority interest valuation under the assumption that its shares are freely tradable on a public market exchange. In other words, the capitalization rate developed using the ACAPM is applicable to the marketable minority interest level of value. Most valuation writers agree with this assertion. Recalling the discussion from the Integrated Theory, if there are no additional cash flow or earnings benefits available to financial buyers for a controlling interest in the company, the resulting indication of value may also approximate a financial control value.

In each specific application, the ACAPM capitalization rate may be further adjusted to reflect an appropriate marketability discount for the specific securities being valued if they are nonmarketable minority interests. If applicable, an appropriate control premium may be considered if the securities represent control over the subject company. In practice, many appraisers make these adjustments to their estimations of earnings at the enterprise level.

---

[132] Recall that sensitivity of conclusions to changes in key assumptions is a fact of life in business appraisal. Other things being equal, the lower the discount rate, the greater the sensitivity of resulting ACAPM multiples to small changes in risk or expected growth. Appraisers using the ACAPM as part of developing WACC should keep this fact in mind. WACCs (discount rates based on total capital, rather than equity) are lower than equity discount rates if leverage is positive, and are generally more sensitive to small changes in assumptions than equity capitalization rates.

The discussions regarding r in Chapter 3 suggest that the ACAPM capitalization rate should apply to the net income of business enterprises in single-period income capitalization methods, particularly when the analyst develops the long-term growth rate of core earnings, or G_e, for use in the capitalization rate. And the ACAPM discount rate would be applicable to the net cash flow of enterprises, particularly for periods during which earnings are expected to be retained to fuel growth (i.e., DPO < 100%).

The level of debate on this issue has been substantial, with some suggesting, rather adamantly, that r is applicable only to net cash flow, and with others, like me, suggesting that it might be applicable either to net income or to net cash flow.

Ibbotson data is collection of realized returns, which, in the aggregate, are used to estimate investors' required returns. Realized returns on portfolios of publicly traded stocks are the result of dividends paid by the portfolio companies and changes in their stock prices, and are only tangentially related to the financial performance (whether measured as cash flow or net earnings) of those portfolio companies in the context of the overall market. Therefore, discount rates derived from Ibbotson data cannot be emphatically described as applicable to either cash flow or net earnings based on such comparisons. The most important elements of a discount rate application are consistency and a clear explanation of the underlying assumptions regarding a particular application (i.e., earnings are assumed to be distributed or reinvested at the discount rate).

Ibbotson data measure market returns from stocks and bonds. Appraisers use these returns as a basis to establish required returns in valuations. The companies studied reflect a wide range of industries and companies employing a wide range of dividend payment policies (from zero to virtually all earnings over time). It should be clear from the discussions both in this chapter and Chapter 1 that the markets discount and or capitalize relevant cash flows, whether net income or net cash flow. And appraisers should do the same.

THE ACAPM AND
SHAREHOLDER LEVEL VALUATIONS

As we conclude this discussion of the Adjusted Capital Asset Pricing Model for developing enterprise level discount rates, we look now to the shareholder level valuation concepts. The *Quantitative Marketability Discount Model* (QMDM) is introduced in Chapter 7. At this point we observe:

- In the context of the Integrated Theory of Business Valuation, R_{mm} is the discount rate applicable to the marketable minority level of (normalized) enterprise cash flows. Figure 3-11 is reproduced as Figure 6-4.

	Conceptual Math	Relationships	Value Implications
Marketable Minority Value	$\dfrac{CF_{e(mm)}}{R_{mm} - G_{mm}}$	$G_v = R_{mm}$	V_{mm}

Figure 6-4

- In Chapter 3 we introduced the shareholder level of value in relationship to the marketable minority level. R_{hp} was defined as the required holding period return at the shareholder level, or conceptually:

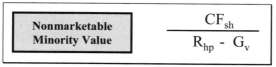

Nonmarketable Minority Value	$\dfrac{CF_{sh}}{R_{hp} - G_v}$

Figure 6-5

- R_{hp} is a function of the enterprise (ACAPM) discount rate and HPP, or the extra risk factors attributable to ownership of illiquid interests (relative to as-if or freely traded interests). We will discuss R_{hp} in more depth in Chapter 7; however, it is appropriate to see it in the context of the enterprise level ACAPM discount rate before proceeding.

$$R_{hp} = R_{mm} + HPP$$

- Finally, we can observe that to the extent that the ACAPM discount (R_{mm}) rate is sensitive to changes in assumptions, R_{hp} will be similarly sensitive, since its base is R_{mm}.

The ACAPM develops discount rates (and capitalization rates) applicable at the marketable minority interest level of value. It is therefore an appropriate base from which to develop the required holding period return of the Quantitative Marketability Discount Model, which was developed to help appraisers develop marketability discounts in the context of enterprise appraisals. The basis of comparison in the valuation of nonmarketable minority interests is the relevant universe of publicly traded securities. By beginning with the base equity discount rate of the ACAPM and adding increments of return for shareholder level risks, the subject nonmarketable minority interest is rendered comparable, from an investment viewpoint, with the relevant universe of alternative investments.

JUDGMENT AND REASONABLENESS AND THE ACAPM

Theoretical issues aside, the development of capitalization rates is enhanced by the experience, knowledge, and valuation judgment of the business appraiser. Experience is important if it is good experience. Long ago, I defined business valuation experience as "grappling with issues and growing in the process." There is a world of difference in the experience of two appraisers, where one has 10 years of grappling and growing and the other has the same year of experience repeated 10 times. Knowledge is a function of relevant experience, classroom education, seminar learning, self-learning, on-the-job training, and many other factors.

Valuation judgment is the exercise of knowledge and experience in the context of specific valuation situations. And valuation judgment is required, because the range of judgment is potentially very broad. This range can be placed into perspective in Figure 6-6, where five discount rates and capitalization rates are developed by four hypothetical appraisers and the author.

The Beginning of the Range of Judgment

In order to illustrate the beginning point of the range of appraiser judgment, we assume that all five appraisers agree on issues that are themselves matters of judgment.

- First, all appraisers use the ACAPM (or, if they prefer, a build-up method based on CAPM).

- Next, all appraisers agree that *beta* should be equal to 1.0, that company-specific risk factors require an additional risk premium of 2.0%, and that the expected long-term growth of earnings is 6%. All Treasury rates are as of November 8, 2002, which is the agreed upon valuation date.

- In addition, all appraisers agree that the appropriate time horizon for estimating the equity risk premium is 1926-2001, and that Ibbotson Associates *2002 Yearbook: Market Results for 1926-2001* is the appropriate source of rate of return data.[133]

- Finally, there is complete agreement that the expected net income of the enterprise is $1.0 million based on sales of $10 million.

Figure 6-6 illustrates the range of value indications that can be developed based solely on the appraisers' decisions related to these two questions:

- What is the appropriate Treasury rate to be used as the risk-free base rate for the build-up of a discount rate?

- Should equity risk premiums be based on arithmetic mean returns (the average of one-year returns over the horizon period), geometric returns (the cumulative return over the horizon period), or on some rolling average of returns (effectively an averaging of the arithmetic and geometric returns)? The answer to this question influences the selection of both the equity risk premium and the small stock premium.

---

[133] *Stocks, Bonds, Bills, and Inflation: 2002 Yearbook Market Results for 1926-2001* (Chicago, IL: Ibbotson Associates, 2002). The basic return figures used in this analysis are found on page 31 of this source.

With total agreement on the fundamentals of the enterprise, and near total agreement on some very important areas where judgment is exercised, one might think, regardless of the answers to the above questions, the resulting value indications for the five appraisers should be similar. However, such is not the case.

- The first appraiser is the author. The common stock and small stock premiums were developed through an analysis that effectively blends the arithmetic and geometric returns in the Ibbotson data series.[134] This appraiser uses the 20-year Treasury rate (as of November 8, 2002) as the basis for a discount rate of 15.1% and a capitalization rate of 8.1%, with a resulting price/earnings multiple of 12.4x.

- Appraiser #2 uses the 10-year Treasury rate as recommended in the second edition of the Copeland text, arguably the best-selling valuation book ever.[135] He also used the geometric mean returns for both the equity risk premium and the common stock premium as suggested by the Copeland text in the second edition. With only these changes, Appraiser #2 values the enterprise at $19.6 million, or 58% higher than Mercer.

- Appraiser #3 follows the recommendation for using the 10-year Treasury rate and the rolling average of returns as found in the third edition of the Copeland text.[136] Note that the third edition changed its recommendation to using rolling average returns from the geometric mean return recommended in the second edition. Appraiser #3's conclusion of $14.2 million is much closer to the author than Appraiser #2, who had not yet read Copeland's third edition.

---

[134]   This analysis was first set forth by Michael Julius (formerly of Mercer Capital) in "Market Returns In Rolling Multi-Year Holding Periods: An Alternative Interpretation of the Ibbotson Data," *Business Valuation Review*, Vol. 15, No. 2 (1996): pp. 57-71. Analysts at Mercer Capital began using the methodology set forth by Julius several years prior to the publication of his article in 1996.

[135]   Tom Copeland, Tim Koller, and Jack Murrin, *Valuation: Measuring and Managing the Value of Companies*, 2nd ed. (New York: John Wiley & Sons, Inc., 1995), pp. 258-264.

[136]   Tom Copeland, Tim Koller, and Jack Murrin, *Valuation: Measuring and Managing the Value of Companies*, 3rd ed. (New York: John Wiley & Sons, Inc., 2000), pp. 214-224.

- Appraiser #4 read Ibbotson Associates latest *Yearbook* and uses the 20-year Treasury rate and the 1926-2001 arithmetic mean return.[137] Appraiser #4 reached a value indication of only $9.6 million, or 23% *below* the value derived by Mercer.

- Appraiser #5 is an eclectic sort, taking guidance where he finds it and using that which he finds pleasing. Appraiser # 5 used one of the "reasonable alternatives" mentioned in both of the Copeland editions, i.e., T-Bills, as his choice the for the Treasury rate. In addition, he used the geometric mean returns as recommended in Copeland's second edition. Appraiser #5 developed a discount rate of 9.4%, a price/earnings multiple of 42x, and a conclusion of $41.7 million.

Readers should note that since the publication of the most recent issue of *Cost of Capital*, Shannon Pratt has revised his position on the issue of using the arithmetic mean. In a recent article, Dr. Pratt concluded that the use of the arithmetic mean returns tended to overstate discount rates in the current market environment and therefore, to understate value. He now suggests that the common stock premium should be about 1.25% less than the arithmetic mean.[138] In so doing, he has moved much closer to the positions of Copeland and Mercer Capital of using historical rolling average returns.

---

[137] Shannon P. Pratt, "Build-up Models," *Cost of Capital Estimation and Applications*, 2nd ed. (New York: John Wiley & Sons, Inc., 2002), pp. 57-69.

"The Long Run Perspective," *Stocks, Bonds, Bills, and Inflation: 2000 Yearbook Market Results for 1926-1999* (Chicago, IL: Ibbotson Associates, 2000).

[138] Shannon P. Pratt, "Editors Column," *Shannon Pratt's Business Valuation Update*, Vol. 10, No. 1, January 2004, p. 1. In the same Editor's Column, Pratt reported on a recent article by Roger Ibbotson and Peng Chen in which Ibbotson and Chen concluded that their equity risk premium estimates are about 1.25% lower than historical estimates. Ibbotson and Chen, "Long-Run Stock Returns: Participating in the Real Economy," *Financial Analysts Journal*, Vol. 59, No. 1 (January/February 2003), pp 88-98. Nevertheless the current guidance in the Ibbotson *Valuation Edition 2004 Yearbook* clearly recommends the use of arithmetic mean returns. (Chicago, IL, Ibbotson Associates, 2004) p. 71.

Discount Rate and Capitalization Rate Development Illustration of Beginning Range of Judgment		Copeland 2nd Edition	Copeland 3rd Edition	Ibbotson	Available Choices
Risk Free Rate Return Premium	Mercer 20 Yr Tr/ Rolling Avg Return	"Reasonable" T-Bills Rolling Avg Return	Recommended 10 Yr Tr/ Rolling Avg Return	20 Yr Tr/ Ibbotson Arithmetic	T-Bills Geometric Mean Return
Risk-Free Rates (11/08/02)	4.9%	3.9%	3.9%	4.9%	1.2%
Common Stock Premium (Ibbotson 1926-2000)	6.2%	5.4%	6.2%	7.0%	5.4%
Beta	1.00	1.00	1.00	1.00	1.00
Beta Adjusted Common Stock Premium	6.2%	5.4%	6.2%	7.0%	5.4%
Small Company Premium (Ibbotson)	3.0%	1.8%	3.0%	4.6%	1.8%
Specific Company Risk	1.0%	1.0%	1.0%	1.0%	1.0%
Net Cash Flow Discount Rate	15.1%	12.1%	14.1%	17.5%	9.4%
Less: Expected Growth Rate	7.0%	7.0%	7.0%	7.0%	7.0%
Net Cash Flow Capitalization Rate	8.1%	5.1%	7.1%	10.5%	2.4%
Expected Net Cash Flow for Next Period	$1,000,000	$1,000,000	$1,000,000	$1,000,000	$1,000,000
Implied Multiple of Next Year's Expected CF	12.39	19.60	14.20	9.60	41.67
Implied Values of Enterprise Equity	$12,392,000	$19,600,000	$14,200,000	$9,600,000	$41,667,000
% Difference from Mercer		58%	15%	-23%	236%

Figure 6-6

The point of the illustration in Figure 6-6 is that five appraisers who agree completely on the fundamental analysis of a subject company can develop widely disparate valuation indications based solely on their selections of risk-free rates and average return series from Ibbotson Associates (or other sources). We make the following observations about the beginning range of judgment reflected in this analysis. Indications of value were developed that:

- Values range from $9.6 million to $41.7 million

- Discount rates range from 9.4% to 17.5% and capitalization rates from 2.4% to 10.5% solely on changes of assumptions regarding equity premiums and the appropriate risk-free rate.

Given this wide range of possibilities in developing capitalization rates, how can an appraiser know that he or she is "right" when coming to a conclusion with respect to a specific capitalization rate (or discount rate)? The range of judgment is wide, indeed. As noted above, experience and knowledge assist in the application of judgment. Through experience and study of available information in data bases, appraisers gather evidence regarding capitalization rates from observed pricing of real transactions.

There are now a number of data sources where appraisers can obtain information regarding the valuation parameters of actual transactions in public and private companies. These include, among others, the following:

- *Control Premium Study.*[139] This reference provides certain valuation multiples regarding transactions in public company change of control transactions. For purposes of this discussion, I am referring to this information rather than the observed control premiums that give the study its name.

- *Mergerstat/Shannon Pratt's Control Premium Study*[140]

- *Pratt's Stats*[141]

- *Done Deals*[142]

- *BizComps*[143]

In addition, there are industry-specific databases providing transactional detail for industry groupings such as banks, media companies, printing companies, engineering companies, and the like. Appraisers should search to find relevant transactional information as a basis to test the reasonableness of valuation indications from other methods, as well as to develop indications directly from relevant transactional evidence.

In addition, appraisers can make comparisons of valuation conclusions with pricing measures taken from guideline company groups selected for their appraisals, yields on similar investments, or comparisons with pricing in the current mergers and acquisitions market (even if not as specifically comparable as desired).

---

[139] *Control Premium Study* (Santa Monica, CA: *Mergerstat®*).

[140] *Mergerstat/Shannon Pratt's Control Premium Study.* Available at www.bvmarketdata.com.

[141] "Pratt's Stats," (Business Valuation Resources, LLC), www.bvmarketdata.com (accessed May 19, 2004).

[142] "Done Deals Online," (Thompson/Practitioners Publishing Company), www.donedeals.com/pDONHome.asp (accessed May 19, 2004).

[143] Jack R. Sanders, *Bizcomps* (San Diego, CA, Pacific Services, Inc.). Also available at www.bvmarketdata.com.

In the final analysis, appraisers must bring to bear their best background, knowledge and experience in the selection of capitalization rates for specific valuation requirements. In other words, they must exercise appraiser judgment.

For example, no transactional evidence was provided regarding Figure 6-6. Suppose there had been numerous change-of-control transactions in the industry. Excluding three outliers, assume there were some 20 transactions in the last couple of years for which price (total capital) to sales data was available. The average and median price/sales multiples were both $1.00 per dollar of sales, and the range was from $1.00 to $1.50 per dollar of sales. Appraisers #1, #3, and #4 reached conclusions in or very near the range of judgment indicated by the transactional evidence. Appraiser #2 missed that range by a considerable margin. Finally, Appraiser #5 reached a conclusion that was not even in the same ballpark.

All too many valuation reports conclude with statements similar to the following:

> Based on our analysis of all the relevant factors related to American Soap Company, Inc., it is our opinion that the fair market value of American's common stock is $100 per share. This conclusion is rendered in connection with (stated purpose), and is rendered on a controlling (or minority) interest basis as of December 31, 2003.

Such a conclusion, while technically proper, omits an important step that can help readers of appraisal reports understand the reasonableness of their conclusions. In my opinion, appraisal reports should include a further statement by appraisers indicating why the concluded value is reasonable. In other words, appraisal reports should generally include what we call "tests of reasonableness." The proof can consist of simple comparisons with comparative reference points, including:

- Median or average guideline company multiples across appropriate valuation parameters (sales, EBITDA, EBIT, pre-tax income, net income, book value, etc.).

- Transactions involving the subject company's own stock.

- Comparisons with transaction multiples from the sale of reasonably similar businesses.

- Tests of the returns available to investors who purchase the business or business interest at the appraised value. While the discounted cash flow method may not be used in every case, it is also possible to reverse-engineer a valuation conclusion. Given a conclusion, the appraiser can make reasonable assumptions about expected future earnings (even in the absence of management forecasts), and about the financing that might reasonably be available for a purchase of the business (pricing and terms). These assumptions can form the basis for a forecast of projected earnings and cash flows, including debt service. Internal rates of return can then be calculated based on varying assumptions about earnings margins and growth, financing terms, and the like. These internal rates of return can then be compared with market rates of return for venture capital investors or other groups of investors as tests of reasonableness of the conclusions of value.

- Tests of the sensitivity of the conclusion to changes in key inputs.

- Other comparisons that can help readers understand the reasonableness of the conclusion(s), including the use of common sense.

Comparisons such as these help readers and appraisers place the conclusions of reports into perspective. If a valuation conclusion stands out as relatively high or low, the appraiser and readers should be comfortable that this relative comparison is reasonable in light of the total analysis of the report.

When appraisers provide recurring appraisals of the same company (e.g., for Employee Stock Ownership Plans, gift tax purposes, buy-sell agreements, or other corporate purposes), it is equally important to relate the current appraisal with prior conclusions. In addition to illustrating the reasonableness of the current appraisal in relationship to the market or other familiar contexts, the appraiser should also illustrate its reasonableness in comparison to previous appraisals.

This section concludes with a quote from a brief article I wrote for *Business Valuation Review* in 1988 that reflects policies already in effect at that time at Mercer Capital.

> We believe a further procedure is necessary with recurring valuation assignments to: 1) insure the intellectual honesty of the analyst (and the firm); 2) allow the reader to understand the basis for significant methodological shifts; and 3) provide the perspective a reader needs to anchor the reasonableness of the current conclusion, not only today, but in light of historical results.

The current methodology is summarized in a table in the report. The table includes all methodologies considered, valuation indicators derived, and weights assigned to each. All discounts or premiums to market multiples applied in the various methodologies are disclosed in the table, as are all marketability or minority interest discounts. The prior year conclusions (one or two years) are then displayed next to the current year data, and changes are noted. Finally, comparative data such as the effective price/earnings, price/sales or price/book value ratios implied by the conclusions, and relevant public market comparisons are included.

The procedure requires the analyst to discuss specific reasons for significant methodological shifts, changes in weightings applied to methodologies, of changes in fundamental comparisons, or marketability/minority discounts. While [a foolish] consistency has been called "the hobgoblin of little minds," *this methodology requires careful consideration and justification of methodological changes and weighting shifts.*

When this procedure is applied consistently within a firm, it will inevitably and appropriately *highlight "outlier" conclusions, and will, over time, help develop consistency of procedures and conservatism of results. In addition, the procedure adds credibility to the conclusions in the current report, in discussions with clients, and occasionally, in courtroom testimony regarding the valuations.*[144] (emphasis in original)

CONCLUSION

The Adjusted Capital Asset Pricing Model is based on the Capital Asset Pricing Method. It is the most widely used tool for developing discount rates and capitalization rates for closely held enterprises. The ACAPM develops R_{mm} for the Gordon Model and is the base discount rate for the Integrated Theory of Business Valuation.

---

[144] Z. Christopher Mercer, "Issues in Recurring Valuations: Methodological Comparisons from Year-to-Year," *Business Valuation Review*, Vol. 7, No. 4 (1988): pp. 171-173.

Having reached these conclusions, it is important to understand that the ACAPM must be developed in the context of exercising common sense, informed judgment, and reasonableness. And there is considerable room for the exercise of judgment. However, appraisers should not make judgments in a vacuum. My friend and business partner, Ken Patton, ASA, has observed many times: "It is quite possible to make the 'right' decisions every time and to achieve an absolutely wrong conclusion 'or result'." These thoughts regarding the range of judgment are presented in the chapter on the Adjusting Capital Asset Pricing Model intentionally. They illustrate the need to exercise common sense as well as the need to test the reasonableness of valuation judgments made.

Appendix 6-A

NET INCOME VS. NET CASH FLOW AND THE ACAPM

Shannon Pratt suggests that net cash flow is the preferred economic income measure to which the ACAPM cost of capital should be applied. At the beginning of Chapter 2 of the second edition of *Cost of Capital,* he writes:

> For the purpose of this chapter, we will assume that the measure of economic income to which cost of capital will be applied is *net cash flow* (sometimes called *free cash flow*). Net cash flow is discretionary cash available to be paid out to capital stakeholders (e.g., dividends, withdrawals, discretionary bonuses) without jeopardizing the projected ongoing operations of the business....
>
> Net cash flow is the measure of economic income on which most financial analysts today prefer to focus for both valuation and capital investment selection. We explain the reasons for this preference in more detail in Chapter 3. Net cash flow represents money available to stakeholders. Most analysts prefer this measure of income because it obviates owners' discretionary disposal of company funds. Although the contemporary literature of corporate finance widely embraces a preference for net cash flow as the relevant economic income variable to which to apply cost of capital for valuation and decision making, *there is still a contingent of analysts who like to focus on accounting income.* [emphasis in this paragraph added] [145]

The footnote at the end of this quote cites *Valuing Financial Institutions* and my December 1989 ACAPM article. I did not realize that I was a part of such a "contingent of analysts."

---

[145] Ibid, p. 9. Note that the issue of "obviating" owners' discretionary use of corporate funds is not an issue in the context of the Integrated Theory. Marketable minority *(enterprise)* value indications are developed after normalizing for any such discretionary owner expenses or uses of funds. The valuation impact of disproportionate distributions of funds to selected stakeholders is appropriately considered in developing nonmarketable minority values based on expected cash flows at the *shareholder level.*

There must be some way to reconcile the views that 1) net cash flow is *the measure* and 2) that net income is sometimes or even often an acceptable measure. Let's move forward in *Cost of Capital* for the promised discussion in Pratt's Chapter 3.[146] Pratt suggests that the 'conceptual' reason for preferring net cash flow is that it represents the expectations of investors. He then states that the "empirical" reason for preferring net cash flow is that we have historical rate of return information based on net cash flow.

> The entire discussion in Pratt's Chapter 3 is based on a quotation from *Valuation Edition 2002 Yearbook* published by Ibbotson Associates. The quoted portion suggests that 'Ibbotson clearly states' the rationale for preferring net cash flow (free cash flow): There are several things to note about free cash flow. First, it is an after-tax concept. While the equation starts with earnings before interest and taxes (EBIT), this number is tax-adjusted to get to an after-tax value. The equation starts with tax-adjusted EBIT because we want to focus on cash flows independently of capital structure. We must therefore start with earnings before interest expenses and then tax adjust those earnings. Secondly, pure accounting adjustments need to be added back into the analysis. It is for this reason that depreciation and deferred tax expense are added back into the after-tax EBIT. Finally, cash flows necessary to keep the company going forward must be subtracted from the equation. These cash flows represent necessary capital expenditures to maintain plant, property, and equipment or other capital expenditures that arise out of the ordinary course of business. Another common subtraction is that the entity in question will remain a long-term going concern that will grow over time. As companies grow, they accumulate additional accounts receivable and other working elements that require additional cash to support.

> Free cash flow is the relevant cash flow stream because it represents the broadest level of earnings that can be generated by the asset. With free cash flows as the starting point, the owners of a firm can decide how much of the cash flow stream should be diverted toward new ventures, capital expenditures, interest payments, and dividend payments. *It is incorrect to focus on earnings as the cash flow stream to be valued*

---

[146] It is nice to be quoted. However, most of the time it is better to be misquoted than not to be quoted at all. I am not really suggesting that Pratt is misquoting me here, but misunderstanding me a bit.

> *because earnings contain a number of accounting adjustments and already include the impact of the capital structure.* [emphasis added] [147]

Since there are no other citations in *Cost of Capital,* it is instructive to review the context within which the quoted paragraphs are presented.   Chapter 1 of *Valuation Edition 2002 Yearbook* is a short, introductory chapter to business valuation.   It notes that there are three approaches to valuation, the income approach, the market approach, and the asset approach. Interestingly, within the income approach, the discounted cash flow method is essentially the only method mentioned.   The entire discussion of the single-period income capitalization method is found in the following sentences:

> While the basic concept of the income approach to valuation is fairly straightforward, implementing it can be quite arduous.   The two most commonly used methods for applying the income approach are the discounted cash flow (DCF) and capitalization of earnings methods....The capitalization of earnings method takes the same discount rate the DCF uses, but subtracts the company's expected annual growth rate. This is most appropriate when a company's current operations are indicative of its future operations.[148]

It should now be clear that Ibbotson Associates, and therefore, Pratt, are considering the DCF method almost in the entirety when discussing that net cash flow is the more appropriate economic measure of earnings.   However, I believe that by number of appraisals prepared by valuation analysts, the use of single-period income capitalization methods is more common than the use of the DCF method.   While this belief is unsupported by formal survey, it is based on examining many valuation reports prepared by analysts around the country, and by discussions with appraisers at many appraisal-related conferences over a many-year period.

Ibbotson Associates is a valued and highly regarded vendor of rate of return-related empirical data. To the best of my knowledge, however, the firm does not provide valuation services directly and lacks experience in the valuation of privately owned companies or their securities, i.e., *in the application of its data in*

---

[147] Ibid, p. 19. See also the entire discussion on this issue in: *Stocks, Bonds, Bills and Inflation, Valuation Edition 2002 Yearbook* (Chicago, Ibbotson Associates, 2002). Chapter 1 is titled "Business Valuation," and begins on page 9. The section quoted in Pratt is found at page 13.

[148] Ibid, p. 12.

actual valuation applications. While I appreciate being informed about the sources of data and how the data are derived, I do not look to Ibbotson Associates (or any other vendor of valuation data) for directions regarding their application in actual valuations. See the more detailed discussion of the net income vs. net cash flow issue in Chapter 1.

DIRECT CAPITALIZATION METHOD

In my opinion, it is inappropriate for a vendor of valuation data to discuss, in such direct and didactic terms as in the emphasized portion of the quotation above, what is correct or incorrect *in the application of the appraisal process.* The objective of an appraisal is to present a credible, reasonable, and believable opinion of value. Business appraisers, not data vendors, value businesses.

There are many commonly accepted "theoretical impurities" that are part of common appraisal practice, including, at least, the following:

- The use of *any method* other than one that forecasts all future benefits and discounts them to the present. After all, valuation is the present value of all expected future benefits. So why do we use single-period income capitalizations, market-based methods, or asset-based methods at all? We do so because different methods provide differing perspectives on value that can assist the appraiser in reaching valuation conclusions.

  To carry this analogy a bit further, if it is "incorrect" to capitalize net income when applying the income approach, it could be argued that it is therefore incorrect to capitalize net income when using the market approach – even when using market multiples. Yet public stock analysts and business appraisers do this every day. Why do we not see price/cash flow multiples just like we see price/earnings multiples? The reason is simple – cash flow is far more difficult for analysts to forecast than are earnings. And capital expenditures are "bunchy" and can create substantial swings from year-to-year. But thoughtful stock analysts definitely know about cash flow requirements and reinvestment and dividend policies when they discuss *price/earnings* multiples and *price(total capital)/sales* multiples, and *price (total capital)/EBITDA* multiples. Note that none of these multiples have anything to do with net cash flow per Pratt or free cash flow per Ibbotson. And yet, stocks get priced every day, with resulting implied discount rates.

- *Within the income approach*, using market-based (usually current multiples) as the basis for determining the terminal value in a discounted cash flow (or earnings) method. This fairly common mixture of income and market approach techniques is certainly not "pure" in a theoretical sense, and some would suggest that it is even incorrect. However, it is used by many, if not "most analysts," at least occasionally because it grounds the terminal value calculation in terms of current market multiples, which are observable and which represent prices actually being paid by investors.

- With a *single-period income capitalization method*, using any income measure other than the discretely forecasted benefit for the next period. Measures other than "next year's" benefit are commonly used by appraisers. As noted earlier, in developing what we call *ongoing earning power*, analysts often use trailing twelve month earnings, averages of historical earnings, weighted averages of historical earnings, earnings based on historical *margins*, rather than actual dollar earnings, averages including forecasts for the coming year, and others, in addition to the specific forecast for next year. And some appraisers develop earnings indications using techniques above and multiply the derived indication by (1 + G%) for their final indication of ongoing earning power. All of these techniques are well within the range of appraiser judgment and are not right or wrong. The appraiser who argues that another is wrong on theoretical grounds for one method will likely find himself equally wrong on theoretical grounds for another. Appraisers' implementations of valuation methodologies are ultimately "right" or "wrong" based on the valuation conclusions that are developed using them.[149]

Each of the "theoretical impurities" noted above represent generally accepted valuation methods used by business appraisers every day. To this list, I would add *the application of the ACAPM capitalization rate to the net income* (rather than the net cash flow or free cash flow) of a business enterprise, particularly when using the (single-period capitalization of income method.

---

[149] Ongoing earning power is the base level of earnings that is capitalized in a direct capitalization method and, implicitly, from which earnings are expected to grow into perpetuity at the selected G_e. Note that the implied forecast of earnings (and cash flows) resulting from this method will often differ from a specific forecast of earnings that might be developed using the discounted cash flow or future earnings methods.

In addition to the theoretical discussions in Chapters 3 and 6, compelling arguments can be made that the ACAPM, or build-up discount rate should be applicable to the net income of firms for at least the following reasons:

> In a 1992 article in *Business Valuation Review*, we developed an adjustment factor under the (incorrect) assumption that it would be appropriate to adjust r based on whether the analyst was considering net income or net cash flow. That adjustment factor was proven to be small, if applicable, and within the range of judgment routinely applied by appraisers.[150] The discussion in Chapter 1 states that it is not r that should be adjusted, but the g in the ACAPM capitalization rate – and again, the adjustment factors would normally be relatively small and within the range of judgment routinely applied by appraisers.
>
> As we have further seen, either adjustment factor could be swamped by other decisions made by appraisers related to expected growth, specific company risk, *beta*, and cash flow estimation.
>
> Based on having examined hundreds of closely held businesses over the last 25 years or so, there is a relatively close correlation between net income and net cash flow for many closely held businesses, suggesting that for those companies, the application of the ACAPM discount rate to net income would be appropriate.
>
> In spite of assertions that "most analysts" focus on net cash flow rather than net income, many, if not most stock analysts seem to focus on estimates of earnings per share (i.e., net income per share, or EPS) more so than specific estimates of periodic net cash flow. EPS estimates (for the current year, for next year, and for the next five or more years) are far more widely available than are estimates of net cash flow per share.
>
> The stock analysts who publish earnings forecasts and expected future valuations (price targets) have available to them the very same historical return data used by business appraisers who value closely held business interests.[151]

---

[150] Z. Christopher Mercer, "Adjusted Capitalization Rates for the Differences Between Net Income and Net Free Cash Flow," *Business Valuation Review*, Vol. 11, No. 4, (1992) pp. 201 - 207.

[151] Does the stock market punish public stocks for missing net cash flow targets? That is not the way the institutional fabric of our markets work at the present time.

Embedded within every price/earnings multiple for public companies is an R, or discount rate. When we use the ACAPM to develop a discount rate, we are using historical returns from public securities to estimate an R. Could they be the same R? Or sufficiently similar that we hardly know the difference in application, particularly when applied in the context of an overall analysis that examines historical earnings and cash flows? I think so.

Business appraisers have been using the ACAPM, or build-up, or CAPM-related discount rates for years. And business appraisers have quite often, in all likelihood, applied these discount rates to the estimates of ongoing earning power of business enterprises based on net income than to indications based on net cash flow, particularly when using the direct capitalization of earnings method within the income approach.

In the final analysis, business appraisers have employed the ACAPM discount rate to capitalize indications of net income to achieve credible valuation results for many years. In my opinion, it is perfectly acceptable valuation methodology to use indications of the net income of business enterprises as the income measure for capitalization using the discount rate developed with the Adjusted Capital Asset Pricing Model, or other build-up methods based on the CAPM.

With respect to discounted cash flow versus discounted future earnings, when discrete forecasts of earnings and cash flows are made, it may well be preferable to apply the ACAPM discount rate to expected net cash flows, particularly during a discrete forecast period calling for losses or heavy capital expenditures. The appraiser then must make an appropriate decision regarding the method used to determine a terminal value.

AN EXERCISE IN LOGIC

Hopefully, an exercise in logic will end the debate on the net income vs. net cash flow question. Assume for the moment that there are two distinct discount rates, one applicable to net cash flow (R_{ncf}) and the other applicable to net income (R_{ni}). Assume further that the dividend payout ratio of an enterprise is constant, but less than 100%. In other words, some earnings are retained and reinvested.

It should be clear that for the example enterprise:

$$NCF < NI$$

There are two expressions of value for the enterprise, both of which must yield an identical value, or V_0.

$$V_0 = \frac{NCF_1}{R_{ncf} - g} = \frac{NI_1}{R_{ni} - g}$$

The implicit assumption of these suggesting that the discount rates any differ is that g is constant for both expressions and the g's are identical.

Under these assumptions:

$$R_{NCF} + a = R_{NI}$$

- a is an appropriate adjustment factor that can be estimated.

- a, then, is an increment of return for investments based on net cash flow. What does a do? It provides the required rate of return, which is R_{ni}. However a is a non-economic factor. The only way to achieve the target rate of return if cash flows are reinvested is to accelerate the future growth of those cash flows. This was the essence of the analysis of Chart 1-2 in Chapter 1. We now rewrite the valuation equation:

$$V_0 = \frac{NCF}{R - g_{ncf}} = \frac{NI}{R - g_{ni}}$$

Now, for value equality and common sense to hold it should be clear that:

$$G_{ncf} > g_{ni}$$

Appendix 6-B

HISTORICAL ASIDE

As a profession, business appraisers are sometimes slow to accept changes or clarifications of theoretical issues. But once accepted, we tend to forget that things were ever different. For example:

- As noted in Chapter 3, prior to about 1990 the now ubiquitous levels of value charts had not been published in a valuation book or article. It is clear that the concepts were known by more than a few appraisers prior to their publication; however, general industry understanding normally does not develop prior to publication, which is the catalyst for broad understanding. Today, the conceptual levels of value are an integral part of valuation theory and practice. However, as indicated in earlier chapters, some disagreement remains over the configuration of this conceptual chart as our collective understanding continues to evolve. See Chapter 10.

- Prior to late 1989, there was not a clearly developed, published analysis of how the CAPM could be adjusted to develop discount rates and capitalization rates in the valuation of closely held businesses. See, however, the 1984 publication by Roger J. Grabowski, ASA who wrote a precursor description of the ACAPM which, unfortunately, we did not see until 2004. [152] We developed the ACAPM at Mercer Capital in the late 1980s because we had struggled with the concepts and because there was not a clear exposition of how to develop a capitalization rate using the CAPM as a base.*

* If any reader locates or knows of any early articles or expositions in valuation texts regarding the ACAPM, please let us know so that we can give it appropriate attribution.

---

[152] Grabowski, Roger J. (developer), *Closely Held Corporations Valuation*, (1984, Steven C. Dilley's Tax Workshops, Inc.), pp. 81-83.

Chapter 7

The Quantitative Marketability Discount Model

INTRODUCTION

The Quantitative Marketability Discount Model (QMDM) was developed to assist appraisers in the process of developing marketability discounts applicable to indications of value at the marketable minority interest level.[153] The QMDM is a discounted cash flow (present value) model that values illiquid interests of privately owned businesses based on their expected shareholder level cash flows and the risks associated with those cash flows.

In the fourth edition of *Valuing a Business,* Pratt/Reilly/Schweihs reiterate the validity of considering the value of minority interests in the context of expected cash flows to investors: "Ultimately, of course, the value of the nonmarketable minority interest is the present value of the benefits it will produce for its owner. This fact is recognized in the Quantitative Marketability Discount Model."[154]

The QMDM was developed to address the limitations of what is commonly called "benchmark analysis." Restricted stock transactions data and pre-IPO transaction data have been abused and misrepresented for too long. Average discounts derived from a series of transactions which have nothing in common with closely held minority interests are not proxies for marketability discounts. However, if we *look through* the transactions data, instead of just *at* it, we can learn a great deal from the behavior of investors in illiquid interests. Such observation is highly instructive as to the derivation of marketability discounts for minority

---

[153] Z. Christopher Mercer, *Quantifying Marketability Discounts: Developing and Supporting Marketability Discounts in the Appraisal of Closely Held Business Interests* (Memphis, TN: Peabody Publishing, LP, 1997).

[154] Shannon P. Pratt, Robert F. Reilly, and Robert P. Schweihs, *Valuing a Business: The Analysis and Appraisal of Closely Held Companies,* 4th ed. (New York, NY: McGraw-Hill, 2000), p. 411.

interests in closely held business enterprises. This chapter will therefore briefly examine how restricted stock transactions, and the information they do provide, can assist appraisers in developing marketability discounts.

COMMON QUESTIONS

1.   What is the source of value of an *interest* in a business enterprise?

2.   If a minority interest is worth less than its pro rata share of an enterprise, what are the sources of this diminution in value?

3.   Is the often lower value of minority interests (relative to pro rata enterprise value) a function of "lack of power" of minority shareholders?

    a.   Do minority shareholders of public enterprises have any more "power" in terms of voting rights or ability to control management than do shareholders of private enterprises?

    b.   Is the "lack of power" of minority investments in private enterprises more akin to a lack of liquidity (inability to sell at will) than to the ability to exercise control over a business?

4.   What are the economic factors that give rise to the marketability discount?

5.   Does the QMDM measure only the marketability discount or does it capture the minority interest discount as well?

6.   What assumptions are necessary to value illiquid interests in private enterprises that do *not* pay dividends?

7.   What assumptions are necessary to value illiquid interests in private enterprises that *do* pay dividends?

8.   What is the impact of expected sub-optimal growth to the controlling shareholder? To the minority shareholder?

9.   Why is the concept of the expected holding period an integral element in the valuation of illiquid minority interests of enterprises?

10. What is the relationship between the discount rates of minority shareholders of business enterprises and the discount rates of the enterprises themselves?

11. What valuation information is provided by a restricted stock discount?

   a. Evidence re: marketability discounts for private companies (note: if you chose this answer, what evidence?)

   b. None directly. A restricted stock discount is a valuation result, not a valuation driver.

12. What relevant economic evidence do restricted stock transactions provide to assist appraisers in valuing illiquid minority interests of business enterprises?

13. Do guideline public company multiples yield marketable minority or controlling interest level of value indications?

CONCEPTUAL OVERVIEW OF THE QMDM

The QMDM was developed to assist appraisers in the valuation of illiquid minority interests of privately held (or public) entities. As should be clear from the development and discussion of the Integrated Theory in earlier chapters, the value of illiquid minority interests of enterprises should be considered in the context of the value of the relevant enterprises.

The marketability discount can be viewed as one of the conceptual adjustments enabling appraisers to address or to develop indications of value at differing levels of value. In order to understand the nature and significance of the QMDM, it is appropriate to place the marketability discount into context within the levels of value framework. In that framework we distinguish between enterprise and shareholder cash flows in defining enterprise and shareholder levels of value. *Enterprise levels* relate to the cash flows of enterprises. The *shareholder level* relates to that derivative portion of enterprise cash flows that are expected to be attributable to their illiquid, minority interests.

Begin With Enterprise Value

Recall the discussion of the basic discounted cash flow model and its relationship to the Gordon Model (Chapter 1). The value of an enterprise is the (present) value of all expected future cash flows of an enterprise discounted to the present at an appropriate discount rate. The value of a public security reflects this present value. Minority (public) shareholders of public companies enjoy the continual benefit of the present value of all expected future cash flows through the institution of the public securities markets. Market quotes are readily available and minority shareholders can monetize interests in approximately three days.

This paradigm breaks down when there is no active market for the minority interests of an enterprise. The enterprise exists; however its (as-if) public, or enterprise, value cannot be ascertained daily in *The Wall Street Journal*.

Business appraisers are retained to determine enterprise values of private companies (or their values can be determined by market exposure and sale). Appraisers seek to determine, by the application of one or more valuation methods, the present value of the expected future cash flows of enterprises.

Some readers of *Quantifying Marketability Discounts* have suggested that the QMDM actually measures both the minority interest discount and the marketability discount. If one thinks in terms of the traditional, three-tiered levels of value chart (at the left side of Figure 7-1), it should be clear why we postulate that the QMDM begins with value at the marketable minority level of value.

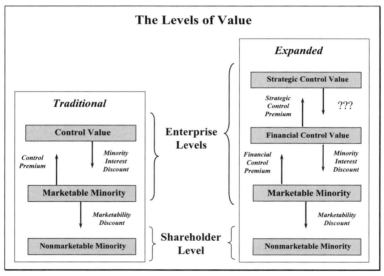

Figure 7-1

The controlling interest level of value is an enterprise value. However, so is the marketable minority level of value – because the expected cash flows of the enterprise are capitalized daily by the public stock markets. The QMDM begins at the marketable minority level of value to avoid confusion between the minority interest discount and the marketability discount.

Confusion between the controlling interest levels of value and the marketable minority interest level of value should be mitigated in many valuation situations because of the relatively small differences, if any, between the financial control level of value and the marketable minority level of value in many circumstances. As discussed at some length in Chapter 3, logic and observation suggest that the so-called marketable minority, or as-if-freely-traded level of value for public companies is very similar, if not identical to the financial control level of value, as seen in the more detailed levels of value chart presented in Chapter 3. In the context of the Integrated Theory, there would be significant differences between the financial control value and the marketable minority value only in circumstances where typical financial buyers could expect to enhance cash flows and would be willing to share (or give) that benefit with the selling shareholders.

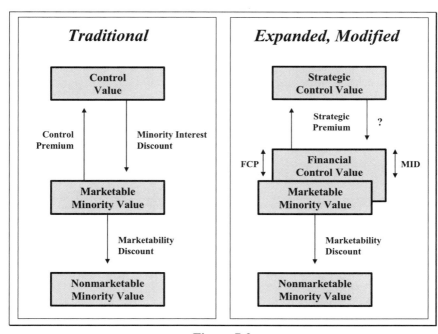

Figure 7-2

There is little evidence in the public securities markets suggesting that the value of publicly traded shares reflect significant penalties for "lack of control." This observation is the crux of the Nath Hypothesis, published in an article in *Business Valuation Review* in 1990, that said public guideline company analysis yielded valuation indications at the control/marketable minority level of value.[155]

In any event, to the extent that the minority interest discount might be misspecified in an appraisal, by focusing on the expected cash flows to be received by investors in illiquid minority interests, the QMDM assists appraisers in developing reasonable values for those interests despite such misspecification.

Nonmarketable Minority Interest Values

Business appraisers are often asked to determine the (fair market or other) value of illiquid, minority interests of enterprises.[156] According to the conceptual levels of value discussed in previous chapters, this is normally accomplished by first determining the marketable minority value of an enterprise, and then applying an appropriate marketability discount to arrive at the indicated nonmarketable minority interest value of a particular interest.

Recall the discussion in earlier chapters of the basic discounted cash flow model as applied to illiquid, minority interests of enterprises.

$$V_{sh,0} = \frac{CF_{sh,1}}{(1+R_{hp})} + \frac{CF_{sh,2}}{(1+R_{hp})} + \dots + \frac{CF_{sh,n}}{1+R^n} = \frac{CF_{sh}}{R_{hp}-G_v}$$

Value of Illiquid Interest in Enterprise (Value to Shareholder)

Equation 7-1

---

[155] See the more detailed discussion of this topic and the overall concept of the levels of value in Chapter 3, which introduces the Integrated Theory, and in Chapter 10, which addresses positions advanced by various appraisers regarding the levels of value.

[156] The QMDM addresses the issue of the minority interest versus the marketability discount in two ways. First, by beginning with a carefully determined indication of value at the marketability minority level of value, the issue of the minority interest discount should be avoided in the process of determining the marketability discount. If the marketable minority and financial control values are coincident, this implies that the minority interest discount is zero. And second, the QMDM provides a modeling assumption enabling the appraiser to specify an appropriate discount or premium if it is expected that the terminal value cash flow will be achieved at a level of value other than marketable minority.

This model illustrates the conclusion quoted earlier from Pratt/Reilly/Schweihs: "Ultimately, of course, the value of the nonmarketable minority interest is the present value of the benefits it will produce for its owner."

Enterprise and Shareholder Values

We have now examined what might appear to be two discounted cash flow models – one attributable to enterprises and the other to interests in them. They are, however, reflective of the same model. Enterprise cash flows determine the value of enterprises. For public securities the value of all future cash flows is continually available in the public markets. For private companies, that value is available upon sale, and during periods prior to a sale, those expected cash flows are available for reinvestment, distribution, or to offer for sale.

That benefit (of access to enterprise value) is not readily available to holders of illiquid, minority interests of enterprises. The value of such interests is the present value of *that portion of enterprise cash flows* expected to be available to the minority shareholders.

Any method of developing the value of illiquid, minority interests that does not focus on the expected cash flows available to shareholders, the risks associated with those cash flows, and the holding periods over which the shareholder cash flows are expected to be received, will result in an appropriate result only by chance.

Conceptual Illustration of Chance

It is common sense and core financial theory that investors evaluate investments on the basis of their expected cash flows to the investors. If there is no compromise to the liquidity of a given investment, then an investor's returns and risks are the same as the risks of the enterprise. However, if liquidity is impaired, the cash flows to the investor could be less, and the risk associated with the cash flows could be greater. We have shown the following conceptual "valuations" of both the enterprise and shareholder levels.

$$V_{mm} = \frac{CF_{e(mm)}}{R_{mm}-G_{mm}}$$

Conceptual Representation of Enterprise Value

$$V_{sh} = \frac{CF_{sh}}{R_{hp}-G_v}$$

Conceptual Representation of Shareholder Value

Equation 7-2

We learned in Chapter 3 that the Marketability Discount (MD) can be represented in terms of these two values, V_{mm} and V_{sh}.

$$MD = \left(1 - \left(\frac{V_{sh}}{V_{mm}}\right)\right) = \left(1 - \left(\frac{\dfrac{CF_{sh}}{R_{hp} - G_v}}{\dfrac{CF_{e(mm)}}{R_{mm} - G_{mm}}}\right)\right)$$

Equation 7-3

Examining these conceptual representations, it is clear that the marketability discount is a function of the relationship between enterprise value and shareholder value. It can further be seen that any divergence between these two values results from one or more of four sources:

• Differences in cash flows	$CF_{sh} \leq CF_{e(mm)}$
• Differences in risk	$R_{hp} \geq R$
• Differences in growth in value	$G_{mm} \leq G_v \leq R$
• Differences in the expected holding periods	$HP < $ Perpetuity

If the value to the shareholder is equal to the value of the enterprise, the factor V_{sh}/V_{mm} is equal to 1.0 and the marketability discount is zero.

In light of this discussion, consider two forms of benchmark analysis often used by appraisers in estimating marketability discounts:

- *Comparisons with averages of discounts found in restricted stock studies or pre-IPO studies* (Simple Benchmark Analysis). Assume that a group of restricted stock studies reflects an average restricted stock discount of 35%. By making comparisons of a particular valuation situation to this average, what information can be gleaned regarding the following factors that cause differences between enterprise and shareholder values?

    - What are the expected differences between effective receipt of 100% of enterprise cash flows ($CF_{e(mm)}$ capitalized value always available) and the actual distributions expected from the particular minority interest (CF_{sh})?

- What is the appropriate discount rate for expected shareholder cash flows (R_{hp}) relative to the enterprise discount rate (R)?

- What are the differences between the expected growth in earnings and value between the enterprise and the interest?

- What is the impact of holding period assumptions for the illiquid interest relative to the perpetuity capitalization implicit in V_{mm} (or relative to the holding period assumptions in the actual restricted stock transactions)?

- Finally, to the extent that the analyst is able to answer the above questions, how is he or she able to assess the impact of any of the differences on the marketability discount being estimated and, therefore, on the value of illiquid minority interests?

- *Comparisons with individual restricted stock transactions from the limited databases of restricted stock transactions.* Assume that the analyst performs a guideline company analysis using an available restricted stock transaction database, none of which have more than a few hundred transactions covering a period of 20 or more years. Now ask the same questions above regarding simple benchmark analysis, which focuses on the averages of the various studies.

It should be clear that benchmark analysis cannot help appraisers answer the critical questions that account for divergences between enterprise and shareholder value in particular valuation situations. So the use of benchmark analysis can only be expected to lead to the appropriate marketability discount by chance. And chance is not good enough. When viewed through the lens of the Integrated Theory, benchmark analysis cannot address, much less answer, critical questions.

Practical Illustration of Chance

Consider the following enterprise valuation situation:

- Enterprise Earnings (CF_1) $0.10 per share
- Expected Growth in Earnings (G_e)   6.0%
- Enterprise Discount Rate (R)   16.0%

Applying the Gordon Model, we obtain an enterprise value of $1.00 per share ($V_{mm} = \dfrac{CF_1}{R - G_E}$; therefore $V_{mm} = \dfrac{\$0.10}{16\% - 6\%} = \$1.00$). Now we ask the question: What should the appropriate marketability discount be? Any appraiser would, of course, respond: "It depends on the facts and the circumstances."

For this practical illustration of the inadequacy of benchmark analysis we can use the basic discounted cash flow model to look at a broad range of possible circumstances relative to our assumed enterprise valuation. Consider the following range of assumptions:

- $CF_{sh} \leq CF_{mm}$ A range of distributions to shareholders from 0% (no distributions) to 100% (total distributions) is considered. To simplify the example it is assumed that all cash flows not distributed to shareholders are "leaked" as extra compensation to the controlling shareholder. Therefore the expected growth in value (G_v) is equal to the expected growth rate in earnings (G_e), since there is no reinvestment of cash flows to provide more rapid growth. To make the impact of this assumption clear, look at the upper portion of Figure 7-3 to the line where R_{hp} is 16.0%, which is equal to R. If 100% of cash flows are distributed (far right) the calculated marketability discount is 0%. If there are no distributors (0% of cash flows to shareholders) the calculated marketability discount is 36.3%

• $R_{hp} \geq R$ We introduced the concept of the holding period premium (HPP) in Chapter 3. (R_{hp} - R) is the extra compensation required by investors for accepting illiquidity for the expected holding period. The example addresses a range of holding period premiums of 0% to 4%, providing a range of R_{hp} from 16% (R) to 20%.

• Holding Period   Calculations are made for two possible expected holding periods, five years and 10 years.

Based on the above assumptions, we have directly calculated the present values of the expected cash flows to shareholders under the full range of assumptions and then calculated the implied marketability discounts over the range. For example, if there are no distributions, HPP = 4% (so R_{hp} = 20.0%), and the expected holding period is 10 years, the value to the shareholder is $0.29 per share, calculated as follows:

$$\left(\frac{\$1.00 \times (1+6\%)^{10}}{(1+20\%)^{10}} = \$0.29 \right)$$

Equation 7-4

The implied marketability discount is therefore 71%, or $[\, 1 - \frac{\$0.29}{\$1.00} \,]$.

The implied marketability discount is 46% if the holding period is assumed to be five years. The implied marketability discount for a 10-year expected holding period with all other assumptions the same is 71%. The following two tables calculate the full range of marketability discounts for the range of assumptions for five and 10 years expected holding periods. The "correct" marketability discounts are shown in boxes in the context of shaded areas to reflect the "standard" range of benchmark analysis discounts of 35% to 45 %.

5 Year

Implied Marketability Discounts -- Holding Period   5 Years

Percentage of Enterprise Cash Flows Received Each Year by Minority Shareholders

R_{hp}	0.0%	10.0%	20.0%	30.0%	40.0%	50.0%	60.0%	70.0%	80.0%	90.0%	100.0%
16.0%	36.3%	32.7%	29.0%	25.4%	21.8%	18.1%	14.5%	10.9%	7.3%	3.6%	0.0%
17.0%	39.0%	35.4%	31.9%	28.3%	24.8%	21.3%	17.7%	14.2%	10.6%	7.1%	3.5%
18.0%	41.5%	38.0%	34.6%	31.1%	27.7%	24.2%	20.8%	17.3%	13.8%	10.4%	6.9%
19.0%	43.9%	40.5%	37.2%	33.8%	30.4%	27.0%	23.7%	20.3%	16.9%	13.5%	10.1%
20.0%	46.2%	42.9%	39.6%	36.3%	33.0%	29.7%	26.4%	23.1%	19.8%	16.5%	13.2%

10 Year

Implied Marketability Discounts -- Holding Period   10 Years

Percentage of Enterprise Cash Flows Received Each Year by Minority Shareholders

R_{hp}	0.0%	10.0%	20.0%	30.0%	40.0%	50.0%	60.0%	70.0%	80.0%	90.0%	100.0%
16.0%	59.4%	53.5%	47.5%	41.6%	35.6%	29.7%	23.8%	17.8%	11.9%	5.9%	0.0%
17.0%	62.7%	57.0%	51.3%	45.6%	39.9%	34.2%	28.5%	22.8%	17.1%	11.4%	5.7%
18.0%	65.8%	60.3%	54.8%	49.3%	43.9%	38.4%	32.9%	27.4%	21.9%	16.4%	11.0%
19.0%	68.6%	63.3%	58.0%	52.7%	47.5%	42.2%	36.9%	31.6%	26.4%	21.1%	15.8%
20.0%	71.1%	66.0%	60.9%	55.8%	50.8%	45.7%	40.6%	35.5%	30.5%	25.4%	20.3%

Figure 7-3

Figure 7-3 illustrates that benchmark analysis will yield the appropriate marketability discount only by chance. Looking at both tables, it is evident that the usual range of marketability discounts of 35-45% represents only a limited set of potential assumptions regarding risk and expected distributions. *Simple benchmark analysis effectively forces the facts and circumstances into a predetermined range of results, rather than allowing the facts and circumstances to determine the results.*

This point can be illustrated by examining summary statistics regarding the various restricted stock studies that are frequently cited by appraisers in support of marketability discounts. Figure 7-4 summarizes key statistics for the restricted stock studies, and is reproduced from *Quantifying Marketability Discounts: Revised Reprint* in the chapter about restricted stock studies.[157]

Summary Results of Nine Restricted Stock Studies						
Study	Number of Observations	Medians	Means	Standard Deviations	Range Low	High
1 SEC Institutional Investor Study	398	24%	26%	na	(15%)	80%
2 Gelman Study	89	33%	33%	na	<15%	>40%
3 Moroney Study	146	34%	35%	18%	(30%)	90%
4 Maher Study	34	33%	35%	18%	3%	76%
5 Trout Study	60	na	34%	na	na	na
6 Stryker/Pittock Study	28	45%	na	na	7%	91%
7 Willamette Management Assoc.	33	31%	na	na	na	na
8 Silber Study	69	na	34%	24%	(13%)	84%
9 Hall/Polacek Study	100+	na	23%	na	na	na
Averages		33.0%	31.4%			

Figure 7-4

As should be clear from casual observation, the range of discounts for the studies for which information is available is wide, indeed. And the standard deviations are quite large in relationship to the measures of central tendency. The nature of the underlying data can be understood even more clearly in the scatter diagram of the discounts from available studies (Figure 7-5).

---

[157] Z. Christopher Mercer, *Quantifying Marketability Discounts* (Peabody Publishing, Memphis TN 1997), p. 45.

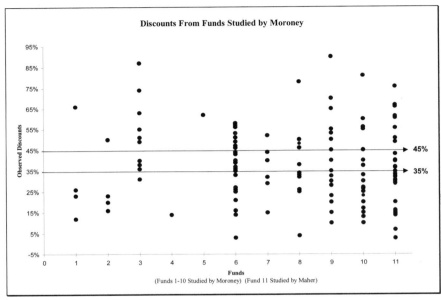

Figure 7-5

The diagram provides clear and visual evidence that the early studies do not support a blanket 35% marketability discount. Further, the studies do not support a "benchmark range" of 35% to 45% for marketability discounts, which would include averages related to pre-IPO Studies. While we will not spend time in this book discussing these studies, they have the same issues with dispersion of observations as do the restricted stock studies. For example, the scatter diagram for the Emory pre-IPO studies available through the publication of *Quantifying Marketability Discounts: Revised Reprint* in 2001 is reproduced as Figure 7-6.[158]

[158] Ibid, p. 92.

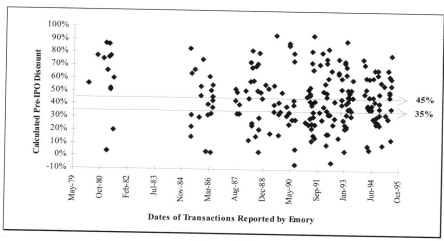

Figure 7-6

Benchmark analysis, with its limited use of average statistics, whether from averages of studies or averages from a few transactions (using guideline company analysis) can achieve the appropriate marketability discount only by chance. Indeed, it would seem, based on observation of the scatter diagrams for both the restricted stock and pre-IPO studies above, that these transactions occurred in the so-called "benchmark range" of about 35% to 45% only by chance.

GENERAL ASSUMPTIONS OF THE QMDM

In the typical presentation of the QMDM, it is assumed that a marketable minority interest indication of value for an enterprise is equated to $1.00, and all calculations are made to determine an appropriate range of implied marketability discounts in relationship to the $1.00 of assumed enterprise value. The concluded (percentage) marketability discount is then applied to the actual indication of fair market value developed by the appraiser in his or her enterprise level valuation. In other words, the model calculates the present value of expected future benefits to shareholders for an investment and determines the implied marketability discount based on the difference between the derived shareholders' value and the marketable minority value.

To be clear, the QMDM provides a *direct* valuation of minority interests based on expected future cash flows *to the interests*. This valuation is performed in the context of relevant enterprise valuations, where enterprise values are based on the capitalization of *enterprise* cash flows. At its essence, the QMDM quantifies the value impact of divergences between the benefit of effective receipt of all enterprise cash flows (through the ability to sell in the public markets or as captured by the Gordon Model at the marketable minority level) and the actual cash flows minority shareholders may expect to receive (which may be less then, even substantially less than, enterprise cash flows).

In applying the QMDM, it is recommended that dividends for tax pass-through entities (S corporations, limited liability companies, and limited and/or general partnerships) be converted to C corporation equivalency. This conversion places all dividends on a comparable basis, and avoids overstating or understating the economic dividends/distributions to shareholders based on a failure to consider the actual out-of-pocket taxes that must be paid by the owner of an interest in a tax pass-through entity.

The typical assumption made when using the QMDM is that liquidity from a nonmarketable investment will occur at the marketable minority interest level of value – which, as has been discussed in several chapters in this book, may well approximate the financial control value in many instances. Liquidity may or may not occur at this level of value; however, we believe it is a reasonable assumption to make in many, if not most, appraisals. Liquidity can occur in a variety of ways:

- Through a potential future sale of the business at a possible premium to the then-marketable minority value.

- Through a sale to third parties on less favorable terms at a discount to the marketable minority level.

- Through stock repurchases by the subject company on favorable or unfavorable terms.

- If the company is of sufficient size and attractiveness, through an initial public offering of its shares.

Assuming liquidity at the marketable minority level of value can be seen as a way of balancing these various possible outcomes without bias when no specific liquidity events are anticipated. It is important to note that in the context of the QMDM, the assumed liquidity event is "expected" within the expected holding period of the investment. In other words, in the absence of specific, known prospects for liquidity, the analyst must estimate a holding period within which to consider the expectation of liquidity. Depending on some fact patterns, expected holding periods may be relatively short. In other cases, they may be fairly lengthy. In any event, the longer the expected holding period, the greater the probability that favorable liquidity outcomes may arise (or unfavorable outcomes avoided). On the other hand, the longer the expected holding period, the longer the period of illiquidity, and the greater the risk. The balancing of these factors is an unavoidable fact of life when investing in or valuing illiquid minority interests.

Since originally introduced, the QMDM has been updated to allow the analyst to make a specific assumption regarding the level of value at which liquidity is expected to occur.[159] In the *QMDM Companion* to *Quantifying Marketability Discounts* (*QMDM Companion*) the appraiser is able to make a specific assumption about the level of value at which liquidity is expected to be achieved.

INTRODUCTION TO THE FIVE QMDM ASSUMPTIONS

There are five key assumptions in the QMDM. At this point, we state them with a brief introduction. The assumptions will then be considered in the context of financial and valuation theory. The assumptions are:

1. *The expected growth rate in value.* From a concluded indication of value at the marketable minority level of value, the appraiser must make an assumption about the reasonable expectations for growth in that (marketable minority) value over the duration of the expected holding period.

---

[159] The QMDM was summarized in a calculation diskette in 1997. The Model has been updated and a brief tutorial provided in the current version. The Model is available through Mercer Capital (electronically) at www.mercercapital.com or Wiley Publishing, Inc., Indianapolis, IN (Z. Christopher Mercer, "Marketability Discounts Software: Quantifying Marketability Discount Modeling," ISBN: 0-471-10598-8).

2. *The expected dividend (or distribution) yield.* Many closely held companies do not pay dividends, and the expectation regarding future dividends may be for more of the same. However, many other private entities do pay regular dividends. To facilitate calculation in the *QMDM Companion*, the expected dividend is expressed as a percentage of the marketable minority value.

3. *The expected growth rate in the dividend.* The dividend will not necessarily be expected to grow at the same rate as the underlying growth in value. This assumption allows the appraiser to consider the impact of various potential dividend policies over the expected holding period.

4. *The expected holding period (range).* Other things being equal, as noted above, a dollar tomorrow is worth less than a dollar today – so the longer the expected holding period without liquidity, the lower the value today. Since the expected holding period is almost never known with certainty, the QMDM allows the appraiser to express this assumption in terms of a reasonable range of expected holding periods.[160]

5. *The required holding period return (range).* Given an expected stream of future payments (or a single, lump-sum payment represented by a terminal value), that stream can be converted into present dollars by the application of an appropriate discount rate. This discount rate is the underlying equity discount rate for the enterprise with the additional consideration of risks of the holding period not present with a marketable security. As with the expected holding period, the QMDM enables the appraiser to consider a reasonable range of discount rates based upon the assumed range of holding period premiums (HPP) relative to the base equity discount rate (R). In other words, $R_{hp} = R + HPP$, as will be discussed further below.

---

[160] For those who might desire to ignore the holding period assumption, it should become clear as we progress that the specification of *any* marketability discount carries with it an implied holding period assumption (or a range of assumptions).

The QMDM requires the appraiser to reach (hopefully) reasonable and supportable conclusions regarding each of the five key assumptions of the model. The assumptions are made in the context of the underlying marketable minority appraisals and the particular facts and circumstances that are relevant to the interests being appraised. When appraisers make assumptions that are reasonable both individually and in relationship to each other (in the context of the facts and circumstances of an appraisal), the resulting conclusions should also be reasonable.

The focus on ranges of expected holding periods and of discount rates appears to trouble some observers of the QMDM. This focus on ranges, however, is directly analogous to the use of sensitivity analysis with the discounted cash flow method in valuing enterprises. In fact, a sensitivity analysis in table form is a common feature in DCF valuations at the enterprise level. These sensitivity tables illustrate changes in value based on ranges of assumptions regarding discount rates, terminal value multiples, or other key assumptions of the indicated analyses.

THE QMDM ASSUMPTIONS: INITIAL PERSPECTIVE

Because the QMDM is a discounted cash flow model, we have asserted that the model is developed in the mainstream of financial theory. And the five key assumptions of the model have now been introduced. Equation 7-5, which segregates the discounted cash flow model for enterprise valuation into two components, is reproduced here for reference. The left component represents the Present Value of Interim Cash Flows (PVICF) through a finite period ending with Year f. The right component is the Present Value of The Terminal Value (PVTV) calculated at the end of Year f.[161]

$$V_0 = \left(\frac{CF_1}{(1+r)^1} + \frac{CF_2}{(1+r)^2} + \frac{CF_3}{(1+r)^3} + \dots + \frac{CF_f}{(1+r)^f} \right) + \left(\frac{CF_{f+1}/(r-g)}{(1+r)^f} \right)$$

PVICF   PVTV

Equation 7-5

---

[161] I am grateful to Travis W. Harms, CFA, CPA/ABV, who has helped me immeasurably with the algebraic and mathematical insights in this section. He is also co-author of Chapter 1.

This formula can be rearranged as follows:

$$V_e = \sum_{i=1}^{f} \left[\frac{CF(1+g_e)^i}{(1+r)^i} \right] + \left[\frac{CF(1+g_e)^{(f+1)}/(r-g)}{(1+r)^f} \right]$$

$$\underbrace{\hspace{3cm}}_{\textbf{PVICF}} \qquad \underbrace{\hspace{3cm}}_{\textbf{PVTV}}$$

Equation 7-6

This arrangement of the enterprise DCF model helps focus on the relevant investment assumptions:

1. V_e is the value of the enterprise at time period zero at the marketable minority interest level of value.

2. g_e is the expected growth rate in core earnings before consideration of the reinvestment of cash flows. Recall that this growth rate is the Appraisers' G from Chapter 1.

3. CF is the current, base level of cash flows, so for the interim forecast period, cash flows are capitalized beginning with those of the next period ($CF_1 = CF * (1 + g_e)$).

4. r is the discount rate applicable to the cash flows, CF.

5. The duration of the forecast for the enterprise is into perpetuity, given that all expected future cash flows beyond Year f are discounted to the present.

As has been previously demonstrated, if g_e is constant and if all future cash flows are reinvested in the enterprise at r, the expected growth rate in value, or g_v, will be equal to the discount rate, r.[162]

In the next equation, the QMDM is specified in terms analogous to the enterprise DCF model to determine the Value to a Shareholder (V_{sh}) as opposed to the Value of the Enterprise (V_0).

---

[162] Alternatively, to the extent any portion of the cash flows are distributed, under optimal reinvestment assumptions, the expected growth in value will be reduced by the dividend yield ($g_v = r -$ Dividend Yield%).

$$V_{sh} = \overset{f}{\underset{i=1}{Sum}} \left[\frac{CF_{sh}(1+g_d)^i}{(1+R_{hp})^i} \right] + \left[\frac{V_e(1+g_v)^i}{(1+R_{hp})^f} \right]$$

PVICF   PVTV

Equation 7-7

This arrangement of the QMDM helps focus on the key assumptions of the model:

1. g_v is the expected growth rate in value (of the enterprise for the duration of the expected holding period). Recall that the growth of value may differ from the discount rate in private companies under a number of circumstances, including the payment of non-pro rata distributions to selected shareholders and expected reinvestment of retained cash flows at less than the discount rate. Because of these divergences from the public model, it is necessary to specify g_v in order to avoid overvaluation of minority interests in private companies.

2. CF_{sh} represents the expected dividend stream to be received by the holder of an illiquid interest of an enterprise. Note that CF_{sh} will be less than CF of the enterprise to the extent that distributions are less than 100% of enterprise cash flows – i.e., in the normal case.

3. g_d is the expected growth rate of the dividend stream, CF_{sh}.

4. The holding period for this investment is to the end of Year f, a finite period of time, rather than forever, as in the case of the public market equivalent valuation at the marketable minority level.

5. R_{hp} is the required holding period return for the expected holding period ending in Year f. R_{hp} consists of r, the equity discount rate of the firm, plus any holding period premium(s) caused by risks at the shareholder level (*HPP*) over and above those at the enterprise level (r). In other words, $R_{hp} = r + HPP$.

These are the *very same* assumptions (or results) found in the enterprise valuation equation. This can be seen in the following example. Consider the case where 100% of enterprise cash flows will be distributed to shareholders pro rata. We further assume that the enterprise engages in no other equity-related transactions, that there are no changes in capital structure, and no change in market multiples for purposes of the illustration.

- CF_{sh} is identical to the CF of the enterprise.

- R_{hp} would be equal to r, since there would be no incremental, shareholder-level risks of receipt of the cash flows. Any such incremental risks are assumed away.[163] Under this assumption set, the expected cash flows of minority or controlling shareholders would be identical.

- g_d would be equal to g_e, since all earnings are being distributed. There will be no growth in value from reinvested cash flows. As a result, the present value of interim cash flows would be equal under the enterprise or shareholder formulation.

- Finally, the terminal values would also be identical under both formulations. This can be shown algebraically, but the practical proof will be shown below in the discussion of the base case. The shareholder formulation calls for the current value of the enterprise to grow at g_v. Since all cash flows are being paid out (i.e., there is no reinvestment to augment growth in value), g_e and g_v would necessarily be equivalent. This ensures the equivalency of values of the two terminal value calculations.

It should now be clear that the QMDM is offered in the mainstream of financial theory. A number of critics have attempted to dismiss the QMDM as a "simple" discounted cash flow model. If so, it is the same "simple" discounted cash flow model used to value business enterprises. Appraisers using the model, or indeed, any quantitative, rate of return analysis, must make assumptions at the shareholder level similar to those made at the enterprise level to value expected enterprise cash flows.

---

[163] There could be some conceivable risks that could cause R_{hp} to be greater than R, e.g., restrictions on transfer for some shares relative to others with no such restrictions. Such risks are assumed away for this discussion. If they exist in actual appraisal situations, their impact should be appropriately considered in the QMDM assumptions.

EXPANDING ON THE FIVE ASSUMPTIONS OF THE QMDM

One of the most valuable aspects of the QMDM is the framework provided for the discussion of marketability discounts. By defining a small number (five) of well-defined parameters with consistent and predictable relationships to the resulting discount, appraisers and other interested parties have an elegant means of defining the area(s) of disagreement and debating the relative merits of each position. The clarity and specificity provided by this framework often serve to uncover implicit (and unspecified) assumptions of the parties, which can lead to resolution or an understanding of the impact of the various assumptions on the resulting discount.

The five assumptions of the QMDM are discussed in some detail below. Since different assumptions define different investments and since investments can vary widely in their characteristics, it should not be surprising that the use of the QMDM can yield a wide range of potential marketability discounts – each appropriate for the investment defined.

Assumption #1: Expected Growth in Value (g_v)

If an investment is appreciating, that growth will provide a portion of the realized return during the holding period. Growth potential should be evaluated in the context of management's business plan, historical growth, and external factors, such as changing industry conditions.

For public companies, the expected growth in value should be equal to the difference between the expected (or required) return on equity and the expected dividend yield (dividends plus capital appreciation). The (minority) investor ultimately has no other means to meet his or her return requirement. To this point there are two concepts of growth for the public markets. The first is the long-term expected growth of earnings, or g. The second is the long-term expected growth in value, which is r, or the discount rate. We now introduce a third concept of growth from the viewpoint of shareholders, the expected growth in value of the enterprise or g_v, because g_v for investors in illiquid minority interests may be less than the theoretical expectation of r. Deviations from public equivalent expectations are commonly caused by two factors:

- *Cash flow leakage from the enterprise, sometimes referred to as agency costs.* Leakage often takes the form of excessive owner compensation, or non-pro rata distributions.

- *Suboptimal reinvestment decisions, or expected reinvestment at rates less than the discount rate of the enterprise.* Suboptimal reinvestment is often evidenced by the accumulation of excessive cash balances or other non-operating assets.[164]

If there are cash flow leakages resulting from, for example, above-market compensation to a majority shareholder, the "leaked" cash flows are not available for reinvestment in the business and are not received by minority shareholders. So leakage results in a loss of return opportunity for investors in illiquid interests and is reflected in lower expected growth for the business. As a result, the expected growth in value of the enterprise, or g_v, must be specified in the QMDM.

A similar loss of return opportunity occurs if cash flows are reinvested in a business but at suboptimal (i.e., below r) rates. Companies that retain earnings and accumulate large amounts of low yielding cash are the most common examples of suboptimal reinvestment. Suboptimal reinvestment lowers growth potential, and therefore, the expected growth rate in value, g_v.

Practically, we have found it helpful to analyze expected growth rates in value along a continuum ranging from the expected growth in enterprise earnings at the low end to the enterprise-level required return (less any expected dividend yield) at the high end. While this range is not necessarily definitive, the expected growth in enterprise earnings is appropriate if all the enterprise-level cash flows are expected to leak out of the business; while for well-run private companies with no cash flow leakage and optimal dividend policies, the enterprise-level required return may be appropriate. Explicit assumptions regarding leakage and reinvestment rates may be used to specify appropriate estimates of growth in value within this range.

Expected growth in value and the marketability discount are negatively correlated. Other things being equal, as expected capital appreciation increases, marketability discounts decrease.

---

[164] These factors are considered by some appraisers related to the minority interest discount rather than the marketability discount. This criticism is addressed in a later section of this chapter.

Assumption #2: Expected Dividend Yield ($D\%$)

Holding period returns are also influenced by interim cash flows. Recall that $r = D/P + G_v$. Stated alternatively, shareholder returns are comprised or dividend yields (D/P) plus capital appreciation (g_v).

Dividends and other holding period cash flows should be evaluated in the context of historical (and expected) payout policy, a company's ability to distribute cash, and the cash needs implied by the business plan. The direct consideration of dividends is one of the most important aspects of the QMDM. Appraisers who employ benchmark analysis have no objective means of considering the often considerable impact of dividends on the value of illiquid interests. Virtually none of the companies engaging in restricted stock transactions analyzed in the various restricted stock studies pay dividends. Consequently, even if other problems with benchmark analysis or guideline company analysis using restricted stock studies can be overcome, absent the QMDM, the appraiser has no realistic means of assessing the valuation impact of expected dividends. Dividends are considered in the QMDM *over the relevant expected holding period.*

A failure to consider expected dividends in the valuation of illiquid minority interests is tantamount to ignoring interim cash flows in discounted cash flow models used to value enterprises. An appraiser who ignores such interim (enterprise) cash flows would advance a flawed analysis. They are specific and quantifiable and have a specific impact on the present value of an enterprise.

Likewise, an appraiser who chooses to treat dividends in a purely subjective fashion would also advance a flawed analysis. Expected dividends are quantifiable and have a specific impact on the present value of an interest in an enterprise.

As with growth in value, holding period cash distributions and marketability discounts are negatively correlated. Other things being equal, a higher expected dividend will create more present value and lower marketability discounts.

Assumption #3: Expected Growth in Dividends ($g_{D\%}$)

Holding period returns are further influenced by the expected growth in interim cash flows. In our application of the QMDM, the expected growth in dividends often ranges from 0% if a constant dollar dividend is expected, to the expected growth in enterprise-level earnings if a constant payout ratio is expected, to the expected growth in value if a constant dividend yield is expected. Specific facts and circumstances may occasionally warrant different assumptions. Although the dividend growth does not have a material impact on valuation conclusions in many appraisals, it is especially important in situations with relatively high dividends and relatively long expected holding periods. It must be specified for completeness of the projection of interim cash flows to shareholders.

As with the dividend yield, the expected growth in dividends and marketability discounts are negatively correlated.

Assumption #4: Expected Holding Period (HP)

Without an active market, an investor must hold a given investment for an uncertain length of time until a liquidity event occurs. In our experience, expected holding periods are reasonably related to historical ownership policies, buy/sell agreements, management or ownership succession plans, likely exit strategies for the controlling owners, and potential opportunities for the favorable sale of the underlying assets.

The expected holding period assumption is sometimes criticized as unduly difficult to estimate. However, the essence of investment is uncertainty. No one can know the unknowable; however, investment decisions and appraiser assumptions must be made in the face of this uncertainty.

Yogi Berra once observed: "It's hard to predict the future because it hasn't happened yet." However, investors must make decisions every day in the face of uncertainty by evaluating future prospects and charging higher required returns as uncertainties increase. Appraisers cannot ignore the potential duration of the expected holding period when valuing illiquid minority interests. To do so is not only inconsistent with rational investment decision-making (and valuation theory), it is also irresponsible.[165]

Any time a form of benchmark analysis is used or when comparisons are made with guideline transactions, implicit holding period assumptions are being made – those reflective of the expectations of market participants engaging in restricted stock or pre-IPO transactions. Unfortunately, one size does not fit all in valuation.

We have found that reasonable assumptions can be made if the factors above are considered in the context of the appraiser's general experience. Even a rather broad range supported by pertinent considerations specific to the subject interest is superior to no direct consideration of the effect of the holding period at all. The expected holding period has a direct and quantifiable impact on the valuation of illiquid minority interests. It is simply not possible to gauge this impact subjectively.

In general, longer holding periods without liquidity imply higher marketability discounts.

Assumption #5: Required Holding Period Return (R_{hp})

To compensate for illiquidity, an investor expects a premium return in excess of that provided by liquid alternatives. One of the most useful aspects of the restricted stock studies is the evidence supporting the notion that investors in illiquid securities require premium returns relative to otherwise identical liquid alternatives (and that such premiums are generally not trivial).

---

[165] In a teleconference, Lance S. Hall, ASA advanced a novel idea. Illiquid minority interests are marketable – all holders have to do is dump them into the same illiquid markets in which they were purchased and get money back on the same basis as the investments were purchased. This suggestion related to the need to estimate holding periods. The problem is that the suggestion is contrary to the purpose of investing in illiquid investments, which is to realize their expected benefits over their expected terms of investment (i.e., expected holding periods). Teleconference: *Discounts for Lack of Marketability: Critique of the Bajaj Approach,* April 27, 2004. Sponsored by Business Valuation Resources, LLC. Panelists: Lance S. Hall, ASA; Z. Christopher Mercer, ASA, CFA; Robert P. Oliver, ASA. Moderator: Dr. Shannon Pratt, CFA, FASA, MCBA.

The essence of a restricted stock transaction can be summarized: If shares of public companies are issued with restrictions relative to their freely traded shares, and there are no other differences in the freely traded and restricted shares, restricted stock transactions tend to occur at discounts to the freely traded prices of issuing companies.[166]

These discounts are price concessions required by investors that create a higher expected return for the holder of the restricted shares relative to the expected return attributable to the freely traded shares. In other words, for any given level of future performance until the restricted shares become marketable, the restricted shareholders will achieve a higher rate of return. The *future value* at that date will be the same for all shareholders but the restricted shareholders have a *lower present value*, or cost, because of the discount. Stated another way, investors holding restricted stock tend to have higher required returns than investors holding otherwise identical, freely traded shares. The difference between the higher required return of restricted stock investors and the public company discount rates is the premium in return charged for bearing the risks of future illiquidity.

The restricted stock studies indicate that, on average, investors acquiring stocks subject to the minimum holding periods of Rule 144 had annual required returns in the high teens (at the lowest), and even into the higher 20s and low 30s.[167]

As noted previously, R_{hp}, the required holding period return of the QMDM, can be defined as:

$$R_{hp} = R + HPP$$

Equation 7-8

R is the enterprise discount rate utilized in or implied by an appraiser's conclusion of value for a subject business at the marketable minority level of value. *HPP* is the holding period premium (or sum of premiums) applicable to risks anticipated by the shareholder *in addition to the risks of the enterprise*. Such risks include the potential for a long and indeterminate holding period until liquidity is expected, uncertainties over distributions, and numerous others. Note that if *HPP* is equal

---

[166] Since only a very small portion of companies that have issued restricted stock in private placements pay any dividends to shareholders, the available evidence does not allow a testing of whether discounts would be mitigated dramatically by substantial distributions.

[167] See the discussion above regarding the overall results of the restricted stock studies.

to zero, and there are no incremental risks to the shareholder, then $R_{hp} = R$. This situation could possibly occur if a business was distributing 100% of its earnings and a continuation of this policy was a certainty. Under that circumstance, there might be little or no marketability discount. This was close to the economic situation in the now-famous Tax Court case, *Estate of Gross v. Commissioner.* [168]

In our application of the QMDM, we strive to relate the expected holding period return to the expected return of the enterprise and the specific characteristics of the subject illiquid interest. These factors include the uncertainty related to the timing and favorability of exit from the investment, the uncertainties associated with the receipt of expected shareholder-level cash flows, and various monitoring or agency costs. While the premiums assigned are certainly items of valuation judgment, such assumptions are really no different than specific company risk estimates typically found in business appraisals at the enterprise level.

We find it interesting that some of the same appraisers who routinely estimate *specific company risks* in CAPM-related, or build-up, methods when developing *enterprise-level* discount rates, choose to criticize the QMDM because analogous, *shareholder-specific risks* are estimated. Those who would so criticize the QMDM are, in effect, criticizing all discounted cash flow methodologies. They do not seem to recognize the inconsistency of their positions.

The argument goes something like this: When an appraiser specifies specific risk, he or she is, in effect, specifying the marketability discount, because when all other factors are known, this assumption is determinative of the result. And the argument has an element of truth. If the expected cash flows are known (whether for an enterprise or for a shareholder's interest in that enterprise), once the discount rate is specified, the result is known. However, note the following:

- *Appraisers do not begin with the end result when appraising enterprises.* They make forecasts of expected enterprise cash flows and they make good faith estimates of discount rates, inclusive of specific risks attributable to the enterprise not otherwise accounted for by their CAPM-related discount rates. Valuation conclusions at the marketable minority level are the result of this process (assuming that control adjustments have not been made to the expected cash flows).

- *Appraisers do not begin with the end result when appraising illiquid interests in enterprises.* When employing the QMDM, forecasts of

---

[168] *Gross v. Commissioner*, T.C. Memo. 1999-254, affd. 272 F.3d 333 (6th Cir. 2001).

expected cash flows attributable to the relevant interests of enterprises are made, as are good faith estimates of the required holding period returns, inclusive of shareholder-specific risks over and above their enterprise discount rates. Valuation conclusions at the nonmarketable minority level are the result of this process, and the marketability discount is determined by the relationship between the nonmarketable minority value and the marketable minority value.

The exact premiums applicable to various enterprise-level or shareholder-level discount rates are inherently imprecise and require the exercise of appraiser judgment. That judgment is rendered in the context of knowledge of alternative markets and rates of return and with common sense, informed judgment, and reasonableness – three critical factors noted in Revenue Ruling 59-60. We have found it possible to develop reasonable discount rates for enterprise valuations over the years on this basis. And, for the last 10 years or so, we have found it possible to develop reasonable required holding period returns for shareholder-level valuations in the process of developing marketability discounts.

Required holding period returns for the QMDM can be assessed in the context of alternative investments, including venture capital investments, illiquid investments in real estate limited partnerships, and implied rates of return embedded in restricted stock transactions (see below).

As with any present value analysis, the value of the subject interest is negatively correlated with the discount rate.

THE BASE CASE FOR THE QMDM

In *Quantifying Marketability Discounts*, we introduced the QMDM with a base case to illustrate the model. In this book, we will discuss that same base case in three parts, and will then provide three realistic applications of the QMDM in the following section. The three parts of the base case are:

- The conceptual overview originally presented.

- A practical illustration of the base case indicating exactly how the QMDM values the example security and why the concluded value differs from the marketable minority value. In other words, the components of the marketability discount will be analyzed.

- The base case in the context of the *QMDM Companion.*

At the conclusion of this section, readers should be able to understand both the conceptual and the mechanical operation of the QMDM.

The base case presented in this chapter is the same case presented in *Quantifying Marketability Discounts* in 1997 and in 2001. The concluded marketability discount is 71%. Because this base case is outside the "normal range" of 35% to 45% or so, some readers inferred that the QMDM was designed to achieve high discounts. Not so. The QMDM is designed to achieve appropriate discounts based on relevant facts and circumstances.

Following the base case discussion, three examples of the QMDM in action are provided. We then address the use of the QMDM in non-tax (i.e., real world) transactions. Finally, we comment briefly on criticisms of the QMDM.

Base Case Conceptual Overview

The QMDM is most frequently used in the context of the valuation of a company at the marketable minority level. The assumptions of the base case are summarized in Figure 7-7. A discount rate of 16% is developed using the Adjusted Capital Asset Pricing Model The expected growth rate of earnings (g_e) is 6%. The Figure illustrates the development of the discount rate, the associated capitalization rate, and the relevant multiple of earnings. With expected earnings of $0.10 per share next year, the concluded marketable minority value is $1.00 per share.

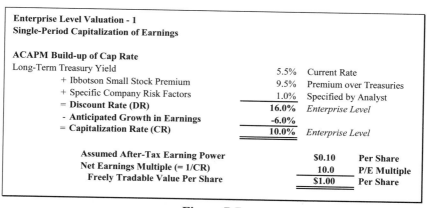

Figure 7-7

Based on the assumed facts and circumstances surrounding the enterprise valuation, which are unstated except as otherwise noted below, the following conclusions have been reached with respect to the five key assumptions of the QMDM.

- *Expected Growth Rate of Value = 6%.* The build-up above assumes an annual earnings growth of 6%. It is assumed that all cash flows (until the end of the holding period) are distributed to the majority shareholder as excess compensation. The economic effect of this assumption is that there will be no retained earnings for reinvestment, and therefore, the expected growth in value will be equal to the expected (long-term) growth rate of earnings, or 6%. The non-pro rata distribution of earnings (management leakage) creates an agency cost for (nonmarketable) minority shareholders that must be taken into account in their valuation.

- *Expected Dividend Yield = 0%.* Since all available earnings of the enterprise are being paid to the controlling shareholder, no net earnings will be available for distribution to all shareholders.

- *Expected Growth in Dividends = 0%.* Since there is no expectation for dividends, there is no expectation for future growth in dividends.

- *Expected Holding Period = 10 years.* Normally, analysts applying the QMDM use a reasonable range of holding periods. In the present example, the holding period is assumed to be exactly 10 years. Given the base value of $1.00 per share, the expected growth rate of value of 6% per year, and the expected holding period of 10 years, the only expected minority shareholder benefit is the expected terminal cash flow of $1.79 per share ($1.00 x $(1 + 6\%)^{10}$). This terminal cash flow is a marketable minority level value indication given the base from which it is derived, which is the marketable minority interest basis.

- *Required Holding Period (Rate of) Return = 20% per year.* The required holding period rate of return is a discount rate applicable to the cash flows from the subject illiquid investment from the perspective of the minority shareholder. The required holding period return reflects the investor's required rate of return, or the opportunity cost of investing in the subject company versus another, similar investment that has immediate market liquidity. Relative to the enterprise discount rate of 16%, the required holding period return of 20% represents a holding period premium (HPP) of 4%.

To be clear at the outset, the QMDM begins at the marketable minority level of value. That value is then assumed to grow at G_v. It further assumes that the terminal value, to be received at the end of the expected holding period, will be at the then-marketable minority value. If another expectation is more realistic, certain modeling assumptions in the QMDM can adjust for them. For purposes of the present discussion, however, we assume that the terminal value cash flow will be at the marketable minority value.

Each of the key assumptions will be addressed below and perspectives on their general reasonableness will be provided. The specific assumptions of the base case are shown in graphically in Figure 7-8.

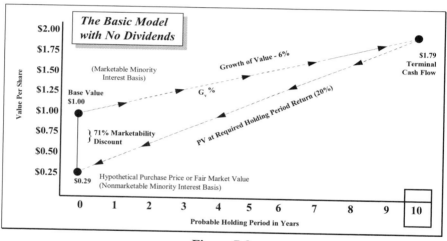

Figure 7-8

Given these assumptions, the QMDM values the subject interest at $0.29 per share. The $0.29 per share represents the present value of the terminal cash flow of $1.79 per share (the result of $1.00 growing at 6% compounded for 10 years) to be received 10 years out, discounted to the present at the required holding period return of 20%.

The implied marketability discount based on this analysis is 71% (the percentage difference between $1 per share enterprise value on a marketable minority interest basis and the indicated fair market value if $0.29 per share on a nonmarketable minority interest basis).

Algebraically, the resulting marketability discount, MD, can be seen as:

$$MD = \left\{ 1 - \left[\frac{\text{Shareholder's Value}}{\text{Enterprise Value}} \right] \right\} \%$$

or

$$1 - \left[\frac{\text{Value of Expected Cash Flows to Minority Shareholder}}{\text{Value of Expected Cash Flows in Context of Ongoing Business}} \right] \%$$

or, substituting numbers from the example

$$MD = \left[1 - \frac{\$0.29}{\$1.00} \right]$$

$$= \quad (1 - 0.29) \ \%$$

$$= \quad 71\%$$

Figure 7-9

Given the assumptions, the value of a minority interest is a straightforward application of present value concepts. The discount of 71% is the net impact of the factors that differentiate the postulated nonmarketable minority interest from a freely tradable interest, where the freely tradable value is $1 per share. A rational buyer (i.e., the hypothetical willing buyer) would pay no more than $0.29 per share for the stipulated investment. Alternatively, a rational seller (i.e., the hypothetical willing seller) would realize these facts. A hypothetical transaction could occur at the derived price of $0.29 per share.

In the absence of a hypothetical transaction, the hypothetical willing seller becomes, in effect, the buyer who is faced with the same investment situation as the hypothetical willing buyer. It should be clear at the outset that the QMDM considers both hypothetical willing buyers and hypothetical willing sellers in the context of fair market value. Importantly, the QMDM also offers a practical tool to assist real buyers and sellers of illiquid minority interests.

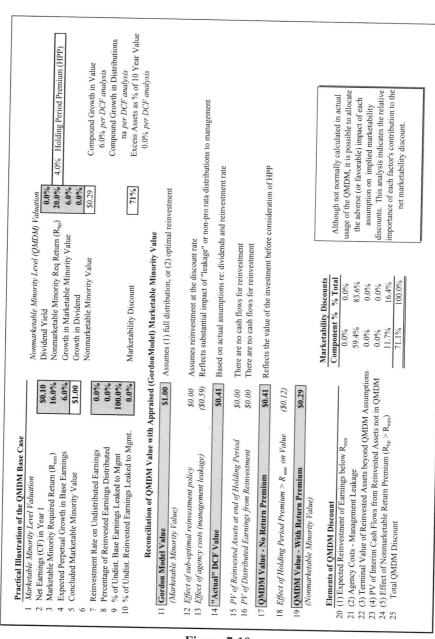

Figure 7-10

Base Case Practical Illustration

The QMDM is a discounted cash flow model. In the base case, there is only one cash flow, the terminal cash flow. Figure 7-10 sets forth the base case in a different form. We will focus on the aspects of the Figure that are most important to understanding the components of the concluded marketability discount of 71%.

Several observations can be made from the practical illustration of the base case presented in Figure 7-10. First, the assumptions are exactly the same as in the conceptual presentation (see Lines 1-10). Second, four separate values are calculated in lines 11-19:

- *The Gordon Model Value (Line 11)*. This is equal to $1.00 (per share). This valuation at the marketable minority level assumes that all cash flows are reinvested in the enterprise at the discount rate of 16%. The fact that they are not going to be reinvested, but rather paid out in excess owner compensation *(Line 9)*, does not change the value of the enterprise. The expected earnings of $0.10 have been normalized to reflect this adjustment.

- *"Actual" DCF Value (Line 14)*. This value is based on the actual assumptions regarding dividends (none), reinvestment rate (none), and enterprise discount rate (16%). It calculates the value of the cash flows expected by the minority shareholder, which is $0.41 (per share) before consideration of a holding period premium for illiquidity risks. This can be confirmed as follows: The expected future value remains at $1.79. The present value is the future value discounted to the present at the enterprise discount rate ($1.79 / (1 + 16\%)^{10} = \$0.41$). As a result, as seen in the bottom box of the chart at line 21, the marketability discount would be 59% before consideration of the holding period premium to reflect shareholder risks.

- *QMDM Value – No Return Premium (HPP) (Line 17)*. In the present example, with assumed growth in value of exactly 6%, which corresponds with the assumed growth in earnings, this value is identical to the "Actual" DCF Value, or $0.41 per share. There are potential elements of DCF value that may not be considered explicitly in the QMDM. These can result, for example, from a misspecification of the expected growth rate. There is no misspecification in this example, so there is no divergence from the actual DCF value.

- *QMDM Value – With Return Premium (HPP) (Line 19).* The QMDM value is $0.29 (per share), which, as noted above, is the present value of the expected terminal value of $1.79 (per share) discounted to the present at the required holding period return of 20%, which includes a holding period premium (HPP) of 4%. The difference in value between the "Actual" DCF Value (and the QMDM Value – No HPP), represents the diminution in value resulting from the isolated impact of the assumed HPP of 4%. The increase in the discount rate by the 4% HPP reduces value by an additional $0.12 per share (Line 18), therefore increasing marketability discount by another 12% (Line 24).

This practical illustration of the base case is confirming of the algebraic representation of the enterprise and shareholder values above. This illustration also proves that we have accounted for all of the cash flows of the enterprise when applying the QMDM. We begin with the enterprise cash flows, and then determine the portion of those cash flows that will be applicable to minority shareholders (and the reasons for any diminution). By way of further illustration, if the assumptions are changed such that all cash flows are reinvested at the discount rate of 16% and no HPP is assumed, then the QMDM value is equal to the Gordon Model value, both equal to $1.00 (per share), and the calculated marketability discount would be zero.

The practical illustration of the base case suggests that the components of the marketability discount can be identified and quantified.

- *Agency Costs.* Leakage of cash flow to a controlling shareholder reduced value by $0.59 per share to $0.41 per share. So we see that the divergence of cash flows to shareholder (no distribution) relative to total availability (through the availability of capitalized enterprise cash flows) creates a substantial differential between shareholder and enterprise values. In this example, agency costs comprise about 84% of the total marketability discount of 71% (Line 24).

- *Holding Period Premium > 0%.* The assumption of a holding period premium (*HPP*) of 4.0% raised the shareholder's discount rate (R_{hp}) to 20% relative to $R = 16\%$. As seen above this incremented risk premium reduced value (relative to $1.00 per share of enterprise value) by $0.12 per share (or about 16% of the total marketability discount of 71%).

At this stage we need to make an important point. Some have suggested that the QMDM, by capturing the effect of agency costs, is really quantifying portions of the minority interest discount rather than the marketability discount. After all, they say, leakage of cash flows to management is a direct result of lack of control and not lack of marketability.

Recall the discussion of Chapter 3 regarding this issue. Minority shareholders of public companies do not have control over enterprise cash flows or their distribution. Yet there is no market price penalty for this lack of control in the public securities markets. Why? Because collectively, public shareholders have *substantial control* collectively in terms of focusing management attention on shareholder returns. And individually, public shareholders have the control to achieve liquidity by selling their shares in the public markets. It is the absence of the market mechanism, and not a lack of control over enterprises, that creates the divergences between enterprise and shareholder values. Therefore, logically, it is appropriate to capture the impact of agency costs as an element of the marketability discount.[169]

Base Case in the *QMDM Companion*

The five base case assumptions are entered into the *QMDM Companion* in Figure 7-11. In addition to the five key assumptions of the QMDM, the spreadsheet allows for two important modeling assumptions. In cases where there are dividends or distributions, the appraiser can specify their receipt at the end or at mid-year for each forecast year. And, as noted earlier, there is an input for the appraiser's assumption if liquidity is expected to be achieved at a premium or discount to the expected marketable minority value. In the base case, liquidity is assumed to be at the marketable minority level, so the modeling input is 0%, reflecting no premium or discount to that value level.

A more detailed discussion of the QMDM is found in the 2004 edition of *Quantifying Marketability Discounts* presented in E-Book format, and accompanied by the *QMDM Companion*. The 2004 edition provides an overview of the QMDM in the context of the Integrated Theory.[170]

---

[169] This highlights the importance of making appropriate Type 2I normalizing adjustments on the development of the marketable minority indication of value (to which the marketability discount is applied). See the discussion of normalizing adjustments in Chapter 4.

[170] *Quantifying Marketability Discounts* 2004 Edition and the *QMDM Companion* are available at www.mercercaptial.com.

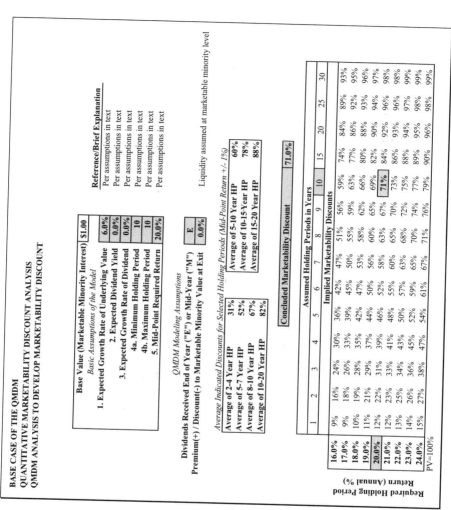

Figure 7-11

When the base case assumptions are applied, the QMDM calculates an implied marketability discount of 71%, as shown at the intersection of a 20% required holding period return and a 10-year holding period.

Initial Questions About the Base Case

The base case was presented under very specific assumptions. Readers might ask several questions regarding this case, or for that matter, any situation in which an appraiser uses the QMDM.

How do we know the growth rate of value (g_v)? We estimate g_v based upon the facts at hand. The enterprise level valuation provides critical information necessary to answer this question. The outlook for a firm's dividend policy, core earnings growth, and prospects for suboptimal reinvestment or cash flow leakage help the appraiser estimate g_v.

Why is the growth rate of value applied to the marketable minority interest valuation indication? The growth rate of value in the QMDM is applied to the marketable minority interest base value for three primary reasons:

- First, the appraiser is grounded in the growth expectations of the enterprise as a result of preparing the initial indication of value at this level. The marketable minority value is an enterprise value that sets the value context for minority investors. This is the most logical vantage point from which to view expectations for future growth in value, because earnings growth expectations are necessarily embedded in the underlying valuation at this point.

- Second, we believe that this concept of growth most closely approximates the thinking of hypothetical and real investors in nonmarketable minority interests of businesses.

- Finally, the QMDM assumes liquidity will be achieved at the marketable minority level (unless the appraiser specifies otherwise). The rationale for this position is discussed in the next section, Simulating the Thinking of Hypothetical Investors.

How do we know that the holding period is exactly 10 years? In the vast majority of valuation cases, the length of the holding period for a minority investment will not be known with certainty. It might end up being, after all, shorter or longer. Business appraisers cannot be expected to know the unknowable. However, based upon the facts and circumstances that exist relative to specific investments, real-life purchasers must address the holding period question. Can it be answered with precision? Not necessarily, but the facts will provide evidence to suggest that the holding period may be very short, very long, or something in between. Risk-averse investors will consider this information in their pricing decisions. After all, real-life investors make investment decisions based upon available information. Hypothetical willing buyers and sellers (and appraisers) must do the same. The fact that the expected holding period cannot be known with certainty is no basis for criticizing the QMDM or for criticizing appraisers who make a good faith effort to estimate the holding period in the face of uncertainty.

How do we know that liquidity can be achieved at the end of the holding period at the marketable minority level? We do not, of course, but we can assess the probabilities. Will liquidity be available from an initial public offering of the entity's shares? What is the likelihood that the company will be sold outright at a controlling interest value? And if so, will a premium valuation be achieved? What is the likelihood that the current illiquidity discount implicit in these calculations will still be present at a future date? While specific calculations may not be made, investors assess the probabilities, at least in a general sense.

How do we determine the investor's required rate of return during the holding period (R_{hp})? We can start with known market rates of return, but must add increments of return for the risks of the holding period (i.e., exact a premium return) for both illiquidity and uncertainty.

Again, the marketability discount implied by the QMDM base case analysis is 71%. In this case, the derivation of a marketability discount was fairly straightforward. The basic model assumed liquidity would come at the marketable minority interest level of value, in exactly 10 years. But it might not. Hypothetical willing buyers must consider, relative to a certain sale at $1.79 per share in 10 years, several other possibilities.

Figure 7-12 provides an enhancement of the terminal point of Figure 7-9. In the context of this Figure, we can address the questions of hypothetical willing buyers (and sellers).

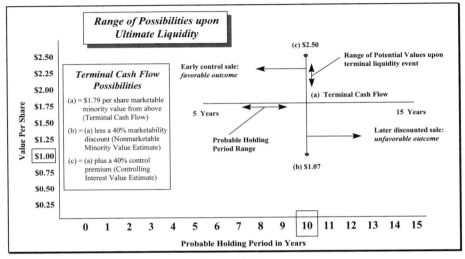

Figure 7-12

This Figure and discussion incorporate return calculations summarized in Figure 7-13.

What is the likelihood that the sale would occur at the strategic control level of value, say $2.50 per share after applying an assumed control premium of 40% to the expected $1.79 per share (maintaining our assumption of liquidity in exactly 10 years)? That would be favorable. In fact, an investor who buys at $0.29 per share, holds for 10 years, and sells for $2.50 per share would experience a compound rate of return of 24%, rather than the required holding period return of 20%. This would clearly be a favorable event.

What is the likelihood that the sale will be discounted, say by a marketability discount of 40% (or the operation of a shareholders' agreement), yielding proceeds of only $1.07 per share in 10 years? In this event, the investor who pays $0.29 per share would experience a compound rate of return of 14%. That would be unfavorable, at least relative to the expected holding period return of 20%, but not a disaster in the context of this single investment or in an assumed portfolio of investments.

What is the likelihood of achieving liquidity in less than 10 years? Consider the same assumptions about pricing as above and examine the implied returns for the hypothetical investor who sells in five, rather than 10 years. The marketable minority interest value would be $1.34 per share ($1 per share growing at 6% per year).

Sell at a control price of $1.88 per share (40% control premium). The investor's annual return would be 45%, which would be spectacular.

1. Sell at a discounted price of $0.80 per share (marketability discount of 40%). The investor's annual return would be about 23%, and still more favorable than the required holding period return of 20%.

2. Clearly, achieving liquidity earlier than expected is generally favorable to the hypothetical willing buyer.

What is the likelihood that liquidity will not occur until after the expected 10-year period? Let's assume that liquidity is achieved in 15 years. The marketable minority interest value would be $2.40 per share.

1. Sell at a control price of $3.36 per share (40% premium). The investor's annual return would be 18%, or modestly below the required holding period return (20%).

2. Sell at a discounted price of $1.44 per share (40% marketability discount). The investor's annual return would be 11%, again, below the required return of 20%, but not a disaster.

CALCULATED EXPECTED RATES OF RETURNS
Assuming Exit (Liquidity) at Assumed Control, Marketable Minority and
Nonmarketable Minority Values Over Varying Expected Holding Periods
Base Case Investment (6% Growth, No Expected Dividends)

Purchase Price $0.29 Per Share Expected Holding Period (in Years)	6% Growth Expected Per Share Enterprise Value*	40% Implied Control Value	Control Premium Rate of Return if Liquidity Achieved in Year	Compound Return Liquidity Occurs at the Marketable Minority Interest Level*	40% Implied Minority Value	Marketability Discount Rate of Return if Liquidity Achieved in Year
0	$1.00	$1.40	na	na	na	na
1	$1.06	$1.48	410%	266%	$0.64	121%
2	$1.12	$1.57	133%	97%	$0.67	52%
3	$1.19	$1.67	79%	60%	$0.71	35%
4	$1.26	$1.77	57%	44%	$0.76	27%
5	$1.34	$1.87	45%	36%	$0.80	23%
6	$1.42	$1.99	38%	30%	$0.85	20%
7	$1.50	$2.11	33%	27%	$0.90	18%
8	$1.59	$2.23	29%	24%	$0.96	16%
9	$1.69	$2.37	26%	22%	$1.01	15%
10	$1.79	$2.51	24%	20%	$1.07	14%
11	$1.90	$2.66	22%	19%	$1.14	13%
12	$2.01	$2.82	21%	18%	$1.21	13%
13	$2.13	$2.99	20%	17%	$1.28	12%
14	$2.26	$3.17	19%	16%	$1.36	12%
15	$2.40	$3.36	18%	15%	$1.44	11%
16	$2.54	$3.56	17%	15%	$1.52	11%
17	$2.69	$3.77	16%	14%	$1.62	11%
18	$2.85	$4.00	16%	14%	$1.71	10%
19	$3.03	$4.24	15%	13%	$1.82	10%
20	$3.21	$4.49	15%	13%	$1.92	10%

* Enterprise value estimated at the hypothetical, marketable minority interest level

Figure 7-13

Simulating the Thinking of Hypothetical Investors

Figure 7-13 depicts the base case range of possibilities in more quantitative terms. Both the qualitative pictures of Figures 7-7 and 7-11 and the quantitative results shown above are helpful as we attempt to simulate the thinking of hypothetical investors as they deal with the reality of nonmarketable minority interests in business entities.

Are we suggesting that every hypothetical or real investor makes the detailed calculations shown in Figure 7-13? No. In *Estate of Lauder*, an expert was criticized by the Court for making complex calculations:

> We are not convinced that the market would engage in the rigid type of analysis that Dr. Blaydon followed in arriving at his estimate of the discount to be applied to reflect lack of liquidity.[171]

But whether a hypothetical investor makes detailed calculations or not, the issues are factored into the decision-making process in a qualitative sense. We now introduce Mr. Hypothetical Willing Buyer, a client of the author, who was provided with the base case as an investment opportunity. When he finally agreed to the deal at $0.29 per share, this is what he told me:

> I know that I want to earn about 20% per year on any investment that can tie up my money and is not likely to produce dividends. That seems pretty reasonable. I'd like to get more, but I can live with 20%.

> How long will my money be tied up? I don't have any idea, but, based on the history of the business, my guess is that it will be a long time, maybe 10 years or so. No one in senior management will be anywhere close to retirement before then. Maybe, by then, the company will be big enough to have an IPO, or maybe they'll sell the company. At any rate, if I pay $0.29 per share today, I can get my 20% over this period if the base value just keeps on growing at about 6%. They've done that for a long time, and there seems to be plenty of market potential to keep it up.

> But you know, if I had to hold for even 15 years, and can sell at any kind of reasonable price, I'll probably make 10% or 12%. And who knows, maybe they'll surprise me and sell the whole company in the next few years. I'd make out like a bandit if that happened!

> So, I guess I can't get hurt too badly by this deal, and I've got a shot at some pretty sporty returns if something favorable happens.

> What the heck, I'll do this deal for $0.29 per share. That's my price.

---

[171] *Estate of Lauder v. Commissioner*, 68 T.C.M. (CCH) 985 (1994), footnote 27.

Every time a hypothetical or real investor makes an investment in the nonmarketable stock (or ownership units) of a closely held company (or other entity), he or she is faced with a similar range of possibilities. Investment decisions are ultimately made in the face of uncertainty based upon the specific facts and circumstances of each investment.

The QMDM assists appraisers in their efforts to simulate the thought process of hypothetical willing buyers and sellers. This simulation process is necessarily very specific and uses calculations that individual investors might not make. The purpose of the analysis, however, is to simulate the decision-making process in such a fashion that we can deal, specifically, with the kinds of factors that are generally acknowledged to have an impact on the value of investments, at both the enterprise and shareholder levels, and on marketability discounts.

Do hypothetical or real willing buyers and willing sellers enter into transactions in the face of the kinds of uncertainties outlined above? Yes, they do. We have observed many arms' length transactions in the shares of closely held companies where real investors invested real money in illiquid shares or ownership interests. Can appraisers simulate that thinking and quantify marketability discounts? Yes, we can.

This is not a leap of faith. In the enterprise valuations that all appraisers conduct, we attempt to simulate the collective thinking of the public markets that would result in market pricing for a closely held company under the assumption that there is a free and active market for its shares. In the alternative, we are simulating the thinking of buyers of controlling interests in companies. The typical appraisal report is filled with tables, analyses, calculations, and projections, all of which relate to the *facts and circumstances faced by the companies being valued at the valuation date.* The methodologies outlined in this book are designed to provide that same analytical rigor to valuation *at the shareholder level, where the facts and circumstances faced by the hypothetical investor may differ from those faced by investors in freely marketable securities.*

EXAMPLES OF THE QMDM IN ACTION

The five assumptions of the QMDM are applicable to all valuation scenarios, and their specification forces the appraiser (and the reader of the appraisal report) to deal specifically with the underlying economic factors giving rise to the marketability discount. Differences of opinion are likely to exist with respect to the estimation of one or more of the parameters, but this framework pushes the parties to carefully analyze the specific facts and circumstances of the subject company to support their assumptions. Isn't this what courts (and other users of appraisal reports) have been demanding in marketability discount analyses?

Three examples of the QMDM in use are provided for perspective and to illustrate the ability of the Model to enable appraisers to address widely disparate fact patterns with consistency and confidence. The summary tables which present the QMDM results were developed using the *QMDM Companion*. Each example involves small, minority interests of the respective enterprises.

Example #1: A Real Estate Limited Partnership

In our first example, a real estate limited partnership owns raw land that is expected to grow in value at about 6% per year according to the real estate appraiser. The expected holding period is fairly lengthy, eight to 10 years. Liquidity will likely come as development approaches the properties. The appraiser has determined that a required holding period return of 20% is appropriate, partially because of burdensome features of the limited partnership agreement. There are no dividends, with the property generating just enough cash flow to pay expected expenses. *Note that there are no guideline transactions in any of the restricted stock studies that are reasonably comparable to this situation.* The results of the QMDM calculations for this example are show in Figure 7-14.

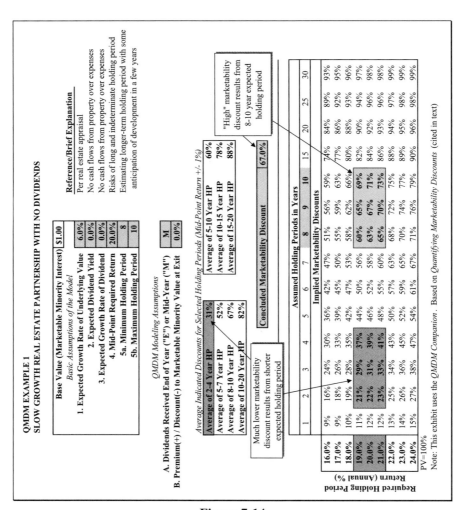

Figure 7-14

Under the indicated assumptions, the midpoint marketability discount for the eight to 10-year expected holding period is 67%. Such a discount would be appropriate for an investment with the described characteristics. Note, however, that if the appropriate holding period assumption had been two to four years, the appropriate marketability discount would have been 31%. This simple illustration should make it clear that appraisers cannot ignore the outlook for the holding period when valuing illiquid minority interests.

Example #2: High-Distribution Family Limited Partnership

In our second example, a family limited partnership holds an attractive, well-maintained, high-occupancy apartment building. Values are growing at about 3% to 4% per year per the real estate appraisers. The partnership units receive distributions of 10% (of pro rata value) per year, and rent increases and a near-term pay-off of partnership debt suggest that distributions will grow at 3% to 4% per year. There is a long history of distributions, and expectations that they will continue. The expected holding period is 10 to 15 years based on current family ownership and long-term plans. The required holding period return of 17% is mitigated by the high level and predictability of distributions. *Note that there are no guideline transactions in any of the restricted stock studies that are reasonably comparable to this situation (because it is a partnership and substantial dividends are expected).* The results of the QMDM calculations for this example are shown in Figure 7-15.

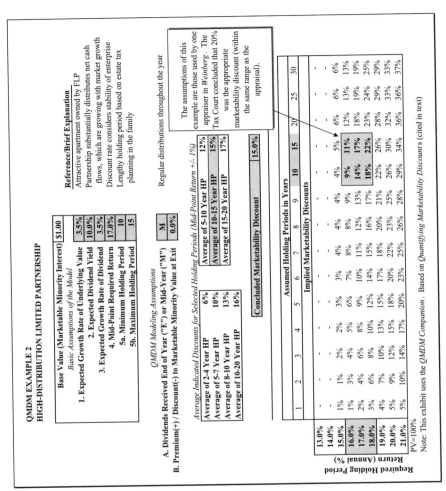

Figure 7-15

Under the indicated assumptions, the appropriate marketability discount is 15% for the 10-to-15-year holding period. Such a discount would be appropriate for an investment with the indicated characteristics. Interestingly, Example #2 reflects the assumptions made by one appraiser using the QMDM for the partnership valued in *Weinberg*.[172] In that decision, the Court commented that small changes in assumptions using the QMDM can yield large changes in results, which some have viewed as a key criticism of the Model.

Examining the calculations in Figure 7-15, it should be clear that *small changes* in assumptions (an increase of a year or two in the expected holding period or an increase of a percentage point in the required holding period return) do not have large impacts on the calculated results. Even more interesting in *Weinberg*, after commenting about the assumptions, the Court held that the appropriate marketability discount was 20%, or clearly within the range of judgment based on the indicated assumptions (the highlighted box shown in Figure 7-13). We find it fascinating that appraisers who cite *Weinberg's* criticism of the QMDM almost never note that the appraiser using the QMDM won the marketability discount issue. The other expert's marketability discount was 35% (surprise). The Court's conclusion was much closer to the QMDM result than to the result of restricted stock and pre-IPO benchmark analysis used by the other appraisers.

---

[172] *Estate of Etta H. Weinberg, et al., v. Commissioner*, T.C. Memo. 2000-51. In *Weinberg*, the Court made a hypothetical calculation and increased the expected holding period by five years from 10-to-15 years to 15-to-20 years, and increased the discount rate by 3%. The combination of these changes would have increased the calculated marketability discount from 15% (used by one appraiser) to 30%. Big changes in DCF assumptions create big changes in results.

See also Mercer Capital's *E-Law Newsletter* 2000-03 & 04, "*Weinberg et al. v. Commissioner* - It's Not About the Marketability Discount," March 13, 2000, and "It's Not About Marketability, It's About Minority Interest," *Valuation Strategies*, July/August 2000.

Example #3: Rapidly Growing C Corporation

In our third and final example, the subject enterprise is a rapidly growing C corporation with revenues of $50 million and a net income margin of 10%. This is a well-run, attractive company in an expanding service industry, and management expects to be able to maintain margins and to grow. All earnings are being reinvested into the company to finance its growth, and there are realistic expectations for 15% compound growth for the next 10 years or more. Management intends to continue to build the company, but a sale or even an IPO could be possible over the next decade as the controlling shareholders may desire liquidity. There are no expectations, however, for any near-term sale. The required holding period return of 20% represents a premium to the enterprise's discount rate to reflect the numerous uncertainties and risks of illiquid minority ownership over and above the risks of the company. The appraiser estimated the holding period to be within the fairly broad range of five to 10 years. The results of the QMDM calculations are shown in Figure 7-16.

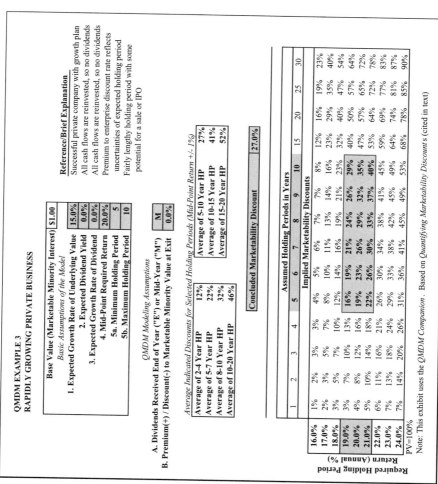

Figure 7-16

Under the indicated assumptions for Example #3, the appraiser determined the appropriate marketability discount to be 27%, which is the mid-point of the calculated discounts for the five-to-10-year expected holding period. While there are no expectations for dividends from the subject company, the minority shareholder can expect significant capital appreciation and reasonable prospects for eventual liquidity. The highlighted range of discounts is broad, but it is the relevant range. Within that range, the appraiser must decide the discount, just as a real-life investor would decide the price he or she would pay based on the overall facts and circumstances.

Summary of the Examples

The three examples above illustrate three widely different investments in illiquid, minority interests of business enterprises. With historical benchmark analysis, where marketability discounts are estimated to be 35%, plus or minus a bit, or even 35% to 45%, plus or minus a bit, it would be impossible to estimate the appropriate marketability discounts for any of the examples with any degree of confidence. Further, even if an appraiser wanted to use restricted stock studies to conduct guideline company analysis, there would be no comparable transactions for either Example #1 or Example #2, because none of the transactions involve entities owning only land or real estate. While guideline companies might be found for the company in Example #3 in a restricted stock database, few, if any of them would be in the same industry, and all of the supposedly guideline transactions would have occurred years ago, and perhaps, many years ago.

Interestingly, the average discount for the three examples is about 35% (15% plus 27% plus 67% divided by 3), but none of the marketability discounts fit comfortably within the so-called benchmark ranges. It should be clear from the wide range of potential investment situations illustrated by the three examples above, that appraisers need tools to address them with credibility. The QMDM is that tool.

APPLICABILITY OF THE QMDM TO NON-TAX SITUATIONS

The marketability discount literature has historically focused almost exclusively on the gift and estate tax arena. Yet we have seen numerous instances of the QMDM's application in non-tax situations, for example, when actual buyers and sellers are negotiating transactions in illiquid business interests. We have found that the QMDM is able to move from the hypothetical world of tax compliance to the real world of dispute resolution, economic planning, and capital investment. Actual buyers and sellers frequently remark that the parameters of the QMDM effectively mimic the considerations in their own real-life investment discipline, while not a single party to a real-life transaction in substantial illiquid interests has yet made reference to any statistic from the published IPO and restricted stock studies.

Kenneth W. Patton, ASA, President of Mercer Capital, wrote an article regarding application of the QMDM in non-tax situations.[173] In that article, he recounted actual applications of the QMDM to the development and resolution of buy-sell agreements among extended family members holding fractional interests in a large number of real estate partnerships, and a public company's purchase of a significant minority interest in a closely held company that was not in its core business. In each instance, the dollar amounts were significant, the transactions were complex, and the negotiations included participants with a variety of backgrounds (often nonfinancial). Application of the QMDM lends credibility to the valuation process, and contributes to the resolution of negotiations – the ultimate test of a valuation method.

---

[173] Kenneth W. Patton, "The QMDM in Action in Non-Tax Situations," Mercer Capital's *E-Law Business Valuation Perspective,* Issue 2002-09, December 13, 2002.

CRITICISMS OF THE QMDM

Since its first public exposure in 1994, the QMDM has been criticized by both fellow appraisers and the Tax Court.[174] The various criticisms fall into two general categories:

- The QMDM measures something other than the marketability discount. Some observers believe that the QMDM captures elements that relate to lack of control rather than lack of marketability.

- The QMDM is overly sensitive to changes in the five assumed parameters.

---

[174] We have addressed all known criticisms in writing in many articles in the *Business Valuation Review*, *Valuation Strategies*, and in issues of *Value Matters*[TM], Mercer Capital's electronic newsletter. I was asked by the Court in a recent case about the Tax Court's criticisms of the QMDM. In my response, I noted that the thrust of the Court's criticisms in *Weinberg* and *Janda* were related to the *assumptions* made by appraisers using the QMDM, and not so much about the Model itself.

Eric Engstrom, "An Examination of the QMDM," *Shannon Pratt's Business Valuation Update*, March 2001, pp. 7-8.

Z. Christopher Mercer, "Mercer Responds to Engstrom Analysis," *Shannon Pratt's Business Valuation Update*, March 2001, pp. 9-10.

Jay B. Abrams, *Quantitative Business Valuation* (New York, McGraw-Hill, 2001). Mr. Abrams criticized the QMDM in his book. My detailed response to that criticism can be found in his book since he was kind enough to offer me space for rebuttal.

Z. Christopher Mercer, "The QMDM and Estimating Required Rates of Return for Restricted Stocks of Public Companies," *Business Valuation Review*, June 2001, pp. 5-9.

Lance S. Hall, and Espen Robak, "Bringing Sanity to Marketability Discounts," *Valuation Strategies*, July/August 2001, pp. 6-13, 45-46.

Z. Christopher Mercer and Nicholas J. Heinz, "Marketability Discounts: Back to Reality," *Valuation Strategies*, November/December 2001, pp. 34-40.

Abrams, Jay B., "Problems in the QMDM and Comparison to Economic Components Model: A Response to Chris Mercer," *Business Valuation Review*, June 2002, pp. 83-93.

Lance S. Hall and David M. Eckstein, "The Case of the Black-Box Model vs. Empirical Data." *Valuation Strategies*, July/August 2002, pp. 36-37.

Z. Christopher Mercer, "QMDM:QED," *Valuation Strategies*, July/August 2002, pp. 37-38.

An additional criticism is that the QMDM requires assumptions to be made.[175] However, *all* valuation methods (including the discounted cash flow method and market methods for valuing enterprises, and benchmark analysis related to pre-IPO and restricted stock studies for interests in enterprises) require assumptions. So, this can hardly be a legitimate criticism of any valuation method. As with assumptions made using other valuation methods, assumptions for the QMDM must be made in the context of the facts and circumstances of each appraisal and with the exercise of common sense, informed judgment, and reasonableness. The beauty of the QMDM is that it illustrates the sensitivity of conclusions to changes in assumptions in a very visual way, as can be clearly seen in the base case and in the three examples above.

Criticism #1: Does the QMDM Measure only the Marketability Discount?

As discussed previously, the expected growth in value assumption of the QMDM allows the appraiser to incorporate judgments regarding cash flow leakage from the enterprise and suboptimal reinvestment during the expected holding period into the determination of the marketability discount. Some critics have suggested that such adjustments relate to the subject interest's lack of control rather than the lack of marketability.[176] After all, would not such negative influences on value be eliminated if the subject interest exercised control over the enterprise?

This criticism reflects an inconsistent approach to the levels of value framework. While it is true that controlling shareholders of private companies do not suffer the indignities of expected cash flow leakage (and may be the beneficiaries), neither do minority shareholders in public companies (i.e., the marketable minority level of value). The discipline of the marketplace prevents public company managements from routinely denying shareholders the benefits of pro rata distribution of cash flows and/or optimal reinvestment. In other words, if management of a public company routinely made suboptimal reinvestment decisions and/or paid itself substantially above-market compensation (cash flow leakage), the minority shareholders could take advantage of their liquidity and sell

---

[175] The articles cited above indicating criticisms of the QMDM include the criticism of Mr. Jay B. Abrams, ASA, CPA. Mr. Abrams' criticism relates to the misunderstanding of the magnitude of the holding period premiums employed when using the QMDM. This criticism is addressed in the section examining restricted stock studies, where the magnitude of HPP is discussed at length.

[176] See, for example, Engstrom. Supra. Dr. Mukesh Bajaj has also made this assertion publicly at appraisal conferences; however, we are not aware of any instance where he has addressed this issue in writing.

the shares. Such selling would ultimately lead to "under-priced" stock – in turn leading to the potential for an unsolicited takeover of the company, and installation of new management.[177]

Controlling shareholders of private companies are in an interesting situation with respect to future suboptimal reinvestment. The current values of their businesses reflect the assumption of optimal reinvestment. However, if they knowingly expect to make suboptimal reinvestments, the loss of opportunity for returns will be borne by them as well as by any minority shareholders. In those cases, the value of the business from the controlling shareholders' viewpoints will exceed the value of their expected business plans.[178]

The ability of public minority shareholders to achieve liquidity is generally sufficient to enforce management discipline and prevent expected cash flow leakage and suboptimal reinvestment even without control of the enterprise by individual, minority shareholders. Both public and private shareholders lack "control." As a result, considerations of both cash flow leakage and suboptimal reinvestment are appropriately included in the determination of the marketability discount.[179]

While it is beyond the scope of this chapter (see Chapter 4), the QMDM assumes that appraisers make normalizing adjustments to enterprise cash flows to eliminate the effects of nonrecurring events as well as discretionary management expenses (cash flow leakage). If it were not so, the resulting valuation indications would not be marketable minority indications – for the reasons outlined in the paragraphs above. Some appraisers want to call such adjustments "control adjustments" because minority shareholders of private companies lack the power to eliminate leakages. However, public minority shareholders have this same lack of control. Lack of control is not the issue. The real issue, and the relevant basis

---

[177] This is not to say that the managers of public companies never make mistakes or that public companies never endure bad outcomes. Rather, the process described herein prevents management from routinely abusing minority shareholders such that *expectations* regarding cash flow leakage and/or suboptimal reinvestment are unfavorable.

[178] This phenomenon was discussed briefly in Chapter 3. A controlling shareholder's decision to continue making suboptimal reinvestments creates an opportunity cost not only for himself, but for all shareholders.

[179] This discussion assumes that appropriate normalizing earnings adjustments have been made in the enterprise-level valuation. We have discussed this closely related topic in several presentations and speeches in recent years and in an appendix written by Mercer for Pratt's *Cost of Capital*. The subject is further addressed in Chapter 4.

for comparative analysis, is the lack of marketability, which would enable the minority shareholder to avoid the detrimental value impact of leakages.

Criticism #2: Is the QMDM Overly Sensitive to Changes in Assumptions?

Some critics, notably the Tax Court in *Weinberg*, have suggested that the QMDM is overly sensitive to small changes in valuation assumptions, as noted above. Based on the discussion regarding Example #2 above, we respectfully disagree with the Court that the described assumption changes noted in *Weinberg* were "slight variations." Further, the resulting change in the marketability discount is a function only of the basic present value principles used in nearly all appraisals. *The QMDM is no more sensitive to changes in assumptions than any other discounted cash flow model used to provide an indication of value for enterprises.*

In our experience, the sensitivity of the QMDM to changes in assumptions is one of the model's most valuable features. The model's sensitivity to various assumptions is measurable and predictable. By casting the question of the appropriate marketability discount into the light of basic present value analysis of expected economic benefits, the sensitivity of the QMDM forces users to carefully consider and support their rationales for their concluded discounts. Disputes as to the appropriate discount are generally reduced to differences over one or two assumptions. The effect of the various alternative assumptions on the computed discount can be readily determined. Such analysis is difficult, if not impossible, for users of the various benchmarking models.

CONCLUSIONS

We have introduced the QMDM and its five assumptions and have seen the model from three vantage points, a conceptual overview, a practical illustration summarizing the DCF calculations of the model, and four applications of the QMDM spreadsheet, including the base case. Under the assumptions of the base case, the concluded marketability discount is 71%. The purpose of using an example that reached a high discount (relative to historical, restricted stock average discounts) was to indicate that, under appropriate facts and circumstances, marketability discounts can be quite high. We have examined three other quite realistic applications of the QMDM and have seen the ability of the model to address differing facts and circumstances. Finally, we have briefly addressed criticisms of the QMDM, providing the bibliography of criticisms and Mercer responses.

As we stated at the outset of this chapter, the Quantitative Marketability Discount Model has been developed within the context of the Integrated Theory of Business Valuation and basic financial theory.

Critics of the QMDM have been unsuccessful in their criticisms:

- How can anyone realistically argue with the proposition that the value of an illiquid minority interest is the present value of the expected future benefits from that interest discounted to the present at an appropriate discount rate? Present value is, after all, present value.

- How can anyone realistically argue that the QMDM should be dismissed because appraisers using it must make assumptions? Appraisers make assumptions when employing every valuation approach, method, and technique.

- How can anyone realistically argue that the QMDM should be dismissed because the results developed when using it are sensitive to the assumptions made? The sensitivity of appraisal conclusions to the assumptions made is well known. In particular, indications of value developed using the discounted cash flow method are known to be highly sensitive to the assumptions made. The QMDM is but another example of the discounted cash flow method. The QMDM makes the sensitivity to changes in assumptions clearly visible for all to see. We cannot throw the baby out with the bathwater: We still need the baby, i.e., discounted cash flow analysis.

- How can anyone realistically argue that the QMDM should be dismissed because it captures the valuation impact of elements they believe should be considered as part of the minority interest discount – and then provide no means of capturing that valuation impact? It should be clear from the discussions in this book, that the detrimental valuation impact resulting from agency costs, or leakage, or suboptimal reinvestment of enterprise cash flows is, in reality, a function of lack of liquidity (in relationship to minority, publicly traded securities) rather than any lack of control (in relationship to minority, publicly traded securities).

In short, the critics of the QMDM have fallen short for the last decade. It is time for the valuation profession to embrace quantitative, rate of return analysis when valuing illiquid, minority interests of enterprises, just as it does in the valuation of the enterprises themselves.

Appendix 7-A

PERSPECTIVE

In the third edition of *Valuing a Business* by Pratt, Reilly and Schweihs, the authors, describe three general methods for valuing minority interests:[180]

- Proportion of the Enterprise Value Less Discount(s), if Applicable

- Direct Comparison with Sales of Other Minority Interests

- The Bottom-Up Method

Each of the three methods is discussed briefly at this point to place this chapter on the QMDM into perspective:

- "Proportion of the Enterprise Value Less Discount(s), if Applicable." This method calls for estimating the enterprise value of a business, then applying appropriate minority interest and/or marketability discounts. This method has been in common use by appraisers for many years. Appraisers have generally used some form of benchmark analysis, making comparisons or references to restricted stock studies, pre-IPO studies, and other sources in the process of reaching a conclusion regarding the marketability discount. As discussed elsewhere in this book, benchmark analysis has been criticized for its lack of relevance to particular valuation subjects, for the lack of comparability between cited studies and subject interests, and for its inability to distinguish the relative importance of particular facts and circumstances pertinent to subject interests.

- "Direct Comparison with Sales of Other Minority Interests." This method is actually a form of the guideline company method wherein the analyst makes comparisons between a subject minority interest and transactions of other minority interests in the same company, or with comparable minority interests of other companies. Because of the lack of

---

[180] Shannon P. Pratt, Robert F. Reilly, and Robert P. Schweihs, *Valuing a Business*, 3rd ed. (Chicago, IL: Irwin, 1996), pp. 312-315.

active markets for most private companies, this method is seldom definitive of value, although appraisers are always advised to examine arms' length transactions in the stock of the company they are valuing if such transactions are relevant to the value of a subject interest.

- "The 'Bottom-Up' Method." The "bottom-up" method "begins with nothing and builds up whatever elements of value" exist for minority interests, according to Pratt/Reilly/Schweihs:[181]

In most cases, the values the minority interest holder may realize fall into two categories: (1) distributions, usually in the form of dividends, and (2) proceeds to be realized on the sale of the interest. The mechanics of this approach are the same as those discussed in Chapter 9 [Income Approach: Discounted Economic Income Methods], with the expected cash contributions as the economic income returns to be discounted. The steps in this approach are as follows:

1. Project the flow of expected distributions (timing and amounts).

2. Project an amount realizable on sale of the interest (timing and amount).

3. Discount the results of steps 1 and 2 to present value at an appropriate discount rate, reflecting the degrees of uncertainty of realizing the expected returns at the times and in the amounts projected.

Pratt/Reilly/Schweihs have described the Quantitative Marketability Discount Model. They have also placed the QMDM directly within the context of valuation theory under the income approach.

---

[181]   Ibid, pp. 315-316.

Chapter 8
Fair Market Value vs. the Real World

FAIR MARKET VALUE AND THE INTEGRATED THEORY

The Integrated Theory is grounded in the real world of market participants. The Integrated Theory illustrates the normal behavior of the market participants buying and selling business enterprises and interests in them, whether in the public or private markets. And many aspects of less normal behavior can also be explained in the context of the Integrated Theory.

While the Integrated Theory is grounded in the real world of market participants, it is logical to ask what the theory says about fair market value since this is the standard under which a majority of appraisals are rendered. The hypothetical participants in the world of fair market value look at the real-world transactional data, including rational and irrational data points, in their determinations of price. But the definition of fair market value refines the behavior of hypothetical market participants (relative to real-world participants) in several specific ways by eliminating elements of compulsion found in the real world; eliminating knowledge disparities that may exist when real-world market participants engage in transactions; and equating the capacities of hypothetical buyers and sellers.

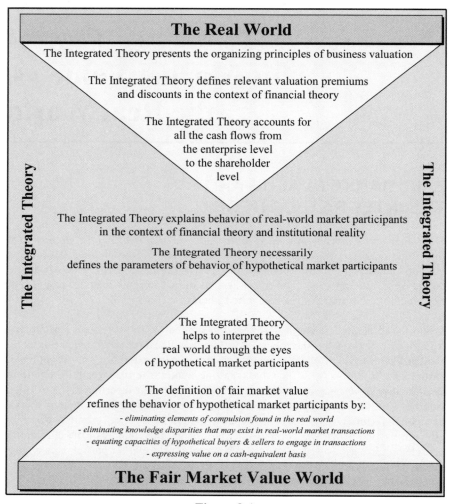

Figure 8-1

The world of fair market value is not the real world.[182] The world of fair market value is a special world in which the participants are expected (defined) to act in specific and predictable ways. It is a world of hypothetical willing buyers and sellers and engaging in hypothetical transactions. The real world is populated by real people, whose actions are unpredictable, and not subject to consistent definition, who engage in actual transactions with unpredictable results. It should come as no surprise that these two worlds, the hypothetical world of fair market value and the real world, are sometimes in conflict over the question of the value of businesses and business interests.

We begin this chapter with a review of the definition of fair market value. The second part of the chapter offers a partial interpretation of the meaning of fair market value from a valuation perspective and looks into the hypothetical world of fair market value.

COMMON QUESTIONS

1.   How can business appraisers test the reasonableness of their valuation assumptions and conclusions?

2.   What is the relationship between the standard of value of fair market value and the strategic control level of value?

FAIR MARKET VALUE DEFINED

Fair market value is known as a "willing buyer and willing seller" concept. Appraisers often recite versions of its definition by rote. Unfortunately, rote recitations overlook or ignore important elements of meaning and nuance in the hypothetical world of fair market value. Revenue Ruling 59-60 (RR 59-60) provides a working definition of fair market value: (the parentheticals [ ] below are added to facilitate discussion).

> 2.2 Section 20.2031-1(b) of the Estate Tax Regulations (section 81.10 of the Estate Tax Regulations 105) and section 25.2512-1 of the Gift Tax Regulations (section 86.19 of Gift Tax Regulations 108) define fair

---

[182]   The genesis of this chapter was an article of the same title as the chapter title. See Z. Christopher Mercer and Terry S. Brown, "Fair Market Value vs. The Real World," *Valuation Strategies*, Vol. 2, No. 4 (1999), pp. 6-15; and "Fair Market Value vs. The Real World," *Business Valuation Review*, Vol. 18, No. 1 (1999): pp. 16-25.

market value, in effect, as [1] the price at which the property would change hands [2] between a willing buyer [3] and a willing seller [4] when the former is not under any compulsion to buy and the latter is not under any compulsion to sell, [5] both parties having reasonable knowledge of the relevant facts. Court decisions frequently state in addition that [6] the hypothetical buyer and seller are assumed to be able, [7] as well as willing, to trade and [8] to be well informed about the property and [9] concerning the market for such property.[183]

This definition provides a bare-bones description of the hypothetical world of fair market value. However, it is almost impossible to cite the definition of fair market value without also noting the eight factors enumerated in RR 59-60 for consideration in a fair market value determination. They are so commonly cited in business appraisal reports that Mercer Capital refers to them as the *Basic Eight* factors (from Section 4.01):

1. The nature of the business and the history of the enterprise from its inception.

2. The economic outlook in general and the condition and outlook of the specific industry in particular.

3. The book value of the stock and the financial condition of the business.

4. The earning capacity of the company.

5. The dividend-paying capacity.

6. Whether or not the enterprise has goodwill or other intangible value.

7. Sales of the stock and the size of the block of stock to be valued.

8. The market price of stocks of corporations engaged in the same or similar line of business having their stocks actively traded in a free and open market, either on an exchange or over-the-counter.

The *Basic Eight* factors of RR 59-60 should be examined in the context of what we call the *Critical Three* factors of common sense, informed judgment, and reasonableness, which "must enter into the process of weighing those factors and determining their aggregate significance." (Section 3.01)

---

[183] Revenue Ruling 59-60, Internal Revenue Bulletin 1959-1 CB 237, IRC Sec. 2031.

The nine parenthetical elements of the definition of fair market value are the focus of this chapter, rather than the *Basic Eight* factors. However, these nine definitional elements are necessarily interpreted in the broad analytical context provided by the *Basic Eight* and under the general umbrella of the *Critical Three* factors of common sense, informed judgment, and reasonableness. And the concept of fair market value that they define must be examined in relation to the real world of actual transactions.

FAIR MARKET VALUE VS. THE REAL WORLD

Conceptual discussions of fair market value can be found in numerous valuation texts.[184] They all recite or paraphrase the definition above, and they all provide good, but short, discussions of the topic. With the Tax Court and other courts increasingly requiring specificity in valuations, business appraisers need to focus more on this definition.

The most comprehensive discussion of fair market value we have identified in (relatively) current valuation literature is in a Canadian text by Ian Campbell, et al., dealing with the Canadian definition of fair market value.[185] Campbell's discussion of fair market value in Canada is quite instructive for American appraisers. It outlines the difference between what in Canada has long been called a *notional market*, in which hypothetical transactions occur, and the *open market*, in which actual transactions occur. As early as 1982, Richard M. Wise, ASA, another Canadian appraiser, wrote:

> The open or actual market should be compared to the notional market outlined above. In real-life, many of the criteria or ideal standards with respect to the notional marketplace simply do not exist. The "perfect" market is often lacking because of a host of variables and unpredictable

---

[184] James H. Zukin, *Financial Valuation: Business and Business Interests* (New York: Maxwell MacMillan, 1990), p. 2-3; Jay E. Fishman and Shannon P. Pratt, *Guide To Business Valuation*, 3rd ed. (Fort Worth, TX: Practitioners Publishing Company, 1993), p. 2-2; Shannon P. Pratt, Robert F. Reilly, and Robert P. Schweihs, *Valuing a Business: The Analysis and Appraisal of Closely Held Companies*, 3rd ed. (Chicago, IL: Richard D. Irwin, 1996), p. 22-24; Z. Christopher Mercer, *Valuing Financial Institutions* (Homewood, IL: Business One Irwin, 1992), pp. 26-27. These citations are from the early to mid-1990s. More current valuation texts also have discussions of fair market value, but they are too numerous to cite here.

[185] Ian R. Campbell, Robert B. Low, and Nora V. Murrant, *The Valuation & Pricing of Privately-Held Business Interests* (Toronto: Ian R. Campbell, 1990), pp. 14-32.

vagaries such as those constantly present in the real world. Therefore, the actual or open marketplace in which "live" transactions take place might bear no resemblance to the ideal, hypothetical (notional) marketplace in which value is determined for income tax purposes[186]

The concept of the notional market was, to the best of our knowledge, first discussed in the U.S. valuation literature in a recent article by Jay Fishman and Bonnie O'Rourke in *Valuation*.[187] The Fishman/O'Rourke piece discusses the definition of fair market value at some length and then compares the "notional market" of U.S. fair market value with the "open market" of the real world. Their article shows how courts have used the fair market value standard differently in marital dissolution cases from the hypothetical (or notional) manner in which it is commonly considered and discussed in the present article.

One of the most complete discussions of the definition of fair market value in the United States is found, not in a valuation text or article, but in the *Internal Revenue Service Valuation Training for Appeals Officers Coursebook*.[188] The *IRS Coursebook* comes with the following caveat:

> This material was described specifically for training purposes only. Under no circumstances should the contents be used or cited as authority for setting or sustaining a technical position.

Appraisers and attorneys should read the *Coursebook*. It deals with many of the elements that will be discussed below.

---

[186]   Richard M. Wise, "Valuation Concepts and Principles: Some Current Thoughts", *Journal of Business Valuation* (1983). Mr. Wise wrote further on this subject in *Financial Litigation - Quantifying Business Damages and Values*, (Toronto: The Canadian Institute of Chartered Accountants, 1987).

[187]   Jay E. Fishman and Bonnie O'Rourke, "Whose Fair Market Value Is It Anyway?" *Valuation*, Vol. 41, No. 1, (1997), pp. 92-103.

[188]   The *IRS Coursebook* is available for downloading from the Internet at *Shannon Pratt's Business Valuation Update* website (www.bvupdate.com). Pratt's website requires a subscription in order to download articles.

The world of fair market value is not the real world. It is a hypothetical world created by the legal standard set out in Revenue Ruling 59-60 and interpreted by appraisers and courts.[189] We offer this comparison of two different worlds.

THE ELEMENTS OF FAIR MARKET VALUE

We now focus on the nine elements noted parenthetically in the definition of RR 59-60 above. While we do not normally use the term *notional*, it should be clear that we are discussing fair market value in similar terms as Campbell, Wise, and Fishman/O'Rourke. Figure 8-2 at the end of this chapter summarizes the comparison of the real world (the open market) and the hypothetical (notional) market of fair market value in a format used by all three writers. Readers are invited to recall the organizing principles, or GRAPES of Value, during this discussion of fair market value.

- *Price* and *Change Hands*. There are several qualifying characteristics that define "the price at which the property would change hands." Note that the definition references the *price*, and not the *proceeds*, of the sale of a property.

  Elsewhere in RR 59-60, the fair market value price is paid in terms of money or money's worth, it is a cash-equivalent concept. It is paid in terms of dollars today or the present value of consideration to be received in the future. Note also that *property changes hands*. A transaction is presumed in the definition of fair market value.

  Appraisers sometimes consider discounts for controlling interests of companies relating to the transactions costs incurred while selling those entities. While such costs are undoubtedly real in actual transactions, the costs are deductible to sellers and therefore reduce proceeds, not price. Other costs, such as those related to deferred hirings or maintenance, for example, may well lower value, and thus, price. Appraisers should

---

[189] We have intentionally not referred in this article to Tax Court decisions or other court cases regarding the definition of fair market value. While the definition is cited in many cases, and numerous cases discuss one or more of its aspects, the purpose of this article is to provide a discussion from a valuation perspective. Business appraisers should provide valuation evidence for consideration by courts, and not the reverse.

therefore distinguish between costs that influence price (value) and proceeds (value less transactions costs).[190]

If fair market value is a cash-equivalent concept, how meaningful are stock-for-stock acquisition transactions in consolidating industries (like banking and auto dealerships, to name two) as a basis for determining the fair market value of an entity on a controlling interest basis for estate tax purposes? It is fairly well known that stock-for-stock deals often have occurred at higher dollar-denominated prices than cash deals.[191] If fair market value is a cash-equivalent price, and if the stock-for-stock value indications exceed the price that could be obtained if an entity were sold in a cash deal, business appraisers attempting to determine the fair market value price should probably take this factor into account.

- *Willing Buyer.* The hypothetical buyer of fair market value fame is a willing buyer. He or she is interested in engaging in a transaction to acquire the subject interest and is inclined to do so "if the price is right." Hypothetical buyers make their determinations of price based on rational financial and economic principles applied in relation to a subject interest. In other words, the hypothetical willing buyer is a rational buyer.

- *Willing Seller.* The hypothetical seller of fair market value is a willing seller.[192] Specific sellers are not always interested in selling, particularly if market conditions are perceived as poor. Yet, they can sometimes be convinced to sell an asset "if the price is right," to obtain liquidity, or to invest in a higher yielding alternative investment. But note that for a seller, the timing must also be right. If the definition of fair market value is to hold up, the contemplated class of willing sellers must be comprised of a group of potential sellers for whom the timing for a (hypothetical) transaction is propitious.

If a hypothetical seller does not sell, he or she has become, in effect, a buyer who acquires (by retaining) a subject interest. Every hypothetical seller is evaluating the same economic and financial factors under

---

[190] See the discussions of the applicability of marketability discounts to controlling interests of enterprises in Chapter 3 and 5.

[191] With the release of SFAS 141 and SFAS 142 and the elimination of pooling accounting for acquisitions, these observed differences may become less distinct.

[192] For an in-depth discussion of the hypothetical willing seller, see Chapter 6 of *Quantifying Marketability Discounts*.

consideration by the relevant group of hypothetical buyers. So the hypothetical willing seller, like the hypothetical willing buyer, is a rational investor. A discussion containing many of the same concepts is found in an article in the *Business Valuation Review*.[193]

The definition of fair market value assumes willing buyers and willing sellers. It could be argued that because someone would not buy a particular interest, it therefore must be next to worthless. Others suggest that because a holder of an interest would not sell, it should be valued dearly. Both positions may at times be correct in the real world, but neither represents fair market value.

The lack of willingness to engage in a transaction by any particular party should not enter into a determination of the fair market value of the subject interest, else the behavioral requirements of the definition are not met. Finding that a seller would not sell because the price is "too low" or that a buyer would not buy because the price is "too high" implies analysis of the motivation of specific sellers or buyers, ignores the need to consider hypothetical sellers and hypothetical buyers, and introduces elements of speculation and subjectivity not contemplated by the definition of fair market value.

Appraisers sometimes use the terms "typical buyers" and "typical sellers" as representatives of hypothetical willing investors. These are important concepts. A specific buyer will likely consider the intrinsic worth of an investment to him or to her. A specific seller will also consider the worth of an investment from his or her unique perspective. Such considerations do not constitute a market. A group of *typical buyers*, on the other hand, collectively represents one side of a market and a group of *typical sellers* represents the other side. Together they create the hypothetical (notional) market of fair market value.

- *No Compulsion.* Neither party is assumed to be under any compulsion to engage in a transaction, nor to be under any duress. This point suggests that although willing to engage in a transaction, the parties are under no pressure to do so. Compulsion to engage in a transaction by a party to a transaction usually works adversely to that party's interests. A

---

[193] J. Peter Lindquist and Brad Bickham, "Analyzing the Needs of the Hypothetical Seller," *Business Valuation Review*, Vol. 16, No. 3 (1997), pp. 137-142. Lindquist and Bickham offer a conceptually similar analytical framework to discuss the hypothetical willing seller.

"motivated buyer" is likely to pay more than a rational price to acquire an asset. On the other hand, a "motivated seller" is likely to sell for less than he or she would otherwise accept for the sale of an asset.[194] Hypothetical buyers and sellers in the fair market value world, being equally uncompelled, can negotiate the price and terms of their deals based on their rational financial and economic consequences.

There is an interesting corollary to the issue of motivation. Appraisers need to be careful to consider the motivations, to the extent possible, of the parties to any transactions being used as guidelines in an appraisal. In terms of the usual discussion, can the parties to a guideline transaction be assumed to have been acting at arms' length? This is a point of investigation (to the extent reasonable or feasible) for appraisers, and a point of questioning for attorneys or other users of appraisal reports.

Recall that we suggested above that attempting to ascertain why specific persons *did not* engage in a transaction is speculative and subjective. Analyzing actual transactions to attempt to ascertain or estimate the motivations of market participants is a far more objective process and can often add value to the process of determining fair market value.

A specific buyer for a subject interest with *strategic or synergistic motivations* may pay a price that is unaffordable to a typical buyer who lacks such opportunities to enter a market. *So fair market value will likely not reflect the highest price that might be obtained.* With reference to the real world, it more probably should reflect the *consensus rational pricing* discerned from a group of buyers with typical motivations to achieve reasonable returns based on the expected cash flows of an investment. At first blush, this is a financial control concept. However, if the enterprise offers potential synergies attractive to several strategic buyers, the group of typical buyers might well be comprised of strategic/control buyers.

This logic also suggests that a transaction in a company's stock may not be indicative of fair market value, even if that transaction occurred between independent parties. The mere fact that the parties were independent of each other says nothing about the motivations of either party. In many, if not most cases, we may never know or understand the actual motivation of the parties. But we can analyze the economics of

---

[194] Nearly everyone is familiar with the use of the term "motivated seller" in the real estate markets.

actual transactions and assess whether they occurred under rational conditions that reflect the elements of fair market value. If a transaction in a subject company or a guideline transaction involving another company cannot be explained rationally, chances are neither is a candidate for inference regarding the fair market value of a particular subject interest.

- *Reasonable Knowledge.* Both parties are assumed to have reasonable knowledge about the relevant facts pertaining to an investment. This is an important assumption, because knowledge about certain companies, interests in companies, or other investments is not generally available to everyone.

The term "fully informed" is often used to describe the state of reasonable knowledge of relevant facts. In real life, we know that buyers and sellers of equity interests are seldom fully informed. Why is it that the surprises after acquisitions are invariably adverse to buyers? From a seller's viewpoint, the refrain that "nothing will change after the merger" is so often wrong as to be laughable. And some of the issues that come to light after transactions are quite "knowable" beforehand, based on reasonable analysis or investigation. They are, however, frequently ignored or overlooked by participants in real-life transactions who might be motivated, compelled, or not quite fully informed.

In addition, implicit in the discussion thus far is a similar level of negotiating ability between hypothetical buyers and sellers. In the real world, it is quite often the case that buyers of companies have more experience in negotiating purchases than sellers, who may never have sold a company before. This phenomenon is quite common in many consolidating industries. Under these circumstances, one could reasonably infer that hypothetical sellers of businesses are ably represented by qualified deal counsel and investment bankers. In other words, bargaining parity between hypothetical buyers and sellers is assumed in the context of fair market value.

Reasonable knowledge and the future. Real life transactions are based on facts and circumstances known up to the minute of their closings, and consider reasonable outlooks for the future. Reasonably, or fully informed does not mean having a crystal ball that eliminates uncertainties by forecasting the future with precision.[195]

Appraisers engaging in *after-the-fact* valuations should not abuse the standard of reasonable knowledge based on facts that clarified themselves shortly or long after an historical valuation date. Attorneys representing the side in a dispute benefited by knowledge of post-valuation date events may *want* to believe that the certainty of those events was reasonably knowable at the valuation date. Independent appraisers do not have this luxury in the context of fair market value determinations.

In some instances, the fact that an event *might* occur in the future is known at the time of a transaction or at a valuation date. What is not generally known is *when* or with *what probability* the event might occur. Appraisers must assess those probabilities and incorporate the risks or potential benefits appropriately in their appraisals – the way that reasonably informed hypothetical willing investors might, based on information available as of a valuation date.

This brief discussion of the reasonable knowledge component of the definition of fair market value should illustrate that following its implied guidance requires the exercise of common sense, informed judgment, and reasonableness by appraisers, and that it will create issues for consideration by users of valuation reports and triers of fact. The remaining elements of the definition enhance this discussion of reasonable knowledge.

- *Able to Trade.* The hypothetical willing buyer and seller are assumed to be able to engage in a transaction. The implication is that each of the parties must have the financial capacity to engage in the subject transaction.

Consider the following example: the subject interest has no market, is worth about $500 thousand, and provides a market yield for similar assets. In the context of such a cash flowing investment, the universe of hypothetical buyers would include individual investors who, in the context of diversified portfolios of investments, would have the ability to

---

[195] Z. Christopher Mercer, "Tax Court Perspectives," *E-Law Newsletter 98-04* (December 10, 1998), www.bizval.com/publications/elaw/archive/elaw9804.htm (accessed May 19, 2004).

purchase an investment in this value range. Such investors would likely be fully taxable individuals or corporations paying taxes at the maximum statutory rate.

If we assume that most rational investors would not place more than 10% or so of their portfolios in any single investment (about the minimum number of investments to achieve reasonable diversification if all the individual investments are publicly traded securities), then we are discussing a group of investors with liquid financial capacity on the order of $5 million or more.

Yet consider that investors are usually willing to place only smaller portions of their wealth in specific illiquid assets. The universe of hypothetical investors for our $500 thousand asset might, in reality, be those with a net worth of $10 million or more who might be willing to place only about 5% of their assets into any single, illiquid security. This universe of investors will likely have higher return requirements and investment expectations for the private security than for publicly traded securities because the additional risks imposed by holding periods of long and indeterminate length.

So, appraisers should consider the universe of hypothetical investors in making their determinations of fair market value. Specifically, appraisers should consider the impact of the investment requirements of the relevant universe of hypothetical investors on the fair market value of particular interests. Attorneys and other users of appraisal reports should have the expectation that such considerations are made, either explicitly or implicitly, in appraisal reports.

- *Willing to Trade.* Both parties must be willing to make the trade. It should be clear that hypothetical investors are rational investors. They engage in transactions and approach the issue of price from a rational economic and financial perspective.

- *The Property Itself.* Both parties are assumed to be well-informed about the property that is the subject of the appraisal. In other words, the parties must have the knowledge and the ability to investigate the potential investment. This aspect of the definition carries the point of being reasonably informed in a general sense to being well-informed in a specific sense.

Gaining such knowledge about a specific property or transaction can be time-consuming and expensive, so it is an important characteristic to consider in an appraisal. Further, the hypothetical investors are negotiating over the economic and financial value of the property itself, and not on the synergies, strategic impetus, or psychological benefit it might provide to a particular buyer.

- *Market for the Property.* The last element of the definition of fair market value carries the concept of "reasonably informed" one step further. Both parties are assumed to be knowledgeable, not only about the specific property, but also about the market for the relevant property. This fact adds a layer of time and expense or experience to the process of investigation by hypothetical buyers. Knowledge about the market for a property assumes an understanding of industry conditions as well as local, regional, and/or national economic conditions.

The markets in which properties trade in the fair market value world are rational markets and consistent markets. This can create occasional disjoints between actual market pricing and fair market value. The Integrated Theory of Business Valuation presented in this book provides a consistent framework for bridging these two worlds. Appraisers must exercise common sense, informed judgment and reasonableness to rationalize market evidence from the real world before it can be applied in determinations of value in the hypothetical world of fair market value.

Our brief discussion of the definitional elements of fair market value found in Revenue Ruling 59-60 makes clear that this standard of value does not lend itself to simplistic interpretation. Appraisers, attorneys, users of valuation reports, and triers of fact have more to consider than glib recitations of the definition of fair market value.

As the business appraisal profession continues to mature, there will be an increasing focus on the elements of the definition of fair market value in valuation reports.

CONCLUSION

Appraisers, attorneys, and users of valuation reports should have more than a superficial understanding of the valuation implications of the standard of value known as fair market value. Fair market value is not the real world. Appraisers, attorneys, and other users of business valuation reports who operate every day in the real world need to continue to develop a better understanding of that other world, the hypothetical market in which fair market value transactions occur. As noted in the *IRS Coursebook*:

> . . . the consideration of any valuation case would ensure that both sides, including their respective appraisers, if any, are employing the correct definition and criteria for determining fair market value. No case is stronger than its weakest link and if the wrong valuation standard is applied, the conclusion will be defective.[196]

It is important for appraisers to focus specifically on the definitional elements of fair market value while describing valuation opinions in their reports. And attorneys and other users of valuation reports should expect this in their reviews of valuation reports.

---

[196] The *IRS Coursebook*, p. 1-9. Available at www.bvupdate.com.

Fair Market Value vs. Real World

	Fair Market Value Hypothetical (Notional) Market	Real World (Open) Markets
Market participants	Market participants are hypothetical buyers and sellers acting in their own self-interests in the manner and on the basis described by the elements below	Market participants are real persons who may act in their own self-interests or not, and whose behavior, while generally assumed to be rational, may not be in specific instances
At arms' length	Arms' length transactions are the standard. The parties are independent of each other and act that way	Actual transactions may or may not occur at arms' length. There may be elements of compulsion, duress, or other unknown motivations or relationships that influence the pricing and terms of actual transactions
Willing to trade	The parties are hypothetical willing buyers and willing sellers who are equally willing to engage in a transaction (subject to reasonable economics). Unwillingness to trade is not a factor	Unwilling participants often preclude transactions from happening in the real world
Reasonable knowledge	Both parties to the transaction are reasonably informed about the property and the market for the property	Parties to a transaction may have different, even widely disparate knowledge concerning the property and/or its market(s)
Absence of compulsion	Neither party is under compulsion or duress such that both are equally uncompelled	Parties negotiate on bases known only to themselves and may engage in transactions involving compulsion or duress on the part of the buyer, the seller or both
Bargaining parity	Both parties have similar bargaining experience and ability	One party may have more experience and/or greater ability in negotiating that gives advantage
Ability to trade (financial capacity)	Both parties have the financial capacity to engage in a transaction. Both are able to trade and neither is disadvantaged by the superior financial capacity of the other	Relative inequality in financial capacity or staying power often puts one side or the other to a transaction in a disadvantageous position
Rational, economic values	Each party approaches a transaction rationally and makes decisions based on financial and economic consequences (costs or benefits). Transactions occur at consensus pricing of rational (hypothetical) investors based solely on the financial and economic characteristics of the subject interest, and not the highest price that might be obtained	Transactions may be influenced by strategic motivations, operating synergies, sentimental values, psychological factors, or other factors, all of which may distort the economics of pricing from the viewpoint of the seller, the buyer, or both. Transaction pricing may or may not reflect rational pricing based solely on the financial and economic characteristics of the subject interest
Cash-equivalent values	Hypothetical transactions are assumed to be conducted in terms of cash, i.e., in terms of money or money's worth, or dollars of present value as of the date of the transaction. The price agreed upon is the value of the subject interest, and not the proceeds of the sale (value minus expenses)	Negotiated deals may contain elements of consideration that disguise their effective economics, including earnouts, puts, debt instruments with above or below market rates and/or terms, or restrictions on the ability to sell stock or debt instruments received by sellers
Rational markets	The market for the subject property is rational and consistent	Real world markets experience booms and panics that can swing value widely or wildly and over very short timeframes
Impact of restrictions	Restrictions, whether legal or contractual, which might preclude a transaction are normally assumed to lapse long enough to permit the transaction; however, the economic impact of the restrictions is considered in determining value	Restrictions can preclude or hinder transactions, or affect their outcomes in unpredictable ways
Transactions occur	Hypothetical buyers and sellers negotiate and a hypothetical transaction consistent with the definition of FMV (and the elements above) occurs. Further, the transaction is assumed to occur as of the valuation date	Real buyers and sellers negotiate. An actual transaction may or may not occur. If a transaction occurs, it may or may not reflect some or all of the elements of FMV, and it may or may not be indicative of the FMV of the traded interest. This point is particularly true the further removed in time an actual transaction and a FMV valuation date regarding the same or a similar interest

Figure 8-2

Appendix 8-A

USING THE DEFINITION OF
FAIR MARKET VALUE
TO CLARIFY A VALUATION

In 1987, Mercer Capital prepared a valuation report regarding the fair market value (FMV) of an interest in a nonmarketable, unsecured debt instrument for an estate. The valuation was disputed by the IRS and the issue was ultimately tried in Federal District Court. The government hired another appraisal firm to prepare a valuation.

The indicated FMVs of the note ranged from $3.0 million (Mercer Capital) to $4.5 million (other appraisal firm). Specific consideration of the elements of the definition of FMV in the note appraisal led to an affirmation of our 1987 appraisal by the Court in 1996. Several of the definitional elements of FMV were discussed in detail at trial.

- *The Nature of the Property.* The note was originally appraised as an undivided one-half interest based on facts known in 1987. The government's appraiser chose to ignore that the fractional nature of the interest could adversely impact value. Documentation for the note consisted of a single page of description. The issuer of the note had subsequently been acquired by Champion International Corporation, a large, publicly traded company.

- *Being Reasonably Informed.* In our 1987 appraisal process, we called and wrote Champion as representatives of the holder of the subject note on several occasions requesting clarification regarding the extent of Champion's corporate guaranties or responsibilities regarding the unsecured note. We ultimately received a one-page letter with a single paragraph in which a junior officer of Champion said that Champion was "responsible" for the note. We did not consider that this unspecific acknowledgment of responsibility rose to the level of protection afforded the holders of Champion's public debt.

- *The Market for Such Property.* We considered that the market for the unsecured note was very thin and populated by hypothetical investors who would take its specific characteristics into consideration in making purchase decisions in a private market transaction. The appraiser retained by the IRS suggested there should be no problem in finding buyers for the note at a minimal yield premium to Champion's public debt.

The Court's conclusion of FMV affirmed our original appraisal issued in 1987, as well as the reappraisal based on the fact that additional documentation relative to the note was found by the executor of the estate shortly prior to trial. The focus on the definitional elements of FMV in our appraisal reports and testimony at trial were critical elements in being able to defend the 1987 valuation.

The point of this case discussion is that the universe of potential investments in sizeable, illiquid, unsecured and unprotected commercial notes was discussed in detail. The concerns of these real-world investors were outlined in the context of financial theory (the GRAPES of Value, if you will). Finally, the notes were valued in the context of the required returns of likely potential (real or hypothetical) investors. The Court reached a conclusion of value at the nexus of facts and circumstances of the case and the hypothetical world in which those facts and circumstances must be interpreted. Thankfully, the Court's conclusion was identical with Mercer Capital's conclusion. May it always be so.

Chapter 9

Economic Value Added, Economic Profit and Market Value Added

INTRODUCTION

It seems that the term Economic Value Added (EVA) that has been widely talked and written about is not so well-understood. In this chapter, we will discuss Economic Value Added and the identical, generic concept – economic profit as well as the concept of Market Value Added (MVA). In the process, we will see how these concepts are related to the more familiar valuation concepts of return on equity, price/earnings multiples, and price/book multiples. Then, we further relate the concepts of Economic Value Added, economic profit, and Market Value Added to our basic valuation theory as it relates to the value of businesses and business interests at the freely traded and nonmarketable minority interest levels.

ECONOMIC VALUE ADDED

Economic Value Added, or EVA, is a registered trademark of Stern-Stewart & Company. EVA has been a subject of discussion at a number of business valuation conferences and has been given regular national prominence by being featured in *Fortune* magazine and other financial publications.

Each time I have examined the concept of EVA, I have come away with the impression that Messieurs Stern and Stewart have done a remarkable job of packaging and marketing age-old wisdom: *firms build value by maximizing the differential between their costs of capital and the actual returns achieved.* They have, however, built a performance measurement system, which is different than a valuation methodology – but performance and valuation are necessarily related. And they have built a sizeable consulting business by establishing a vocabulary, a discipline, and compensation systems geared to encourage managers of many of the larger companies in America to manage them better.

Is maximizing returns what EVA and economic profit are all about? Yes. EVA, economic profit, and the related concept of Market Value Added (the present value of all future EVA or economic profit), essentially boil down to one simple idea:

> *A firm maximizes value to current shareholders by maximizing its return on equity.*[197]

In fairness to Stern-Stewart, there can be considerable discussion over which "return," or how to measure the income stream, and which "equity," or what to include in the definition of equity. And there can be even more discussion about how to develop a firm's cost of capital. But make no mistake; EVA is all about *return on equity*. It is almost as if this is a little-known secret that no one wants to talk about. For example, a recent book by James Grant was extolled as a "must read" by G. Bennett Stewart. In that book, the concept of return on equity (ROE) was mentioned only once, on page 26, in a brief observation of an example company's 15% return on equity.

The Grant book begins:

> The analytical tool called EVA, for Economic Value Added, was commercially developed during the 1980s by the corporate advisory team of G. Bennett Stewart III and Joel Stern. This financial metric gained early acceptance from the corporate financial community because of its innovative way of looking at a firm's real profitability. Unlike traditional measures of corporate profitability – such as net operating profit after tax (NOPAT) and net income – EVA looks at the firm's "residual profitability," net of both the direct cost of debt capital and the *indirect* cost of equity capital. In this way, EVA serves as a modern measure of corporate financial success because it is closely aligned with the shareholder wealth-maximization requirement.[198]

While the name Economic Value Added may be registered, the concepts are not. In fact, other consulting firms have developed similar concepts based on the

---

[197] This statement is made with an obvious caveat: return on equity must be maximized subject to prudent leverage constraints.

[198] James L. Grant, *Foundations of Economic Value Added* (New Hope, PA: Frank J. Fabozzi Associates, 1997).

essential idea that firms build value by maximizing their returns on shareholders' equity. At its heart, EVA is the same as "economic profit" which has been discussed for years, where economic profit is measured as net income, or accounting profits, less the opportunity costs of ownership (i.e., the foregone return from the next best alternative investment).

Business owners, their advisers, and business appraisers can benefit from these insights. There is no magic to building economic value in businesses.

DEFINITIONS

Professor Grant expresses Economic Value Added in general terms as:[199]

EVA = NOPAT - $ Cost of Capital

$ Cost of Capital = [Debt Weight x % After-Tax Debt Cost + Equity Weight x % After Tax Cost of Equity]

NOPAT is a firm's debt-free, net operating profit after tax. Since it will be helpful for the discussion that follows, we will assume an equivalency between NOPAT and *debt free net income*, or DFNI. Cost of capital is traditionally defined.

Professor Grant then expresses Market Value Added as follows (at page 3):

MVA = Firm Value (at market value) - Total Capital (at book value)

MVA = (Debt plus Equity Value) - Total Capital

MVA = PV of Expected Future EVA

---

[199] Ibid, p. 2. The point of the similarity between EVA and economic profit made above is highlighted in a prominent treatise. Economic profit is defined as NOPLAT (net operating profit less adjusted taxes) minus a firm's invested capital (debt plus equity) times its weighted average cost of capital (WACC) – in other words, the same thing as NOPAT in the EVA terminology above. EVA and economic profit are the same concept. See McKinsey & Company, Inc, et al., *Valuation: Measuring and Managing the Value of Companies*, 3rd ed. (New York: John Wiley & Sons, Inc., 2000), pp. 143-145.

EVA is a function of the relationship between a firm's earnings and its cost of capital, and MVA is a function of that firm's expected future EVA. So market value added is clearly a function of a firm's earnings. How earnings are defined and what adjustments are appropriate to earnings are age-old questions of securities analysis.

EVA IS A FUNCTION OF RETURN ON EQUITY

We can see the relationship between return on equity (ROE) and EVA by working with its definitional equation. Since EVA is expressed in terms of dollars (in the United States) we will use the notation $EVA, number the equations and offer brief discussion as the development progresses.

1. $\$EVA = DFNI - \text{Cost of Capital}$

For ease of notation, we can express Cost of Capital by the expression:

$$\text{Cost of Capital} = K_E * BV_E + K_D * BV_D$$

K_E and K_D represent the cost of equity and the after-tax cost of debt, respectively. BV_E and BV_D correspondingly represent the book values of equity and debt.

2. $\$EVA = DFNI - (K_E * BV_E + K_D * BV_D)$ or,

3. $\$EVA = DFNI - K_E * BV_E - K_D * BV_D$

Debt-free net income can be broken into its constituent parts, the portion attributable to equity and the portion attributable to debt. This conceptual relationship can be expressed as:

4. $DFNI = DFNI_E + DFNI_D$ or,

   $= DFNI_E + K_D * BV_D$

But $DFNI_E = \text{Net Income} = NI$ so,

5. $\$EVA = NI + K_D * BV_D - K_E * BV_E - K_D * BV_D$

After canceling out equivalent terms, EVA becomes:

6. $\$EVA = NI - K_E*BV_E$

So $EVA is a function of a firm's net income less its cost of equity capital (K_E*BV_E). This would suggest that $EVA is maximized by maximizing the differential between earnings and the cost of equity capital. Now, we can consider EVA in percentage terms by dividing all parts of Equation 6 by equity, or BV_E.

7. $\%EVA = \$EVA/\ BV_E = NI\ /\ BV_E - (K_E*BV_E/\ BV_E)$ so,

8. $\%EVA = (NI\ /\ BV_E) - K_E$ and finally,

9. $\%EVA = ROE - K_E$

$EVA is a function of earnings in excess of a firm's equity cost of capital and %EVA is a function of a firm's ROE less its percentage equity cost of capital.

Proponents of EVA might argue that this analysis is an oversimplification and that EVA is critically dependent upon how one defines the earnings that are used and, for that matter, the equity Figure that is used in the calculation of ROE. But conceptually it is clear:

A firm maximizes value to current shareholders by maximizing its return on equity.

The analysis of EVA thus far shows that those who employ it are implicitly recognizing the concept that return on equity is an important driver of the value of equity securities. It is pretty basic, but firms maximize value by focusing on returns to their shareholders. In the real world, firms attempt to maximize return on equity and hope that the public markets will award their efforts with premium earnings multiples.   Is this accomplished by a slavish devotion to reported earnings per share under the most liberal and allowable interpretations of GAAP? Hardly not. The market sees through such shenanigans (at least over the longer term), and, hopefully, so do business appraisers in valuing privately owned or public companies.

MARKET VALUE ADDED IS A FUNCTION OF EVA AND ROE

In order to round out our conceptual understanding of EVA, we need to look at the related concept of MVA a bit more closely. Recall that MVA was defined as a firm's value (equity plus debt) less its capital employed (equity plus debt). We can use nomenclature consistent with the analysis above, substituting market value concepts for book value concepts, and express MVA, in dollar terms, as:

10. $\$MVA = (MV_E + MV_D) - (BV_E + BV_D)$

It is fairly common to assume (absent contrary evidence) that the market value of debt is approximately equivalent to the book value of debt. There can, of course, be exceptions to this simplification, but it is generally used in the financial community as a first-blush assumption. Substituting and simplifying yields:

11. $\$MVA = MV_E + BV_D - BV_E - BV_D$ Therefore,

12. $\$MVA = MV_E - BV_E$

It is clear from Equation 12 that $MVA is the surplus of the market's valuation of a firm's equity over the book value of that equity. In other words, MVA is the value premium over the shareholders' historical investment in a firm. If a firm is adding economic value by maximizing its return on equity (and its $EVA), the market may reward it with a large $MVA. If that sounds like a firm's price/book value multiple might be involved, read on as we convert $MVA to %MVA.

13. $\$MVA / BV_E = \%MVA = MV_E / BV_E - BV_E / BV_E$

The market value of a firm's equity divided by its book value is none other than the price/book value ratio, or multiple. This relationship was also noted by Copeland, et al. in their discussion of MVA[200], although that discussion is framed in terms of total capital rather than just equity. So %MVA can be expressed as:

14. $\%MVA = $ Price/Book $- 1$

---

[200]   Ibid, pp. 59-62.

In other words, %MVA is the multiple over a firm's book value of equity that is indicated by the market value of its equity. For example, a price/book multiple of 2.0 would indicate that the market is valuing a firm's equity at 1x greater than the shareholders' historical investment. But where is ROE?

Stated in the terms of our analysis thus far:

Price/Book = MV_E/BV_E Which can be expanded into,

Price/Book = MV_E/NI x NI/BV_E

MV_E/NI is generally known as the price/earnings ratio, or multiple. And, from above, NI/BV_E is identical to ROE. Going back to Equation 14 and substituting, we see that ROE enters into the picture of %MVA (and $MVA) as follows:

15. %MVA = ((Price/Earnings) x ROE) - 1

%MVA is nothing other than the reward (the price/earnings multiple) that the market accords to a firm's ROE. Therefore, %MVA and $MVA are, like %EVA and $EVA, integrally related to a firm's ROE. Once again, our analysis of MVA affirms the basic idea:

A firm maximizes value to current shareholders by maximizing its return on equity.

Since %MVA is a function of both the price/earnings multiple and ROE, it is clear that a firm's value is related to things that management can influence, and things that management cannot influence. Management can influence many aspects of a business that ultimately are reflected in a firm's ROE. However, management cannot influence overall market or industry trends and the impact that those trends may have on prevailing price/earnings multiples or the pricing of individual securities.

BASIC ASSUMPTIONS REVIEW

EVA, and the related concept of economic profit, suggest that maximizing the differential between a firm's incremental investments and its cost of capital will maximize shareholder wealth. Mathematically, we have shown that maximizing EVA and MVA results from maximizing return on equity.

However, some readers are certainly thinking at this point that I must delight in pointing out the obvious. The implication that maximizing $EVA and $MVA are the same as maximizing a firm's return on equity was not obvious – we had to look at the underlying concepts. But the thought that maximizing return on equity (i.e., the shareholders' investment) is the path to maximizing shareholder value should be intuitively obvious. What is not obvious is what happens when companies do not follow value-maximizing strategies.

The following assumptions are implicit in any valuation of expected future cash flows to the equity owners of a business:

- The cash flows (let's assume net earnings for discussion purposes) are reinvested by the company *at the discount rate at which the company was valued, or,*

- The cash flows are distributed to the owners of the business so that they can be reinvested by the owners (at least theoretically) *at the discount rate at which the company was valued, or,*

- Some combination of the first two assumptions occurs.

Business appraisers have known for years that suboptimal reinvestment policies have a depressing impact on the value of a company's illiquid minority shares. Reinvestment at less than a company's required rate of return, assuming no leakage of assets from the company through dividends or excess compensation to owners/managers, reduces a company's expected growth rate of value (relative to the optimal reinvestment outlook), and therefore tends to lower the value of minority shares. We attempt to capture the impact of expected growth in value lower than the required return using the Quantitative Marketability Discount Model. This impact is captured as a component of the marketability discount applied to marketable minority interest value indications. Other appraisers using benchmark analysis have made more subjective judgments to attempt to account for this potential.

THE VALUE OF A BUSINESS

While working on these concepts, I had what can only be described as a BGO – a Blinding Glimpse of the Obvious. The penalty of lower expected future value resulting from less than optimal reinvestment plans has an impact on controlling shareholders, as well. Having made this "discovery," two questions came immediately to mind:

1. Does the expectation of lower than optimal reinvestment policies regarding a company's cash flows impact the value of a company?

2. Or, does the impact of suboptimal reinvestment policies fall on the shareholders of the company over time as a result of the suboptimal business plan, and not on the value of the company, itself?

An example is sometimes worth a thousand or more words. Consider the following valuation situation:

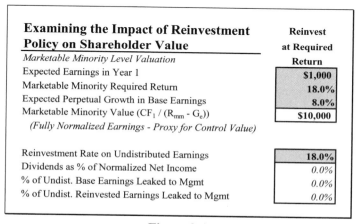

Figure 9-1

This "valuation" is a straightforward application of the Gordon Model. A company's normalized, expected net earnings for next year are capitalized at its discount rate less its expected growth rate in earnings (18% - 8% = 10% which is the capitalization rate. The inverse of the capitalization rate, or 1/10% , is the multiple, or 10x). Expected net earnings of $1.0 million are worth $10.0 million at the marketable minority interest level. No controversy thus far.

The text in the assumptions box suggests that this marketable minority interest value of $10.0 million is a reasonable proxy for a controlling interest value indication. The rationale is straightforward. By assumption, salaries and any other owner-related expenses, as well as any non-recurring items of income or expense have been normalized to a theoretical "public equivalent" level. Unless a buyer of the company can expect to realize increases in cash flows through better management (financial buyers) or changing the cash flows (strategic buyers), no (or very little) premium will be paid to the marketable minority interest value. Under these assumptions, there is no difference in the present value of the business today ($10.0 million), or if it is run according to the above assumptions and sold in 10 years. The importance of this issue will be clarified momentarily.

THE VALUE OF THE BUSINESS PLAN

It should be clear that *the business* is worth $10.0 million. Now, let's look at the expected business plan of the company that has just been valued at $10.0 million. Consider that our company is run by its 100% shareholder (to eliminate minority shareholder issues). Consider further that no excess compensation will be paid to the owner or his relatives, and that there will be no dividends. The only differences between the expected business plan of the owner and the assumptions of the $10.0 valuation are the following:

- The company has historically reinvested its cash flows in cash and other non-operating assets. It can be reasonably assumed that the reinvestment rate for future cash flows will be at the rate of about 5% (net), rather than 18% (the discount rate). In other words, there is an expectation that there will be a suboptimal reinvestment policy for this company for the foreseeable future.

- The company is expected to be sold in 10 years based on the owner's retirement plans.

Just as we valued the *business* (in the context of the market place of willing buyers and sellers), we can value the *business plan* of this owner. In other words, what is the present value of the expected cash flows, given that we are expecting a suboptimal reinvestment plan? Compare the two situations:

	Expected Reinvestment at R_{mm} (Business)	Expected Suboptimal Reinvestment (Business Plan)	Opportunity Cost of Suboptimality
Gordon Model Value (Business Value)	$10,000	$10,000	$0
(Marketable Minority Value/Proxy for Control Value)			
Present Value of Impact of Reinvestment at $<R_{mm}$	$0	($2,499)	($2,499)
Effect of Agency Costs (Management Leakage)	$0		
Concluded DCF Value for 10 Year Investment Horizon	$10,000	$7,501	($2,499)
Components of Value			
Future Value of Base Earnings	$21,589	$21,589	$0
Future Value of Reinvested Earnings (at R_{mm})	$30,749	$17,668	($13,081)
Total Future Value	$52,338	$39,257	($13,081)
Present Value of Future Value at R_{mm}	$10,000	$7,501	($2,499)
(Confirms DCF Valuations Above)			

Figure 9-2

The first column in Figure 9-2, *Expected Reinvestment at R_{mm}*, provides the valuation of the business we first described. The second, *Expected Suboptimal Reinvestment*, indicates *the value of the assumed business plan.* This plan provides for reinvestment of cash flows for the next 10 years at 5%, rather than 18%, and then a sale of the business at the end of the tenth year (valued at that time under the assumption of optimal reinvestment of cash flows.)

The value of the business plan, as described above, is $7.5 million, which is $2.5 million lower than the value of the business. What happened to the missing $2.5 million? We can see by examining the results of the forecasts at the end of 10 years, when the business will be sold.

EVA AND THE INTEGRATED THEORY

By examining the components of value in Figure 9-2, we see that the value of *the business plan* of $7.5 million is lower than the value of *the business* because there will be some $13.1 million fewer *future dollars* at the end of 10 years. In other words, suboptimal reinvestment creates an opportunity cost for the business owner in this example. If he operates the business going forward and reinvests suboptimally, there will be fewer dollars of value in the future than otherwise. Assuming optimal reinvestment, there will be $52.3 million of value at the end of 10 years and only $39.3 million of future value with suboptimal reinvestment. The difference between these figures is $13.1 million, represents the opportunity cost of suboptimal reinvestment. This is the result of suboptimal expected reinvestments in the business rather than reinvestments at the discount rate.

Is the core business worth any less because the current owner plans to reinvest at less than the discount rate? No. Because there are buyers in the market for businesses who will pay for the company based on the assumptions outlined above, which includes an optimal reinvestment policy. This is a confusing point for many business appraisers. They seem to want to adjust the discount rate to reflect the expectation of future suboptimality, but this is a circular process that is never-ending and is not the way that markets work.[201]

---

[201] This analysis raises an interesting point for consideration. Recall that the enterprise discount rate is 18%. The calculations in Figure 9-2 value both the business and the business plan where expected reinvestment of cash flows is at 5%. It could be argued that the expected build-up of cash called for in the business plan would reduce enterprise risk and that, therefore, enterprise value could remain the same. The basic problem with the argument is that there are likely not a sufficient number of potential investors who would be content to invest in a business whose earnings mix represents an increasing build-up of low return assets (and no distributions).

Consider that investors in businesses expect business returns. They can achieve bond returns on their own. Also consider how appraisers typically value companies with substantial excess assets. First, they determine the level of the excess assets and their income statement effects and remove them from the operating balance sheets and income statements. Next, they value the operating entity/assets (at the enterprise discount rate). Finally, they add the value of any excess assets to the operating entity value. If this typical procedure is considered in relationship to the business plan, then Figure 9-2 represents reasonable values for each.

Why should we not adjust the discount rate to account for suboptimal expected reinvestment? Because, today, tomorrow, or at any time in the future, the current owner can:

- Sell the business at the market discount rate and expectations noted above.

- Change the reinvestment policy towards optimality.

- Dividend the cash flows outside the business where they can (actually or theoretically) be reinvested at the discount rate.

A corollary question is: Why would we adjust the discount rate for minority shareholders of this very same company? Because they cannot change the policies or the business plans.

The missing $2.5 million represents a future *opportunity cost* to the business owner above. If there were minority shareholders, it would certainly represent an opportunity cost to them, as well. The economic impact for minority shareholders of expected suboptimal reinvestment policy would be captured by an analysis using the QMDM just as it has been captured above for the controlling shareholders.

Since the $2.5 million is an opportunity cost, it is not one that is paid with a check. It is realized year-by-year as a result of suboptimal reinvestments. This phenomenon is likely responsible for the notion among some business appraisers that there should be a marketability discount applicable to controlling interests of companies. The math and the logic above, I believe, suggest otherwise. It does not seem appropriate to create a "marketability discount" to account for the opportunity cost of suboptimal business plans on the value of a business today.

IMPLICATIONS FOR BUSINESS OWNERS AND THEIR ADVISERS

We chose the example above intentionally. In Mercer Capital's valuation practice, we see many examples of mature companies experiencing relatively slow growth that consistently accumulate assets in the form of excess or non-operating assets (and lower ROEs). The example suggests that there is an economic penalty to this strategy that is not felt by a controlling shareholder today, but is recognizable over time as suboptimal reinvestment continues.

Many slower growing, mature, privately owned companies fit the general description of our example company. The opportunity cost of less than optimal reinvestment or dividend policies can be substantial. And many business owners do not recognize this very real cost as they continue to accumulate excess and non-operating assets in their companies. If they think about it, they may believe that whatever opportunity cost is being incurred is borne by minority shareholders, but this invisible opportunity cost is borne by all shareholders.

What does our example have to do with EVA and MVA? MVA, or market value added, is the differential in the book value of a firm's equity and the market value of its equity. As we saw earlier in Equation 15:

$$\%MVA = Price/Earnings \times ROE - 1$$

The %MVA is determined by the market's (or the appraiser's) price/earnings multiple multiplied by a firm's ROE, or return on equity. If a firm increases its ROE, other things being equal, market value (and %MVA) will rise. If the increase in ROE translates into more rapid growth prospects for an enterprise, the price/earnings multiple may also be increased by the market (or the appraiser).

Business owners need to be aware of the opportunity costs of their incremental reinvestment decisions. From a policy view, more than a few private businesses avoid paying dividends to shareholders in order to avoid the personal income tax consequences of the dividends. Instead, they engage in a practice of accumulating excess assets. The example above shows that the shareholders of companies that do this are paying a considerable "tax" in the form of opportunity losses.

Business appraisers and other advisers to business owners who understand these EVA, economic profit, market value added, and return on equity concepts are in a position to assist their clients in the process of maximizing shareholder wealth.

CONCLUSION

Business owners, their advisers, and, yes, business appraisers, should take an important lesson from this brief analysis of EVA and MVA.

> *A firm maximizes value to existing shareholders by maximizing its return on equity.*

As a result, there should clearly be a focus on ROE in valuation reports of private companies. Low ROEs, other things being equal, yield relatively low price/book multiples, and therefore, relatively low values of $MVA. Alternatively, high ROEs, other things being equal, yield relatively high price/book multiples, and, therefore, relatively high values of $MVA.

The overall point of this review of Economic Value Added (remember, economic profit is the same thing), and Market Value Added (which is, effectively, the premium to a firm's book value reflected by the value of its capitalized earnings) is that shareholder value added is the result of a consistent focus on maximizing the return on equity of a firm.

For now, it should be clear that suboptimal reinvestment policies (i.e., investing at less than a firm's cost of capital) and suboptimal dividend policies (i.e., policies that facilitate the build-up of excess or non-operating assets in an operating business) have very real and substantial economic opportunity costs for shareholders of private (and public) companies.

Chapter 10

The Levels of Value
in Perspective

INTRODUCTION

The conceptual framework generally referred to as the "levels of value" has been developing in the valuation literature since at least the 1980s. Appendix 10-A to this chapter provides the most complete bibliography on the subject that we have been able to develop. Following the presentation of the Integrated Theory, which presents the levels of value in the context of current financial theory, we now step back to examine the development of the conceptual framework in the valuation literature. In addition, other efforts to discuss the levels of value will be noted, together with reconciliation with the Integrated Theory, if possible. Many references to the bibliography will be made by author and number (in Appendix 10-A) rather than in footnote form because of the large number of references in the chapter.

I recognize that many appraisers are not familiar with debates that occurred in the early 1990s because they have entered the business since then. This chapter is written to capture some of the history. The purpose of this chapter is to frame the historical discussion in the context of what is known today and in the context of the Integrated Theory.

COMMON QUESTIONS

1. Using the levels of value framework, can the following phenomena be explained or described?

    a. The existence of control premiums when public companies sell.

    b. Most public companies do not sell in any given period.

    c. Illiquid minority interests often sell for less than their pro rata share of enterprise value.

d.   Private companies often sell for less than public company multiples in their industries.

e.   Private companies often sell at lower relative valuations than public companies in their industries.

f.   A public stock may sometimes sell for higher prices than the entire company is worth.

g.   An illiquid interest in an S corporation could be worth more than an otherwise identical interest in a C corporation. Or Less than.

h.   Strategic buyers may pay more than financial buyers for the same company.

i.   Financial buyers may compete with strategic buyers and win.

THE DEBATE BEGINS: 1990

While the concepts embodied in the levels of value were known by appraisers earlier, the now-familiar levels of value chart first appeared in the valuation literature around 1990 [Mercer, #22; May/Garruto; ed. Zukin, #20]. The original levels of value chart had three levels. Figures 10-1 and 10-2 reproduce the first published levels of value charts.[202] Make no mistake, the concepts underlying the chart were at least generally understood before 1990, and I am certain that the chart existed in appraisal firms considerably prior to that date. For example, Figure 10-2 includes notes regarding how appraisers could develop valuation indications at each level.

---

[202] When I first made the statement about the 1990 publication of the levels of value chart, a number of my colleagues challenged me. I have asked openly for earlier published references to a levels of value chart, but have found none to date. I specifically requested of Shannon Pratt that he research the issue. He was unable to locate an earlier published reference.

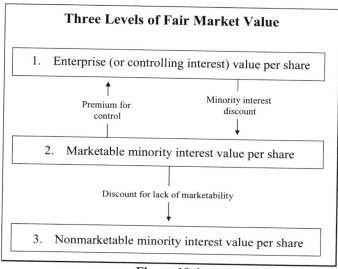

Figure 10-1

Interestingly, Figure 10-1 appeared in a chapter entitled "Valuation Case Study" and not in any of the more theoretically-oriented chapters of the 1990 (initial) edition of *Financial Valuation: Businesses and Business Interests.* [May/Garruto; ed. Zukin, #20].

Figure 10-2 was introduced in my 1990 article in a section called "The General Valuation Model" as follows:

> Prevailing valuation theory uses market-based information to develop capitalization factors in the context of a general model. An explicit assumption of the general model is that the market prices of publicly traded securities represent the trading of marketable minority interests, which for most public market transactions is true by definition. [Mercer, #22, p. 123].

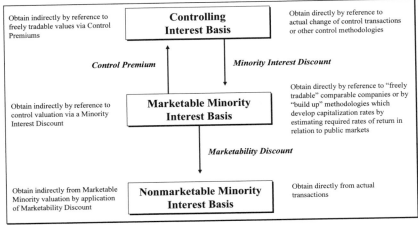

Figure 10-2

So Figures 10-1 and 10-2 illustrated the general levels of value chart. It was so "general" that Michael J. Bolotsky, ASA, CBA referred to the concepts underlying the chart as "prevailing wisdom." [Bolotsky, #5, p. 94]. The levels of value were "general" and "prevailing" but were not written about very much in any formal sense until about 1990.

The first article on the subject, rather than describing, discussing, or affirming the conventional, three-levels of value framework, challenged it. Eric W. Nath, ASA, wrote an article that literally shocked the appraisal industry. It was titled "Control Premiums and Minority Interest Discounts in Private Companies," and appeared in the June 1990 edition of *Business Valuation Review* [Nath, #44]. The central thesis of the Nath article was that public market prices tended to represent controlling interest prices. One consequence of the thesis was that appraisers applying control premiums derived from change of control transactions of public companies to this already control basis would tend to overvalue companies.

At this point, it is appropriate to quote from Nath's first article at some length. Before doing so, however, it is only fair to note that my 1990 article quoted just above was written in response to the Nath article. Apparently I (and the rest of the valuation profession) was comfortable with the general model so long as it was not challenged. After his introduction, Nath addresses the issue of control premiums:

How can buyers justify paying such enormous premiums? There are several answers:

1. The target company's shares may be "undervalued" if the company is mismanaged or otherwise underutilized. To an entrepreneur, such a situation may represent an opportunity to realize a sizeable return if the company can be purchased, even at a premium, and run more efficiently (a la RJR).

2. On the other hand, the company may be very well run and shareholder value may be maximized, but this fact may not be communicated effectively to the stock markets by management. Because the market does not fully understand management's plan for the company it may not value the shares high enough, again representing a financial takeover opportunity.

3. For those companies whose management is maximizing shareholder value, and this is being communicated effectively to the market place, the company may still represent a good takeover candidate for the strategic acquirer. Access to new markets, new technologies or other synergistic benefits may make paying a premium worthwhile to the strategic buyer.

4. And, from time to time, there may indeed be a greater fool who pays too much. Mr. Campeau's troubles with Federated Department Stores is a current example.

I call the first three categories "Primary Takeover Requirements." If a public company does not meet any of these Primary Takeover Requirements, I believe there is little reason to suspect it will be taken over. Why should it be? After all, no one else can make the company run any better, nor squeeze out any more earnings or cash flow, and the stock is correctly priced (assuming a relatively efficient market).

Absent the required takeover conditions in a public company, therefore, it would seem that a control premium would not exist or would be too small to make it worth anyone's time or money to attempt a takeover.

Indeed, corporate managements in recent years have expended large amounts of time and money restructuring their companies in order to avoid being taken over. In effect, restructuring does nothing more than reduce or eliminate whatever potential control premium that may exist that might attract an attack.

If the analysis above is correct, then the only conclusion to be drawn by the appraiser is as follows: any public company being used as a comparative that is not currently "in play" as a takeover target must be assumed to have no control premium, or at least one that is so small as to be immaterial. (Even the price of takeover stocks should presumably reflect takeover value since any takeover offer is evaluated by the market relative to the probability of completion, and bid up to a point that reflects that probability.) [Nath, #44, pp. 40-41]

As mentioned previously, Nath's article was published in the June 1990 issue of *Business Valuation Review*. I responded with the article from which Figure 10-2 was taken in the December 1990 issue. [Mercer, #22] One of the key messages of the Nath article was that appraisers using control premium data applied to public market guideline multiples would tend to overvalue companies. At that point, I agreed with Nath on the point of potential overvaluation. However, my agreement was from another perspective. My article in the December 1989 issue of *Business Valuation Review* raised the issue of potential overvaluation. [Mercer, #21, which introduced the Adjusted Capital Asset Pricing Model]

In the ACAPM article, I suggested that many appraisers failed to make appropriate adjustments to guideline company multiples for differences in risk and expected growth – and therefore tended to overvalue companies as a result.[203] So my response to Nath was colored by this position, even if I did not realize it at the time. Quoting from my response, which in retrospect was somewhat defensive, I noted:

The Nath article disagrees with the fundamental outline of relationships outlined in Exhibit 1 [Figure 10-1]. He *postulates* that "most public companies tend to trade at or near their takeover, or controlling interest values." He goes on to state that "If the argument can be made that public stocks tend to trade at or near their takeover value, then valuation of private *minority* interests using publicly traded stock multiples or

---

[203] This is the concept of the *fundamental adjustment* introduced in Chapter 3 and discussed at length in Chapter 5.

discount rates will require discounts for *both* lack of liquidity (i.e., marketability) *and* lack of control. [Mercer, #22, pp. 123-124]

Nath discussed five problems with control premiums in his article. I addressed each of the problems through the filter of differences in risk and expected growth and attempted to "explain away" the real issues raised by Nath. My 1990 article concluded:

> The Nath article offers an interesting challenge to prevailing valuation theory by suggesting that the prices of publicly held companies reflect controlling interest values rather than minority interest values. The postulate has a fair amount of intuitive appeal; however, we remain unconvinced of its general validity based upon the rationale of this article and general experience in representing buyers and sellers of companies in change of control transactions. [Mercer, #22, p. 125].

Nath concluded that minority interests valued using publicly traded stock multiples would require discounts for lack of control (minority interest discounts) and lack of liquidity (marketability discounts). I concluded that public guideline multiples yielded marketable minority values and that only a marketability discount was appropriate to reach the nonmarketable minority level of value. Interestingly, we were both right (and wrong a little). The reconciliation of the two views was provided in one form in Chapter 3 and follows in another later in this chapter.

LEVELS OF VALUE UNTIL 1995

The debate over the levels of value continued for some time. Between 1990 and 1995, several articles addressing the levels of value were published in *Business Valuation Review*. For now, we focus on two additional articles, which came to be viewed as part of a serial debate involving Nath, Mercer, Bolotsky, and Dr. Wayne C. Jankowske, CPA, ASA.

The Bolotsky Article

Bolotsky's article took the Nath article and my articles as the point of departure for discussion. To provide a flavor of the article, its conclusion is quoted here:

> As noted in earlier sections of this article, we found some merit in the basic arguments of Mr. Nath; however, we disagreed in whole or in part with most of his conclusions (the Nath Hypotheses).

At the same time, we found Prevailing Wisdom to be generally incomplete although, for the most part, not flawed as far as it goes. However, we also feel that Prevailing Wisdom does not go nearly far enough, in that it relies on only two key attributes to explain shareholder-level value differences, when in reality there are at least four, and perhaps more, key attributes. We introduced a new analytical framework for assessing shareholder-level value differentials, one that relies on four key attributes and allows for the inclusion of additional key attributes. At the same time, we recognized that there are currently few, if any, market-based data sources to shed light on the magnitude of the information-related key attributes.

We considered and explained part of the tendency of Prevailing Wisdom to overvalue private company ownership interests for fair market value purposes.

We attempted to synthesize the conclusions of Prevailing Wisdom and the Nath Hypotheses in a manner that illuminates a range of possible circumstances rather than the "black or white" implications of one point of view or the other.

We hope that, at least, this article has been thought provoking and generates additional dialogue in the form of both Letters to the Editor and future articles. [Bolotsky, #5, pp. 94-110]

With the benefit of hindsight, the Bolotsky article was more insightful than I thought at the time it was written. During the 1990s, most appraisers were looking at the world of value through a variety of shades of tinted glasses – and many of us (including me) read and/or participated in the growing debate over levels of value through our own colored glasses.

Bolotsky proposed an analytical framework for assessing "Prevailing Wisdom" and the "Nath Hypothesis." The insights it provides are helpful today in reconciling issues regarding the levels of value.

From the current perspective, Bolotsky's proposed "analytical framework" is, in reality, a call for consideration of factors other than "pure illiquidity" in developing marketability discounts. Buyers and sellers of public minority interests lack control and have the ability to obtain liquidity in (now) three days. They have access to substantial publicly filed information that should be generally reliable based on compliance with SEC disclosure requirements.

He suggests that buyers and sellers of minority interests of private companies have limited ownership rights (and lack control) and very low liquidity in the absence of any market for their shares. He summarizes their rights regarding information access as very limited for sellers and even more limited for buyers, and similarly regarding information reliability. In the Bolotsky framework, buyers and sellers of 100% control have total control and limited liquidity (suggesting some impairment in the value of capitalized earnings for such limitations – a point with which we disagree). The seller of 100% control has total information access and complete information reliability, and these attributes vary among buyers.

Bolotsky then provides three illustrations (which I have summarized) in the context of the traditional three-level levels of value chart [Bolotsky #5]. My comments are presented in parentheticals.

- *Going from public minority value to private company 100% control value.* 100% control value begins with the public minority value, adjusts value for differences between ownership rights (+), for differences in liquidity which is limited for control (-), for differences in information access (+), and for differences in information reliability (+).

    [Note that this framework makes no adjustment to value relating to potential differences in cash flow or expected growth in cash flow between the two levels. Implicit in any increment in value then, is a reduction in the discount rate. Recall that $(V = CF / (R - G))$. If neither CF nor G are changed, the only way for V to increase is for R to decrease. However, as discussed at several points in this book, market forces will tend to cause no change in R for financial buyers of controlling interests, so the only way for buyers to justify higher prices is by improving cash flows and/or expected growth and sharing some or all of that benefit with sellers. So the analytical framework proposed by Bolotsky does not explain differences between public minority values and financial control sales. And it does not explain the often substantial differences in strategic control values and public minority values reflected in public company acquisitions.]

- *Going from public minority value to private company minority value.* Private company minority value begins with the public minority price and makes no adjustment for ownership rights, which are alike. Adjustments are made for differences in liquidity (-), differences in information access (-), and differences between information reliability (-).

  [Again, there is no adjustment in the Bolotsky framework to account for differences in expected cash flow between the marketable minority level and the nonmarketable minority level. However, these differences are material. Recall that the public minority shareholder has "instant" liquidity, which is reflected in the ability to obtain the market's consensus value of the expected cash flows of the enterprise (the market price) in three days. While the public minority shareholder does not control enterprise cash flows, he has access to their capitalized value at any time. The private company minority shareholder has access only to those cash flows expected to be distributed by the company over the expected holding period of the investment. These differences must be considered in any adjustment from public minority to private minority values.]

- *Going from private company 100% control value to private minority value.* Private company minority value (nonmarketable minority) begins with 100% control value and decreases value for differences in ownership rights (control). Further adjustments are made for differences in liquidity, because Bolotsky views 100% control as more liquid than a minority interest (-), for differences in information access (-), and for differences in information reliability (-).

  [Once again, no adjustments are made in this framework for the potentially substantial differences in cash flows to be received by minority shareholders versus 100% control of cash flows available to the 100% control shareholder.]

Bolotsky ends the levels of value analogy with the following:

> The three scenarios discussed above correspond to three of the common guideline company methodologies utilized in Prevailing Wisdom. As you can see, the positive and negative adjustments required are often quite difference from the "Premium for Control" and "DLOM" of Prevailing Wisdom. [Bolotsky, #5, p.102]

The 1991 Bolotsky analytical framework provides interesting insights. Most importantly, it recognized that differences in value between ownership interests at different "levels" are accounted for by more than differences in cash flows at the various levels of value (or for the various ownership characteristics). Unfortunately, the framework then proceeded to ignore differences in cash flows – unless it can be implicitly assumed that ownership control gives access to cash flows. And then, it does not account for public minority shareholders' access to the capitalized value of cash flows on an "instant" basis.

I should point out that this review of the Bolotsky article is occurring some 13 years after it was written. My criticisms and observations have the benefit of years of grappling with the issues and, hopefully, growing in the process. And these observations are being made in the context of an understanding of valuation and valuation relationships that I did not enjoy at the time he wrote the article in 1991.

When Nath wrote his article, he concluded that public minority multiples applied to private company earnings yielded controlling interest value indications. He then suggested that the nonmarketable minority value would be achieved by applying successive minority interest and marketability discounts. Bolotsky reached an important conclusion in 1991 when discussing the Nath Hypothesis that I simply missed until a few years ago, when I thought that I had probably developed it for the first time. The reconciliation of the Nath Hypothesis lies in the application of a minority interest discount of zero to the controlling interest value. Bolotsky said in 1991:

> Therefore, in determining a private company minority interest value in the above scenario [using public guideline analysis], the valuator has only two reasonable choices:
>
> 1. Begin with the public minority price, that is, the as-if-freely-traded value, and adjust for the differences in key attributes between a public minority value and a private minority value (i.e., differences in liquidity only in the framework of Prevailing

Wisdom or differences in liquidity and information in the framework we introduced earlier), or

2. Begin with the control price, which happens to be the same as the public minority price, subtract the value of the appropriate premium between the two prices, which by definition is zero, to derive the as-if-freely-traded value, and then proceed as in number (1.) above.

Either way, you end up with the same conclusion, a conclusion that necessarily relies on a premium of zero and which implies that a premium should not be subtracted from the as-if-freely-traded value in any circumstances, but rather only from the control value. Another way of stating the above is that we can't have it both ways, with no control premium when that helps us and instead with a positive premium when that helps us. One can't first make a case for having a zero control premium over the public price, as Mr. Nath did in justifying the use of public prices with no premium for the valuation of entire private companies; then again make a case for a zero control premium, as Mr. Nath did in arguing that the starting point in a public guideline company approach represents a control price even though it is based on evidence from minority trades; and then turn around and state that, when backing out the very same control premium to derive the as-if-freely-traded value, the premium should suddenly transform from an amount of zero to a positive amount. We can't have it both ways. Or, as Mr. Mercer aptly stated, there are far easier and more realistic ways of justifying the often significant value differences between public minority blocks and private minority blocks based on company-level differences in risk and growth. [Bolotsky, #5, p.107].

We were all struggling in the early 1990s, but Bolotsky showed a much keener perception on this point than did the rest of us. Current comments or criticisms aside, the Bolotsky article was important in the development of our collective understanding of the levels of value.

The Jankowske Article

Jankowske took the Nath, Mercer and Bolotsky articles as his point of departure. [Jankowske, #16, p. 143]. Quoting from his conclusion [with Mercer comments in parentheticals]:

> This article states that guideline firm valuation ratios applied to a subject firm's shares should be adjusted for known attribute differences among the firms. Such adjustments should reflect differences at both the enterprise and shareholder level.
>
> > [Jankowske's conclusion seems to overstate the key point that he made in his 1991 article: "The important point to recognize is that both company-level and shareholder-level differences should be reflected in the appraisal." [Jankowske, #15, p. 142]. None of us know how to parse public company data to account for public-private differences at the shareholder level.]
>
> When it is agreed that discounts for minority interests may vary with facts and circumstances, it then becomes plausible that the minority discount appropriate for a public firm may be less than (or sometimes greater than) the minority discount appropriate for a subject firm.
>
> > [As I read Jankowske's article today, it appears that one of his key concerns was that appraisers appropriately consider all of the differences between public guideline companies and subject private companies. He focuses on fundamental adjustments that may be necessary to public multiples to apply them to private companies. These would not be part of any minority interest or marketability discount. In terms introduced in Chapter 5, fundamental adjustments "adjust the levels of value" to the appropriate point for private companies. Further, the differences he seems concerned about between public and private minority interests "include differences in legal and contractual protection, agency costs, relative incentives, and differential economic benefits." [Jankowske, #15, p. 141] These concerns were as legitimate in 1991 as they are today. However, in the context of the valuation of minority interests, they relate to the marketability discount. The adverse impact of most, if not all of these differences is avoided by public minority shareholders as result of their ability to sell their shares at will in the public markets.]

To say that a greater DFMI (discount for minority interest) cannot be taken for the subject firm is to make an important mistake in logic. It is logically flawed to assume that since both are labeled "minority interests," both must be the same for purposes of valuation. In point of fact, minority interests in public firms tend to differ from minority interests in private firms.

> [My comments immediately above apply to this focus on the differences of public and private minority interests.]

> It has been suggested in this article that varying degrees of the minority interest discount could be incorporated directly into the prevailing framework. It is logical to take an additional minority interest discount if minority shareholders of a public guideline firm experience fewer disadvantages than their counterparts in a subject firm. Failure to recognize these differences within some framework is likely to produce inaccurate estimates of value.

At this point, it appears that the reconciliation of the Integrated Theory with Jankowske's article lies in the fact that he is asking appraisers to be certain to consider many of the same issues in their appraisals of illiquid minority interests as are discussed in this book in the context of the marketability discount.

1995 ASA Advanced Business Valuation Conference

The Nath-Mercer-Bolotsky-Jankowske series of articles was a topic of considerable discussion among appraisers. The four of us were asked to address the issue at the International Conference of the American Society of Appraisers held in Denver in June 1995. At that conference, we addressed the question: "Is the 'Levels of Value' Concept Still Viable?" [Bolotsky, et al., #6]. We prepared the handout materials in advance, and shared our papers with each other prior to the session.

- Nath introduced a "new" levels of value chart. In valuing a private company, Nath suggested a three-way method to develop the controlling interest value of a private company considering the potential for an IPO (guideline company method), the value of the company if 100% of its equity were sold, and liquidation value. After correlating these values, he then suggested applying appropriate minority interest and marketability discounts. Nath's concepts are further discussed below.

- Bolotsky continued to discuss concepts of value driven by liquidity and power. He concluded regarding the levels of value chart:

  > It is a useful representation of reality in the right market conditions for the right companies. However, used blindly and universally, without an assessment of whether the appraisal-date market conditions support its validity at that point in time, and without an assessment of whether the subject company's own characteristics appear to support its validity for that company, it can produce distorted value conclusions. In any case, the model can be improved by a consideration of the other ownership attributes that can influence value, as detailed in my September 1991 *Business Valuation Review* article. [Bolotsky, #5]

- Jankowske provided a thoughtful paper that focused on a number of possible exceptions or pricing anomalies that could call the levels of value into question: He concluded:

  > While perhaps useful as a tool of communication, the Levels of Value Concept may require serious rethinking if it is to be useful to appraisers who draw insights from modern economic thought. In my opinion, adjustments should be made along a Levels of Value Continuum that reflect economic value drivers. Such continuum would identify two levels of control: financial control value and strategic control value.

  > Under this approach, adjustments for control and marketability would be viewed as different "tracks," unconstrained by present notions as to their relative importance. Consequently, we may find situations in which marketable-minority value is greater than, equal to or less than either of the two levels of control value. [Jankowske, #16]

- I discussed the levels of value as a conceptual framework and concluded that it was a viable economic theory:

> The chart above [essentially Figure 10-1] shows three distinct Levels of Value for purposes of discussion and illustration. An alternate depiction is of two extremes of value, with the "controlling interest" block representing the value of 100% of an enterprise (the highest value), and the "non-marketable minority interest" block representing the value of a very small minority interest (the lowest value). Between the highest and lowest values are a variety of gradations of value.
>
> For example, appraisers must often deal with "control blocks" representing less than 100% ownership and with minority interests with differing characteristics that affect marketability and value. The use of appraiser judgment is always necessary in real life situations. Illustrations like the chart above simply provide a framework for the exercise of that judgment consistent with valid financial and valuation theory, objective market evidence, and experience.
>
> The Levels of Value concept is a model used to explain economic and financial reality. The model is a simplified picture or map of the normal valuation relationships that exist in the real world. McConnell stated that "theories which do not fit the facts are simply not good theories." The alternative statement would be that theories that do fit the facts (all the facts) are probably pretty good theories. The Levels of Value model generally fits the facts. It is a good theory or model.

Jankowske's calling for a fourth level of value that distinguished between financial control and strategic control echoed Nath's original thesis. Appraisers discussed these specific concepts for some time prior to 1995; however, no one had published a different levels of value chart. In response to all the papers, I introduced some hand-prepared overhead slides at the session. That chart is reproduced (in much prettier form) as Figure 10-3 using terminology consistent with this book.

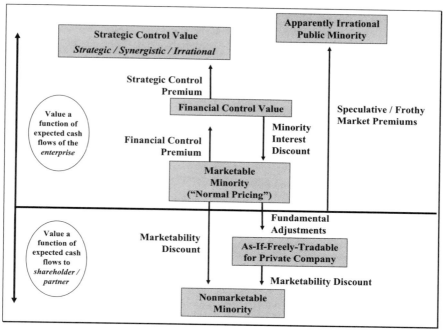

Figure 10-3

This hand-prepared levels of value chart was based on experience and intuition. With it, I attempted to explain the various valuation circumstances that some thought called the levels of value framework into question. Without the benefit of the Integrated Theory, but clearly benefiting from early thinking about the subject, this chart addressed several questions or issues.

- The potential differences between financial and strategic control valuation concepts were identified. A distinction was drawn between financial control premiums and strategic/synergistic (and even irrational) control premiums. As previously mentioned, both Nath and Jankowske had discussed these concepts.

- The minority interest discount was identified as relating to financial control value and not strategic control value. This recognition led to my articles and speeches (beginning in 1996) on the potential to overstate minority interest discounts by referring to (strategic) control premium data in *Mergerstat Review* or elsewhere. [Mercer #27, #30]

- A clear distinction was drawn between enterprise and shareholder level valuation concepts. We first utilized (an early version of) the Quantitative Marketability Discount Model in appraisals in 1994 at Mercer Capital. I first addressed the QMDM at the ASA Advanced Business Valuation Conference in San Diego in the Fall of 1994. So we were beginning to develop the Integrated Theory even then.

- The concept of the fundamental adjustment was identified as adjusting the levels of value for private companies in relationship to publicly traded guideline groups. The 1989 ACAPM article [Mercer, #21] discussed the fundamental adjustment and the fact that appraisers who failed to adjust for fundamental differences (in risk and expected growth in earnings) often "fixed" their appraisals by subtracting a "marketability discount" applicable to controlling interests. In 1994, I wrote an article on this topic. [Mercer, #26. See also Mercer #22, #24; Goeldner, #11, #12] Jankowske discussed the fundamental adjustment in writing as early as 1991, as noted above.

- Finally, some appraisers had attempted to dismiss the entire levels of value framework because they saw public stock prices in excess of enterprise values for individual companies in the stock markets. So the chart recognized that publicly traded (minority) stocks could trade at values in excess of either their financial or strategic control values. I used the term "speculative/frothy market premiums" to describe this concept. Recognition that irrationality or speculation could push prices beyond the real of rational, financial concepts (based on the GRAPES of Value discussed in Chapter 2) was important. Mark Lee, CFA, provided excellent insight on this issue in an article in 2001. [Lee, #19]

Importantly, however, the 1995 chart did not address Nath's thesis that the market prices of public companies tended to illustrate control values. That took more time and thought and the development of the Integrated Theory (although, as noted in the earlier discussion, Bolotsky had already recognized the conceptual key to reconciliation).

LEVELS OF VALUE: 1995 TO THE PRESENT

Escalating interest regarding the levels of value can be seen in the number of articles in the bibliography that deal with one or more aspects of the concept. This interest has been driven by intellectual curiosity as well as by the need to support valuations with clients and in courts. For example, a central issue in *Estate of Jung* was whether the discounted cash flow method of valuation yielded a marketable minority or controlling interest value indication.[204] While this was a 1993 case, it took time for the debate to spread. In reviewing the case in *Quantifying Marketability Discounts* (in 1997), I noted:

> The underlying question raised here is whether a valuation conclusion developed using a discounted cash flow or other form of discounted future earnings model is a controlling interest or a marketable minority interest level indication of value.

> As should be clear from the discussion in Exhibit 8-2 regarding the Adjusted Capital Asset Pricing Model, the discount rate typically used in DCF (or DFE, discounted future earnings) methods is applicable at the marketable minority interest level of value. As such, the DCF method is a marketable minority interest valuation method. However, numerous appraisers would argue that the implied cause of the change in value in moving from the marketable minority interest to the controlling interest level of value is not a change in the underlying discount rate, but a change in investors' perceptions of the earnings stream.

> Appraisers who make controlling interest adjustments to a subject company's earning stream (like owner salary adjustments or the elimination of certain non-recurring items) can make a legitimate claim that their DCF or DFE methods provide controlling interest valuation methods....[205]

---

[204] *Estate of Mildred Herschede Jung v. Commissioner*, 101. T.C. 412 (1993). This case is summarized in Chapter 4 of *Quantifying Marketability Discounts*.

[205] Author's Note: This was written in late 1995 or 1996, before we concluded that such *normalizing adjustments* are not control-adjustments, but adjustments necessary to value a company at the marketable minority level. In practice, analysts at Mercer Capital made such normalizing adjustments and considered resulting value indications to be at the marketable minority level of value. The theory, however, was still formulating.

The message is important: appraisers need to be crystal clear about the theoretical justifications underlying valuation methods and equally clear when valuation adjustments might change the level of value to which a particular method might apply.

There is some legitimate confusion on this question among appraisers and the Tax Court, and the question needs to be addressed at more length in a credible forum.

The need for a clearer understanding of the levels of value was apparent based on the number of articles and speeches that addressed the issue during the late 1990s.

The levels of value was again a topic of discussion in 2001 at the 20th Annual Advanced Business Valuation Conference of the American Society of Appraisers in Seattle. The panelists included Dr. Shannon Pratt (moderator), Michael Bolotsky, Eric Nath, Mary McCarter, and Carla Glass. Timothy R. Lee of Mercer Capital, while not a panelist, spoke from the floor at Dr. Pratt's request. The Seattle session and its accompanying handout materials provide the backdrop for bringing the levels of value debate to the present.

Chapter 3 introduced the Integrated Theory and provided an in-depth discussion and analysis of the levels of value. Each level of value was defined and described in the context of current financial theory. The discussion in Chapter 3, however, could appear to be at odds with other views regarding the levels of value, some of which were advanced in the 2001 Seattle session.

Some of the panelists apparently believed that there were problems with the levels of value framework that need to be resolved (Pratt, Bolotsky, McCarter), while others made comments that were consistent with the traditional concepts (Nath, Glass). It was suggested that Nath and I disagree substantially on the issue of levels of value. However, based on his handout material, comments, and personal conversations with him, our thinking seems more closely aligned than some may believe.

SUMMARY OF LEVELS OF VALUE SESSION BY PRESENTER AT THE ASA 2001 BUSINESS VALUATION CONFERENCE

Dr. Shannon P. Pratt, CFA, FASA, MCBA

Pratt stated that control premiums (and implied minority interest discounts), on average, are smaller if negative premiums are considered. This distinction is now clearly indicated in the *Mergerstat/Shannon Pratt's Control Premium Study*. He supported his comments with an article by Mark Lee, CFA, parts of which were included in the session handouts [Lee, #19].

The Lee article elaborated on key points regarding control premiums and minority interest discounts found in earlier articles by Nath [Nath, #44] and by Mercer [Mercer, #27, in which a four-level chart was published], and in a speech by Steve Garber, ASA [Garber, #10]. The Lee article provided a four-level, levels of value chart. The handout material also reproduced the four-level chart from the *Guide to Business Valuations* [Fishman et al., #8]. That the four-level chart for the levels of value is becoming accepted is reflected by the fact that it is published twice in the fourth edition of *Valuing a Business* [Pratt/Reilly/Schweihs, #57]. The first chart is identical to the Fishman/Pratt chart, and the second is a reproduction of the chart in Mercer, #27, which was developed from one of the levels of value charts I prepared for the 1995 Denver ASA Conference. That chart is presented in Figure 10-4 adjacent to the original three level, levels of value chart.

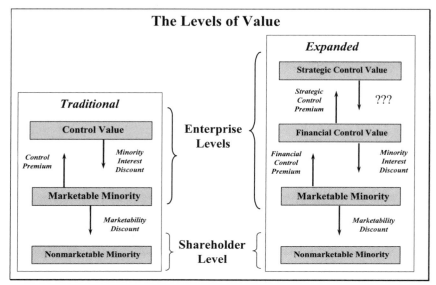

Figure 10-4
Comparison of Original and Expanded Levels of Value Charts

With broader publication of the four-level chart shown in Figure 10-4, there has been a growing acceptance among appraisers that there can be a distinction between financial and strategic buyers of companies and, therefore, a difference between financial and strategic control values.

Pratt suggested that there is a need for consensus regarding the concept of a marketability discount applicable to controlling interests. However, neither he nor anyone else has yet made a convincing argument for the existence of such a discount.[206] If value can be represented conceptually by CF/(R-G), and if CF represents the normalized cash flows of a financial buyer, R is the appropriate discount rate, and G is the expected growth rate of those cash flows, any such discount is considered in the already-specified value components. [Mercer, #26, #29, #32 and the discussion of the Integrated Theory of Chapter 3 of this book]. In fact, although such a discount is mentioned in the Fishman/Pratt exhibit [Fishman/Pratt, #8], there is no block or symbolic representation of the discount.

---

[206] See the discussion in Chapter 3 and 5 regarding marketability discounts applicable to controlling interests in companies. See in particular the sidebar comments by Dr. Pratt on this issue in Chapter 5 and my reply in the accompanying text.

Pratt's Discussion of Article by
Mark Lee, CFA

In addition to providing a four-level level of value chart, Pratt also reproduced a Figure from the Mark Lee article relating to the relationship of the stock market and the M&A market. That Figure is reproduced as Figure 10-5.

Figure 10-5
Schematic Relationship of Stock Market and M&A Market[207]

In introducing what is Figure 10-5 in this chapter in his article, Lee drew clear distinctions between the stock markets and the M&A markets [Lee, 2001, #19]:

> The circle in the chart above is the M&A Market. The box is the stock market. (The sizes of the two are not proportionate.)
>
> If a potential acquirer believes that it can create sufficient added economic benefits, the acquisition value of the company will exceed its market value. The additional economic benefit can pay for the cost of the acquisition premium. These are the transactions reported in the Control Premium Study and similar publications.

---

[207] Lee, M. Mark, "Control Premiums and Minority Discounts: the Need for Specific Economic Analysis," *Shannon Pratt's Business Valuation Update*, August 2001 (obtained on-line at www.bvresources.com. Chart reproduced as published with the addition of the arrows indicating that the M&A market and stock market can move independent of each other, which is a key point of the Lee analysis.

Most publicly traded companies are not taken over in a given year. Generally, there is no market available that can create benefits large enough to justify payment of the premium required for the acquisition of these companies in view of other alternatives.

If there is no market available to sell a company at a premium to its stock market value, then there is little or no acquisition premium, much less a "theoretical" premium based on an average of acquisitions of dissimilar companies.

In emerging industries, such as the Internet in 1998 and 1999, the value of the common stock of a corporation as a whole often is less than the aggregate market value of common stock trading as minority interests. While the new industry is viewed as very attractive for investment, individual corporations are perceived as too risky. As a result, individual and institutional investors will pay more for minority interests as part of a diversified industry portfolio than individual acquirers will pay for the entire company.

Similarly, many companies spin off units or sell them in an IPO rather than sell the units in the M&A market because a higher price can be obtained in the market than in an M&A transaction.

The stock market is a market for minority interests in common stock. The principal buyers and sellers are individuals, mutual funds, and financial institutions. The market is highly liquid, individual investment horizons may be short, and risk tolerances can be greater than in illiquid markets. Financing is often readily available from banks and brokers at short-term money rates. Investors are generally passive. Individual investments are purchased as part of diversified portfolios, which leads to greater tolerance for risk.

The M&A market is a market for whole companies. The principal buyers and sellers are controlling stockholders, corporations, and LBO houses. The market is not liquid; as a result, individual investment horizons tend to be longer. Risk tolerances in the short term tend to be lower than in a liquid market. Transactions are financed using long-term debt from banks, insurance companies, mezzanine funds, equity of large corporations, and private equity funds. M&A investors take an active role in managing their companies.

The relationship of the two markets is not linear. Linearity presupposes that acquisition premiums apply in all situations and that acquisition premiums are roughly the same amount generally or in each industry.

This brief introduction of Lee's 2001 article leads to two observations:

- It should be clear from the excerpted text of Lee's article that Lee is talking about the same concepts that led me to observe that "apparently irrational" behavior could cause the public minority price to exceed that of even a strategic level value (look back at Figure 10-3). Lee adds the insight that the seemingly irrational behavior of individuals in paying very high prices for emerging companies may not be so irrational when viewed as purchases in the context of diversified portfolios of investments.

- It should also be clear that Lee believes that the M&A market and the stock market are substantially different in nature, and that the investors in the two markets may have quite different investment horizons and risk tolerances.

The Lee article admonishes appraisers that the existence of and the magnitude of any acquisition premium (strategic control premium in the vocabulary of this book) is dependent on the facts and circumstances of an appraisal situation. He observes that the discounted cash flow method should be used to determine a subject company's stand-alone value – in the absence of expected synergies. And he refers to this stand-alone value as "enterprise value," which corresponds to the financial control value in the context of this book.

Lee's observations are important to this discussion of the levels of value. Although he does not discuss the magnitude of control premiums (financial control premiums), he makes it clear that the blind application of acquisition premiums (strategic/synergistic control premiums) is improper and would normally lead to overvaluation. He affirms Nath's observation that, since most public companies are not taken over in any given year, M&A market participants must not see sufficient potential benefit to warrant acquisitions. This suggests that there are no (or very small) financial control premiums that would be generally applicable.

Finally, Lee's logic supports the proposition that there is no marketability discount applicable to controlling interests in companies, although he does not make that point in the article. Enterprise values are based on enterprise cash flows, and those are the cash flows used by M&A market participants to assess the value enterprises.

Michael J. Bolotsky, ASA, CBA

Bolotsky started with observations of the need to improve the analysis of issues related to risk and growth. However, he did not fully integrate the idea into his discussion of the levels of value that followed. Bolotsky presented the same charts at this session that he used in the 1995 session, attempting to explain the levels of value in the context of the concepts of liquidity and power. He used two charts to attempt to explain two observations from the markets. These charts are reproduced as Figure 10-6 for comparison with the more traditional levels of value chart.

Controlling interest values in public companies sometimes are higher than freely traded minority values ("Normal Times" on the Figure).

Freely traded minority values are sometimes in excess of the value of 100% of the enterprise ("Unusual Times" on the Figure).

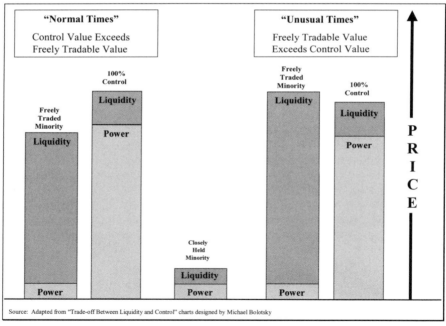

Figure 10-6
Bolotsky 1995 and 2001: Trade-off Between Liquidity and Control

From my reading, Bolotsky may believe that the more traditional levels of value chart "worked" in the 1970s and 1980s, did not work in the 1990s, and may or may not work today. He seeks to explain differences in observed pricing in the marketplace based on relative degrees of "liquidity" and "power."

Neither in his 1995 presentation nor in the 2001 session did Bolotsky explain how an appraiser would be able to value an enterprise based on an examination of these factors. He called for further research on the issue in 1990, and that research has not been forthcoming. Further, Bolotsky's trade-off concept ignores the fact that the public securities markets and the market for controlling interests of companies are different markets. Investors in the public markets may have different investment objectives, time horizons, and immediate needs for the availability of liquidity than investors in whole companies.

Figure 10-6 indicates relatively little "power" for a public shareholder and substantial "liquidity" in either "normal times" or "unusual times." While it is true that minority shareholders in a public company cannot generally influence management of the enterprise directly, it is also true that they can tap into the capitalized value of 100% of the company's cash flows via the mechanism of the public markets and receive cash in three days. And collectively, public shareholders can exert great "power" when they express displeasure with managements and sell their shares. This is an alternative source of "power" for minority shareholders that cumulatively drives the stock price – and ultimately, the actions of management.

The high degree of "power" indicated for the 100% control situation delivers the benefit of 100% of the cash flows of the business. Regarding the low degree of "liquidity" for the 100% control situation, I have pointed out before that buyers (and holders) enjoy the normal degree of liquidity for companies. Companies trade in different markets than the public securities markets, and a comparison of relative liquidity between the two is essentially irrelevant. It certainly does not explain why companies pay the prices they pay for other companies any more than does the acquisition of "power." See also the discussion in Chapter 3 regarding the perquisites of control.

Eric W. Nath, ASA

Nath presented a chart titled "Level of Value in Private Companies Based on Owners' Options for Exit or Liquidity." Nath's analysis examines value from the perspective of a controlling owner and a minority owner, and is consistent with his 1995 presentation. As the title suggests, he looks at the different liquidity options available for controlling and noncontrolling shareholders. As I have indicated on many occasions now, I believe there is a logical reconciliation between Nath's idea and the more traditional levels of value concepts.

Nath recognizes several options available for a controlling shareholder, including sale of a company, liquidation, or IPO. He suggests that the method providing the highest value, whether an estimate of value if taken public, or the value based on M&A transactions, or the value based on capitalized income or DCF, represents the value of control. However, the "value of control," while providing excellent advice for the controlling business owner, may not represent fair market value, particularly if fair market value is interpreted to be a value based on financial returns, rather than value based on strategic or synergistic considerations. In this case, Nath's methodology would yield an indication of investment value to the owner rather than the fair market value. This issue exists whenever appraisers use strategic acquisition multiples as a basis for determining the fair market value of controlling interests, and is clearly an area where appraiser knowledge is evolving.

As discussed earlier in this chapter, Nath caused many in the appraisal profession, including me, to think seriously about the levels of value when he wrote his thoughtful first article in 1990 [Nath, #44], and in his articles since then [Nath, #45, #46]. He argued that the freely traded price in the public marketplace most likely represented a controlling interest, rather than a minority interest price. As we have studied the question over time and worked with the financial theory underlying the various levels of value, I began to realize that Nath and I might be saying very much the same thing.[208]   The conceptual reconciliation of what Bolotsky referred to as "the Nath Hypothesis" [Bolotsky, #5] and the more traditional levels of value is discussed below.

---

[208]   In fairness, I am now saying what he said a long time ago, at least in part.

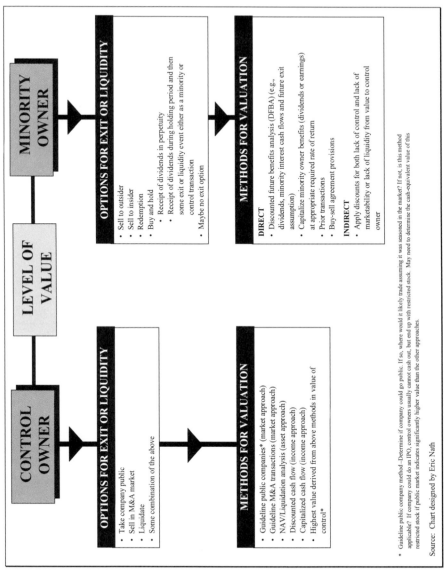

Figure 10-7

Nath 1995 and expanded 2001: Level of Value in Private Companies Based on Owners' Options for Exit or Liquidity

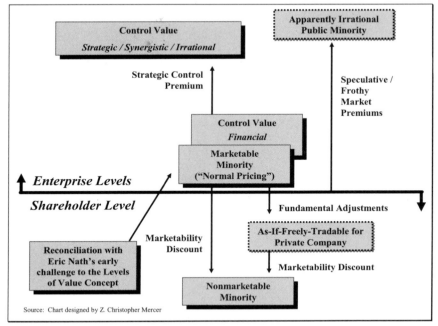

Figure 10-8
Mercer 1999: Reconciliation with Nath's Level of Value Concept

Nath advocates what he refers to as "direct" methods for valuing minority interests of private companies. These methods include a discounted future benefits analysis (such as dividends, minority interest cash flows and future exit assumptions). His chart, in fact, describes the essence of the QMDM (at the bottom right of Figure 10-7). Nath stated during the 2001 presentation that he regularly uses the QMDM, and his presentation provides solid support for quantitative, rate of return analysis in valuing illiquid minority interests in private companies.

Regarding his "indirect" methods of minority interest valuation, Nath suggests applying discounts for lack of control and lack of marketability from the value to the control owner. As I have observed before, this methodology is consistent with the more traditional levels of value concepts. However, note in Figure 10-8 that the minority interest discount may be zero or quite small.

It took several years, but the so-called Mercer-Nath "dispute" over the levels of value is, I believe, over. We now have a logical and a theoretical reconciliation of the issue.

Mary B. McCarter, CFA, ASA

McCarter provided a chart titled "Basis of Value" (reproduced as Figure 10-9) that discusses the traditional levels of value in relationship to Bolotsky's power and liquidity concepts. In fact, reading the chart, the difference between the marketable minority value and the nonmarketable minority value is the marketability discount. Further, one can achieve a nonmarketable minority interest value by beginning with a control value and reducing it sequentially by a minority interest discount and a marketability discount.

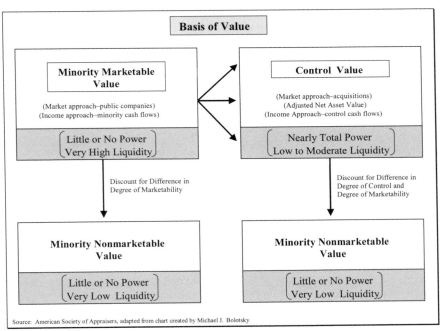

Figure 10-9
McCarter 2001: Basis of Value

Arrows on the chart seem to indicate that the marketable minority value may be less than, equal to, or greater than the control value. At its essence, this chart is a restatement of the traditional levels of value with an attempt to explain apparent market anomalies (like Bolotsky in Figure 10-6 and Mercer in Figure 10-2). Comparing McCarter's Figure 10-9 with Figure 10-2 and ignoring the parenthetical comments regarding liquidity and power, it is clear that Figure 10-9 is a subset of Figure 10-2.

Interestingly, the suggestion that public minority shareholders and holders of illiquid minority interests share the attribute of "little or no power" is consistent with the discussion above relating to the fact that the difference between the two levels of value relates to the lack of marketability.

Carla Glass, ASA did not present a particular level of value chart. Rather, she posed questions and made observations for the panel and audience.

All in all, while one objective of the 2001 ASA Advanced Business Valuation Conference may have been to call traditional levels of value concepts into question, the comments and handout materials, in my opinion, ultimately affirm these concepts. Every variation of the levels of value chart used by panelists other than Bolotsky conform (or can be reconciled) with the framework presented in this book. And McCarter used Bolotsky's propositions, at least partially, to conform her thoughts to the same concepts.

CONCLUSION

We hope that the Integrated Theory of Business Valuation presented in Chapter 3 and the discussion of this chapter will enhance understanding of the levels of value in the appraisal community.

Appendix 10-A

LEVELS OF VALUE
PARTIAL BIBLIOGRAPHY

We prepared this Bibliography in 2004 and have made every effort to be comprehensive; however, we realize that we may have inadvertently overlooked articles that should appear here. If that is the case, please inform us of those additions by e-mailing us at **mcm@mercercapital.com** and we will add those articles to the list and post a more complete Bibliography to our website (www.mercercapital.com).

Due to space considerations, this bibliography contains only a partial list of the presentations that have been presented on the subject of "Levels of Value."

1.   **Abrams**, Jay B., "Discount for Lack of Marketability: A Theoretical Model," *Business Valuation Review*, Vol. 13, No. 3 (September 1994).

2.   ———, "Letter to the Editor," *Business Valuation Review*, Vol. 14, No. 1 (March 1995).

3.   **Abrams**, Jay B., "Chapter 7: Adjusting for Levels of Control and Marketability," *Quantitative Business Valuation: A Mathematical Approach For Today's Professional*, New York, NY: McGraw-Hill, 2001.

4.   **Annin**, Michael, "Understanding and Quantifying Control Premiums: The Value of Control vs. Synergies or Strategic Advantages," *The Journal of Business Valuation*, 1999.

5.   **Bolotsky**, Michael J., "Adjustments for Differences in Ownership Rights, Liquidity, Information Access, and Information Reliability: An Assessment of 'Prevailing Wisdom' versus the 'Nath Hypotheses'," *Business Valuation Review*, Vol. 10, No. 3 (September 1991).

6. **Bolotsky**, Michael J., **Jankowske**, Wayne C., **Mercer**, Z. Christopher, and **Nath**, Eric. W., "Is the 'Levels of Value' Concept Still Viable?" (Panel discussion at the American Society of Appraisers International Appraisal Conference, Denver, CO, June 20, 1995).

7. **Evans**, Frank C., "Making Sense of Rates of Return and Multiples," *Business Valuation Review*, Vol. 18, No. 2 (June 1999).

8. **Fishman**, Jay, **et al.,** *PPC'S Guide To Business Valuations*, Fort Worth, TX: Practitioners Publishing Company, annual editions since about 1990.

9. **Fowler**, Bradley A., "How Do You Handle It?," *Business Valuation Review*, Vol. 12, No. 4 (December 1993).

10. **Garber**, Steven D., "Control vs. Acquisition Premiums: Is There a Difference?" (Presentation at the American Society of Appraisers International Appraisal Conference, Maui, HI, June 23, 1998).

11. **Goeldner**, Richard W., II, "Bridging the Gap Between Public and Private Market Multiples," *Business Valuation Review*, Vol. 17, No. 3 (September 1998).

12. ———,"Adjusting Market Multiples of Public Guideline Companies for the Closely Held Business" (Presentation at the 18th Annual Advanced Business Valuation Conference, New Orleans, LA, October 29, 1999).

13. **Hertzel**, Michael and **Smith**, Richard L., "Market Discounts and Shareholder Gains for Placing Equity Privately," *The Journal of Finance*, Vol. 48, No. 2 (June 1993).

14. **Hood**, L. Paul, Jr., Esq., "*Janda*: Valuation and Marketability Discounts – 'Damned If You Do' Valuation," *E-Law Business Valuation Perspective*, Issue 2001-02 (February 13, 2001).

15. **Jankowske**, Wayne C., "Valuing Minority Interests in Relation to Guideline Firms," *Business Valuation Review*, Vol. 10, No. 4 (December 1991).

16. ———, "Frameworks for Analysis of Control Premiums," *Business Valuation Review*, Vol. 14, No. 1 (March 1995).

17. **Jeffries,** Spencer J. and **Johnson**, Bruce A., *Comprehensive Guide for the Valuation of Family Limited Partnerships*, Dallas, TX: Partnership Profiles, Inc., 2001.

18. **Jeffries**, Spencer J., "Family Limited Partnerships: How to Support Your Valuation Before the IRS Comes Knocking" (Presentation at the 20th Annual Advanced Business Valuation Conference, Seattle, WA, October 26, 2001).

19. **Lee**, Mark, "Control Premiums and Minority Discounts: the Need for Specific Economic Analysis," *Shannon Pratt's Business Valuation Update*, August 2001.

20. **May**, Richard C. and **Garruto**, Loren B., *Financial Valuation: Businesses and Business Interests* (2000 Update with Cumulative Index), New York, NY: Warren Gorham & Lamont/RIA Group, 2001. James H. Zukin edited the original volume and all updates up to and including the 1996 Update.

21. **Mercer**, Z. Christopher, "The Adjusted Capital Asset Pricing Model For Developing Capitalization Rates: An Extension of Previous 'Build-Up' Methodologies Based Upon the Capital Asset Pricing Model," *Business Valuation Review*, Vol. 8, No. 4 (December 1989).

22. ———, "Do Public Company (Minority) Transactions Yield Controlling Interest or Minority Interest Pricing Data?," *Business Valuation Review*, Vol. 9, No. 4 (December 1990).

23. ———, *Valuing Financial Institutions*, Homewood, IL: Business One Irwin, 1992.

24. ———, "Adjusted Capitalization Rates for the Differences Between Net Income and Net Free Cash Flow," *Business Valuation Review*, December 1992.

25. ———, "Quantitative Marketability Discount Methodology," *The Journal of Business Valuation*, November 1994.

26. ———, "Should 'Marketability Discounts' be Applied to Controlling Interests of Private Companies?," *Business Valuation Review*, Vol. 13, No. 2 (June 1994).

27. ———, "A Brief Review of Control Premiums and Minority Interest Discounts," *The Journal of Business Valuation*, 1996.

28. ———, "Are Marketability Discounts Applicable to Controlling Interests in Private Companies?," *Valuation Strategies*, November/December 1997.

29. ———, *Quantifying Marketability Discounts: Developing and Supporting Marketability Discounts in the Appraisal of Closely Held Business Interests*, Memphis, TN: Peabody Publishing, LP, 1997.

30. ———, "Understanding and Quantifying Control Premiums: The Value of Control vs. Synergies or Strategic Advantages – Part II," *The Journal of Business Valuation*, 1999.

31. ———, "Theoretical Determinants of Value in the Context of 'Levels of Value'," Audio Tape, Mercer Capital, 1999. Available at 1-800-769-0967.

32. ———, "The Quantitative Marketability Discount Revisited," *E-Law Business Valuation Perspective*, Issue 2000-01 (January 11, 2000).

33. ———, "*Weinberg et al. v. Commissioner* – It's Not About the Marketability Discount," *E-Law Business Valuation Perspective*, Issue 2000-03 & 2000-04 (March 13, 2000).

34. ———, "The Quantitative Marketability Discount Model Revisited," *Valuation Strategies*, March/April, 2000.

35. ———, "Fair Market Value and Income Statement Adjustments," *E-Law Business Valuation Perspective*, Issue 2000-05 (April 3, 2000).

36. ———, "It's Not About Marketability, It's About Minority Interest," *Valuation Strategies*, July/August, 2000.

37. ———, "Restricted Stock Studies' Typical Results Do Not Provide 'Benchmark' for Determining Marketability Discounts – But They Do Help!," *E-Law Business Valuation Perspective*, Issue 2000-09 (September 19, 2000).

38. ———, "A Review of Current Business Valuation Textbooks on the Topic of Marketability Discounts," *E-Law Business Valuation Perspective*, Issue 2000-11 (November 21, 2000).

39. ———, "*Janda v. Commissioner* – The QMDM Appears in Tax Court Again," *E-Law Business Valuation Perspective*, Issue 2001-01 (February 5, 2001).

40. ———, "Quantitative, Rate of Return Analysis vs. Benchmark Analysis in Developing Marketability Discounts," *Valuation Strategies*, March/April, 2001.

41. ———, "Appendix D: Developing Cost of Capital (Capitalization Rates and Discount Rates) Using ValuSource PRO Software," *Cost Of Capital: Estimation And Applications*, New York, NY: John Wiley & Sons, Inc., 2001.

42. ———, *Quantifying Marketability Discounts: Developing and Supporting Marketability Discounts in the Appraisal of Closely Held Business Interests, Revised Reprint*, Memphis, TN: Peabody Publishing, LP, 2001.

43. **Mercer**, Z. Christopher, and **Julius**, J. Michael, "Selling Partial Ownership Interests: Levels of Value," *Mergers And Acquisitions Handbook For Small And Midsize Companies*, New York, NY: John Wiley & Sons, Inc. edited by Thomas L. West and Jeffrey D. Jones, 1997.

44. **Nath**, Eric. W., "Control Premiums and Minority Interest Discounts in Private Companies," *Business Valuation Review*, Vol. 9, No. 2 (June 1990).

45. ———, "A Tale of Two Markets," *Business Valuation Review*, Vol. 13, No. 3 (September 1994).

46. ———, "How Public Guideline Companies Represent 'Control' Value for a Private Company," *Business Valuation Review*, Vol. 16, No. 4 (December 1997).

47. **Phillips**, John R. and Freeman, Neill W., "Do Privately-Held Controlling Interests Sell for Less?," *Business Valuation Review*, Vol. 14, No. 3 (September, 1995).

48. ———, "What is the Marketability Discount for Controlling Interests?," *Business Valuation Review*, Vol. 18, No. 1 (March 1999).

49. **Pratt**, Shannon P., *Valuing A Business*, Homewood, IL: Dow Jones – Irwin, 1981.

50. ———, *Valuing A Business*, 2nd ed., Homewood, IL: Dow Jones – Irwin, 1989.

51. ———, "Public Market Values Inflated in Comparison with Private Companies," *Shannon Pratt's Business Valuation Update*, November 1997.

52. ———, "The Oxymoron of 'Control, Marketable'," *Shannon Pratt's Business Valuation Update*, October 1999.

53. ———, "Discount Rates Based on CAPM Don't Always Lead to Minority Value," *Shannon Pratt's Business Valuation Update*, March 2001.

54. ———, *Business Valuation Discounts & Premiums*, New York, NY: John Wiley & Sons, 2001.

55. **Pratt**, Shannon P., **Reilly**, Robert F., and **Schweihs**, Robert P., *Valuing Small Businesses And Professional Practices*, 2nd ed., Homewood, IL: Business One Irwin, 1993.

56. ———, *Valuing A Business*, 3rd ed., Chicago, IL: Irwin, 1996.

57. ———, *Valuing A Business*, 4th ed., New York, NY: McGraw-Hill, 2000.

58. **Pratt**, Shannon P., **et al.**, "Levels of Value – A Panel" (Panel discussion at the 20th Annual Advanced Business Valuation Conference, Seattle, WA, October 26, 2001).

59. **Simpson**, David W., "Minority Interest and Marketability Discounts: A Perspective, Part I," *Business Valuation Review*, Vol. 10, No. 1 (March 1991).

60. **Vance**, Charles, "Capitalization Rates," *Business Valuation Review*, Vol. 20, No. 1 (March, 2001).

61. **Wiggins**, C. Donald, "Matching Cash Flows and Discount Rates in Discounted Cash Flow Appraisals," *Business Valuation Review*, Vol. 18, No. 1 (March 1999).

H

Hall, Lance S., 277, 306
Harms, Travis W., 1, 269
Holding Period Premium, 261
Holding Period Premium, 122, 125, 278, 287
HPP
  See Holding Period Premium, 122
Hypothetical Investors, 294

I

Ibbotson Associates, 34, 37, 176, 184, 213, 218, 221, 228, 242, 243
Income Approach, 42, 216
Income Statement Adjustments
  Control Adjustments. *See* Control Adjustments
  Control Adjustments Defined, 142
  Discount Rate, 147
  Normalizing Adjustments. *See* Normalizing Adjustments
  Normalizing Adjustments Defined, 141
  Value Impact, 158–63
Integrated Theory of Business Valuation
  Acquisition Pricing for CFOs, 135–40
  Conceptual Math, 132, 145, 204
  Control Levels of Value, 92–95
  Defined, 87
  Enterprise Levels vs. Shareholder Level of Value, 118–21
  Financial Control Level of Value, 95–99
  Financial Control Premium, 100
  Gordon Model, 84
  Marketability Discount, 126–27
  Marketable Minority Interest Level of Value, 88–92
  Strategic Control Level of Value, 112
IRS Coursebook, 318, 327

J

Jankowske, Wayne C., 359, 361
Jung, Estate of, 365

K

King, David W., 220
Knowledge, 69

L

Lee, Mark, 92, 364, 369
Levels of Value, 86–87
  Bibliography, 379–84
  Bolotsky
    1991 Article, 353–358
    1995 ASA Presentation, 361
    2001 ASA Presentation, 372–73
  Early History, 348
  Jankowske
    1995 Article, 361
    1995 ASA Presentation, 361
  Lee Article, 369
  McCarter 2001 ASA Presentation, 377–78
  Mercer 1995 ASA Presentation, 362
  Nath
    1990 Article, 350–52
    1995 ASA Presentation, 360
    2001 ASA Presentation, 374–76
  Pratt 2001 ASA Presentation, 367–71
Long-Term Expect Growth Rate in Earnings, 29
Long-Term Growth Rate in Cash Flow, 30

M

Market Approach, 42
Market Value Added. *See* MVA
Marketability Discount, 53, 87, 119, 126–27
  Applicable to Controlling Interest, 127–31, 197–200
  Benchmark Range, 264
  Equation, 126